796.357   Anderson, Dave
AND
           Pennant races

$24.95

DATE			

Pennant Races

Pennant Races

BASEBALL AT ITS BEST

Dave Anderson

Doubleday
NEW YORK LONDON TORONTO SYDNEY AUCKLAND

PUBLISHED BY DOUBLEDAY

a division of Bantam Doubleday Dell Publishing Group, Inc.
1540 Broadway, New York, New York 10036

D O U B L E D A Y and the portrayal of an anchor with a dolphin
are trademarks of Doubleday,
a division of Bantam Doubleday Dell Publishing Group, Inc.

BOOK DESIGN BY CLAIRE NAYLON VACCARO

Library of Congress Cataloging-in-Publication Data

Anderson, Dave.
Pennant races : baseball at its best / Dave Anderson.
p.   cm.
1. Baseball—United States—History.   I. Title.   II. Title: Pennant races.
GV863.A1A5   1994
796.357'0973—dc20   93-30514
                                       CIP

ISBN 0-385-42573-2

1   3   5   7   9   10   8   6   4   2

Contents

Introduction

I was reading newspaper accounts of a pennant race in the New York Public Library's microfilm room when a middle-aged man noticed I was looking at a sports page.

"What year is that?" he asked.

"Nineteen fifty-one," I said.

"A terrible year," he said. "If you're a Brooklyn boy, that was a terrible year."

Not so terrible, I thought, for a Giants fan.

BUT A PENNANT race does not consist of Bobby Thomson's home run, or Bucky Dent's home run, or Gabby Hartnett's home run. It's the games leading up to those homers that make pennant races great. It's the day-by-day, night-by-night struggle over weeks, sometimes months. That's what I've tried to re-create here. It's all those smaller moments that most baseball fans don't remember or never knew.

For me, a pennant race has always been baseball at its best. Better than the World Series, better than a League Championship Series.

The World Series is acted out on a big stage, as if the games belong in a time capsule. The National League and American League Championship Series provide an audition for that big stage. But in the World Series or an LCS, a team has already won something. If a team didn't win its divisional race, or if it didn't win its league pennant in the years before 1969 (when each league was split into two divisions), it didn't win anything.

The World Series or an LCS is played in anywhere from four to seven games. But a pennant race is a season-long ordeal: game after game, week after week, month after month (with an occasional playoff to break a tie). The longer and tighter it is, the better it is.

In the World Series or an LCS, there's no need for the players or the fans to watch the scoreboard for the progress of out-of-town games. But in a pennant race, the scoreboard is the X factor, its silently changing numbers heightening the tension. In baseball's early years, fans responded to pennant races by flocking to downtown game-boards where men with megaphones read Western Union messages and shouted, "Cobb singled" while a peg was placed at first base on the board. Now pennant race games are on television three time zones and three hours apart, as they were in the 1991 struggle between the Atlanta Braves and the Los Angeles Dodgers; as they were in the last pure pennant race, the 1993 duel between the Braves and the San Francisco Giants.

In selecting the pennant races for this book, I've tried to choose those with the most theatrical dimension:

The two races in 1908 that the Tigers and the Cubs won two days apart two weeks after Fred Merkle's boner.

The 1920 Cleveland Indians who finally won only four days after eight Chicago White Sox players had been indicted for fixing the 1919 World Series, only two months after the August death of shortstop Ray Chapman, and despite Babe Ruth's then-record fifty-four homers in his first season with the Yankees.

The 1934 "Gashouse Gang" St. Louis Cardinals who benefited from the backfire of Giant manager Bill Terry's remark "Is Brooklyn still in the league?"

Gabby Hartnett's 1938 homer in Wrigley Field's twilight.

The 1940 "Cry Baby" Indians, who lost their mutiny and then lost the pennant to a Tigers pitcher they had never heard of.

The 1941 Brooklyn Dodgers with Leo Durocher at his loudest.

The 1944 St. Louis Browns, the symbol of World War II rejects.

The 1948 Indians, who rode Lou Bourdreau's bat and Bill Veeck's showmanship.

The 1949 Yankees who prevailed despite Joe DiMaggio's injuries and illness.

The 1951 New York Giants, finally winning on Bobby Thomson's playoff home run off Ralph Branca after the Brooklyn Dodgers had been thirteen and one-half games ahead between games of an August 11 doubleheader.

The 1964 Philadelphia Phillies blowing a lead of six and one-half games with only twelve games remaining.

The 1967 scramble among the Boston Red Sox, Detroit Tigers, Minnesota Twins and White Sox that the California Angels decided.

The 1978 Yankee comeback that outlasted the Red Sox' eight-game winning streak to force a tie.

The 1991 Braves who overtook the Dodgers in the first cable-television pennant race.

The 1993 Braves who won when the Giants lost their season's finale in Los Angeles.

If you're wondering why the 1969 Mets or Boston's 1914 Miracle Braves aren't included, those teams won in comebacks, not in pennant races. Those Mets won their division by eight games. Those Miracle Braves, who were in last place not only on July 4 but as late as July 19, won by ten and one-half games.

To me, the essence of a pennant race is the tension that multiplies during the last few days of the season, if not the last day.

If one or two of your favorite pennant races isn't there, maybe it's my mistake, but I tried to choose the races with the best plots.

To re-create these races, I searched newspaper microfilm in the New York Public Library as well as dozens of books, magazines, and my own personal baseball files of half a century. More important, I interviewed nearly one hundred players, managers, coaches, and front office executives who were central characters in these pennant races. They provided insights to reflections that they had never discussed with sportswriters at the time.

If you enjoy this book, thank them.

1908

Merkle's Boner, Cobb's Wedding

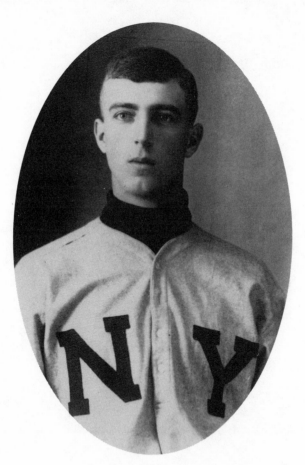

Fred Merkle. *National Baseball Library and Archive, Cooperstown, N.Y.*

IF NINETEEN-YEAR-OLD Fred Merkle had not taken a long lead off first base, Al Bridwell might not have stepped out of the batter's box and stared. If Bridwell's stare had not prompted Merkle to take a shorter lead, the New York Giant rookie might have been closer to second base in the ninth inning when Bridwell's line drive hopped across the outfield grass for an apparent single. If Merkle had been closer to second, he might have stepped on the bag instead of veering toward the Giants' centerfield clubhouse at the Polo Grounds as Moose McCormick trotted across home plate for what appeared to be a 2–1 victory over the Chicago Cubs for John McGraw's team.

Maybe then Fred Merkle, a friendly young man who deserved better, would not have been tortured by the nickname "Bonehead" for the rest of his life.

Then again, if Johnny Evers had not been so small and skinny at five-nine and 125 pounds, he might not have been so wily in reading the rule book with the hope of gaining an edge. If this Cub second baseman with the lantern jaw had not tried to get the same call three weeks earlier in Pittsburgh with the same plate umpire, Hank O'Day, he might not have dared to pull it with O'Day at such an important moment while surrounded by hundreds of another team's fans in another team's ballpark.

But history never has "if" footnotes. Much of what happened on September 23, 1908, still remains clouded, but Johnny Evers stood on second base holding a baseball aloft and Fred Merkle was ruled out in what has endured for nearly a century as baseball's most controversial moment in baseball's most controversial pennant race.

Johnny Evers had already been chiseled into baseball literature by sportswriter Franklin P. Adams for turning double plays with shortstop Joe Tinker and Frank Chance, the Cubs' manager–first baseman. Told one day that his column in the *New York Mail* was eight lines short, Adams, later a panelist on the popular radio show "Information Please," quickly wrote a poem titled "Baseball's Sad Lexicon":

These are the saddest of possible words,
Tinker to Evers to Chance.
Trio of bear cubs and fleeter than birds,
Tinker to Evers to Chance.
Ruthlessly pricking our gonfalon bubble,
Making a Giant hit into a double,
Words that are weighty with nothing but trouble,
Tinker to Evers to Chance.

Ironically, the little second baseman who pricked the Giants' gonfalon bubble had grown up as a Giants fan in upstate Troy, New York, a Hudson River city where the Giants franchise had originated shortly before his birth there. When he weighed only 105 pounds as a Cub rookie in 1902, he was dubbed the "Little Trojan." But he irritated teammates and opponents alike. He and Tinker, also a rookie in 1902, soon stopped talking to each other. In reporting the Cubs' sweep of a doubleheader the day before Merkle's boner, W. W. Aulick of *The New York Times* wrote:

"Now the truculent, scowling, slouching, complainful but nevertheless ball-playing Little Evers must be walked, which gift calls up the only smile that lights up his sorrowful face all afternoon."

After the controversial force-out, Johnny Evers must have smiled again. His quick thinking had wasted nine brilliant innings by Christy Mathewson, the era's premier pitcher in his premier season. The right-hander known as "Matty" and "Big Six" had dueled Jack Pfiester, known as "Jack the Giant Killer" for his mastery of McGraw's team. Then twenty-eight years old, lean and handsome at six-two and 195 pounds, Mathewson would lead the National League that season with a 37–11 record, a 1.43 earned run average, 11 shutouts, 259 strikeouts in 391 innings, and 34 complete games in 44 starts. His 5 saves, unearthed decades later by modern statisticians, would share the league lead with those of his thirty-seven-year-old teammate Joe (Iron Man) McGinnity.

Even more important to baseball's popularity, Christy Mathewson had changed the image of the era's ballplayers. To many people, major league baseball players were thought of mostly as hard-drinking hayseeds. But this Bucknell College graduate had style and substance.

Johnny Evers. *National Baseball Library and Archive, Cooperstown, N.Y.*

In those years, city "blue laws" prohibited major league games on Sunday in New York, Brooklyn, Boston, Philadelphia, and Pittsburgh. But when the Giants were playing on Sunday in Chicago, Cincinnati, or St. Louis, where Sunday games were allowed, Mathewson didn't put on his uniform.

Before the controversial game remembered for Merkle's boner, John McGraw's young Giants team was in first place, but only six percentage points ahead of the Cubs. Merkle had appeared in only thirty-seven previous games, some at first base, some in the outfield, some as a pinch hitter.

Against Pfiester that afternoon, Merkle, batting seventh, was hitless in his first two official at-bats. With two out and leftfielder Harry (Moose) McCormick on first base in the ninth, Merkle lined a long single into rightfield, sending McCormick to third with the potential winning run. In the batter's box now, Al Bridwell, a little twenty-four-year-old shortstop who hit .285 that season, noticed Merkle taking a long lead off first base. If the rookie was picked off for the third out, McCormick would be stranded.

"I saw Merkle edging pretty far off first, almost as if he were trying to steal," Bridwell would say years later. "That didn't make any sense. So I stepped out of the box and looked at him and he went back and stood on the bag. I often think that if I hadn't done that, everything would have turned out all right. Well, the first pitch came in to me, a fastball waist high right over the plate, and I promptly drilled a line drive past Johnny Evers into right-centerfield, a clean single."

Bridwell hurried to first base as McCormick ran home. The Giants had won, 2–1. Or so their 22,000 fans thought as hundreds streamed onto the field.

"As soon as a game at the Polo Grounds ended, the ushers would open the gates from the stands to the field, and the people would all pour out and rush at you," another Giant rookie that season, Fred Snodgrass, told Lawrence Ritter in *The Glory of Their Times* years later. "All they wanted to do was touch you, or congratulate you, or maybe cuss you out a bit. But because of that, we bench-warmers made it a practice to sprint from the bench to the clubhouse as fast as we could. Fred Merkle was so used to sitting on the bench all during the game and then at the end of the game jumping with the rest of us and taking off as fast as he could for the clubhouse beyond centerfield, that on this particular day he did it by force of habit and never gave it a second thought."

Out near second base, Johnny Evers had a second thought. Noticing that Merkle had not touched second base, the accepted practice on a game-winning hit at the time, Evers called for the ball from center-fielder Solly Hofman.

What happened then has never been clearly determined. Many of the Giants and some sportswriters contended that Joe McGinnity, coaching at third base, sensed what Evers had in mind, intercepted Hofman's throw, and heaved the ball into the bleachers. The Cubs' version is that Evers somehow obtained the real ball, if not another ball. Getting base umpire Bob Emslie's attention, Evers then stepped on second base, thereby forcing Merkle for the third out and erasing McCormick's winning run.

Merkle years later was quoted as saying, "I started across the grass for the clubhouse. Matty was near me. When Evers began shouting for the ball, Matty noticed something was wrong. Matty caught me by the arm and told me to wait a minute. We walked over toward second base and Matty spoke to Emslie, 'How about this, Bob, is there any trouble with the score of the play?' 'It's all right,' Emslie said. 'You've got the game. I don't see anything wrong with the play.' We were confident we had won the game."

Mathewson was quoted in the New York *Globe* at the time as saying, "When I saw Merkle leave the basepath, I ran after him and brought him back to second base, so as to make our lead unquestion-able. He was on second base after McGinnity tossed away the ball, following his tussle with the Chicago players. Maybe Evers got the ball and touched the base afterward. If he did, it didn't prove anything. I can state positively that no force play was made before Merkle got to the base."

Whatever did happen, thousands of fans now filled the infield and outfield. Cub manager Frank Chance stormed into the umpires' coop to confront Hank O'Day, then considered the NL's best, and Emslie.

Chance argued that Merkle had been forced at second, the score was still 1–1, and with so many people on the field making it impossi-ble to continue the game, the Cubs should win by forfeit. Perhaps fearing a wild reaction by the Giants fans, O'Day declined to an-nounce a decision then and there. The departing spectators assumed the Giants had won. But at ten o'clock that night, O'Day ruled that Merkle was out and that the game had ended in a 1–1 tie.

"If Merkle was out," John McGraw yelled, "O'Day should have cleared the field and gone on with the game. But Merkle wasn't out. We won and they can't take it away from us."

In a letter to National League president Harry Pulliam, Cubs president Charles Murphy cited the decision rendered in a game at Pittsburgh September 4 between the Cubs and the Pirates when "precisely the same contingency arose." That protest by the Cubs, wrote Murphy, "was not allowed because the single umpire who officiated said he had not seen the play." O'Day had been the umpire that day in Pittsburgh when Evers appealed a similar force-out of rookie first baseman Warren Gill.

There were two out in the ninth in Pittsburgh, and the bases were loaded, when rookie outfielder Owen (Chief) Wilson lined Mordecai (Three Finger) Brown's first pitch past Evers, scoring Fred Clarke for a 1–0 victory. Gill ran to within about thirty feet of second base, then veered toward the Pirates' bench. Evers called for the ball, stepped on second, then turned to see O'Day, the game's only umpire, leaving the field, his back turned. Evers chased him, but the umpire ignored the appeal.

"Clarke was over the plate," O'Day told Evers. "His run counted anyway."

Evers was correct in his application of the rule that base runners traditionally ignored when a game suddenly ended, but O'Day had not seen Gill turn away. The umpire couldn't call what he didn't see, and he didn't try to ascertain what Gill had or had not done. Although the Cubs' protest was disallowed, it branded the play into the memories of both Evers and O'Day.

"I'm glad now we protested," said Chance, "but I never expected the play to come up again."

In the Merkle case, according to O'Day's report, the Giant base runner indeed had not touched second, McGinnity had "interfered," and umpire Emslie had ruled that Merkle was out, erasing McCormick's run. The difference this time was that O'Day had seen Merkle veer toward the clubhouse without stepping on second base.

"I did not ask to have the field cleared," O'Day wrote in explaining why the game was not resumed immediately after the controversy, "as it was too dark to complete play."

The next day, Pulliam, stylish in a high starched collar in his office in the St. James Building in midtown Manhattan, upheld O'Day's decision that the game had ended in a 1–1 tie. Pulliam also announced that if a replay was necessary to decide the pennant, it would occur at the Polo Grounds on Thursday, October 8, the day after the completion of the regular schedule.

Pulliam's ruling riled McGraw, his players, and Giants president John T. Brush, who issued a stinging statement:

"This matter has only just begun. I propose to call in this time for keeps and we will find out whether we are operating this league on a sporting basis or as a sideshow at the expense of the public. There was not a man of the vast crowd who saw the game but knows the Giants won. I am going to convince the National League that a national affair like this annual championship contest, which has been in existence since 1876, is not to be jobbed off like diamonds on the installment plan. I am willing to take my medicine whenever I am wrong, but I am not going to be dealt out of a game which I believe to be as honestly won as any with which I have had anything to do as an owner."

Not that the Giants doubted they would win the pennant. Only hours after Pulliam's ruling on Thursday morning, Mathewson, appearing in relief in the seventh inning, preserved a 5–4 victory over the Cubs.

Early that afternoon, the Cubs tried to pursue their claim of a forfeit victory. Insisting that Wednesday's tie should have been replayed as soon as possible, Chance put his team on the field at 1:30, the time that a doubleheader would have begun. As soon as Andy Coakley, a twenty-five-year-old righthander purchased earlier that month from the Cincinnati Reds, threw five pitches over the plate, Chance claimed a forfeit.

"Not only did the Giants forfeit this game," Chance said, "but they're subject to a $1,000 fine for refusing to play. Until that fine is paid, the Giants must forfeit every game."

Chance and the Cubs filed a forfeit claim, but Pulliam's decision had ordered an October 8 replay, if necessary, not an immediate replay. And the Giants had not been officially notified of the National League president's ruling until noon. By 1:30, only a few Giant players had arrived at the Polo Grounds, and neither O'Day nor Emslie was there to umpire. By the time of the originally scheduled three o'clock game, about 22,000 customers had arrived. To deter the crowd from any disorderly demonstrations over Pulliam's decision, dozens of New York's finest were on duty. Under police order, none of the fans were allowed to stand in the outer areas of the outfield. But the police couldn't prevent the Giants from razzing O'Day.

"Hey, Hank," yelled catcher Roger Bresnahan, "why don't you wear a 'C' on your shirt?"

From the Giants' dugout, McGraw jabbered with Evers throughout the early innings. By the seventh, Giant lefthander George (Hooks) Wiltse was breezing along with a 5–1 lead. But after third baseman Harry Steinfeldt's leadoff single, an error by Giant third baseman Art Devlin, Tinker's single, and catcher Johnny Kling's two-run triple, McGraw waved in Mathewson from the bullpen.

Pinch hitter Del Howard singled for another run before Matty preserved a 5–4 victory that lifted the Giants into first place by one game. But the Giants and the Cubs had just begun to fight, and Chicago, as well as the nation, was watching two pennant races.

THE YEAR BEFORE, Ty Cobb, then a twenty-year-old outfielder for the Detroit Tigers, had led the American League with a .350 batting average, 116 runs batted in, 212 hits, and 49 stolen bases. When the Tigers were swept by the Cubs in the World Series, he batted a flimsy .200. Although hooted as the "World Series lemon" by Chicago fans, at age twenty-one in 1908 he demanded a $5,000 contract, more than double his $2,400 salary. Frank Navin, the Tigers owner who had offered him $3,000, objected. To the Tigers, their club owner was known as "the Chinaman" for his cold expression.

"Who does Cobb think he is?" Navin snapped. "Less than three years in the league and he's trying to play God. I'm not giving in. Cobb is not bigger than baseball."

Maybe not, but Navin eventually gave in. After a spring training holdout, Cobb virtually got what he wanted: a $4,000 base salary plus an $800 bonus if he batted .300.

"I wanted security," Cobb explained. "I didn't know when I'd be hurt and forced out of baseball. I wanted to give my best to the game, but in return I wanted all that was coming to me. The prospect of being just another muscle-worker did not appeal to me. I had more ambition than that. If Navin hadn't given in, I would have quit baseball and gone to college. Nobody really believed I was serious, but I was."

No matter what Ty Cobb did, in baseball or in life, he was always serious. He was so serious about getting married during the 1908 season, he jumped the club.

He deserted the Tigers on August 4 without permission, went to Augusta, Georgia, for his wedding to hazel-eyed Charlotte Lombard, then rejoined the Tigers on August 9, hitting a triple and a single. Some of his teammates resented his absence, especially when he wasn't fined or suspended and later when his league-leading batting average skidded. Over twenty-three at-bats in six games, he produced only three hits.

"The demon Ty Cobb is a demon no more," proclaimed a Detroit dispatch in the Cleveland *Plain Dealer*. "He is a dub hitter, according to the local population and the dope."

Hughie Jennings, the popular Tiger manager, wisely knew that disciplining Cobb for getting married might have made the situation worse, not better. Jennings understood ballplayers. Known for his piercing fingers-in-the-mouth whistle and bellowing "Eee-yah" yell while standing on one leg and lifting both arms high in the third-base coach's box, he was loved by his players. He often handed them cigars, either in appreciation of a victory or to puff away a loss. He knew that Cobb was already a special baseball player. And soon the rightfielder was out of his slump and leading the league in hitting. Although his average was down, fluctuating around .333, so were averages throughout the AL in a season dominated by five future Hall of Fame pitchers: spitballer Ed Walsh, who would win forty games and pitch 464 innings; aging Cy Young; young Walter Johnson, who shut out the Yankees three times in a span of four days; lanky righthander Addie Joss; and fun-loving lefthander Rube Waddell.

Ty Cobb slides ahead of Frank (Home Run) Baker's tag. *National Baseball Library and Archive, Cooperstown, N.Y.*

Cobb was a precocious and pugnacious player who antagonized many of his teammates with his loner lifestyle. When he was a rookie in 1906, one of his few friends among the Tigers was Wild Bill Donovan, the Tigers' ace. But many of his older teammates chased him from the batting cage with snarls of "Get to the outfield, sandlotter." He sometimes found his bats broken or sawed in half.

Out of Royston, Georgia, Cobb had been sold to the Tigers by the Augusta, Georgia, minor league club only three weeks after a family tragedy. His father, William Cobb, the county school commissioner, had been shot dead by his mother, the strikingly beautiful Amanda Chitwood Cobb. She told a jury that she mistook her husband, who often traveled by horse and buggy to nearby towns for two or three days, for a midnight prowler on the porch roof outside their second-floor bedroom. While townspeople gossiped that she had been entertaining a lover at the time, she was acquitted. His father's violent death was believed to be one reason for Cobb's intense nature.

By the end of the 1907 season, Cobb was wearing a derby and spiffy suits while driving a Chalmers, his first automobile. But for all his baseball skills, many of his teammates still didn't like him.

Leftfielder Matty McIntyre and his road-trip roommate, Twilight Ed Killian, once locked Cobb out of the hotel bathroom the Tigers shared. When the team was in Detroit, the older players roomed at the Brunswick, a rowdy hotel–burlesque theater. Cobb lived at a more sedate hotel a few blocks away. When one of the young Tiger pitchers, Eddie Willett, joined Cobb there, McIntyre, as the leader of the antagonists, tried to intimidate both of his younger teammates.

"We're going to run Cobb off the club and you too if you stay friends with him," McIntyre told Willett. "Either move out and hang around with us or you're finished."

Willett moved out. Knowing the others might gang up on him now, Cobb's answer, as he told Al Stump for his autobiography, *My Life in Baseball*, was to "keep a weapon of a lethal nature close by me at all times." Even so he was bloodied in a brutal clubhouse brawl with Charlie (Boss) Schmidt, the Tigers' burly catcher. Because of the ill feeling, the Tigers considered trading Cobb in 1907 to the Cleveland Naps for outfielder Elmer Flick (the 1905 American League batting champion with a .305 average) or to the New York Highlanders for righthander Billy Hogg (whose promising career would end after the 1908 season).

"We've had too many fights," Hughie Jennings explained. "We need harmony on this team, not brawling."

Fortunately for Jennings and the Tigers, neither deal materialized. But during that 1907 season, centerfielder Sam Crawford quietly encouraged his older teammates to haze the young outfielder who had upstaged him as the Tigers' best hitter. One day in batting practice Cobb turned on Crawford.

"You big bastard," Cobb yelled, "you've been making trouble for me long enough. Now put up your hands. Go ahead, I'm calling you."

Crawford backed down. He knew Cobb was serious. He remembered Cobb's reaction in a similar situation. In the final week of his 1906 rookie season Cobb played centerfield because Crawford was hurt. Cobb soon realized that leftfielder Matty McIntyre wasn't backing him up on balls hit between them. On the next ball in the gap, Cobb didn't budge. The ball went for a home run off Ed Siever, another Cobb tormentor. In the dugout Siever cursed Cobb, who challenged him. Siever backed down. That night in the hotel lobby Cobb spotted Siever about to sucker-punch him. Cobb flattened him first. Cobb later developed a close friendship with Boss Schmidt, who had waxed him in the clubhouse, but his relationship with McIntyre never changed.

"Matty McIntyre," Cobb would say years later, "died in 1920 without ever shaking my hand or letting bygones be bygones."

As the 1908 season progressed, Cobb was one of three marquee names in the three-team pennant race. Napoleon Lajoie, born in Woonsocket, Rhode Island, to French-Canadian immigrants, was so popular that in 1903 the Cleveland team was nicknamed the Naps for him in a vote of its fans. Now thirty-four years old, the manager–second baseman had been Cobb's idol, a three-time batting champion whose .422 average in 1901 remains the American League record. When this turn-of-the-century role model endorsed a chewing tobacco, hundreds of kids got sick trying it. He had been the second player to endorse Louisville Slugger bats, Honus Wagner having been the first. For a $75 fee, Cobb would be the third. The other name on the marquee was Ed Walsh, the White Sox workhorse, a handsome twenty-seven-year-old righthander. Once a Pennsylvania coal miner, he threw the dreaded, but then legal, spitball, his slippery "eel ball," as some called it.

"I think Walsh's spitball disintegrated on the way to the plate and the catcher put it back together again," Sam Crawford once said. "I swear, when it went past the plate, just the spit went by."

Now, as Cobb, nicknamed the "Georgia Peach" by sportswriter Grantland Rice that season, awaited a doubleheader with the Phila-

Napoleon Lajoie. *National Baseball Library and Archive, Cooperstown, N.Y.*

delphia Athletics on Friday, September 25, at Navin Field, the Naps, who had ascended into first place with a ten-game winning streak, had a lead of one and one-half games. The second-place White Sox were primarily the same celebrated "Hitless Wonders" who had won the 1906 World Series. The Tigers were third, two games out, but they seemed to respect the White Sox more than they did the Naps.

"I think the best way to beat the Sox is to play wild ball against them," Cobb had said on the train returning from St. Louis the previous week. "Take any and every kind of chance. If you play stereotyped baseball against them, you play right into their hands. Run wild and do everything least expected and least logical and you have a chance of beating them."

With the Tigers, Naps, and White Sox competing, the Midwest had never been so involved in baseball's pennant races. In 1904 the Boston Pilgrims had edged the New York Highlanders for the American League pennant on Jack Chesbro's wild pitch on the last day of the season. But now fans in Detroit and Cleveland as well as fans of both Chicago teams and the New York Giants were gathering at downtown scoreboards in the late afternoon to check the progress of that day's games as the batter-by-batter reports clattered over Western Union telegraph wires. With every posted inning, the phrase "pennant race" was becoming part of America's vocabulary. In the opener of the Tigers' doubleheader that Friday afternoon, Eddie Summers, the Tiger rookie righthander, stopped the Athletics, 7–2, on six hits.

"Why don't you pitch the second game?" a teammate suggested.

"Yeah, give me that ball," Summers agreed. "I can do it."

He did, blanking the A's, 1–0, on two hits over ten innings in a duel with Biff Schlitzer, another rookie. In the Tiger tenth, first baseman Claude Rossman drilled a line drive to right center for an inside-the-park homer. After he slid across the plate, fans tried to lift him to their shoulders. In the commotion, his uniform shirt was torn and his cap disappeared. As hundreds of fans waited outside the Tigers' club-house, Rossman and Summers ducked out a back door to a waiting automobile. With the White Sox idle, the Tigers moved to within one-half game of first place when the Washington Senators suddenly scored five runs off righthander Charlie Chech in the ninth for a 6–1 victory over the Naps.

During the Senators' rally, Frank DeHaas Robison, the former owner of the Naps, was sitting in his suburban Cleveland home listening to a friend describe the play-by-play over the telephone.

As the Senators completed their five-run burst, Robison, once Cleveland's leading streetcar magnate, dropped the telephone receiver and sunk into a stupor, his mustache limp, his narrow face ashen. Hours later, he died. The pennant race had victimized one of the Naps' most celebrated rooters.

But in Chicago the stern White Sox manager, Fielder Jones, a centerfielder who was the first to position other outfielders, wasn't impressed with the Tigers' surge.

"Detroit is welcome to the two games as long as they had to pitch Summers in both of them," Jones said. "Summers is the only pitcher left on the Detroit team who shows reliable form and he can't pitch often enough from now until the end of the season to save Detroit."

Jones was forgetting righthander Wild Bill Donovan, who stopped the A's, 3–2, on Saturday. But the Naps edged the Senators, 5–4, on Walter Johnson's throwing error. The White Sox routed the Yankees, 12–0.

With the Naps idle Sunday, hundreds of fans rode the train from

Cleveland to Detroit, hoping to see the Tigers lose. But the Tigers jumped into first place by one percentage point as righthander George Mullin puzzled the A's, 5–2. In the third McIntyre doubled and Crawford walked. Cobb doubled down the rightfield line for one run. On Rossman's grounder, Crawford was thrown out at the plate as Cobb took third. During a double steal, Cobb escaped from a rundown when A's pitcher Jack Coombs got in his way, and he scored with catcher Mike Powers chasing him across the plate. When the White Sox workhorse, Ed Walsh, blanked the Red Sox, 3–0, only four percentage points separated the top three teams. White Sox owner Charles Comiskey already was planning to enlarge South Side Park for the World Series.

"We'll have three rows of boxes in front of the pavilions," he said. "We'll have circus seats in front of the main grandstand. We're just waiting for the flash."

Comiskey was confident. So was Lajoie. And the Philadelphia Athletics' owner-manager, Connie Mack, in his high starched collar, wasn't that impressed with the Tigers.

"I don't know that Detroit has its nerve back," the A's owner-manager said. "They don't seem to be as confident as they might. What has helped them is young Bush at shortstop. He's a wonder. I guess he beat us out of two games. If Detroit wins the pennant, it can thank Bush."

Owen (Donie) Bush, who had been brought up from the minors in early September, would not be eligible for the World Series if the Tigers were to win the pennant. But at five-six and 140 pounds, the nineteen-year-old rookie had solidified their infield and provided unexpected punch. Monday against the Senators he scored from first base on Crawford's double in a 4–1 victory behind lefthander Ed Killian's six-hitter. When rain washed out the second game of their doubleheader, the Tigers were one-half game ahead of the Naps, who had also been rained out.

Darkness in Chicago halted the White Sox and the Red Sox at 2–2 after ten innings, a game notable for the passions it inspired. As rookie umpire John Kerin left the field, he suffered a broken nose when slugged between the eyes by a fan protesting a controversial call.

With the White Sox trailing, 2–1, in the seventh, leftfielder Patsy Dougherty was on second and second baseman George Davis was on first. Pinch hitter Jiggs Donahue grounded to Red Sox shortstop Heinie Wagner, who threw to third baseman Harry Lord, an apparent easy force play. But the ball hit Dougherty's arm and ricocheted to the grandstand. Dougherty dashed across the plate with the apparent tying run. Davis hurried to third, Donahue to second. Not so fast. Kerin, the base umpire just up from the American Association, ruled Dougherty out for interference, nullifying the run.

"He just had his arm up," White Sox manager Fielder Jones argued. "When you slide, your arms go up."

"He put up his arm to hit the ball," Kerin told him. "He deliberately interfered with the throw."

"How could he have deliberately interfered with the throw?" Jones yelled. "He had his back to the throw."

Jones now was out too. Out of the game. Plate umpire Tommy Connolly ordered Davis to return to second and Donahue to first. White Sox shortstop Freddy Parent doubled, scoring Davis for a 2–2 score. But to the White Sox fans, Kerin's call cost two runs, turning what would have been a 3–2 victory into a 2–2 tie. As the game ended, a man hopped onto the field and struck Kerin from behind. He then disappeared into the crowd, but not before he was recognized by White Sox first baseman Frank Isbell. The assailant turned out to be Robert Cantwell, a thirty-two-year-old Chicago attorney.

With that tie in Chicago and rain in both Detroit and Cleveland, each of the three contenders now had a Tuesday doubleheader. In Detroit the Senators' young Walter Johnson would start and finish both games. The long-armed righthander had joined the Senators at age nineteen the year before out of an Idaho semipro league. The first time Ty Cobb faced him, the Tiger outfielder struck out.

"That kid's fastball," Cobb said, "looks like bird shot."

Johnson would win 416 games, second only to Cy Young's 511, pitch a record 110 shutouts and amass 3,508 strikeouts, a record that would last until Nolan Ryan broke it. Three weeks earlier Johnson had shut out the Highlanders three times in a span of four days: 3–0 on six hits on Friday, 6–0 on four hits on Saturday, and 4–0 on two hits on Monday. But in this doubleheader with the Tigers, he would lose both games, 4–1 on righthander Ed Willett's three-hitter and 7–3 as Ed Summers, on three days' rest after his nineteen-inning doubleheader, scattered fourteen hits. The Naps swept the A's, 5–4 on righthander Charles (Heinie) Berger's four-hitter and 9–0 on righthander Bob (Dusty) Rhoads's eight-hitter. The White Sox swept the Red Sox, 5–1 and 2–0. Ed Walsh, on only one day's rest after his Sunday shutout, pitched both games, a three-hitter in an hour and forty-six minutes and a four-hitter in an hour and thirty-five minutes.

Wednesday the Tigers maintained their one-half-game lead as

Mullin held off the Senators, 7–5, in the late innings while the Naps stopped the A's, 6–1, on Chech's six-hitter. The idle White Sox now were one and one-half games behind, but Fielder Jones was looking to Friday's opener of a two-game series in Cleveland.

"We expect to eliminate the Naps from the pennant race," the White Sox manager-center fielder said. "If we can beat the Naps both games, it will pretty nearly mean that the heart will have been taken out of Lajoie's men. Then all we have to do is clean up the Tigers next week in Chicago and the pennant is ours."

Each team had five games remaining. The Tigers had two with the fourth-place St. Louis Browns in Detroit, then three in Chicago. The White Sox would go to Cleveland for two, then return to Chicago for the three with the Tigers while the Naps were closing their season in St. Louis with three. Because the Naps had never finished higher than third in their seven previous seasons, Cleveland was aglow with anticipation. White Sox owner Charles Comiskey had arrogantly predicted that his team would not lose another game. But the Naps' ace, articulate Addie Joss, who four weeks earlier had been deprived of a no-hitter by Cobb's first-inning single, would put his 23–11 record against Ed Walsh's 39–14 record in Friday's opener. In the Cleveland *Plain Dealer*, a "Rooters Club" notice appeared:

> Every loyal rooter must respond to the call of duty, which summons him to League Park for these two games. Come out with your lungs expanded and your voice prepared for the greatest sessions of rooting that Cleveland has ever known. Bring your horns and bells and noise-makers. The war songs will be distributed in the first-base pavilion and you are expected to report there not later than 1:30 p.m. Join the Rooters Club! Be a Rooter Root!
>
> Charles P. Salen, President.

THE PREVIOUS FRIDAY afternoon, John McGraw had chosen the opener of a doubleheader with the Cincinnati Reds for the big-league baptism of eighteen-year-old lefthander Rube Marquard, just purchased from Indianapolis of the American Association for $11,000, then a record price for a minor leaguer. Over his Hall of Fame career Marquard would win 201 games, including 19 in a row in his 26–11 record in 1912, but he wasn't ready to justify his instant nickname of "the $11,000 Beauty."

"This kid was so nervous, he couldn't do a single thing right," Hans Lobert, the Red third baseman, once said. "He hit the first man up in the ribs, then I tripled, then Bob Bescher tripled, all in the first inning, and suddenly they started calling the $11,000 Beauty the $11,000 Lemon. Just a kid, you know. It was rough."

The Giants lost, 7–1. In the second game the Giants lost again, 5–2, when Joe (Iron Man) McGinnity, who had pitched and won three doubleheaders in 1903 while working 434 innings, didn't last the second inning. With the Cubs winning in Brooklyn, 5–1, the Giants dropped into a second-place tie with the Pittsburgh Pirates, each one-half game behind. Saturday the Giants rebounded, sweeping the Reds, 6–2 and 3–2, behind Mathewson and righthander Leon (Red) Ames, but at Washington Park in Brooklyn the Cubs also won a double-header. After twenty-five-year-old righthander Ed Reulbach needed only an hour and forty-five minutes for a 5–0 five-hitter in the opener, he approached manager Frank Chance.

"Let me pitch the second game too," he said.

In only an hour and fifteen minutes, Reulbach spun a 3–0 three-hitter, the only pitcher in major league history ever to work two shutouts in the same doubleheader. He would produce a 24–7 season, his best, but Big Ed was always overshadowed on the Cub staff by Mordecai (Three Finger) Brown, a future Hall of Famer whose physical handicap proved to be a baseball blessing. As a seven-year-old Indiana farm boy, Brown had caught his right hand in a corn grinder. His forefinger and little finger were reduced to stubs. Most of his mangled middle finger was saved, but it was crooked. To his teammates, he was known as "Miner." He had worked in a coal mine before he realized that his stubbed fingers helped him spin a curveball. In a doubleheader sweep of the Giants that lifted the Cubs into a tie for first place the day before Merkle's boner, Brown had been credited with both victories. He saved the 4–3 opener in relief and completed the 3–1 second game.

"Miner had plenty of nerve, ability, and willingness to work at all times under any conditions," Evers once said. "The crowds never bothered him. There was never a finer character. He was charitable and friendly to his foes and ever willing to help a youngster breaking in."

In the controversy over Merkle's boner, Chicago was hardly charitable and friendly to its New York rivals. In the *Chicago Tribune*, the National League office was charged with "years of weak-kneed vacillating policy toward" the Giant club and McGraw in particular. But ever since McGraw took command of the Giants in 1902, he had questioned Harry Pulliam's judgment. When the NL owners reelected Pulliam after the 1907 season, the vote was 7–1, with the Giants the lone dissenter. Now, with Pulliam upholding the 1–1 tie that hung over the pennant race as possibly requiring a tie-breaking playoff, the Giants were angrier than ever at him.

Pending that possible playoff, the Giants had eleven games remaining, the Cubs only six. For the Giants, the season would end the following Wednesday, October 7, after four games with the Phillies at the Polo Grounds, three in Philadelphia, and three with the Boston Doves, owned by John Dovey, at the Polo Grounds. For the Cubs, about to play five games in Cincinnati, the season would end on Sunday, October 4, in Chicago against the forgotten contender, the Pittsburgh Pirates.

During the harangue between the Giants and the Cubs over Merkle's boner, the Pirates had quietly stayed in the race. John (Honus) Wagner, their thirty-four-year-old shortstop, would be one of five charter members of the Hall of Fame with Babe Ruth, Ty Cobb, Cy Young, and Walter Johnson. In 1908 he would lead the National League with a .354 average, 201 hits, 39 doubles, 19 triples, 109 runs batted in, and 53 stolen bases. Over his career he would win eight batting titles and hit over .300 in seventeen seasons. Many of his contemporaries considered the Flying Dutchman baseball's best player, even better than Ty Cobb.

"Cobb was great, but not the greatest," one of Cobb's teammates, Sam Crawford, once said. "The greatest all-around player who ever lived was Honus Wagner. He could play any position except pitcher and be the best in the league at it. He was a wonderful fielder, very quick, terrific arm. He looked so awkward, bowlegged, barrel-chested, about two hundred pounds, a big man. But he could run like a scared rabbit. He was a good team man and had the sweetest disposition in the world."

Wagner, stocky at five-eleven and 200 pounds, grew up working in the coal mines outside Pittsburgh and, except for three early seasons with the Louisville Colonels before that NL franchise merged with the Pirates, he never left the area. His highest salary was $10,000, but at his peak he turned down offers to jump to the AL and remained in Pittsburgh for fifty-six seasons, including thirty-nine as a coach. In later years, he lived near Forbes Field and after a game he often stopped at neighborhood taverns on the way home.

"He never had to buy an Iron City beer," Ralph Kiner, the Pirate slugger who remembered him as a coach, would say years later. "Honus Wagner was a civic treasure in Pittsburgh."

His baseball card turned into a financial treasure, bringing $450,000 at a 1992 collectors' auction. He is believed to be the first player to have his signature branded on the barrel of a Louisville Slugger bat. But that season Wagner was the only Pirate with a .300 average. Fred Clarke, the Hall of Fame manager-outfielder who had a .312 career average, batted .265, and tiny third baseman Tommy Leach batted .259. But the Pirates had the NL's most balanced staff. Nick Maddox, who had pitched the Pirates' first no-hitter the year before, would be 23–8, Vic Willis 23–11. Howie Camnitz would be 16–9, Sam Leever 15–7 and Al (Lefty) Leifield 15–14.

The Giants, in contrast, now could depend on only one pitcher, Mathewson, but he was weary. Hooks Wiltse would post a 23–14 record but he, Red Ames, aging Joe McGinnity, and rookie right-hander Otis (Doc) Crandall were erratic. As for Rube Marquard, at eighteen he appeared to be too young to trust.

The Cubs not only had Three Finger Brown and Ed Reulbach in top form, but they learned that Jack Pfiester's arm problem had been cured. After pitching in the Merkle game, his left elbow was sore. The large tendon from the shoulder to the wrist had slipped off the point of the elbow. While his teammates traveled to Cincinnati, he detoured to Youngstown, Ohio, to see a healer known as Bonesetter Reese.

"He felt around the elbow with his fingers," Pfiester reported. "He located the tendon and snapped it back into place."

Monday umpire Bill Klem let the Giants and the Phillies slog through rain. Wiltse was shelled early in what appeared to be a 6–5 loss as Roger Bresnahan popped up with two out in the ninth. But short-stop Dave Shean slipped on the wet grass, the ball fell, and Bresnahan hustled into second base. Mike Donlin's triple tied the score, then outfielder Cy Seymour's single lifted the Giants into first place over the idle Cubs. In a Tuesday doubleheader Mathewson stopped the Phillies, 6–2, but Crandall, battered 7–0, was no match for a new name, Harry Coveleski, a twenty-two-year-old lefthander just up from the minors.

When Three Finger Brown, supported by Tinker's two-run homer, stopped the Reds, 6–2, the Cubs regained first place. But the Pirates, sweeping a doubleheader in St. Louis, were a close third, only .004 away.

Wednesday the Giants jumped back into first on Ames's six-hitter, 2–1. Vic Willis lifted the Pirates into second, 5–0, as the Cubs lost to the Reds, 6–5, in the ninth. With the bases loaded, third baseman Hans

Lobert's single off Orval Overall knocked in the tying and winning runs. Knowing that Evers would be watching, Red outfielder Dode Paskert, running from first base, carefully stepped on second and Lobert crossed first before turning to the clubhouse. Merkle's boner had taught base runners a lesson.

"I'm sorry I got that hit," the bowlegged Lobert joked. "I had my eyes shut and couldn't see what I was doing."

Thursday in Philadelphia the Giants split. Mathewson won, 4–3, but Coveleski outpitched Wiltse, 4–3. With the Pirates idle, the Cubs now had a chance to tie for second place. Before warming up, Big Ed Reulbach ate a few chocolate bon-bons and washed them down with water.

"Why the bon-bons?" a newspaperman asked.

"That's what Joe Gans had for energy before his lightweight title fight with Battling Nelson in California a few weeks ago," Reulbach said.

"Gans lost."

"I won't."

Reulbach stopped the Reds, 6–0, on a two-hitter, his third consecutive shutout, tying the Cubs with the Pirates for second place. Friday afternoon Brown's four-hitter blanked the Reds, 5–0, while Ames stopped the Phillies, 7–2, but the Pirates, the forgotten team in this hectic pennant race, swept a doubleheader from the Cardinals, 7–4 and 2–1, and took over first place in the standings:

Pirates	97–55	.6381—	(Games to play: 2)
Giants	95–54	.6375 ½	(Games to play: 5)
Cubs	96–55	.6347 ½	(Games to play: 3)

In the National League office, Harry Pulliam, after more than a week of deliberation, disallowed the Cubs' forfeit claim the day after the Merkle controversy but expanded on his earlier ruling justifying the 1–1 tie. According to Pulliam, "There was no evidence to show Merkle touched second base," and in none of the affidavits was it claimed that Merkle touched second base. Pulliam refused to repudiate "my umpires simply to condone the undisputed blunder" of Merkle in not touching second base.

"O'Day reported that Merkle did not touch second base," Pulliam stated. "This play in question, missed by Emslie, was seen by O'Day, who being the umpire-in-chief, ruled that the run did not count."

Saturday the Giants lost to Harry Coveleski, 3–2, for the third time in five days. Those three losses to baseball's newly nicknamed "Giant Killer," a rookie with a 4–1 record, would haunt McGraw.

"The next year we ran Coveleski out of the league," Fred Snodgrass once said. "McGraw found out Coveleski always carried a piece of bologna in his back pocket and chewed on it secretly, ashamed of his habit. McGraw started yelling, 'Hey, give us a chew of that bologna, will you?' This so upset him, he never beat us again. Other teams found out about it and started doing the same thing and it chased him back to the minors."

Harry Coveleski, the older brother of Hall of Famer Stan Coveleski, didn't return to the big leagues until 1914 with the Detroit Tigers, winning twenty-two, twenty-two, and twenty-one games over three seasons. But in 1908 his three victories in five days over the Giants kept the Pirates and Cubs alive.

That same Saturday the Pirates held first place, winning again in St. Louis, 3–2. Reulbach breezed by the Reds, 16–2, before the Cubs took the train to Chicago for their Sunday, October 4, showdown with the Pirates, the final game for each team, Three Finger Brown pitching against Vic Willis. With the Giants idle and long before the rule that any rained-out games affecting the pennant race must be played, this was the situation:

If the Pirates (98–55) won, they would clinch the National League pennant and render the Merkle controversy inconsequential.

If the Cubs (97–55) won, they would clinch no worse than a tie with the Giants (95–55), and the Pirates would be eliminated. If the Cubs won and the Giants were rained out of any of their three games with the Boston Doves, the Cubs would clinch.

If the Cubs won and the Giants won their three games with the Doves, the 1–1 tie created by the Merkle controversy would be replayed Thursday at the Polo Grounds.

To thwart the possibility of rain Sunday in Chicago, what was known formally as the "diamond tarpaulin cover" was spread across the West Side Grounds infield. Mounted on wheels, the huge tarred canvas, owned by Pirate owner Barney Dreyfuss and invented by Pirate manager Fred Clarke, had been trucked in for the occasion by Cub owner Charles Murphy.

Nothing but the best for this Pirates–Cubs showdown.

IN 1906 THE White Sox Hitless Wonders had won the World Series from the Cubs, four games to two, after batting only .230 as a team during the season with only seven homers. Now, as the 1908 White Sox awaited Big Ed Walsh's duel with the Naps' ace, righthander Addie Joss, on Friday, October 2, at League Park, they were even more hitless. Their team average of .224 again would be the lowest in the American League and they would hit a total of only three homers: one by Fielder Jones, one by first baseman Frank Isbell, and one by Ed Walsh himself.

"They can't hit, they can't field very well, they are not great base runners, they look like a second-division team," Joss had said a few weeks earlier. "And yet play against them and you find out what they can do to you."

What they could do is make a run or two stand up. In winning the 1906 pennant by three games over the Yankees, the White Sox pitching staff had fired thirty-two shutouts. This season their twenty-three shutouts would share the league lead, with Walsh contributing eleven. But manager Fielder Jones had other quality pitchers. Frank Smith, a hard-drinking righthander known as "Deserter" because he had jumped the club in July to resume his off-season job as a piano mover, had pitched a 1–0 no-hitter against the A's on September 20. Another righthander, Doc White, alias Dr. Guy Harrison White, a Georgetown graduate in dental surgery, had led the league with twenty-seven wins the year before. Two years earlier he had led the league with a 1.52 earned run average.

But to Joss, the Hitless Wonders in the batting order were the reason the White Sox had an opportunity to win their second pennant in three years.

"The Sox are game to the core," Joss said. "They can stand the gaff with the best of them. They have the spirit and they have the inside play. When you go in the box against Chicago, you know you've got to pitch. That is perhaps the greatest secret of their success. They always make the pitcher pitch. Hahn, Dougherty, Jones, and that bunch won't swing at anything unless it's right over the plate. A pitcher who can cut the plate can beat them."

Cut the plate. That Friday afternoon in Cleveland both Addie Joss and Ed Walsh cut the plate as few opposing pitchers in baseball history ever have.

Inspired by the Rooters Club message in the *Plain Dealer*, more than 11,000 people bulged League Park beyond its capacity. They were soon rewarded. In the Nap third, centerfielder Joe Birmingham led off with a single to right. Hoping to steal second, he edged into a long lead off first. Walsh turned, threw, and had him picked off. But as Birmingham slid into second, first baseman Frank Isbell's throw hit him, and the ball rolled into left field. Birmingham hurried to third. Shortstop George Perring grounded to short, Birmingham holding third. Joss was up next.

"I never saw Walsh have so much," Joss would say later. "I tried to bunt, and actually could not get my bat out in time."

Joss struck out. With leftfielder Wilbur Good up, one of Walsh's spitballs slid off the heel of catcher Ossee Schreckengost's glove, just far enough for Birmingham to score on the passed ball. Inning after inning, Joss made that one run stand up. In the Naps' dugout, his superstitious teammates not only weren't talking to the lanky six-two righthander with the pinwheel delivery, they weren't even looking at him. Joss was superstitious too. Before going out to pitch the eighth, he knocked on wood, the wooden wall behind the bench. In the press box Western Union telegraphers were listening to incoming Morse code dots and dashes.

"Hasn't anyone reached first base?" one message requested.

"Wait until the end of the game," the telegrapher answered.

In the eighth and ninth, Joss continued to cut the plate. When he retired John Anderson, the last of three pinch hitters, to complete his 1–0 triumph, he had pitched not only a no-hitter but a perfect game. The front page of Saturday morning's *Plain Dealer* would shout:

CLEVELAND FANS SEE GREATEST GAME
IN HISTORY OF BIG-LEAGUE BASEBALL

None of the White Sox batters reached first base. No hits, no errors, no bases on balls, no batter hit by a pitch. Only the third perfect game in major league history. In 1880 John Montgomery Ward of Providence had blanked Buffalo, 5–0. In 1904 Cy Young of the Red Sox had blanked the Philadelphia A's, 3–0.

"I did not try for such a record," Joss was saying now in the Naps' clubhouse. "All I was doing was trying to beat Chicago, for the game meant much to us, and Walsh was pitching the game of his life."

In only eight innings, Walsh had struck out fifteen, an American League record. He had allowed only four hits, but Joss had pitched a perfect game. When it ended, dozens of fans jumped onto the field, hoping to lift the Nap pitcher onto their shoulders in celebration. But he dashed off the mound and quickly escaped into the clubhouse.

"I was taking no chances," Joss explained. "Suppose they had let me drop. The season is not over yet."

Of the dozen perfect games in major league history, Joss's masterpiece is the only one to have occurred during the heat of a pennant race. It also was the third no-hitter in this pennant race. His teammate Bob Rhoads and White Sox righthander Frank Smith had pitched theirs two weeks earlier. Even more important to the Naps, the perfect game kept them one-half game behind the Tigers while dropping the White Sox two and one-half games back.

"I'm sorry we lost," Walsh said, "but seeing that we did lose, I'm glad Addie took down a record that goes to so few. I guess way down in my heart I was glad when 'Silk' O'Loughlin called Anderson out at first in the ninth. I pitched a fairly good game, but Joss pitched better. I'struck out fifteen, but they got four hits off me and we got none. I passed a man and he passed none. That shows how much better ball Addie pitched."

Only two of Joss's pitches were hit hard: Jones's hot grounder that Lajoie snared in the third inning and Walsh's liner to leftfielder Good in the sixth. Lajoie, sniffling with a cold contracted during Thursday's workout in a chilly rain, also scooped Walsh's hopper over Joss's head in the third.

When word of Joss's perfect game arrived in Detroit, the Tigers were struggling even though Cobb's two-run single in the first had knocked out thirty-one-year-old lefthander Rube Waddell, the

Ed Walsh and Addie Joss. *National Baseball Library and Archive, Cooperstown, N.Y.*

Browns' best when he was sober. In his 19–14 record, Waddell, as eccentric as he was thirsty, was seldom as effective on the road this season as in St. Louis, where the Browns arranged for him to be shepherded across the Mississippi between starts. There, with his caretakers virtually holding him on a leash, he would happily fish the southern Illinois lakes. On a road trip, in contrast, the future Hall of Famer found familiar bartenders everywhere, as he had in Detroit the night before Friday's game. But going into the bottom of the ninth, the Tigers still trailed, 6–5. Donie Bush led off with a single and scored on Sam Crawford's double off the leftfield wall. Cobb bunted, but when Crawford kept running for home, little righthander Harry Howell threw him out. On Rossman's double down the leftfield line, Cobb turned third. Umpire Jack Sheridan waved Cobb back, presumably because he believed the ball had bounced into the crowd. Instead of scoring first and arguing later, Cobb stopped to challenge Sheridan's ruling. Jennings rushed out, grabbed Cobb, and all but carried him across the plate while debating Sheridan.

"Egan was in position," Jennings yelled. "Ask him."

Sheridan walked out to the young base umpire, Jack Egan, who told him the ball had not gone into the crowd.

"The run counts," Sheridan ruled. "Detroit wins."

In the clubhouse Jennings reminded Cobb, "Score first, then argue." With that 7–6 comeback, the Tigers retained first place by one-half game. Saturday they jumped one and one-half games ahead with their tenth straight victory, Wild Bill Donovan's 6–0 seven-hitter, while the Naps were losing. Inspired by Joss's masterpiece, a record 20,729 customers overflowed League Park as Glenn Liebhardt and Frank Smith warmed up. Smith's catcher would be dependable Billy Sullivan, who had missed several games because of a split thumb on his throwing hand. Schreckengost had fractured a finger in Friday's loss. Sullivan, traveling to Cleveland on a hunch that he might be able to help, had strolled into the White Sox clubhouse just after Joss's perfect game.

"What are you doing here?" somebody asked.

"I came here to get on base," he replied.

Sullivan did just that. Although his right hand was bandaged, he had two singles, scored a run, and stole a base as the White Sox held a 3–2 lead in the seventh. When the Naps loaded the bases with one out, Fielder Jones waved Ed Walsh in from the bullpen. Bill Hinchman, replacing the ailing Elmer Flick in left field, clunked a dinky grounder to Perring, who got the force at the plate. Now Lajoie was up, with the

League Park crowd howling for a hit. Lajoie already had two doubles. On a two-two count, Lajoie was expecting another spitball. Three times Sullivan called for a curveball, three times Walsh shook him off. Sullivan finally called for a fastball. Walsh nodded. Walsh brought the ball up to his mouth, pretending to moisten it, but threw a low fastball. Thinking a low spitball would break down for ball four, Lajoie stared at the pitch.

"Strike three," plate umpire Silk O'Loughlin bellowed.

Lajoie dropped his head, then dropped his bat. In the top of the ninth Jones was on the White Sox bench when he was handed a yellow envelope, a telegram sent to the League Park press box from White Sox fans in Chicago watching a gameboard.

"Five hundred fans in Coliseum Hall," it read, "congratulate Walsh for striking out Lajoie. Answer."

Walsh's spitball answered it. With two out in the Nap ninth, Hinchman singled. Lajoie had another opportunity. This time Walsh got him to hit a high fly that Fielder Jones settled under for the final out. But even with the 3–2 victory, the White Sox hopes were dim. Even if the White Sox swept three from the Tigers in Chicago, they wouldn't win the pennant unless the Naps lost two out of three in St. Louis. For the Naps to win, they had to take two while the White Sox were sweeping, or they had to win three while the White Sox took two of three. Even if the Naps swept three in St. Louis, the Tigers would win with two out of three in Chicago.

But when the Tigers and White Sox arrived in Chicago on Sunday for that afternoon's game, they were upstaged there by the Cubs–Pirates showdown.

WITH THE NATIONAL League pennant at stake, 30,247 stormed Chicago's wooden West Side Grounds, the largest crowd in baseball history at the time. Thousands more were turned back by policemen occasionally swinging billy clubs. In Pittsburgh an estimated 50,000 people filled two squares along Fifth Avenue, listening for word from men with megaphones atop newspaper buildings. In New York about 5,000 people gathered at the Polo Grounds to watch the gameboard simulating the Cubs–Pirates game, the same board used outside Madison Square Garden to record the progress of Giant games. Three Finger Brown had pitched Friday after having pitched Tuesday and he had lost to Vic Willis, 1–0, in 10 innings in their previous matchup. But the 175-pound, five-ten righthander with the strangely spinning curveball won, 5–2, allowing seven hits and driving in a run with a sixth-inning single. Almost as quickly as the Pirates were in the pennant race, now they were out of it.

"Bosh to those 202 hits and all that stuff," Honus Wagner said. "What does it all amount to when we didn't win that game. I'm going to kill eleven thousand birds this Winter to try to forget it."

Wagner and the other Pirates had another lament: with part of the overflow crowd standing beyond the outfielders, the Cubs hit four balls into the spectators for ground-rule doubles that ordinarily would have been outs. Even more unfortunate, with the bases loaded, Pirates first baseman Eddie Abbaticchio, baseball's first celebrated Italian player, hit a line drive that was ruled foul and struck a woman. When she sued the Cubs for damages, she testified that the ball had been fair.

Now the Cubs had to wait while the Giants had to win. But the Doves were peaceful. Ames and McGinnity combined Monday for a 7–2 two-hitter. Wiltse fired a 4–1 six-hitter. Even before Ames completed a 7–2 eight-hitter Wednesday, the Cubs had gathered at the LaSalle Street station to board the Twentieth Century Limited for Thursday's replay in New York, but manager Frank Chance, the Peerless Leader who often was referred to simply as "the P.L.," had a worry.

"Is Kling here yet?" he asked.

Johnny Kling, baseball's premier defensive catcher, had gone to Kansas City on business Monday but hadn't returned in time for Wednesday morning's workout. Three hours later, his train chugged in only an hour before the Cubs departed. With the Giants still playing, the Cubs weren't informed of the final score in New York until the Twentieth Century Limited stopped in Elkhart, Indiana, where more than two hundred fans had assembled.

"Three Finger, Three Finger," they chanted, referring to their home state hero. "Three Finger."

Brown emerged onto the platform of the last car, but the fans wouldn't leave until he held up his mangled hand that had won three games in six days. Jack Pfiester, healed by Bonesetter Reese and celebrated as "Jack the Giant Killer" until Harry Coveleski usurped his nickname, would be the Cubs' starter tomorrow against Christy Mathewson, with Brown in the bullpen if needed. Another reason why Frank Chance, sitting in the dining car, sounded confident.

"Whoever heard of the Cubs," their manager said, "losing a game they had to have?"

IN 1871, ITS wooden homes and stores a tinderbox from weeks without rain, Chicago was charred by a wind-swept fire that lasted nearly two days and killed three hundred people. Two generations later, the city and its spirit rebuilt, Chicago, not to mention baseball, had never had a day like this. While the Cubs were eliminating the Pirates at the West Side Grounds on Sunday, October 4, before at least 30,247 fans, South Side Park bulged with an estimated 22,000 customers, 7,000 more than capacity. When the gates to the fifty-cent and twenty-five-cent benches were locked shortly after two o'clock, hundreds, if not thousands, of disappointed fans tore down the wooden fences and overran the field. Some were banging dishpans or garbage can lids as background music to their heckling. But two of the Tigers had come prepared. Boss Schmidt and Bill Coughlin had brought a bushel basket of tomatoes to the ballpark and now were firing them, one by one, into the crowd.

Despite the tomato splattering, the White Sox fans were quickly rewarded. In a typical Hitless Wonder inning, the White Sox pasted together three runs in the first without a hit off righthander Ed Killian.

Ed Hahn opened with a walk. Fielder Jones bunted, but when Schmidt, trying for a force play, threw to second, Donie Bush was off the bag. Frank Isbell bunted, both runners moving up. Patsy Dougherty grounded to second baseman Jerry (Red) Downs, but Rossman muffed the throw, Hahn scoring. George Davis lofted a sacrifice fly, Jones scoring. Freddy Parent walked. On a double steal, Dougherty scored when Bush fumbled Schmidt's throw. Those were all the runs Frank Smith got, his Hitless Wonder teammates getting only one hit off Killian, a single by Parent in the fourth. But those were all the runs Smith needed in a 3–1 win.

"Chicago deserved to win," Charles Comiskey would brag later, perhaps thinking of the Cubs' victory that eliminated the Pirates that same day. "Chicago is the greatest ball town in the world."

The White Sox still needed a sweep, but the Naps, frustrated by a 3–3 tie in St. Louis, were complaining about umpire Jack Egan's call in the ninth that nullified what would have been the winning run.

With perfect-game pitcher Addie Joss, who had relieved Heinie Berger, on third and Bill Bradley on second with two out, Bill Hinchman's liner up the middle was smothered by Bobby Wallace, but the Brown shortstop's throw pulled first baseman Tom Jones's foot off the bag. Most observers also thought Hinchman clearly beat the throw. Joss had crossed home plate and Bradley, who had rounded third, was about to be trapped in a rundown when Egan signaled that Hinchman was out.

Many of the Naps rushed Egan, but Lajoie, not wanting to risk being ejected, walked to second base without saying a word.

"As sure as I'm alive," Tom Jones said later, "Hinchman beat that throw. I was thunderstruck when Egan called him out."

In the Monday morning *Plain Dealer*, an editorial asked, "Why Does Ban Johnson Force Egan upon the Naps?" In criticizing the American League president, the editorial accepted Billy Evans, Tommy Connolly, Frank (Silk) O'Loughlin, and Jack Sheridan as capable umpires, but not Egan, who had aroused the Naps throughout the season with other controversial calls.

"Ever since we had words with Egan in Washington early in the season," Bradley said, "he's had it in for us and he's given us the worst of it. Had we won in nine innings, Joss would have come right back at these fellows tomorrow. The championship really hinges on that rotten decision."

The tie created a Monday doubleheader. In the opener, another controversial call by Egan, this time at home plate, provided the Browns with one of their runs in a 3–1 victory.

When the White Sox battered twenty-four-game winner Eddie Summers, 6–1, behind Ed Walsh's six-hitter and fortieth victory with some of the Cubs watching, the Naps were eliminated. "I honestly believe," Lajoie would say years later, "that the 1908 race took more out of me than three ordinary seasons." Even though the Naps took the second game of Monday's doubleheader, 5–3, the best they could do now was produce a 90–64 record, a .584 percentage. Because the Tigers and White Sox had played fewer games due to ties that were never replayed, the winner of the Tuesday, October 6, season finale in Chicago would win the pennant.

If the Tigers won the finale, their 90–63 record would create a .586 percentage, two points ahead of the Naps.

If the White Sox won the finale, their 89–63 record would create a .586 percentage, two points ahead of the Naps.

Knowing the pennant would be at stake in the South Side Park finale, Hugh Jennings addressed the Tigers that Tuesday morning in the manager's suite at the Lexington Hotel.

"That talk," one Tiger said later, "would have instilled the fighting spirit of a lion in a yellow rabbit."

As the Tigers' bus rolled through Chicago's dusty streets, Jennings felt confident. He liked the way his players were talking. He liked the set of their jaws, the look in their eyes. He knew their fighting blood was up. But he also knew that his starting pitcher, Wild Bill Donovan, had phoned trainer Harry Tuthill during the night.

"My arm hurts so much I can't get to sleep," Donovan said. "I need a rubdown."

The year before, Donovan had produced a 25–4 record. Now he was merely 17–7, good but not great. But when the game began, Donovan's mind and maybe his arm were quickly soothed. His team-mates jumped on righthander Doc White in the first inning. Matty McIntyre singled. Donie Bush struck out, but Sam Crawford doubled into the crowd in rightfield. Ty Cobb, whose .324 average would win the second of his record twelve batting titles, tripled to left center. After only four batters, Jones waved for his workhorse. Ed Walsh was about to pitch in his seventh game in ten days, including two days when the White Sox didn't play. The day before, he had pitched a 6–1 four-hitter. Saturday he had pitched the last two and one-third innings, preserving a 3–2 victory. Friday he had lost a 1–0 classic to Addie Joss's perfect game. The previous Tuesday he had pitched and won both games of a doubleheader, 5–1 and 2–0, allowing only seven hits. The Sunday before that, he had pitched a 3–0 shutout.

Over his record 464 innings Walsh would lead the league with 40 wins, six saves, 42 complete games, and 269 strikeouts (while walking only 56). Of his fifteen losses, the Hitless Wonders had been runless in six and truly hitless in one. In his 9–3 record since September 10, each of his losses had occurred when the Sox were shut out on three hits, one hit, and no hits.

But now the coal miner known as Big Ed was being asked to pitch again, his seventeenth relief appearance in addition to his forty-nine starts. All over South Side Park the fans were pleading for Big Ed to stop the Tigers' rally. Three runs already were more than the Hitless Wonders were likely to get. Any more Tiger runs and the White Sox cause surely would be hopeless. But the coal miner's spitball wasn't dipping. Claude Rossman beat out a grounder off Isbell's glove and Herman (Germany) Schaefer singled. By the time Wild Bill Donovan walked to the mound, he had a 4–0 lead and another overflow crowd of 23,000 had been silenced.

"I was worried on the bus," Donovan would say later, "but once I threw to Hahn, I knew I was all right."

Ira Thomas knew too. Thomas was catching because Schmidt had a

36

damaged finger. "I've seen speed," Thomas would say later, "but nothing like Donovan had today. His jumpball was fooling the Sox all day and his change of pace had them helpless." Donovan pitched a two-hitter with nine strikeouts as the Tigers won, 7–0, on a barrage of fourteen hits: Crawford four, Cobb and McIntyre each three, Bush and Schaefer each two. After the final out, Jones, Isbell, and Davis shook hands with several of the Tigers.

"We've got to hand it to you, Bill," Davis said to Donovan. "Nobody in the world could have beaten you."

Big Ed Walsh had departed in the fifth inning. His head drooping in disappointment, when he neared the White Sox bench he flung himself onto the ground. By then the muttering had already begun among White Sox fans and some of their players. They were second-guessing Jones for starting Doc White instead of Frank Smith with the pennant at stake. White, who had stopped the Tigers on Sunday with a 3–1 five-hitter to lift his record to 18–12, had only one day's rest. At least Smith had two days' rest even though he had a shaky 16–17 record.

Those who knew Jones knew that the White Sox manager despised Smith for having jumped the club in midseason. Jones believed that Smith's desertion cost the White Sox the pennant. But not choosing Smith may have cost Jones his job. Whatever the reason, Comiskey fired him.

The Naps, with a 5–1 victory in their finale in St. Louis, finished second, only one-half game out: 90–64 to the Tigers' 90–63, with the White Sox at 88–64. Only the Naps completed the 154-game schedule. The Tigers played 153 games, the White Sox 152, but in those years, unlike today, unplayed games that affected the pennant race were not played. Had the Tigers lost their other game and the White Sox won their two other games, there would have been a three-way tie.

The Naps, as such, would never come close again. The next two seasons, they would finish in sixth and then in fifth place. Addie Joss's career 1.88 earned run average still ranks second to Ed Walsh's 1.82, but in 1911, his arm gone, he would die at age thirty-one of tubercular meningitis.

Back at the Lexington Hotel in Chicago that Tuesday evening, the Tigers were celebrating their second straight American League pennant with a champagne dinner. When they heard Jennings's quick walk in the corridor, they stood, held their glasses high, shouted "Eee-yah, eee-yah," and greeted him with an ovation. Jennings reminded them of his midseason promise: if they won the pennant, each player would

The Polo Grounds during the Cubs–Giants rivalry. *National Baseball Library and Archive, Cooperstown, N.Y.*

receive a tuxedo as a present. Thinking of the winters in Scranton, Pennsylvania, where he lived, third baseman Bill Coughlin grunted.

"I'd prefer an overcoat," he said.

After dinner, the Tigers continued their celebration on a late train out of LaSalle Street station. When it arrived at the Michigan Central station in Detroit the next morning at 7:15, hundreds of Tiger fans were waiting. One by one, Jennings and the players appeared. Some fans hoisted Donovan onto their shoulders during the serenade of "Michigan, My Michigan" by the red-coated Ancient and Honorable Artillery Band and the blue-coated Schmemman Band.

Soon the Tigers were sitting in decorated open cars for the ride to city hall, where Hugh Jennings didn't hide his dislike for the Naps.

"I would rather have lost it, if it had to be lost," the Tiger manager said, "to the White Sox than to any other team in the world."

But now the Tigers had to wait to see whether the Cubs or the Giants would be their opponents in the World Series that would open in Detroit.

NO GAME IN baseball had ever been quite like it, the first pennant playoff. No game had ever stirred the emotions quite like it. When all the tickets at the Polo Grounds had been sold more than two hours before the three o'clock start, thousands climbed the fences. Some even climbed the elevated train structure out on Eighth Avenue beyond the centerfield fence. One fan, fireman Henry McBride, fell to his death from a rusty girder at the 155th Street station. To maintain order, policemen turned fire hoses on the overflow spectators. As Mathewson and Pfiester began to warm up, the Giants had an idea that hinted of their desperation: Iron Man McGinnity would pick a fight with Chance early in the game.

If both were ejected by the umpires, the Giants wouldn't miss their aging pitcher nearly as much as the Cubs would miss their first baseman and manager. McGinnity cursed Chance, stepped on his feet, pushed him, even spit on him. Realizing that he was being baited, Chance wisely walked away.

Pfiester wasn't himself. In the first, he plunked the Giants' leadoff man, Fred Tenney, with a pitch. Buck Herzog walked. Roger Bresnahan's strikeout created a double play as Herzog was run down between first and second. But when Turkey Mike Donlin doubled down the first-base line, Chance waved his glove at the bullpen for Three-Finger Brown, who struck out Cy Seymour.

Through two innings, Mathewson set the Cubs down in order. His fans were yelling "Matty! Matty!" But in the third Joe Tinker, who batted .421 against Mathewson that season, led off with a triple. Johnny Kling's single made it 1–1. Brown sacrificed. With two out, McGraw ordered Evers walked intentionally. Rightfielder Frank (Wildfire) Schulte doubled down the third-base line into the crowd, Kling scoring. Chance doubled into the rightfield corner, Evers and Schulte scoring for 4–1.

The Giants added a run in the sixth, but Brown, allowing only four hits, breezed to a 4–2 victory for the National League pennant. The Cubs would go to Detroit for the World Series, which they would win from the Tigers in five games. But when baseball historians think of 1908, they think primarily of Fred Merkle's boner.

"It's criminal," McGraw explained, "to say that Merkle is stupid and to blame the loss of the pennant on him. In the first place, he is one of the smartest and best players on this club and in not touching second base, he merely did as he had seen veteran players do ever since he's been in the league. In the second place, he didn't cost us the pennant. We lost a dozen games we should have won this year. Yes, two dozen. Any one of them could have saved the pennant for us. Besides, we were robbed of the pennant and you can't say Merkle did that."

Even so, when the Giants didn't win the pennant, their fans blamed Merkle for not having touched second base.

During a vaudeville act in a Broadway theater, a comedian joked, "I call my cane 'Merkle' because it has a bone head." When the gag appeared in the newspapers, the fans jumped on it. Merkle had a nickname that he would always be remembered by, no matter how good a ballplayer he was. Over his sixteen major league seasons, mostly with the Giants, he was a solid .273 hitter who in 1911 had 49 stolen bases. After he emerged as the Giants' first baseman in 1910, he often was consulted by McGraw, his occasional bridge partner.

"Mr. McGraw never asked Matty, he never asked me," John (Chief) Meyers, a Giant catcher of that era, once said. "He'd say, 'Fred, what do you think of this?' Bonehead, what a misnomer. One of the smartest men in baseball, Fred Merkle."

Not one of the luckiest. As a first baseman with the Giants, Dodgers, and Cubs, he was in five World Series, and as a coach with the 1926 Yankees he was in another World Series, all with the losing team. In the decisive seventh game of the 1912 World Series between the Giants and the Boston Red Sox, his tenth-inning single off Smoky Joe Wood drove in the go-ahead run for a 2–1 lead with Christy Mathewson pitching. Three more outs and Bonehead Merkle would be measured for a new nickname.

In the bottom of the tenth, Giant centerfielder Fred Snodgrass dropped leadoff pinch hitter Clyde Engle's routine fly ball for a two-base error. With one out, Matty walked second baseman Steve Yerkes, but he then got Tris Speaker to lift a high pop foul near the first-base line. Merkle, transfixed momentarily, broke late. Seeing his teammate's hesitation, catcher Chief Meyers dashed to get to the ball. It dropped between them.

With a reprieve, Speaker singled, Engle scoring the tying run and Yerkes hurrying to third. Duffy Lewis was walked intentionally to set up a force play at home. Moments later Yerkes scored the Series-winning run on third baseman Larry Gardner's sacrifice fly to left. Snodgrass would be remembered for his $30,000 muff, the sum representing the difference between the World Series swag to be shared by the winning and losing teams. But once again a Merkle misadventure had cost the Giants.

"Snodgrass didn't lose the game," McGraw said. "It was lost when Merkle didn't catch Speaker's foul. We were all yelling at him from the bench that it was his ball but the crowd made so much noise he couldn't hear us. Besides, he should have caught it without anybody yelling at him."

Bonehead Merkle had done it again. But his 1908 mistake had

affected more than the Giants, more than just him. For ordering the tie game replayed, National League president Harry Pulliam, whose office was in New York, was besieged by criticism from McGraw, the Giants, and the Giants' fans. Once the city editor of the *Louisville Commercial*, he was a sensitive man who enjoyed his solitude. Too sensitive to ignore the criticism that accompanied the job he had taken in 1903.

Only two months after the December hearing that resulted in the exile from baseball of Dr. William Creamer, the Giants' club physician, over the alleged bribe offer to Bill Klem before the playoff game, Pulliam took a leave of absence from the NL office. He reportedly was suffering from a mental breakdown. On July 25, 1909, he committed suicide.

But for Fred Merkle, that fallen foul ball in the 1912 World Series was soon forgotten, unlike the enduring memory of his 1908 involvement in what has endured as the most controversial game in baseball's most controversial pennant race. More than half a century later, Al Bridwell, whose line drive past Johnny Evers had triggered the controversy, told Lawrence Ritter that he wished he had never hit Jack Pfiester's first pitch.

"I wish I'd struck out instead," Bridwell said. "If I'd done that, then it would have spared Fred a lot of unfair humiliation. Yes, I wish I'd struck out. It would have been better all around."

In the years before Fred Merkle died in 1956 in Daytona Beach, Florida, at age sixty-seven, he was a recluse in the back room of a fishing tackle shop. He seldom discussed what happened on September 23, 1908, at the Polo Grounds when he veered to the Giants' centerfield clubhouse instead of stepping on second base. But in 1950 he talked to John McCallum of the Newspaper Enterprise Association.

"I suppose when I die," he said, "they'll put on my tombstone, 'Here Lies Bonehead Merkle.' "

1920

Death, Disgrace, and the Babe

Ray Chapman. *National Baseball Library and Archive,*
Cooperstown, N.Y.

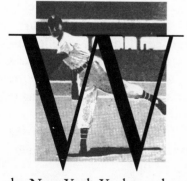

HEREVER THE CLEVELAND Indians were, Ray Chapman would assemble what was known as "the quartet" and lead the singing. On trains, in hotels, sometimes in the clubhouse. Now, on August 16, 1920, on an elevated train rattling through uptown Manhattan to the Polo Grounds for a game with the New York Yankees, the popular shortstop looked around at his teammates' grim faces.

"I know why we haven't been winning," he said. "We haven't been singing."

In his tenor voice, Chapman began warbling "Dear Ol' Pal o' Mine" and soon outfielder Jack Graney, catcher Steve O'Neill, and first baseman Doc Johnston were singing along with the others. Only a week earlier the first-place Indians were four and one-half games ahead of the Yankees and five games ahead of the Chicago White Sox. But they lost four straight to the Yankees in Cleveland before splitting a two-game weekend series there with the St. Louis Browns. As the Indians, with a 71–40 record, walked into the visiting team's clubhouse on this humid, heavy Monday afternoon for the opener of a three-game series with the Yankees, they were only four percentage points ahead of the White Sox, only one-half game ahead of the Yankees.

"Mays is pitching," said Chapman, still trying to relax his teammates. "I'll do the fielding and you do the hitting."

Carl Mays was one of baseball's most feared righthanders. He threw a "submarine ball," an underhand fastball that veered upward across the plate. As a young righthander with the Boston Red Sox, he had a 22–9 record in 1917 and a 21–13 record in 1918 while developing a reputation for throwing at batters. Ty Cobb once asked him, "Do you try to hit me?"

"What do you think?"

"I think you do."

"If you think I do, Ty, that makes me a better pitcher," Mays said. "As long as you're feeling that way, I'm more effective."

After a 1919 disagreement with Red Sox general manager Ed Barrow over payment of a fine, Mays deserted the team and demanded to be traded. To prevent other players from making similar demands, Ban Johnson, the American League president, ruled that no team was allowed to make a deal for Mays, but owner Harry Frazee quickly traded him to the Yankees for $40,000 and two obscure pitchers. Before the 1920 season Frazee, who needed money to finance his Broadway plays, also dealt Babe Ruth to the Yankees. And as Mays took the mound against the Indians, he had an 18–8 record while the Babe's forty-two homers had already far surpassed the major league record of twenty-nine, which he had set the year before.

In the soft rain of the second inning, Steve O'Neill, one of the singers on the elevated train, hit a home run into the leftfield bleachers. In the fourth the Indians extended their lead to 3–0.

As the fifth inning began, the rain had stopped. Chapman, the leadoff batter, leaned over the plate in his usual crouch and took an inside pitch. Ball one. Mays, uncoiling out of his underhand windup, fired a fastball, aiming it high and inside. As if hypnotized, Chapman never moved. The ball smashed into the shortstop's left temple. Seeing the ball bounce toward him, Mays assumed it had struck Chapman's bat. He grabbed the ball and tossed it to first baseman Wally Pipp for what he thought was the first out. But in the batter's box, Chapman, his face distorted by pain, his left ear oozing blood, had dropped to the dirt. Muddy Ruel, the Yankee catcher, appeared transfixed, but plate umpire Tommy Connolly yanked off his mask.

"We need a doctor," Connolly yelled. "Is there a doctor in the house?"

Hurrying onto the field, Dr. Joseph Cascio, who was on the staff at St. Lawrence Hospital, rushed to where Chapman had crumpled. Revived by ice packs on his head, Chapman soon wobbled to his feet as the fans applauded. But when he tried to speak, he couldn't. He agreed to go to the Indians' clubhouse in centerfield for treatment, but waved off those around him. He didn't want any help. His roommate Jack Graney and another teammate accompanied him anyway.

Near second base, Chapman's legs buckled. Grabbing him, his two teammates draped his arms around their shoulders and carried him to the clubhouse, where Dr. Cascio determined that emergency surgery was necessary to relieve pressure on Chapman's brain. Soon an ambulance from St. Lawrence Hospital, less than a mile away on West 163rd Street, was speeding through the streets, its siren blaring.

On the field, Harry Lunte, a utility infielder, had trotted to first base to run for Chapman while Mays, displaying the ball that had struck Chapman, told Connolly to look at a scuff mark on it. Mays would say later that the pitch had "sailed" more inside than he intended because the ball was scuffed. That season some AL club owners, in a cost-saving plea, had complained to Ban Johnson that too many scuffed baseballs were being thrown out of play by umpires.

"Keep balls in the game as much as possible," Johnson ordered his umpires, "except those which are dangerous."

But an active AL umpire, Billy Evans, wrote in his syndicated column after Chapman's beaning that "no pitcher in the A.L. resorted to trickery more than Mays in attempting to rough a ball to get a break on it which would make it more difficult to hit." Evans remembered how in previous seasons Mays "constantly used to drag the ball across the pitching rubber to rough the surface," prompting rules banning such scuffing.

When the game resumed, the Indians held on for a 4–3 victory that opened a half-game lead on the White Sox, idle that day. In the Yankee clubhouse Mays, annoyed that he had not pitched the Yankees into first place, explained that he had been "as wild as a hawk and the ball was wet" during the early innings. When he asked about Chapman's condition, he was told that an ambulance had taken him to St. Lawrence Hospital shortly before the game ended. In the clubhouse Chapman had looked up at the Indian trainer, Percy Smallwood, and pointed to his finger.

"Ring," he said faintly.

Smallwood realized that Chapman wanted the diamond ring that his wife, Kate, had given him. Smallwood went to the trunk where the players kept their valuables, found the ring, and slid it onto the ring finger of Chapman's left hand.

"Don't call Kate," he said now. "But if you do, tell her I'm all right."

Kate Chapman, the daughter of M. B. Daly, the owner of the East Ohio Gas Company in Cleveland, was expecting their first child. Less than a year after their October 29 wedding, they also were awaiting the completion of their new home. Around the time of his marriage Chapman had agreed to play one more year for the Indians before settling down in his father-in-law's business.

"I want to help give Cleveland the first pennant it ever had," Chapman had said. "Then I'll talk about quitting."

But now Tris Speaker, the Indians' manager and centerfielder, had phoned Kate Chapman about her husband's beaning. Hoping to ease her fears, Speaker told her that he himself had been beaned in 1916, but was playing in ten days. He assured her that the doctors intended to delay a decision on surgery until she arrived in New York the following morning. Kate and a friend, Jane McMahon, boarded the overnight train from Cleveland while doctors monitored her husband's condition. X-rays showed a depressed fracture, with a piece of bone pressing against the brain. When Chapman's pulse dropped that evening, the doctors told Speaker that they couldn't wait until the morning to operate. He agreed. Shortly after midnight, at 12:29 A.M., Chapman underwent surgery by a team of five doctors, led by Dr. T. M. Merrigan, the hospital's surgical director. One hour and fifteen minutes later, the operation was over. Merrigan had found blood clots. He also had found lacerations on the right side of the brain where the shock had forced the brain against the skull. In the process, the surgeons had removed a loose piece of skull about an inch and one-half square. In the recovery room, Chapman's pulse rose. He was breathing easier. But his condition was still listed as critical.

Speaker returned to the Ansonia Hotel at Broadway and 72nd Street where several teammates, unable to sleep, were sitting in the lobby waiting for definite word of Ray Chapman's condition. Shortly before dawn, word arrived: he had died at 4:40 A.M. of an intercranial hemorrhage.

In their grief, some Indians wept, some prayed, some remembered how their pal had always been so cheerful, how he had led the singing on the train ride to the Polo Grounds less than twenty-four hours earlier, how their star shortstop had been the innocent victim of Carl Mays's dreaded submarine ball.

"Mays has a freak delivery," Jack Graney said. "His fastball has a sudden dip to it that never gives a batter a chance to dodge."

At ten o'clock that morning Kate Chapman's train arrived at Grand Central Station, where a Philadelphia priest, Father Connors, a longtime friend of Ray, met her. They rode together in a taxi to the Ansonia Hotel where Speaker and a few other players were waiting in the manager's room. When she walked in and saw them staring at her, she knew.

"He's dead, isn't he?" she said.

Speaker nodded and she fainted.

On learning of Chapman's death, the Yankees had postponed the Tuesday afternoon game. In the morning Mark Roth, a member of the Yankee office staff, had knocked on the door of Carl Mays's apartment where he lived with his wife, Freddie, and their three-week-old daughter. Mays answered the door.

"I've got some bad news," Roth said. "Ray Chapman died at five o'clock this morning."

Stunned and shaken, Mays slowly closed the door. Soon he was contacted by the police and by a Yankee lawyer, who advised him to go to the Manhattan district attorney's office. There he described what had happened to John F. Joyce, who was in charge of the homicide bureau.

"It was a straight fastball and not a curved one," Mays said. "When Chapman came to bat, I got the signal for a straight fastball which I delivered. It was a little too close and I saw Chapman duck his head in an effort to get out of the path of the ball. He was too late, however, and a second later he fell to the ground. It was the most regrettable incident of my career and I would give anything if I could undo what had happened."

Joyce quickly ruled Chapman's death "purely accidental" and told Mays he could go home.

Miller Huggins, the Yankee manager, tried to absolve Mays, saying, "Chapman's left foot may have caught in the muddy ground, which prevented him from stepping out of the way." According to Indian righthander Ray Caldwell, who had pitched for the Yankees for nine seasons, Chapman had "ducked into the pitch; if he hadn't ducked, the ball would've hit him on the shoulder."

Those theories did not soften the situation: Ray Chapman had been killed by a pitched ball.

That evening Chapman's body, in a white pine casket, was rolled on a trunk wagon through Grand Central Station and placed aboard the Lake Shore Limited for its return to Cleveland and Friday's funeral. In the terminal, hundreds of people stood with heads bared. That afternoon more than three thousand people had visited the James F. McGowan Funeral Home not far from the Polo Grounds, but Mays did not. He decided not to phone Kate Chapman and not to go to the funeral parlor.

"I knew," the pitcher later explained, "that the sight of his silent form would haunt me as long as I live."

The death was already haunting Mays. When he returned home from the D.A.'s office, his wife told him of two threatening phone calls from baseball fans. Red Sox and Detroit Tiger players were talking about a petition to ban him from baseball, and the St. Louis Browns were considering not playing against the Yankees if Mays pitched. In his seven seasons, he had hit sixty-six batters, including two other Indians in 1920, first baseman Doc Johnston and leftfielder Charlie Jamieson. Another factor in the sorrowful reaction to Chapman's death was the popular shortstop's reputation. He was described by sportswriter Bill Slocum as possessing "qualities of sterling manhood" even in arguments with umpires.

"Ray never protested unless he felt justified," umpire Billy Evans recalled. "One time after he debated a call, he came up to me the next inning and said, 'I guess you win that one, Bill. Everybody on the team saw the play as you did. Seems as though I must have been wrong.'"

By the time Chapman's body arrived in Cleveland on Thursday morning, more than two hundred floral pieces had been delivered to the Daly home. But on Wednesday afternoon the Indians had resumed the season, riding the elevated train to the Polo Grounds without their singing shortstop. With the American flag and the smaller flags atop the grandstand at half-mast, Yankee first baseman Wally Pipp hit an inside-the-park home run off Jim Bagby in the ninth inning for a 4–3 victory that narrowed the Indians' lead over both the White Sox and the Yankees to one-half game. Both teams wore black armbands on the uniforms, but Carl Mays was conspicuous by his absence.

Thursday afternoon Babe Ruth hit his forty-third homer but the Indian cleanup hitter, rightfielder Elmer Smith, hit a homer and the new shortstop, Harry Lunte, had two hits. The Indians won, 4–3. When they boarded the Lake Shore Limited that evening to return to Cleveland for Friday's funeral, they had a one-game lead on the White Sox.

Originally, the funeral mass was to have been in the Daly family's parish church, St. Philomena's, but it was transferred to St. John's Cathedral to accommodate the expected throng of mourners. Thousands stood outside. As the casket entered the cathedral, two small boys, their hands clasped, peeked past the adults in front of them. One of the boys tossed a white carnation, hoping it would land on the casket, but it fell to the floor among the pallbearers' feet.

"That's all right," the other boy was heard to say. "You threw it anyway."

Outside the cathedral later, Ban Johnson, who was being pressured to discipline Mays, said, "I could not conscientiously attempt to make any trouble for Mr. Mays after listening to Father Scullen's wonderful sermon, but it is my honest belief that Mr. Mays will never pitch again. From what I have learned, he is greatly affected and may never be capable, temperamentally, of pitching again. I also know the feeling against him to be so bitter among members of other teams that it would be unadvisable for him to attempt to pitch this year at any rate." Mays, meanwhile, was reported to be confined to his home, suffering from a nervous breakdown.

That afternoon in Philadelphia, after both teams had stood for two minutes of silence at the start of the fifth inning in Chapman's memory, the White Sox swept a doubleheader from the Athletics to move into a virtual tie for first place with the Indians.

The White Sox were considered baseball's best team, with many of its best players: slugger Shoeless Joe Jackson, second baseman Eddie Collins, third baseman George (Buck) Weaver, centerfielder Happy Felsch, shortstop Swede Risberg, catcher Ray Schalk, and pitchers Eddie Cicotte, Red Faber, Claude Williams, and Dickie Kerr.

Jackson couldn't read or write, but he could hit. At age twenty-two in his first full season with the Indians in 1911, he had batted .408. His career average would be .356, higher than anybody's except Ty Cobb's .367 and Roger Hornsby's .358.

Cobb, Ruth and Speaker each called Jackson "the greatest natural hitter" they ever saw. Ruth patterned his swing after that of the lefthanded slugger, six-one and 200 pounds, out of Greenville, South Carolina, where he grew up playing baseball barefoot. One day there, after four innings on a field strewn with rocks and broken bottles, he shook his head.

"I can't play anymore," he announced. "Not on this field."

"Are the rocks and glass hurting your feet?" somebody asked.

"Naw, but they're fuzzin' up the ball so I can't throw it."

As the 1920 season developed, Jackson, at thirty-one, was threatening to hit .400 again. Collins, at thirty-three, was having his best season: he would complete it at .369 with 222 hits. He had been baseball's best second baseman since establishing himself with Connie Mack's "$100,000 Infield" on the Philadelphia Athletics teams that from 1910 through 1914 won four pennants in five seasons. Weaver, just turning thirty as baseball's best third baseman, was also having his best season. He would bat .333 with 210 hits. Schalk was baseball's best catcher, defying those who had dismissed him as "too small" at five-nine and 165 pounds. He originated the practice of backing up first base and third base. He once made a putout at second.

William (Kid) Gleason, the fiery manager, also had baseball's best starting rotation. At age thirty-six, righthander Eddie Cicotte was coming off a 29–7 season. Red Faber, a righthander about to turn thirty-two, would go on to win 254 games in a Hall of Fame career. Claude (Lefty) Williams had posted a 23–11 record in 1919 and another lefthander, little Dickie Kerr, only five-seven and 155 pounds, was emerging as a twenty-game winner.

But ever since the White Sox had lost the 1919 World Series to the Cincinnati Reds, gossip about a gambling fix had been heard. Chick Gandil, their first baseman, had mysteriously decided not to report for spring training. Even as the 1920 season progressed, whispers were heard that some members of the White Sox were still doing business with gamblers, although the standings seemed to stifle the rumors.

Over the weekend the White Sox grabbed a two-game lead, winning twice in Washington, while the Indians were losing a Saturday doubleheader in Boston and acknowledging their pitching need by purchasing lefthander Walter Mails from Sacramento of the Pacific Coast League. His nickname was "Duster" because of his wildness in a 1916 trial with the Brooklyn Dodgers, but now he preferred to call himself "the Great" Mails.

On Monday afternoon, August 23, one week after Chapman's beaning, Carl Mays quickly disproved Ban Johnson's theory that he would never pitch again. Encouraged by applause from Yankee fans, he stopped the Tigers, 10–0, then spoke out against his detractors on the Red Sox and Tigers, saying, "Both those clubs have pitchers who have hit more men this year than I have." Mays had hit six, but Bullet Joe Bush of the Red Sox had hit ten and Howard Ehmke of the Tigers had hit nine.

The Indians, meeting without Speaker's knowledge, were circulating a petition that AL teams refuse to play against the Yankees when Mays pitched. Boston, Detroit, St. Louis, and Washington supported the petition, but the White Sox and Connie Mack, the owner-manager of the Philadelphia Athletics, opposed it.

Although the White Sox maintained their two-game lead despite two losses to the Yankees, Speaker apparently was annoyed not only that his players met without consulting him but that they might be more concerned with Mays than they were with the pennant race. "The White Sox are two ahead," he said, "but that's not so bad considering that in our last seventeen games, we've won but five." The next day in Washington, the Indians lost again and dropped into third place.

As the season moved into September, the White Sox suddenly lost three suspicious games in Boston and the Indians regained first place by winning three in Washington, rallying in the finale after the Great Mails had been unable to last two innings in his first start. Now the White Sox were only one-half game behind, the Yankees one game behind. On their train to Cleveland that night of Thursday, September 2, the Indians sat around singing together for the first time since Chapman's death.

The next afternoon, in the Indians' return to League Park, a member of the Naval Reserve unit to which Chapman belonged marched to the shortstop area with a bugle and played taps as the American flag was lowered to half-staff. Supported by an orchestra, one hundred voices sang "Lead Kindly Light" as 15,000 fans stood, many weeping. But when the Indians lost, 1–0, to the Tigers on Ty Cobb's single in the ninth off Harry Coveleski, they were virtually tied with the Yankees.

Over the Labor Day weekend, the Indians edged into a one-game lead over both teams. In a holiday doubleheader with the Browns that attracted an overflow crowd of 23,000, Mails settled down to pitch a seven-hitter in the 7–2 opener before Elmer Smith's third double sparked a two-run ninth-inning rally for a 6–5 victory. But in the morning game, Harry Lunte had pulled a thigh muscle rounding first on a single.

Desperate for a shortstop, Speaker agreed to the purchase of a twenty-one-year-old minor leaguer, Joe Sewell, short on size and experience. At five-six and 155 pounds, he had been playing college baseball at the University of Alabama only four months earlier. But he had been the sensation of the Southern Association season, batting .289 for the New Orleans Pelicans with 19 doubles and 8 triples while scoring 58 runs in 92 games. He seldom struck out.

Sewell, wearing a new suit and new high-button shoes he had purchased in Cincinnati while changing trains, arrived in Cleveland in time for the Indians' biggest series of the year: three games against the Yankees and Babe Ruth with first place at stake. But the Yankees were without Carl Mays.

"We are not taking Mays to Cleveland," Yankee co-owner Cap Huston explained in a statement. "Not because we think there is danger of any trouble, but out of respect to the feeling of the people there. We don't want to offend them. It is largely a matter of sentiment."

In their previous visit to Cleveland, the Yankees had swept four games. Now, in the first inning, the Babe crashed his forty-seventh homer for a 2–0 lead. After that he was walked intentionally three times by Harry Coveleski, who pitched a six-hitter as the Indians rallied to win, 10–4. But the Yankees won the next two games. Ruth's forty-eighth homer propelled Bob Shawkey to a 6–1 victory in Sewell's debut at shortstop, and his two doubles in a 6–2 win contributed to narrowing the Indians' lead to .001, with the White Sox one-half game back.

When the Yankees arrived in Detroit, Mays rejoined them. The Yankees swept three there, with the Babe's forty-ninth homer supporting Mays in a nine-hit 4–2 victory. Stopping in Toledo for an exhibition game, the Babe hit two homers.

"A lad named Meade was pitching for the Toledo club," read the daily United News column that appeared in dozens of newspapers under the Babe's byline. "I hope some A.L. club, not the Yankees, buys him next season."

The Babe was making baseball the national pastime. Nobody had ever hit so many home runs. Nobody had ever hit a baseball so far so often. Over the 1920 season he would bat .376 with 54 homers, 9 triples, and 36 doubles, while driving in 137 runs, scoring 158 runs, and establishing a major league record that still stands, an .847 slugging average (total bases divided by at-bats). Nobody had ever made so much money in baseball—not just his record $20,000 salary but thousands of dollars more from motion pictures, appearances, his syndicated column, and dozens of other fees. And nobody ever had lived so boisterously, at least not so openly and so innocently. He once talked about having been at a party with some "movie people."

"What movie people?" a teammate asked.

"You know, what the hell are their names?"

Their names were Mary Pickford and Douglas Fairbanks, the Madonna and Kevin Costner of their time. But if the Babe didn't know their names, they and everybody else knew his. The day the Babe was hitting those two exhibition homers in Toledo, a New York judge dismissed the Babe's injunction against the Educational Film Association.

According to the judge, "the plaintiff is so famous and public interest in him so intense" that all pictures published about him were a matter of current news and therefore outside the statute forbidding the publication of unauthorized pictures.

Babe Ruth was certainly current news. He had been purchased by the Yankees from Red Sox owner Harry Frazee for $100,000 and a $300,000 loan to secure the mortgage on Fenway Park on January 3, 1920, around the time that the Volstead Act was ruled constitutional. What was known as Prohibition had begun, the prohibition in the

Babe Ruth launches the home run era. *National Baseball Library and Archive, Cooperstown, N.Y.*

United States of the manufacture, sale, import, or export of liquor. In the months that Americans began to visit speakeasies, the Babe had awed them with his home runs. When the first-place Yankees arrived in Chicago for three games with the White Sox, the *Chicago Tribune* wrote of "Tarzan Ruth and the rest of the conquering heroes from Manhattan." But that Thursday the Babe was too anxious to hit little Dickie Kerr, whose lefthanded curveball cut the corners. In five at-bats, Ruth had two singles, but he took only two pitches that were ruled balls. Twice he hit the first pitch, twice he took the first pitch for a strike. With two on in the fifth, a homer would put the Yankees ahead. Kerr curved a called strike, wasted a pitch, curved a swinging strike, curved another pitch that the Babe fouled off, then curved a called third strike. After catcher Ray Schalk tossed the ball toward the mound, the Babe walked out and kicked it. Kerr won, 8–3, while the Indians, with Mails blanking the Senators, 1–0, regained first place by .003.

The next day righthander Urban (Red) Faber stopped the Yankees, 6–4, helped by two-out triples by Eddie Collins, Joe Jackson, and Happy Felsch in the first. The Babe flied out twice, grounded out, and was walked intentionally, but that night he was out and about.

"Ernie Young Announces," the ad in the *Tribune* sports section had blared that morning, "Personal Appearance of Babe Ruth (Himself), the Home Run King, at the Del Weis Gardens, Cottage Grove and the Midway Tonight, Entertainment and Dancing, As Usual."

In Saturday's finale, the White Sox pounded Bob Shawkey in a 15–9 rout as righthander Eddie Cicotte held the Babe to a ninth-inning single. When the Indians beat the Senators, despite three errors in one inning by little Joe Sewell, their first-place lead was one and one-half games over the White Sox and two games over the Yankees who, despite the Babe's record total of fifty-four homers, would not recover from their disaster.

Even with their three-game sweep of the Yankees and their virtual shutout of the Babe, seven members of this White Sox team had begun to be the focus of questions that many of them had hoped never to be asked.

Before an insignificant National League game on August 31 in Chicago between the Cubs and the last-place Philadelphia Phillies, the word out of Detroit was that thousands of dollars had been bet on the last-place Phillies because the game had been fixed by gamblers. The odds suddenly had shifted from 2-to-1 on the Cubs to 6-to-5 on the Phillies. To thwart the rumors, Cub president William L. Veeck ordered manager Fred Mitchell to switch starting pitchers. Instead of using Claude Hendrix, the Cubs started their ace, Grover Cleveland Alexander, but lost anyway, 3–0.

Veeck hoped to keep his investigation quiet, but four days later the Chicago *Herald & Examiner* had a front-page story reporting that $50,000 had been bet on the "fixed" game.

Soon a Cook County grand jury had convened, with Charles

MacDonald, chief judge of the Criminal Courts Division, presiding. In opening the proceedings, Judge MacDonald cited the Cubs–Phillies game but added that the grand jury would explore baseball gambling in general, including the possibility that the 1919 World Series had been fixed.

The embers of that suspected scandal had been smoldering in Chicago ever since the White Sox' stunning loss to the Cincinnati Reds, five games to three. Those embers were about to burst into flames.

On the Sunday after the White Sox' sweep of the Yankees, the *Chicago Tribune* printed a letter on the first page of its sports section from Fred M. Loomis, a prominent Chicago businessman described as "one of Chicago's most enthusiastic baseball followers and a personal friend of several members of the White Sox club." In reality, Loomis had been persuaded by Jim Crusinberry, a *Tribune* sportswriter who suspected the World Series fix but couldn't prove it, to sign a letter that Crusinberry had composed. The headline over the letter read:

IS ANYTHING WRONG WITH SOX?
1919 WORLD SERIES SCANDAL REVIVED;
FAN SEEKS ANSWER TO RUMORS

"Widespread circulation," the letter began, "has been given to reports from various sources that the World Series of last Fall was deliberately and intentionally lost through an alleged conspiracy between certain unnamed members of the Chicago White Sox team and certain gamblers. . . . Where there is so much smoke, there must be fire. . . . The game must be cleaned up and it must be cleaned up at once . . . if baseball is going to survive. . . . There is a perfectly good grand jury located in this county. The citizens and taxpayers of Illinois are maintaining such an institution for the purpose of investigating any alleged infraction of the law. Those who possess evidence of any gambling last Fall in the World Series must come forward so that justice will be done in this case where public confidence seems to have been so flagrantly violated."

When the grand jury began hearing testimony, Charles Comiskey, the White Sox owner known as the "Old Roman," acknowledged having heard the fix rumors but had not pursued them.

"If any of my players are not honest," Comiskey testified, "I'll fire them no matter who they are, and if I can't get honest players to fill their places, I'll close the gates of the park that I have spent a lifetime to build and in which, in the declining years of my life, I take the greatest measure of pride and pleasure."

By now the White Sox, still only one and one-half games behind the Indians, had arrived in Cleveland for a three-game showdown that probably would decide the pennant race. The morning of Thursday's opener, the bold black type of an eight-column headline across the September 23 front page of the *Chicago Tribune* boomed:

BARE "FIXED" WORLD SERIES

According to Assistant State Attorney Hartley Replogle, the 1919 World Series had not been "on the square. From five to seven players on the White Sox team are involved."

The inquiry into the Cubs–Phillies game had resulted in testimony by Buck Herzog, the Cub second baseman who was implicated in that alleged fix.

"Charles L. Herzog, Cubs infielder," Jim Crusinberry reported on the *Tribune*'s front page, "last night unfolded a story, supported by copies of sworn depositions and a letter, that may go far toward clearing up the reports of alleged crookedness in baseball not only in games in which the Cubs were involved, but in the World Series of last Fall."

Although the White Sox were informed of what was happening in Chicago by the time Thursday's game at League Park began, they didn't appear to be distracted.

In extending their winning streak to seven games and closing to within one-half game, they strafed fifteen hits for little Dickie Kerr in a 10–3 rout of Jim Bagby, the Indian ace whose twenty-nine victories had included five over the White Sox. But that afternoon in Chicago the grand jury heard affidavits from two Boston Braves players, Arthur Wilson and Norman Boeckel, who asserted that Giant pitcher Rube Benton had won $3,800 betting on Cincinnati in the World Series after a tip from Hal Chase, a well-traveled first baseman who had been suspended in 1918 for fixing games. The grand jury, aware that it now was close to unraveling the mystery of the White Sox loss to the Reds, extended itself indefinitely and adjourned until Tuesday morning.

"Chicago, New York, Cincinnati, and St. Louis gamblers are bleeding baseball and corrupting players," grand jury foreman Harry H. Brigham said. "We are going the limit on this inquiry. I'm shocked at the rottenness so far revealed."

Thursday night Ban Johnson, who disliked Comiskey, dropped another bombshell: he had heard statements that the White Sox would not dare to win the 1920 pennant because the managers of a gambling syndicate, alleged to have certain players in their power, had forbidden it. The gamblers supposedly had backed the Indians with heavy wagers.

Surrounded now by "fix" stories, the White Sox were shut out by the Great Mails, 2–0, on Friday afternoon, dropping them one and one-half games behind. In the League Park press box, I. H. Sanborn of the *Chicago Tribune* filed a separate story on the White Sox situation.

"Unquestionably," wrote Sanborn, "the grand jury investigation, full reports of which were in the Cleveland paper, have had their effect on the White Sox. It has made those who are not under suspicion mad, but overanxious, as shown by Ray Schalk's failure to make an easy out on Sewell stealing second base in the second inning and by Eddie Collins' striking out on a bad ball in the fifth when a base hit or another base on balls would have broken up the game. One of the players voiced the opinion that the statement by Ban Johnson that the White Sox did not dare to win the pennant might be propaganda to help out the Cleveland club, whose owner is one of the supporters of Johnson, against the White Sox owner, who is his antagonist."

Saturday morning the *Tribune*'s front-page headline blared the "Inside Story of Plot to Buy" the 1919 World Series.

"The gamblers' inside story became public last night," the *Tribune* reported. "The amount actually paid the White Sox players was $15,000 although more was promised.... A few weeks before the close of the 1919 season Abe Attell was approached by Hal Chase and asked whether he could find a gambler who would pay $100,000 to fix the World Series. Attell agreed to put the proposal to Arnold Rothstein.... Attell was chased by Rothstein, but Attell told Chase that Rothstein was agreeable."

According to the *Tribune*, the payments were to be $15,000 after the White Sox lost the opener, $20,000 the morning of the third day, $25,000 the morning of the fourth day, $40,000 after the World Series ended.

By now the names of the White Sox fixers were being whispered: Joe Jackson, Buck Weaver, Happy Felsch, Swede Risberg, Eddie Cicotte, Lefty Williams, utility man Fred McMullin, and Chick Gandil, the first baseman who had decided not to return. Gandil had needed appendectomy surgery the previous Monday in Lufkin, Texas, where he lived.

During the long season the 1919 fix had split the White Sox into two cliques. The innocents hung together, notably Eddie Collins, Ray Schalk, Dickie Kerr, and Red Faber. So did the fixers, although Weaver reportedly hadn't spoken to Cicotte since the World Series ended. But now the fixers were wondering what the next phone call would bring, what the next newspaper headline would say, what would come out of the grand jury Tuesday when Schalk was scheduled to testify.

"It's up to the ballplayers to protect the sport," Schalk had said. "If they're going to drag me into this mess, I'm going to go before the grand jury and tell all I know. I'll mention the names of the men on my own team."

When the White Sox picked up Saturday morning's *Plain Dealer* in Cleveland, they read that Harry H. Brigham, the grand jury foreman, had disclosed that "the name of the man" who fixed the 1919 World Series had been given to the grand jury. The name? Nobody was talking yet for the record, but the grand jury had subpoenaed Arnold Rothstein, described as a "millionaire turfman" and owner of Havre de Grace racetrack in Maryland; Sleepy Bill Burns, a lefthanded pitcher with the White Sox and the Reds a decade earlier who had struck it rich in Texas oil; Abe Attell, the world featherweight champion from 1901 to 1912, and "several other sportsmen."

The noose was tightening, but Saturday afternoon Jackson lifted his average to .387, crashing a homer and two doubles, as cool Claude (Lefty) Williams stopped the Indians, 5–1, on five hits. Again the White Sox were only one-half game out of first place. Quietly they boarded a train for Chicago, where Sunday and Monday they would play the Tigers before finishing the season in St. Louis. The Indians were off to St. Louis and Detroit.

When the White Sox got off the train in Chicago, they were confronted by the *Sunday Tribune*'s front-page headline "First Evidence of Money Paid to Sox Bared." The story described a "mystery package" delivered during the World Series by Fred McMullin to Buck Weaver's home. Weaver was out. McMullin waited awhile, then left the package with Weaver's mother-in-law. On his return, Weaver refused to touch the package and stormed around the room. Now, with the team returning under even more clouds of suspicion, nineteen-year-old James T. Farrell, later a celebrated Chicago novelist, sat in a box seat and studied the White Sox during batting and fielding practice.

"It looked the same as always," Farrell would write years later.

"They took their turns at the plate. They took their turns on the field. They seemed calm, no different than they had been on other days before the scandal talk had broken. The crowd was friendly to them and some cheered. But a subtle gloom hung over the fans. The atmosphere of the park was like the muggy weather."

Although edgy inside, Eddie Cicotte pitched as if at a picnic. His seven-hitter stopped the Tigers, 8–1. But the Indians maintained their one-half-game lead. The late Ray Chapman's successor at shortstop, little Joe Sewell, drove in four runs with a double and a single in a 7–5 victory over the Browns, the Indians rallying from a 5–3 deficit after the White Sox' early runs had been posted at Sportsman's Park.

"After the game," Farrell would write of the White Sox victory, "I went under the stands and stood near the steps leading down from the White Sox clubhouse. A small group always collected there to watch the players leave. But on this particular Sunday, there were about two hundred to two hundred and fifty boys waiting. Joe Jackson and Happy Felsch appeared. They were both big men. Jackson was the taller of the two, Felsch the broader. They were sportively dressed in gray silk shirts, white duck trousers, and white shoes. They came down the steps slowly, their faces masked by impassivity.

"They turned and started to walk away. Spontaneously the crowd followed in a slow, disorderly manner. I went with the crowd and trailed about five feet behind Jackson and Felsch. They walked somewhat slowly. A fan called out: 'It ain't true, Joe.'

"The two suspected players did not turn back. They walked on slowly. The crowd took up the cry and more than once men and boys called out and repeated: 'It ain't true, Joe.' The call followed Jackson and Felsch as they walked all the way under the stands to the Thirty-Fifth Street side of the ballpark and went for their parked cars in a soccer field behind the rightfield bleachers. I waited by the exit of the soccer field. Many others also waited. Soon Felsch and Jackson drove out in their sportive roadsters, through the double file of silent fans.

"I went back to the clubhouse. But most of the players had gone. It was almost dark. I went home. I sensed it was true."

Charles Comiskey also sensed it was true, if he didn't already know it was true. That afternoon he acknowledged that after the White Sox had lost the World Series opener, he was concerned that "some one had fixed" some of his players. Monday morning the Philadelphia *North American* reported it was true. Under the front-page headline "The Most Gigantic Sports Swindle in the History of America," sportswriter Jimmy Isaminger quoted Billy Maharg, a roly-poly former major league catcher and boxer who was working in a Ford assembly plant in Philadelphia, as admitting that he and Sleepy Bill Burns, the former White Sox and Red lefthander now in Texas oil, were the pioneers in the conspiracy to throw the 1919 World Series.

"We were all double-crossed by Abe Attell," Maharg asserted, "and I want everybody to know the truth."

According to Maharg, the first, second, and final games were fixed; the offer to fix the World Series had been volunteered by Cicotte to Burns and Maharg in a New York hotel; the eight White Sox players were promised $100,000 but actually received only $10,000; Attell presented a fake telegram, won a fortune for himself and New York gamblers, but did not keep his word with the eight players or with Burns and Maharg; Burns and Maharg lost nearly every dollar they had bet on the third game, which they thought was fixed.

Isaminger's story was reported in Chicago's afternoon papers. When the White Sox trooped into their clubhouse after Dickie Kerr had blanked the Tigers, 2–0, on six hits in their last home game, several copies were spread on tables.

As the other White Sox players silently stared at the headlines and the story, Joe Jackson, who couldn't read or write, stared at his teammates, then dressed quickly and departed. So did Felsch. So did the others. Cicotte returned to his hotel where a tall, soft-spoken man with an easy smile was waiting in the lobby. The man, a detective hired by Ban Johnson, had been tailing the White Sox fixers in recent weeks, trying to convince Cicotte in particular that it would be better to confess, that the law might go easier on him. Now, as the man talked to Cicotte again, the pitcher listened, then went up to his room.

For all the worries of their fixers, the White Sox were still in the pennant race, still only one-half game out of first place.

That afternoon in St. Louis, the Indians won, 8–4, behind Mails as Charlie Jamieson had four hits: two singles, a double, and a homer. With two more games against the Browns on Tuesday and Wednesday, the Indians had an opportunity to increase their lead while the White Sox were idle before going to St. Louis for the final weekend series, a quirk of the schedule that would help create the biggest and blackest headlines in baseball history. Comiskey was usually the first to arrive at the club offices in the morning, but on Tuesday, with no workout scheduled, manager Kid Gleason was waiting for him.

"Why so early?" Comiskey asked.

"Commy, do you want the real truth?" Gleason asked. "If you do, I think I can get it for you today."

"How?"

"Cicotte. I know he's ready to break down. He's weak. He's been stewing with this all summer."

Comiskey sighed.

"Shall I get him?" Gleason asked.

"Go get him."

Gleason went to Cicotte's hotel and brought his ace righthander to the downtown law offices of Alfred Austrian, the White Sox attorney. In the reception room, Gleason motioned for Cicotte to take a chair.

"Wait here, Eddie," the manager said.

Cicotte sat there for twenty minutes, then a secretary led him into an empty inner office where he sat for another twenty minutes, alone with his guilt. By the time he was led into the office where Comiskey, Gleason, and Austrian were sitting, he had crumbled.

"I don't know what you'll think of me, but I got to tell you how I double-crossed you, Mr. Comiskey," he said. "I did double-cross you. I'm a crook. I got $10,000 for being a crook."

Comiskey knew that the truth was out, that the 1919 World Series had been fixed, that his White Sox team would never be the same, that when the grand jury indicted the players, he would be forced to suspend them, that the pennant race was over.

"Don't tell it to me!" Comiskey barked. "Tell it to the grand jury!"

Shortly before noon, according to the *Chicago Tribune* account, Cicotte walked into the Criminal Courts building with Austrian and two bailiffs. In a sixth-floor office he was introduced to Hartley Replogle by Austrian, who suggested, "Come clean with him, Eddie, and he'll take care of you." Replogle slid a legal paper toward the pitcher.

"Sign it," Replogle said assuringly. "Don't worry. We'll see that you'll be all right."

Cicotte unknowingly signed a waiver of immunity, then was ushered into Judge MacDonald's chambers.

"Are you going to tell us everything?" the judge asked. "We want to know about the gamblers."

Cicotte nodded. The judge told Replogle to indict him. Cicotte asked, "What's that mean?"

Replogle reassured him, then Cicotte was led to the grand jury room where he was sworn in.

"Risberg, Gandil, and McMullin were at me for a week before the

World Series started," he began. "They wanted me to go crooked. I didn't know. I needed the money. I had the wife and kids. The wife and kids don't know this. I don't know what they'll think."

He stopped, dropped his head into his hands. When he looked up, tears were in his eyes.

"The eight of us got together in my room three or four days before the games started. Gandil was the master of ceremonies. We talked about throwing the Series, we decided we could get away with it. We agreed to do it. I was thinking of the wife and kids. I'd bought a farm. There was a $4,000 mortgage on it. There isn't any mortgage on it now. I paid it off with the crooked money.

"I told them I had to have the cash in advance. I didn't want any checks. I didn't want any promises. I wanted the money in bills. I wanted it before I pitched a ball.

"We all talked quite a while about it, I and the seven others. Yes, all of us decided to do our best to throw the games to Cincinnati, then Gandil and McMullin took us all, one by one, away from the others and we talked turkey. They asked me my price. I told them $10,000, and I told them that $10,000 was to be paid in advance.

" 'Cash in advance,' I said. 'Cash in advance and nothing else.'

"It was Gandil I was talking to. He wanted to give me some money at the time, the rest after the games were played and lost. But it didn't go with me. I said, 'Cash.' I reminded him, 'Cash in advance, not C.O.D. If you can't trust me, I don't trust you. Pay, or I play ball. Well, the arguments went on for days, the arguments for some now and some later, but I stood pat. I wanted that $10,000 and I got it.

"How I wish I didn't.

"The day before I went to Cincinnati," he went on, "I put it up to them squarely for the last time that there would be nothing doing unless I had the money. That night I found the money under my pillow. There was $10,000. I counted it. I don't know who put it there, but it was there. It was my price. I had sold out Commy. I had sold out the other boys. Sold them for $10,000 to pay off a mortgage on a farm for the wife and kids ... $10,000, what I had asked, what I had demanded ... $10,000 cash in advance, there in my fingers. I had been paid and I went on. I threw the game.

"If I had realized what that meant to me. The taking of that dirty, crooked money. The hours of mental torture, the days and nights of living with an unclean mind, the weeks and months of going along with six of the seven other crooked players, and holding a guilty secret. And of going along with the boys who had stayed straight and clean and honest, boys who had nothing to trouble them. It was hell. I got the $10,000 cash in advance, that's all. The first ball I pitched I wondered if the wife and kiddies would say if they ever found out I was a crook, yet I had the $10,000."

When the grand jury asked him to explain how he had contributed to throwing the games, Cicotte nodded.

"It's easy," he said. "Just a slight hesitation on the player's part will let a man get to base or make a run. I did it by not putting a thing on the ball. You could have read the trademark on it the way I lobbed it over the plate. A baby could have hit 'em. Schalk was wise the moment I started pitching. In one of the games, the first I think, there was a man on first and the Reds' batter hit a slow grounder to me. I could have made a double play on it without any trouble at all, but I was slow, slow enough to prevent the double play. It did not necessarily look crooked on my part. It's hard to tell when a game is on the square and when it's not. A player can make a crooked error that will look on the square as easy as he can make a square one. Sometimes the square ones look crooked.

"Then in the fourth game, which I also lost, on a tap to the box I deliberately threw badly to first, allowing a man to get on. Another time, I intercepted a throw from the outfield and deliberately bobbled it, allowing a run to score. All the runs scored against me were due to my own deliberate errors. In those two games, I did not try to win.

"I've lived a thousand years in the last two months. I would not have done that thing for a million dollars. Now I've lost everything. Job, reputation, everything. My friends all bet on the Sox. I knew it, but I couldn't tell them. I had to double-cross them. I'm through with baseball. I'm going to lose myself if I can and start life over again."

During more than two hours on the stand, Cicotte mentioned Burns and Maharg, but when Judge MacDonald, thinking of Rothstein and Attell, asked him about other gamblers, he declared he didn't know any.

When the door of the grand jury room opened, those outside suddenly were aware that Cicotte had confessed. Ray Schalk had been waiting to testify, but now he left the building. In his Trenier Hotel room, Joe Jackson was worried.

"I heard I'd been indicted," he would say later in the day. "I decided that those rich men couldn't put anything over on me. I called up Judge MacDonald and told him I was an honest man and that he ought to watch this thing.

"He said, 'I know you are not.' He hung up the receiver on me. I thought it over. I figured somebody had squawked."

Jackson phoned MacDonald again. This time the judge asked him to come to the Criminal Courts building. When the White Sox slugger got there, Austrian took the illiterate from Greenville, South Carolina, into an empty office. Jackson insisted he was innocent, but he wanted to tell his story. Austrian warned him not to lie, that Cicotte had already spilled the story. Austrian assured Jackson that the best way to protect himself was to tell everything he knew, that the court was interested in convicting the gamblers, not the ballplayers. Austrian had Jackson sign a waiver of immunity, then took him downstairs to the grand jury room. Jackson was sworn in. One of Hartley Replogle's first questions was, "Did anybody pay you any money to help throw that Series in favor of Cincinnati?"

"They did," Jackson said.

"How much did they pay you?"

"They promised me $20,000 and paid me $5,000."

"Did [Mrs. Jackson] know that you got $5,000 for helping throw these games?"

"She did that night, yes."

"What did she say about it?"

"She said she thought it was an awful thing to do."

When Jackson testified that Lefty Williams had been the intermediary between him and the gamblers, Replogle asked, "When did he promise the $20,000?"

"It was to be paid after each game."

When Jackson testified that he received only $5,000, which Williams tossed on his bed in a dirty envelope after the fourth game, Replogle asked, "What did you say to Williams?"

"I asked him what the hell had come off here?"

"What did he say?"

"He said Gandil said we all got a screw through Abe Attell . . . that we got double-crossed. I don't think Gandil was crossed as much as he crossed us."

"At the end of the first game you didn't get any money, did you?"

"No, I did not. No, sir."

"What did you do then?"

"I asked Gandil, 'What is the trouble?' " He says, 'Everything is all right.' He had it."

"Then you went ahead and threw the second game, thinking you would get it then. Is that right?"

"We went ahead and threw the second game, we went after him again. . . . After the third game, I says, 'Somebody is getting a nice little jazz. Everybody is crossed.' He said Abe Attell and Bill Burns had crossed him."

"Didn't you think it was the right thing for you to go and tell Comiskey about it?"

"I did tell them, 'I'm not going to be in it,' " Jackson testified, meaning the other White Sox players. "I will just get out of that altogether."

"Who did you tell that to?"

"Chick Gandil."

"What did he say?"

"He said I was into it already and I might as well stay in. I said, 'I can go to the boss and have every damn one of you pulled out of the limelight.' He said it wouldn't be well for me if I did that."

"Gandil said to you?"

"Yes, sir."

"What did you say?"

"Well, I told him any time they wanted to have me knocked off, to have me knocked off."

"What did he say?"

"Just laughed."

"Did you see any fake plays made by yourself or anybody [in the fourth game] that would help throw the game?"

"Only the wildness of Cicotte."

"Did you make any intentional errors yourself that day?"

"No, sir. Not during the whole Series."

"Did you bat to win?"

"Yes."

"And did you run the bases to win?"

"Yes, sir."

"And field balls in the outfield to win?"

"I did. I tried to win all the games."

"After the fourth game you went to Cincinnati and you had the $5,000, is that right?"

"Yes, sir."

"Where did you put the $5,000? Did you put it in the bank or keep it on your person?"

"I put it in my pocket."

"Had you ever played crooked baseball before this?"

"No, sir, I never had."

"Weren't you very much peeved that you only got $5,000 and you were promised $20,000?"

"No, I was ashamed of myself."

"Do you remember the last series you played in Boston [this season]? Lost three straight games. Did any of those games look suspicious to you?"

"There was a lot of funny pitching, a lot of walking."

"Who was pitching those games?"

"Kerr and Williams and Cicotte."

"Was Kerr in on this in any way, do you think?"

"I don't think so."

"Did you ever talk to Claude Williams about it since the Series?"

"We were just talking about how funny it looked that Gandil didn't come back, and he must have made an awful lot out of it, crossed up the boys. We both decided he crossed them up."

"You think now Williams may have crossed you too."

"Well, dealing with crooks, you know, you get crooked every way. This is my first experience and last."

Outside the grand jury room, Jackson kept talking. To reporters.

"I never got that $15,000 that was coming to me," he was quoted as saying. "Before we broke up, I climbed Gandil and McMullin about it. They said to me, 'You poor simp, go ahead and squawk. Where do you get off if you do. We'll all say you're a liar. And every honest baseball player in the world will say you're a liar. You're out of luck. Some of the boys were promised a lot more than you and got a lot less.'

"That's why I went down and told Judge MacDonald and told the grand jury what I knew about this frameup.

"And I'm giving you a tip. A lot of these sporting writers that have been roasting me have been talking about the third game of the World Series being square. Let me tell you something. The eight of us did our best to kick it and little Dickie Kerr won the game by his pitching. Because he won it, those gamblers double-crossed us for double-crossing them.

"They've hung it on me, but I don't care what happens now. I guess I'm through with baseball. I wasn't wise enough like Chick to beat them to it.

"Who gave me the money? Lefty Williams slipped it to me the night before I left for Cincinnati and told me I'll get another $15,000 after I deliver the goods. I took Lefty's word for it. Now Risberg threatens to bump me off if I squawk. That's why I had all the bailiffs with me when I left the grand jury room. I'm not under arrest yet and I've got the idea that after what I told them, ol' Joe Jackson isn't going to jail. But I'm not going to get far from my protectors until this blows over. Swede's a hard guy."

Sportswriter Hugh Fullerton of the Chicago *Herald & Examiner* would describe what happened when Jackson moved down the steps of the courthouse.

"The kids with wide eyes and tightening throats watched," Fullerton reported. "And one, bolder than the others, pressed forward and said: 'It ain't so, Joe, is it?' Jackson gulped back a sob. The shame of utter shame flushed his brown face. He choked an instant. 'Yes, kid, I'm afraid it is.' "

But when Jackson was asked to confirm that story, he shook his head.

"When I came out of the courthouse that day, nobody said anything to me," he recalled. "The only one who spoke was a guy who yelled at his friend, 'I told you the big sonuvabitch wore shoes.' I walked right out of there and stepped into my car and drove off."

Even before Jackson had testified, even before the eight indictments, Comiskey had composed a telegram to the fixers:

> You and each of you are hereby notified of your indefinite suspension as a member of the Chicago American League Baseball Club. Your suspension is brought about by information which has just come to me, directly involving you, and each of you, in the baseball scandal now being investigated by the Grand Jury of Cook County resulting from the World Series of 1919.
>
> If you are innocent of any wrongdoing, you, and each of you, will be reinstated; if you are guilty, you will be retired from organized baseball for the rest of your lives if I can accomplish it. Until there is a finality to this investigation, it is due to the public that I take this action even though it costs Chicago the pennant.
>
> Chicago American League BB Club
> By Charles A. Comiskey

Three of the suspended players reacted quickly. Weaver declared he had never received any money and denied any knowledge of a fix.

During the World Series he had batted .324, with no errors in twenty-seven chances.

"Any man who bats .333 is bound to make trouble for the other team in a ballgame," Weaver said. "The best team cannot win a World Series without getting the breaks. The Athletics were the best team in the country in 1914 but they lost four straight to the Boston Nationals because the breaks were all against them. And nobody ever accused them of lying down."

Felsch denied any involvement in the fix, saying, "It's all bunk as far as I'm concerned. I've always been on the square. All I want is a chance to face the jury."

Chick Gandil, recovering from his appendectomy in Texas, wrote a statement that his doctor handed to reporters. "It's a lot of bunk," it read. "Nothing to it. They're trying to make a goat out of somebody. And I'm telling the world, that somebody won't be me."

Lefty Williams, Swede Risberg, and Fred McMullin were not immediately found by reporters.

That afternoon, having heard that Cicotte and Jackson were talking to the grand jury, Eddie Collins drove by the Criminal Courts building with three teammates: Mike Murphy, Amos Strunk, and Nemo Leibold. Outside the courthouse Sam Pass, a friend of theirs, noticed Collins's car.

"They've handed down eight indictments," Pass yelled.

Hopping out of the car, Leibold hugged Collins, then Collins swatted Strunk across the back, and Strunk playfully punched Murphy in the ribs. Collins hurried to a nearby telephone to inform Schalk, Kerr, Faber, and first baseman John (Shano) Collins. That evening they all gathered for dinner at a downtown restaurant.

"Let's go see the Kid," one suggested.

They drove to Gleason's apartment. When their manager wasn't home, they went on to Collins's apartment on the South Side where the party continued into the early hours with cold chicken, cheese, pickles, and beer. The "square" members of the White Sox were celebrating themselves, but tonight that was enough.

"No one will ever know what we put up with all this summer," one who requested anonymity told a *Tribune* reporter. "I know there were many times when things were about to break into a fight, but it never got that far.

"Hardly any of us have talked with any of the fellows, except on the ballfield, since the season opened. Even during spring training, our gang stood in one group, waiting a turn to hit, and the other gang had their own group. We went along and gritted our teeth and played ball. We had to trail along with these fellows all summer and all the time we felt they had thrown us down.

"It was tough. Now the load has been lifted. No wonder we feel like celebrating."

Justice had triumphed. That afternoon in St. Louis the Indians also triumphed, 9–5, opening a one-game lead with Jim Bagby's thirtieth victory. But in Cleveland, as everywhere else in the United States, baseball fans were buzzing about the developments in the Cook County Criminal Courts building. The front page of Wednesday morning's Cleveland *Plain Dealer* resembled a post office "wanted" poster: eight mug shots of the eight indictees along with a blaring headline:

JACKSON AND CICOTTE ADMIT GUILT;
CLEVELAND ALMOST SURE OF PENNANT

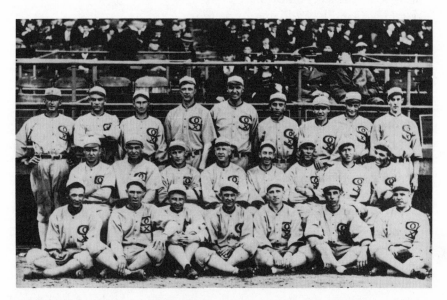

The 1919 Chicago White Sox. (front row) Byrd Lynn, Swede Risberg, Nemo Leibold, Dickie Kerr, Harvey McClellan, Lefty Williams, Eddie Cicotte (middle row) Ray Schalk, Joe Jenkins, Happy Felsch, manager Kid Gleason, Eddie Collins, Shano Collins, Red Faber, Buck Weaver (back row) Joe Jackson, Chick Gandil, Fred McMullin, Grover Lowdermilk, Bill James, Erskine Mayer, Eddie Murphy, John Sullivan, Roy Wilkinson. *National Baseball Library and Archive, Cooperstown, N.Y.*

Around noon the remaining White Sox assembled for a workout, but Kid Gleason called it off. Too cold. He huddled with his coaches to discuss a lineup for Friday's opener in St. Louis of the season-ending three-game series. In the White Sox office, meanwhile, Buck Weaver asked to see Comiskey. When he departed, reporters surrounded him.

"No comment," Weaver said, his head down.

That morning Lefty Williams visited Alfred Austrian's office. Comiskey's attorney suggested that Williams provide a statement that the suspended pitcher later would read to the grand jury. Williams began by recalling that he met at the Warner Hotel in Chicago with Cicotte, Gandil, Weaver, Felsch, and two men "introduced as Brown and Sullivan" from New York.

"They were the gamblers?" Austrian asked.

"They were supposed to be the gamblers, or fellows that were fixing it for the gamblers. One of the two, they didn't say which. I was informed that whether or not I took any action, the games would be fixed."

"Who informed you of that?"

"Chick Gandil," Williams answered.

"Right then and there?"

"No, not right then and there. Just right after that. Just as I got in the hall. So I told them anything they did would be agreeable to me: if it was going to be done anyway, that I had no money. I may as well get what I could. I haven't seen those gamblers from that day to this. I was supposed to get $10,000 after the second game, when we got back to Chicago, but I did not get this until after the fourth game. And he then said the gamblers had called it off, and I figured then that there was a double cross someplace."

"When did Gandil say you would get some money?"

"He didn't say. He didn't make no statement. I was supposed at first to get so much, get $10,000 after the second game," which Williams lost, 4–2. "I didn't receive it until the fourth game. I got only $5,000."

Within hours the Indians would widen their lead to one and one-half games with a 10–2 rout of the Browns for righthander Stanley Coveleski's twenty-fourth victory.

But even though the scandal had riddled Gleason's roster, a White Sox pennant was still possible.

"That's all that's left, three games," Gleason said, sadly. "We'll do what we can to win the flag."

Tuesday night Yankee owners Jake Ruppert and Cap Huston had offered Comiskey "our entire club," including Babe Ruth, to complete the schedule and, if the White Sox were to win the pennant, to oppose the Brooklyn Robins, nicknamed for manager Wilbert Robinson, who would represent the National League in the World Series.

"We are confident," the Ruppert-Huston statement read, "that Cleveland sportsmanship will not permit you to lose by default."

Red Sox owner Harry Frazee declared it "the duty" of each American League club to provide the White Sox with one of its players. But then, as now, a player had to be on a club's roster before September 1 to be eligible for the World Series roster. Comiskey's answer to the Yankee and Red Sox offers was contained in a statement issued by Harry Grabiner, the White Sox secretary.

"We'll play out the schedule," it read, "if we have to get Chinamen to replace the suspended players."

The suspended players were some of baseball's best. For that 1920 season Jackson batted .382, Felsch .338, Weaver .333, Risberg .266. Cicotte had a 21–10 record, Williams a 22–14 record. Along with Faber, who would be 23–13, and Kerr, who would be 21–9, that White Sox team had four 20-game winners. Gleason had Faber and Kerr for the Friday and Saturday games in St. Louis, but for Sunday he now had to consider two lesser righthanders: Roy Wilkinson, who was 7–9 with a 4.03 earned run average and rookie Clarence (Shovel) Hodges, 1–1 in only two previous starts.

Friday afternoon at Sportsman's Park the White Sox batting order had Eddie Murphy at third base, Nemo Leibold in centerfield, Eddie Collins at second base, John (Shano) Collins at first base, Bibb Falk in leftfield, Amos Strunk in rightfield, Harvey McClellan at shortstop, Ray Schalk catching, and Red Faber pitching. Hardly a pennant-winning lineup.

For all his new faces, Gleason couldn't escape the scandal. When he was presented with a bouquet of flowers, a fan yelled, "Give 'em to Cicotte." The White Sox jumped on Frank (Dixie) Davis, the Browns' ace righthander, for three quick runs in the first inning, but Faber was knocked out in the third and the Browns won, 8–6. When the Indians split a doubleheader in Detroit by winning the second game, 10–2, they clinched a tie for the pennant: two games up with two games remaining.

Saturday the White Sox outscored the Browns, 10–7, on Shano Collins's triple and three singles. But that victory merely clinched second place.

In Detroit the Indians won, 10–1, for Jim Bagby's thirty-first victory and Cleveland's first pennant. Almost symbolically, Tris Speaker had three hits. Aware of the gambling cloud that hung over baseball in his second season as the Indians' manager-centerfielder, he had refused to name his starting pitcher until the day of the game. He had kept his team together following the shock of Ray Chapman's death. He had batted .388, driven in 107 runs, scored 137 runs, and led the league with 50 doubles. And the thirty-two-year-old centerfielder known as the Gray Eagle had continued to enhance his defensive reputation.

"You know how an infielder gets down for the pitch?" Joe Sewell would say years later. "Well, you'd get down and the ball would be a hit, a shot, you'd turn, and I never did see Tris Speaker turn. He'd be turned and gone with his back to the plate, the ball, the infield. When he'd turn around again, there would be the ball."

When the Indians finally turned around in 1920 after Ray Chapman's death, after the Yankees suddenly burned out, after the White Sox had been disassembled by disgrace, there was the American League pennant. The dirtying of the White Sox into the Black Sox had stung the nation. In that Saturday morning's Pittsburgh *Dispatch*, sports editor William Reel wrote about a conversation before the 1919 World Series opener with Chick Gandil, his friend for many years.

"Are the Sox going to win?" Reel asked.

"I don't see how we can," Gandil said. "Cicotte is overworked and Williams is an in-and-outer. They are the only pitchers we have. Take a tip from me and don't bet on the White Sox."

To comfort his honest players, Comiskey made up what he termed "the difference" between the winning and losing shares in the 1919 World Series.

"I feel you were deprived of the winner's share in the World Series receipts through no fault of yours," the White Sox owner said. "I do not intend that you shall be penalized."

But according to some honest White Sox, the effort of some of their teammates in 1920 had also been questionable.

"We lost this pennant," backup catcher Byrd Lynn said, "because certain players among those who were indicted didn't want us to win. We soon noticed how carefully they studied the scoreboard, more than even the average player does in a pennant race, and they always made errors which cost us the game when Cleveland and New York were losing. If Cleveland won, we won. If Cleveland lost, we lost. The idea was to keep up the betting odds, but not let us win the pennant."

Eddie Collins supported that theory, charging that two unnamed teammates had failed to put forth their best effort in the 1920 season.

Soon after the eight Chicago indictments, a new whisper surfaced in several New York newspapers: the same gamblers who had arranged for the Black Sox fix had already conspired with some of the Brooklyn Robins to throw the approaching World Series to the Indians. When the headlines appeared, Harry D. Lewis, the Brooklyn district attorney, interrogated many of the Robins, notably Zach Wheat, their future Hall of Fame leftfielder. Lewis quickly announced being satisfied that the players "were on the level." In a best-of-nine World Series, the Indians triumphed, five games to two, without any smoke of suspicion.

Within a month, the scandal would change the major league's structure and soul. On November 12, the major league club owners selected baseball's first commissioner, Kenesaw Mountain Landis, a white-haired, firm-jawed federal judge in Chicago who had fined Standard Oil $29 million in a 1907 antitrust case.

On February 14, 1921, chief prosecutor George Gorman announced the disappearance of the grand jury records, including the confessions of Eddie Cicotte, Joe Jackson, and Lefty Williams.

When the trial began on June 27, the lack of hard evidence resulted in the jury needing only two hours and forty-seven minutes of deliberation and one ballot on August 2 for acquittal. But four months earlier, Landis had put the eight indicted players on baseball's ineligible list. The day after the acquittal, the commissioner issued a statement.

"Regardless of the verdicts of the juries," it read, "no player who entertains proposals or promises to throw a game, no player who sits in conference with a bunch of crooked players and gamblers where the ways and means of throwing games are discussed and does not promptly tell the club about it will ever play professional baseball."

Some of the players, notably Weaver, appealed personally to Landis, without success.

Joe Jackson later appeared in so-called outlaw games in outlaw leagues, but never again in organized baseball as such. Had his career not been stained, Jackson surely would have been voted into the Hall of Fame; if their careers had continued, Buck Weaver, Happy Felsch,

Eddie Cicotte, and Lefty Williams might be honored there now with bronze plaques. But of that team, only Eddie Collins, Ray Schalk, and Red Faber have been inducted.

Of all the pennant races, there's never been one quite like the eternal triangle of events that evolved in 1920: Ray Chapman's death, Babe Ruth's explosion as a slugger with fifty-four homers, and the exposure of the Black Sox scandal.

Me 'n' Paul 'n' Brooklyn

Bill Terry. *National Baseball Library and Archive, Cooperstown, N.Y.*

IN BASEBALL, AS in other sports, foot-in-mouth disease is always arrogant and sometimes embarrassing. Even so, it seldom lingers and decides a pennant race. But in 1934 it did.

In February club executives and managers gathered at the Hotel Roosevelt in New York City for the annual major league meetings. Since the New York Giants had won the 1933 World Series, their manager and first baseman, Bill Terry, who could be gruff, was surrounded in the lobby by sportswriters asking his opinions on the approaching season.

"Anybody want to bet a hat that we don't win again?" Terry asked.

When none of the writers took that bet, Terry said, "Pittsburgh, St. Louis, and Chicago will be the teams to beat." But now silver-haired Roscoe McGowen, who covered the Brooklyn Dodgers for *The New York Times*, had a question.

"How about Brooklyn, Bill?"

"Brooklyn?" the Giant manager said. "Is Brooklyn still in the league?"

The writers smiled. Bill Terry smiled with them.

The Dodgers had finished sixth the previous season, twenty-six and one-half games out of first place. Only the Phillies and the Cubs had finished lower. During the off-season the Dodgers had not made a deal to strengthen the roster. Except for righthander Van Lingle Mungo, none of their players appealed to other clubs. Like everybody else, Terry knew that the Dodgers would not suddenly ascend into contention. But the next day the New York and Brooklyn newspapers duly reported Terry's remark.

"Still in the league?" Dodger fans muttered. "Still in the league?"

Terry's remark inspired hundreds of angry letters with a Brooklyn postmark. It even inspired Dodger general manager Bob Quinn to change managers. Although spring training was about to begin in

Orlando, Florida, Max Carey suddenly was out and Casey Stengel, who had been one of Carey's coaches, was in.

"I'm the first manager," Carey said, "ever fired for not winning the pennant in the wintertime."

Stengel would not win the pennant in the summertime, but Quinn and the Dodger board of directors thought his lively manner would help take the sting out of Terry's remark. Stengel later would prove to be a comic genius whose Yankee teams would win seven World Series and ten American League pennants in twelve seasons from 1949 through 1960 before he provided the early Mets with credibility and comic relief. But in 1934 in Brooklyn he was hired because his popularity among the fans and the sportswriters would hide the shabby dismissal of Carey, the scapegoat for the front office's surrender to the roster's status quo that had provoked Terry's wisecrack.

Not that Terry cared. When he noticed two Dodgers on the same base during a spring training game, he laughed.

"How long have these fellows been down here?" the Giant manager said. "They're in midseason form already."

As the season developed, the Pirates, the Cardinals, and the Cubs were fulfilling Terry's prediction that they would be the teams to beat while the Dodgers tumbled onto their treadmill to sixth place. On Sunday night, May 27, the Pirates were leading the league, with the Cardinals one-half game behind and the Cubs one game behind. In fourth place, the Giants were two games out. The next day the Cardinals moved into first place, the Cardinals of "Me and Paul," pitchers Dizzy Dean and his brother Paul, the Cardinals who would be remembered as much by their nicknames as their real names.

Frank Frisch, the fiery manager and second baseman, had been the Fordham Flash since playing baseball and football in college.

At third base was the Wild Hoss of the Osage (Pepper Martin), at shortstop Leo the Lip, alias the All-America Out (Leo Durocher), at first base Ripper (Jimmy Collins), in leftfield Ducky Wucky (Medwick). The catcher was Spud (Virgil Davis). The other pitchers were Tex (Jim Carleton), Wild Bill (Hallahan), Pop (Jesse Haines), and Dazzy (Clarence Vance).

The only Cardinals without nicknames, but not without skill, were centerfielder Ernie Orsatti, rightfielder Jack Rothrock, and rookie catcher Bill DeLancey.

Another nickname, Daffy, had been attached to Paul Dean, but it was strictly a newspaper nickname to go with Dizzy; Daffy never fit him. None of his teammates called him that. Paul Dean was so quiet, he let his big brother do all the talking for both of them, if not for the entire Cardinal team.

But even in first place, the Cardinals knew that the Giants remained the team to beat for the National League pennant.

"If we was in that other league," Dizzy Dean told Durocher one day early that season, meaning the American League, "we could win the pennant."

"They wouldn't let us in the other league," Durocher said. "They'd say we were a lot of gashouse ballplayers."

With that line, Durocher baptized these Cardinals with their unique nickname that has endured in baseball lore.

"The best thing we had going for us, as far as posterity was concerned, was our name: the Gashouse Gang," Durocher once said. "It gave us an identity. It gave us a personality."

That identity, that personality, had been recognized by Frisch in spring training in Daytona Beach, Florida.

"I'm not going to be a detective and watch over you at night," the manager said in a clubhouse meeting. "Your nights are your own. But your days belong to me. If you'd rather go back to the mines and dig for coal instead of riding around the country in Pullmans and living in the best hotels at the expense of the club, speak up. We haven't any room for softies and no holds are barred. That's the way we're going to play ball."

There has been only one Gashouse Gang, but that's because there has been only one Dizzy Dean.

Shortly after these Cardinals perched in first place, Dizzy decided that his brother Paul, a rookie righthander, deserved more than his $3,000 salary. Diz, who signed a $12,500 contract after a 20–18 record in 1933, had predicted in spring training that "me and Paul will win forty to forty-five games this season." Now that Paul was off to a 4–0 start, Diz threatened to go on strike if Paul's contract was not renegotiated. When the Cardinals arrived in Pittsburgh on June 1 for a weekend series, Dizzy suddenly announced he couldn't pitch. Sore arm.

"I'm satisfied with my own pay, which is what I got last year," Dizzy said. "But Paul must get $2,000 more, or the Cards won't win the pennant. Me and Paul won't pitch anymore under present circumstances."

Frisch told Dizzy, "If you don't want to pitch, go home." Sam

Breadon, the Cardinal owner, assured the manager of his support, and then Frisch called the Dean brothers to a meeting in his Schenley Hotel suite. Apparently the brothers surrendered.

"My arm's getting better fast," Diz said. "I'll throw this ol' arm off to win for Frank and the boys."

Dizzy Dean always did know how to change his story. One day in Brooklyn, three sportswriters from different newspapers had to do a feature story on him. One after the other, Tommy Holmes of the *Brooklyn Eagle*, Bill McCullough of the Brooklyn *Times-Union*, and Roscoe McGowen of *The New York Times* sat with Dizzy in the Cardinal clubhouse. To establish basic facts, each writer asked the same question: Where and when was he born?

"Tommy comes first," Diz later confessed, "and I told him Lucas, Arkansas, January 16, 1911 [the correct place and date]. Then McCullough comes along and I wasn't going to have their bosses bawl him out for gettin' the same story, so I told him I was born at Bond, Mississippi, that's where my wife comes from, and I pick February 22. McGowen wanted the same story, but I give him a break and told him Holdenville, Oklahoma, August 22."

Diz even changed his name. Usually he was Jay Hanna Dean, his actual name. Sometimes he preferred Jerome Herman Dean. But no matter what his name, no matter where and when he was born, he was all pitcher. All competitor.

Pity the hitter who took too much time digging his back foot into the dirt of the batter's box when Diz was pitching. When the batter finally looked up, Diz would be glaring at him and snarling, "You all done? You comfortable? Then send for the groundskeeper and tell him to bring a shovel because that's where they're going to bury you." Whoooom, his fastball flipped that batter upside down, if not inside out. In those years, throwing at batters' heads was more blatant than now. It also was more tolerated by umpires.

"As a ballplayer, Dizzy Dean was a natural phenomenon, like the Grand Canyon or the Great Barrier Reef," wrote Red Smith, the Pulitzer Prize–winning sports columnist of *The New York Times* who in 1934 was working for the St. Louis *Star*. "Nobody ever taught him baseball and he never had to learn. He was just doing what came naturally."

What came naturally was Dizzy Dean's fastball and fast talk. "But if you can do it," he once said, "it ain't braggin'." He could do it. So could his teammates, beginning with Frisch, then in his sixteenth season after having joined the New York Giants out of Fordham in 1919. As a Giant rookie, oddly enough, Frisch had inspired the Cardinal farm system assembled by Branch Rickey, then the Cardinals' president and manager. During that 1919 season Rickey had been offered $350,000, then a stupendous sum, by the Giants for Rogers Hornsby, still considered the best second baseman in baseball history.

"I'll give you Hornsby," Rickey said, "if you give me Frisch and $200,000."

John McGraw, the Giant manager, vetoed the deal. The next day Hornsby was struck in the head by a throw. Hornsby would recover quickly but Rickey didn't.

"I had no Frisch," Rickey would say later, "and, I feared then, no Hornsby."

That's when Rickey decided to search for young players, discover them in towns or big-city sandlots, develop them on minor league teams, and display the best in Cardinal uniforms. That farm system helped produce the Cardinals' first pennant in 1926. After Frisch was acquired from the Giants in a trade for Hornsby prior to the 1927 season, the Cardinals won the 1928 and 1930 pennants. Now, in 1934, the year when moviegoers watched *It Happened One Night* with Clark Gable and Claudette Colbert, the Cardinals were in another pennant race with their farm system products: the Dean brothers, Ripper Collins, Pepper Martin, Joe Medwick, Ernie Orsatti, Tex Carleton, Bill DeLancey.

The Cardinals held first place for nine days in late May and early June but by Sunday night, July 8, as they awaited the All-Star Game at the Polo Grounds in New York, they had dropped to third place, four games behind the Giants. Bill Terry's team was taking charge behind their ace lefthander, Carl Hubbell.

"Hubbell could throw strikes at midnight," Billy Herman, then the Cub second baseman, would say years later. "What a great pitcher and competitor he was. When he was pitching, you hardly ever saw the opposing team sitting back in the dugout. They were all up on the top step watching him operate. He was a marvel to watch, with that screwball, fastball, curve, screwball again, changes of speed, and his control. He didn't have really overpowering stuff but he was an absolute master of what he did have. And he got every last ounce out of his ability. I never saw another pitcher who could so fascinate the opposition as Hubbell did."

Fascinate and frustrate. Then thirty-one years old, Hubbell created in 1934 what has endured as the most memorable moment in All-Star Game history: consecutive strikeouts of Babe Ruth, Lou Gehrig, Jimmie Foxx, Al Simmons, and Joe Cronin.

Hubbell would lead the National League that year with a 2.30 earned run average while producing a 21–12 record, justifying his Depression nickname as the "Meal Ticket" of Terry's staff. But a twenty-three-year-old righthander, Hal Schumacher, would have a 23–10 record and Fat Freddie Fitzsimmons, a thirty-three-year-old righthander, an 18–14 record. Rookie lefthander Al Smith, who would be remembered seven years later as one of the Cleveland Indian pitchers who stopped Joe DiMaggio's fifty-six-game hitting streak, and thirty-seven-year-old Hi Bell were Terry's bullpen pitchers. But in a vital game, Hubbell would be in the bullpen. In an era when relief pitchers weren't used as extensively as they are today, Hubbell's eight saves led the NL that year.

"Bill Terry was one of the great 'pitcher' managers," Hal Schumacher would say years later. "On the days when Hubbell was going to throw between starts, Bill had him throw in the bullpen late in the game. Then if Bill needed him, Hubbell was ready. Bill always knew when to take a pitcher out. You could never talk him out of it."

Terry, who had won the NL batting title with .401 in 1930, would hit .354 in 1934, but at age thirty-seven his home run output would slip to eight from twenty-eight only two years earlier. For power the manager depended on Mel Ott, who would lead the NL with 135 runs batted in and share the lead in home runs with Ripper Collins with thirty-five. Only twenty-five years old, Ott already was in his ninth full season, having arrived at the Polo Grounds on September 1, 1925, as a sixteen-year-old lefthanded hitter out of Gretna, Louisiana, with an unusual batting style. As the pitcher threw, Ott lifted his right foot and swung. Traditionalists predicted that this little teenager, who would grow to only five-nine and 170 pounds, had his foot in the bucket, that he would never make it. John McGraw disagreed. So sure was the Giants' wise old manager, he decided to keep Ott with the Giants rather than risk minor league managers trying to change the kid's style.

"Just keep swinging that way, son," McGraw told him.

During the 1926 season, the seventeen-year-old outfielder mostly sat on the Giant bench next to McGraw, but in his thirty-five games he hit .383. The next year he hit .282 in eighty-two games, with his first homer. But in 1928, at nineteen, he batted .322 with eighteen homers. Master Melvin, as the writers called him, had arrived. In 1929, at twenty, he had 152 runs batted in while smashing 42 homers, many into Ottville, the rightfield stands at the Polo Grounds with its 257-foot rightfield line. Of his 511 career homers, he hit 323 at the Polo Grounds.

Years later, when Ott and Durocher were rival managers, radio announcer Red Barber suggested before a 1946 game at the Polo Grounds that Durocher be a "nice guy for a change," and the Dodger manager bristled.

"Nice guys!" Durocher told sports columnist Frank Graham of the New York *Journal-American*. "Look over there. Do you know a nicer guy than their manager, Mel Ott? Or any of the other Giants? They're the nicest guys in the world. And where are they? In last place. I'm not a nice guy, and I'm in first place. Nobody helped me get there either, except the guys on this ballclub and they ain't nice guys. The nice guys are all over there. In last place."

Midway through the 1948 season, Durocher, who had started the year as the Dodger manager, suddenly succeeded Ott as the Giant manager—still the most startling managerial switch in history. But in 1934 Durocher's way with words had christened the Cardinals as the Gashouse Gang while Ott reigned as the NL's most feared slugger.

Travis Jackson, a future Hall of Famer along with Ott, Terry, and Hubbell, was slowing up at shortstop, but he would hit sixteen homers and drive in 101 runs. Centerfielder Jo-Jo Moore would bat .331 while scoring 106 runs. Some of the Giants were there mostly because of their gloves: catcher Gus Mancuso, second baseman Hughie Critz, and third baseman Johnny Vergez. The leftfielder, George Watkins, would be a disappointment with a .247 average, but the Giants kept rolling along in first place while the Dean brothers kept roiling the Cardinal clubhouse.

On August 12 the Deans were the losing pitchers in a Sunday doubleheader with the Cubs that dropped the third-place Cardinals seven and one-half games behind the Giants.

When the Cardinals rode an overnight train out of St. Louis to Detroit for a Monday exhibition game there, a common occurrence for major league teams in that era, the Deans were not aboard. Dizzy and Paul would come up with the same lame excuse: each had forgotten to pack for the trip.

"Besides," added Diz, "I hurt my arm Sunday."

Frisch wasn't impressed. He fined Diz $100 and Paul $50, explaining, "When the Yankees schedule an exhibition game, Babe Ruth is always present." After the exhibition, which had advertised that the

Dean brothers would coach at third base and first base, the Cardinals returned to St. Louis for the Tuesday opener of a four-game series with the Phillies. In the clubhouse Dizzy confronted Frisch.

"Do those fines stick?" he asked.

"Sure they stick," Frisch said.

"Then we'll take off our uniforms," Dizzy said.

"Yeah, we'll take 'em off," Paul added.

"Then you're both suspended," Frisch said.

Dizzy not only took off his white uniform with two cardinals perched on a yellow bat, he ripped the seams of the shirt and pants. Still storming, he yanked his gray road uniform out of his locker and ripped that apart. Then he and Paul went up to the Sportsman's Park press box and watched the Cardinals win, 5–1.

"Anybody can beat the Phils," Diz said, "but it'll be different when the Giants come in a week from Thursday. It takes me 'n' Paul to stop the Giants, and the Cardinals know it."

Rain washed out Wednesday's game, but Frisch announced that the Dean brothers had been suspended "indefinitely." Despite his bluster, Diz hoped that owner Sam Breadon would refund the $36 fine for destroying the two uniforms.

"I think I can get 'em patched up," he said.

Diz's wife, Pat, annoyed at the $100-a-day fine for her husband, predicted that the brothers would return "in a day or two." Her reason was that the "Dean family needs the money." Against the Phillies, the Cardinals didn't need the Dean family. They swept Thursday's doubleheader with reliever Pop Haines earning his second victory in three days. The next morning Dizzy suddenly arrived at the Chicago office of Commissioner Kenesaw Mountain Landis. Under major league rules, he was entitled to appeal his case.

"I'm being persecuted," Diz said.

Landis ordered a Monday hearing in St. Louis but by Friday afternoon Paul Dean had been reinstated. After a meeting with Breadon, Rickey, and Frisch, the rookie righthander wrote a letter of apology. "I want to make up as much as I can for my mistake," it read in part, "but I also want to make more money next year. But above all I want to keep the Cardinals in the pennant race." That afternoon, relieving in the second inning of a 12–2 victory over the Phillies, the prodigal brother was credited with his thirteenth win. The suspension had cost him $120, including $70 for three days' pay.

While the Cardinals were routing the Boston Braves, 15–0, for

Wild Bill Hallahan on Saturday, Dizzy offered to return, but Breadon told him, "You've placed this in Landis' hands and now we'll let it go until Monday."

After five consecutive victories without Diz, the Cardinals split a Sunday doubleheader with the Braves as Frisch, strapped for pitching, used Pepper Martin in relief, briefly but effectively. In the Monday hearing, Landis ruled that the Cardinals had been within their rights, that the amount of Dizzy's fine and the length of the suspension had not been excessive. Diz agreed to be in uniform the next day.

"So far I've lost $460—a $100 fine, $36 for the two uniforms I destroyed, and $350 for seven days under suspension," he said, his addition not quite accurate. "I can't afford to lose any more money."

In the Tuesday finale against the Braves, the Cardinals won again, 6–2, behind Tex Carleton. When the Giants arrived for a three-game series, Paul Dean started Thursday's opener but lost, 6–3, on Jo-Jo Moore's three-run homer in the ninth. Friday afternoon Dizzy returned in repentance, his shoulders slumping, his head hanging, and his eyes on the dirt mound. Soon he was strutting and taunting the Giant batters. His 5–0 shutout lifted the Cardinals to within five games.

In Saturday's finale, Frisch pressed his luck. Hoping that Diz's arm wasn't too tired, the manager called on him in the seventh inning. This time the Giants jumped on him for four runs, six hits, and a 7–6 loss on Travis Jackson's two-run single in the eighth.

The Dean brothers were back, but the Cardinals were still stumbling. After losing a Labor Day doubleheader in Pittsburgh, they dropped to seven games back. The next day they were to play an exhibition game against the Cardinal farm team in nearby Greensburg, Pennsylvania, but Frisch told Dizzy and his wife to go on to New York ahead of the team so that the Cardinal ace would be rested for Wednesday's game in Brooklyn. When the train was due to leave Pittsburgh, Mrs. Dean was still in the lobby of the Schenley Hotel.

"Dizzy refuses to go to New York tonight," she said. "He's upstairs in a card game with several players."

Perhaps hoping to agitate Frisch in another exhibition game escapade, Diz accompanied his teammates to Greensburg, arrived in New York's Penn Station the next morning, checked into the Commodore Hotel, took the subway to Brooklyn, and stopped the Dodgers, 2–1, on a three-hitter for his twenty-fourth victory. Paul had won fifteen, for a brotherly total of thirty-nine, within easy striking distance of the "forty to forty-five" that Diz had predicted. Although the Cardinals were still mathematically alive, Diz was more concerned about his 1935 salary.

"We'll be well compensated for the work we're doing now," Diz said. "If not, we'll refuse to pitch in the big leagues next year."

The following Monday in Philadelphia, Dizzy won his twenty-fifth, but on Thursday, September 13, the Cardinals were still five and one-half games behind as they opened a four-game series at the Polo Grounds. In a twelve-inning duel, Paul Dean outpitched Freddie Fitzsimmons, 2–0. The next day, Hal Schumacher stopped the Cardinals, 4–1.

"I'm planning on Schumacher," Terry confided, "to open the World Series."

Dizzy Dean agreed. "The Giants are in, there's no use kidding ourselves," he said between poker hands when Saturday's game was rained out. "Me 'n' Paul will beat them tomorrow, but after that it don't matter." Sunday's pitching matchups (J. Dean vs. Schumacher, P. Dean vs. Hubbell) attracted 62,573 customers, at the time the largest crowd in National League history. Just as Diz predicted, he and his brother won both games. Diz needed help from Tex Carleton for his twenty-sixth victory, 5–3. On only two days' rest, Paul prevailed in another extra-inning duel, 3–1, on Pepper Martin's homer off Carl Hubbell in the eleventh. With twelve games remaining, the Cardinals now were three and one-half games behind and Dizzy Dean described Frisch as "the most wonderful manager" in baseball.

Why?

"Because he's the only man who could keep a club in a pennant fight with only two pitchers."

Who were the two?

"Me 'n' Paul."

Not that the Giants seemed concerned. After splitting a Tuesday doubleheader with the Cincinnati Reds, president Horace Stoneham announced that the Giants were accepting World Series ticket orders. After watching Hubbell stop the Reds for his twenty-first victory, Terry had an announcement.

"I'm switching to Hubbell for the World Series opener," the Giant manager said.

To make up two games rained out earlier on their eastern swing, the Cardinals returned to Brooklyn on Friday, September 21, for a doubleheader. At the Cardinals' hotel that morning, Dizzy playfully predicted that the Dodger starters, Tom Zachary and Ray Benge, "will be pitching against one-hit Dean and no-hit Dean today." He wasn't off by much. Diz had a no-hitter broken up with one out in the eighth by rightfielder Ralph Boyle's infield roller and breezed, 13–0, on a three-hitter. In the second game, Paul no-hit the Dodgers, 3–0.

"If I'd known Paul was going to pitch a no-hitter," Diz said with a serious laugh, "I would've pitched one too."

Saturday the Giants lost in Boston while the Cardinals were rained out in Cincinnati, whittling the lead to two and one-half games. Both

Dizzy Dean kisses brother Paul's no-hit baseball. *National Baseball Library and Archive, Cooperstown, N.Y.*

teams split their Sunday doubleheaders, Dizzy finishing both games in relief. Entering the final week of the season, the Giants were off Monday as Cardinal righthander Bill Walker stopped the Cubs at Wrigley Field, 3–1. Returning to St. Louis on Tuesday, Dizzy held off the Pirates, 3–2, for his twenty-eighth victory on a three-run first inning sparked by doubles by Frisch and Collins after the Giants had lost, 4–0, to Curt Davis in Philadelphia. Suddenly the Giants' lead had been sliced to one game. The Giants also were being haunted by a statistical ghost: no major league team had ever gone into September with a seven-game lead and not won the pennant.

Leo Durocher, meanwhile, was about to be haunted by an unofficial statistical ghost: no baseball player had ever gotten married in the final days of a pennant race.

In his usual impetuous manner, the twenty-nine-year-old Durocher had fallen for thirty-two-year-old Grace Dozier, a striking brunette who was Forest City Manufacturing's leading dress designer. She eventually would design her own line of dresses, Carol King, as one of America's most successful businesswomen. Monday she had finally obtained a divorce from Vernon Dozier, whom she married in 1918 and was separated from in 1928. Now, as the season wound down, Durocher, whose first wife, Ruby Hartley, had obtained a divorce several months earlier on charges of cruelty, told Branch Rickey that he planned to be married. The date would be sometime after the season or, if the Cardinals were to win the pennant, after the World Series.

"Why wait?" Rickey asked.

Durocher knew why he wanted to wait. He knew that if he were to be married with the season still on and bobble a few grounders at shortstop, he would hear about it from the fans.

"Do it now," Rickey said. "The marriage will be good for you. Trust me."

Durocher relented. When he told Frisch, the manager sputtered, "Can you imagine a time like this for a wedding?" But on Wednesday morning, September 26, only two days after Dozier's divorce, Durocher, in his best blue suit, and his bride, in a black tailored gown and white ermine cape, entered the municipal building and walked into the office of Judge Edward E. Butler of the Court of Criminal Corrections. As several friends waited for the ceremony to begin, the best man, Cardinal outfielder Ernie Orsatti, entertained them by juggling the box containing the wedding ring. Then the ceremony began.

"I now pronounce you man and wife," the judge said.

That afternoon, with Mrs. Durocher in a box seat, her husband didn't bobble any grounders, but Paul Dean lost, 3–0, to the Pirates on Waite Hoyt's two-hitter. The Giants also lost, 5–4, to the Phillies' Euel (Chief) Moore as Terry used Hubbell and Schumacher in relief. Still one game apart. But the Cardinals had four games to go, the Giants only two, both against the Brooklyn Dodgers on the weekend. The Giants knew they were in jeopardy.

"We just petered out the last three weeks," Schumacher would say years later. "It was a matter of exhaustion. The team went stale. Sometimes it's easier to come on than hold on."

Thursday the Cardinals kept coming on, winning, 8–5, behind Walker. Now the difference was only one-half game. Friday, with only two days' rest, Dizzy blanked the Reds, 4–0, and the pennant race was all even going into single games Saturday and Sunday: the Cardinals in St. Louis against the Reds, the Giants at the Polo Grounds against the Dodgers.

Seven months earlier Bill Terry had wondered if Brooklyn was still in the league. Now the sixth-place Dodgers were part of a pennant race. As a part-time Giant outfielder in 1922 and 1923, Casey Stengel had batted .368 and .339, respectively, but now the Dodger manager's loyalty was to Brooklyn.

"How they want to see those Giants knocked down," Stengel said of his Dodger players. "And we'll do it Saturday and Sunday too. Talk about the Phillies saving Curt Davis and Chief Moore for 'em, we'll have far more dynamite than that in Mungo and Benge. It's nonsense to say that we have nothing to gain by knocking the Giants out of the race. It means a lot to the boys and it means a lot to me. It means a lot to the club. I think I know our fans. If the Cardinals win the pennant because we beat the Giants, they'll be cheering about it all winter. And if the Giants win the pennant because they beat us, the Brooklyn fans will be left without much feeling of pride in their ball team."

When those fans picked up Saturday's *Brooklyn Eagle*, a page-one headline blared: "Dodgers Set To Show They Are In League."

In damp, drizzly weather that Saturday afternoon, only 13,774 customers appeared at the Polo Grounds, most of them having come from Brooklyn on the subway. Van Lingle Mungo would start against Roy Parmelee, a twenty-seven-year-old righthander with a 10–5 record. In the Dodger clubhouse Stengel had reminded his players to wait out Parmelee, who could be wild.

"All right, let's go," Stengel said. "We're still in the league, but let's not be too still."

Mungo was the Dodgers' best pitcher, also their most tempestuous pitcher. "He was as fast as Dizzy Dean, he should've been in the Hall of Fame," his catcher and the Dodger captain, Al Lopez, would say years later. "But his temper hurt him. He'd get mad on the mound. He'd get mad after a few drinks." He'd also get others mad. He once was smuggled out of Cuba when threatened by a machete-waving husband of a nightclub dancer. But that Saturday afternoon Mungo lifted his record to 18–16 with a five-hit 5–1 victory while contributing two singles, scoring the Dodgers' first run, and driving in the second. In St. Louis, meanwhile, Paul Dean, starting against the Reds with only two days' rest, scattered eleven hits in a 6–1 victory, his nineteenth. For the first time since June 5, the Cardinals were in first place.

"Yes, Indeed, Mr. Terry," snickered the Brooklyn *Times-Union*'s front-page headline, "The Dodgers Still Are In The League."

Dizzy Dean, who now would be trying to clinch the pennant with only one day's rest, patted his brother on the back and predicted, "If they give me two or three runs, there ain't gonna be a playoff." When a 2 was posted in the first inning for the Cardinals on the Polo Grounds scoreboard Sunday afternoon, the Brooklyn rooters roared, sure that Diz would win even if the Giants' Freddie Fitzsimmons were to win. Ray Benge, the Dodger starter, was as quiet as Mungo was noisy, a thirty-two-year-old righthander whose 14–12 record would be the best of his career. He fussed and fidgeted on the mound, which Stengel thought might add to the Giants' jitters. He also had two different curveballs.

"He had a small curve that stayed high," Lopez would remember, "and a sharp curve that broke down low."

That afternoon Benge's curveballs didn't break. He was knocked out in the first inning as the Giants scored four quick runs. But the Dodgers kept pecking away. When their two-run rally in the eighth produced a 5–5 tie, three Dodger fans raced through the lower stands. One was grinding an auto claxon. Another rang a cowbell. The third waved a placard proclaiming, "Yes, Brooklyn Is Still in the League." When the Dodgers won in the tenth inning, 8–5, hundreds of their fans rushed onto the field. Some surrounded Stengel, others lifted Lopez onto their shoulders and hurried toward the centerfield clubhouse.

"Let me down, you crazy bastards," yelled Lopez, thinking he would surely fall. "Let me down."

Soon the Dodger captain was dropped gently at the steps to the visitors' clubhouse. But even before the Dodgers won, the Giants knew they were finished. Up on the scoreboard the Cardinals were going into the ninth inning with a 9–0 lead and Dizzy Dean pitching.

"When Cincinnati can stage a nine-run rally," Tommy Holmes wrote in the *Brooklyn Eagle*, "Niagara will flow upward."

Diz quickly completed his seven-hit shutout, emerging as the National League's first thirty-game winner since Grover Alexander of the Philadelphia Phillies in 1917. In the fans' celebration at Sportsman's Park, thousands roamed the field. Some hurried to the mound, including a small boy in a green sweater who put a small block of ice on the rubber.

"Dizzy told me to put it there this morning," the boy was quoted as saying in the St. Louis *Globe-Democrat*. "He said it would be burning up if I didn't. Go ahead and feel it. Even the ice hasn't gotten it cooled down yet."

In the Cardinal clubhouse Ripper Collins was singing, "We're in the money, we're in the money," a popular song from the 1933 Broadway musical *Gold Diggers*. In their World Series triumph over the Detroit Tigers in seven games, a full share would be worth $5,821.19, almost twice Paul Dean's salary. But now the Cardinals were celebrating their remarkable comeback: winning fourteen of their last sixteen games. Dizzy Dean had won his last seven starts, including three in the final six days. For all his salary squabbles, he justified his favorite philosophy: "If you can do it, it ain't braggin'."

At the Polo Grounds, meanwhile, Bill Terry was trying to explain the Giants' collapse in losing five of their last six games.

"I don't know what happened," the Giant manager said. "I guess the best team won. The Deans made the Cardinals a better team. I made some mistakes and I've no criticism of my own club. But if Stengel's team had played as hard all year as it did the last two days, it wouldn't be in sixth place."

With a 71–81 record, the Dodgers had finished sixth on merit, but Casey Stengel was beaming.

"So now Mr. Terry says if we had played hard, we wouldn't finish in sixth place?" the Dodger manager said. "Well, if the season lasted another month and we kept playing him, he'd finish in last place. Maybe the Giants thought we gave 'em a beating. And they're right. But I'm still sorry for them when I think of the beating they still have to take. Wait until their wives realize they're not going to get those new fur coats. I've been through it, and I know."

Gabby Hartnett in the Gloaming

Mace Brown. *UPI Photo*

RIGLEY FIELD WAS thick with twilight. Streaks of shadows from the roof and girders were lengthening across the grass. As the eighth inning ended with the Cubs and Pirates tied, 6–6, the umpires gathered near home plate with the managers, Gabby Hartnett and Pie Traynor.

"One more inning," plate umpire George Barr ruled.

One more turn at bat for the Pirates to increase their lead to one and one-half games. Or one more turn at bat for the Cubs to jump into first place by one-half game. But the Pirates didn't score. In the bottom of the ninth, the Cubs' first two batters quickly departed.

One more out and the game would end in a tie, to be rescheduled the next day as part of a doubleheader.

As the Cub catcher and manager, Gabby Hartnett, dug his spikes into the dirt of the batter's box, twenty-nine-year-old righthander Mace Brown, the National League's best relief pitcher, stared at catcher Al Todd for the sign. The year before, 1937, Brown's record fifty appearances without a complete game had established him as one of the first pitchers to be used primarily in relief; earlier in this 1938 season he had been the first relief pitcher selected in the six-year history of the All-Star Game. At the All-Star break his record was 12–2, but it had dwindled to 15–8 and now he was pitching to preserve a pennant.

"Only a few weeks before," Brown would recall years later, "I saved a game when I threw a curveball to Hartnett and he hit into a double play."

Now, in the gathering gloom of Wednesday, September 28, 1938, Brown threw that same curveball. Hartnett took it. Strike one. Another curveball. Hartnett swung and missed. Strike two.

One more strike and the Pirates, who had been in first place since July 12, again would be one and one-half games ahead.

Two months earlier, thirty-seven-year-old Charles Leo (Gabby) Hartnett had been named Cub manager by owner Philip K. Wrigley, the chewing gum millionaire. Having grown up in Woonsocket, Rhode Island, and Millville, Massachusetts, in a family of fourteen children, Hartnett had joined the Cubs in 1922. With his fist in the air and a smile on his beefy tomato-red face, he had developed Hall of Fame stature. When the Cubs won the 1935 pennant, he was voted the National League's most valuable player. One of his earlier Cub managers, Joe McCarthy, called him the "perfect" catcher.

"He had everything except speed," McCarthy said. "He was super smart. Nobody ever had more hustle. Nobody could throw with him. There have been few great clutch hitters and he was the best."

Hartnett had a sense of humor too. He was the National League catcher in the 1934 All-Star Game when Carl Hubbell struck out Babe Ruth, Lou Gehrig, Jimmie Foxx, Al Simmons, and Joe Cronin in succession. Turning to the American League dugout, he grinned.

"What are you complaining about?" he said. "We have to look at Hubbell's screwball all year."

One day in the Polo Grounds, where the press box hung low from the upper deck behind home plate, Hartnett turned to pursue a high foul. Before focusing on the ball, he found himself staring at two of his friends in the press box.

"Hi, Kenny," he said. "Hi, John."

"You'll drop it," one of them said.

"Bet you fifty I catch it," he said.

They did, and he did. Gabby indeed. "He never stopped talking to hitters," Billy Herman, the Cub second baseman that year, would remember. "I don't know what he said to them, but he never stopped. He was the best catcher I ever saw. Better than Roy Campanella, better than Bill Dickey, better than Mickey Cochrane. He hit .297 lifetime with all those homers."

Hartnett's 236 home runs endured as a career record for catchers until it was surpassed by Campanella, Yogi Berra, Johnny Bench, and Carlton Fisk.

"And he was a great receiver, the best thrower of all time," Herman said. "His throws were right on the bag with something on it. He had a high squeaky voice and if the pitcher was trying to keep a fast runner from getting a big lead, you'd hear him tell the pitcher, 'Let the sonofabitch go.' He didn't care how fast the runner was."

In that era no statistics were kept on how many base runners Hartnett threw out trying to steal. But if one of today's catchers throws out one-third of the base runners, it's a good percentage.

"I saw Al Lopez not long ago," Herman said, referring to a Hall of Fame catcher of that era, "and I asked him, 'What do you think Hartnett's percentage was?' and he said, 'Double that.'"

"He had a terrific arm, the best catcher's arm I've ever seen, better than Johnny Bench's," said Billy Jurges, then the Cub shortstop. "The ball was like a feather when you caught it."

His pitchers cherished his judgment. Not long after Dizzy Dean joined the Cubs in a 1938 trade, he said, "If Gabby would have caught me, I never would have lost a game." And if Dean had accepted Hartnett's judgment, maybe Dean would not have lost a career.

In the 1937 All-Star Game, with Earl Averill at bat, Dean, then with the Cardinals, shook off Hartnett's signal. Hartnett called for another pitch, Dean nodded and threw. Averill lined the ball off Dean's left foot, fracturing the big toe. When Dean tried to pitch before the toe was completely healed, he changed his motion and hurt his arm. He never regained his famous fastball.

During that 1937 season Hartnett turned down a day in his honor at Wrigley Field, along with a new automobile.

"I don't want to be distracted from the business at hand," he explained. "We're trying to win the pennant."

The Cubs finished second that year, three games behind the Giants, but Hartnett had his highest average, .354, in 110 games, his twelfth season (eighth in a row) of at least 100 games. In 1938 the Cubs got off to a good start with Charlie Grimm managing, but on June 9 they dropped out of first place. Two weeks after the All-Star Game, the Cubs were on a fourth-place treadmill, five and one-half games behind the Pirates, with the Giants a close second, and the Reds third. Grimm was fired.

"I was asked to manage the club in June that year," Jurges would say later. "I turned it down."

This time Wrigley offered the job to Hartnett, who didn't turn it down. On July 22, with Grimm now upstairs in the Cub radio booth, Hartnett took command. Not that the change helped that much immediately. On August 15 Hartnett fractured his right thumb as the Cubs slipped six and one-half games behind. He would be out for nearly three weeks. As late as August 22 they were eight games behind the Pirates.

But on Labor Day, the Cubs swept a doubleheader in Pittsburgh, 4–0 behind Bill Lee and 4–2 behind Clay Bryant, the two righthanded starters who would carry the pitching staff. And on September 14, the Pirates lost a doubleheader to the Giants at the Polo Grounds while the Cubs won, 6–3, in Boston on Hartnett's disputed grand slam homer. His thumb healed, Hartnett pulled lefthander Lou Fette's pitch past the leftfield foul pole.

Umpire George (Tiny) Parker called it a fair ball but the Bees, led by manager Casey Stengel, argued that it had been foul.

"It was clearly a foul ball," Chicago sports columnist John Carmichael said at the time, "but the umpire called it a home run."

Blessed by the umpire's mistake, the Cubs had narrowed the Pirates' lead to two and one-half games. But on Sunday, September 18, the Pirates moved three and one-half games ahead on Russ Bauers's four-hitter in Philadelphia while the Cubs lost the first game of a doubleheader in Brooklyn and preserved a 3–3 tie in the second game on Herman's leaping snatch of catcher Gilly Campbell's bases-loaded line drive before darkness descended.

As the Cubs awaited Monday's opener of a four-game series in Philadelphia, the Dodgers' general manager, Larry MacPhail, asked Hartnett to return to Ebbets Field on Friday, supposedly a travel date for the Cubs, to replay the tie.

"I couldn't make up my mind right away," Hartnett would say later. "I asked MacPhail to give me twenty-four hours. He said he would. But I'd been figuring we had to win all three games in our series with the Pirates the next week in Chicago if we were to win the pennant. I had to think of my pitchers. I had to argue with the whole ballclub. They wanted to go back to Brooklyn to play. But I stuck my neck out and turned it down. I felt that we might lose that game just as easy as we could win it. So I took that chance."

That Monday both the Cubs' game in Philadelphia and the Pirates' game at the Polo Grounds were postponed by what is still remembered along the eastern seaboard as the 1938 hurricane. The severe weather also washed out the Tuesday and Wednesday games. Thursday the race resumed. Bill Lee's fourth consecutive shutout, his ninth of the season, and Clay Bryant's eighteenth victory swept the Phillies, 4–0 and 2–1, respectively, but the Pirates won twice in Brooklyn, retaining their three-and-one-half-game lead.

Friday the Cubs stayed in Philadelphia, winning another doubleheader, 4–3 on outfielder Augie Galan's eighth-inning homer and 7–6 on first baseman Jimmy (Ripper) Collins's bases-loaded double in the ninth, a towering fly that outfielder Gib Brack bungled. When the

Pirates lost, 5–4, in twelve innings in Cincinnati, the Cubs were only two games back as they rushed to board their three Pullman railroad cars attached to a milk train that would connect to a faster train in Harrisburg, Pennsylvania.

"Don't worry," traveling secretary Bob Lewis told the players. "We'll be in Chicago in plenty of time for tomorrow's game with the Cardinals."

The day before, the Cardinals were the first baseball team to travel by airplane. After losing a Thursday doubleheader in Boston, the Cardinals peered out the small windows of two United Airlines planes that took them to New York, where they caught an overnight train. But now, on Saturday afternoon at Wrigley Field, Hartnett's homer helped the Cubs rout Lon Warneke, 9–3, for their fifteenth victory in eighteen games while the Pirates' Russ Bauers stopped the Reds, 4–1. In Sunday's games, Bryant, pitching on only two days' rest, earned his nineteenth victory, 7–2, but the Pirates maintained their two-game lead when Charles (Red) Lucas, alias the "Nashville Narcissus," out-dueled Paul Derringer, 5–3.

One week remained. Seven games for the Cubs, eight for the Pirates, several of whom now were sitting in the stands on Monday at Wrigley Field as Big Bill Lee warmed up to oppose the Cardinals.

To his Cubs' teammates, the six-three righthander with the high leg kick was known as "General," a natural nickname for a handsome southern gentleman named Lee who was born in Plaquemine, Louisiana, and would die there. In those years the Cubs spent their early weeks of spring training on Catalina Island off the southern California coast, a vacation retreat for many Hollywood stars.

"Bill was really a good-looking guy with coal-black hair," Phil Cavarretta remembered. "Whenever we were in Catalina, we kept hearing stories that Hollywood people wanted to give him a screen test."

National League hitters wouldn't have missed him. Not quite twenty-nine years old in his fifth season, William Crutcher Lee, Jr., had developed into one of baseball's best pitchers. His curveball was his money pitch. And he was about to put together one of baseball history's most remarkable pennant race performances. With several Pirates watching that Monday afternoon, Lee's streak of scoreless innings ended at thirty-seven and one-third, but he stopped the Cardinals, 6–3, for his twenty-first victory, slicing the Pirates' lead to one and one-half games. With an eight-game winning streak, the Cubs had won seventeen of twenty games as Lee and Bryant combined for ten of those victories. But the Pirates and their manager, Pie Traynor, didn't seem concerned.

"I'm going to play my three aces," Traynor said before Tuesday's opener. "Jim Tobin, Bob Klinger, and Russ Bauers."

Despite the Cubs' streak, the Pirates had won eight of ten games, with those three starters accounting for six of the eight.

"And what would we have done without Mace Brown?" Traynor said. "He's been in almost fifty games, almost all in relief."

Hartnett, as he confessed later, "stuck my neck out" again. Dizzy Dean, his twenty-seven-year-old right arm aching and his once famous fastball only a memory, hadn't pitched since September 13, hadn't started since August 13, but Hartnett selected him to open the Pirates series. Andy Lotshaw, the Cubs' longtime trainer, rubbed Diz's right shoulder and arm with hot ointment.

"His shoulder and arm," teammate Phil Cavarretta remembered, "was as red as a lobster."

Without a fastball, Dean used a sidearm delivery to fool the Pirates with what he called his "nothing ball," a pitch that was the speed of a change-up for most pitchers. In the Pirate dugout, Bauers, who would start Friday's game, kept shaking his head. "Diz doesn't have enough to hit," he muttered. Even so, going into the ninth, Diz had a 2–0 lead, the Cubs having jumped on righthander Jim Tobin for a run in the third on Collins's triple and Jurges's single before adding another run in the sixth. But even before Diz plunked shortstop Arky Vaughan with a pitch to open the ninth, Hartnett had Bill Lee throwing in the bullpen.

"If we needed a pitcher," Hartnett later explained, "that was the spot for the best we had."

With Vaughan on first, the Pirates' cleanup hitter, first baseman Gus Suhr, popped up. Woody Jensen, pinch-hitting for Floyd (Pep) Young, forced Vaughan at second. Two out. But third baseman Lee (Jeep) Handley drilled a double off the leftfield wall, Jensen stopping at third. His mask off, Hartnett glanced over at Lee in the bullpen along the leftfield line as he walked out to the mound.

"Al Todd was up," Hartnett later explained. "He always hit Dean pretty good, even when Diz had his stuff, and Diz didn't have a thing then. Not only that, but Todd never hit Lee very well. So even though Lee hadn't been a steady relief pitcher, I called him in. My neck was out again. I'll say this for Diz, he never complained. He said I'd done the right thing, that he'd lost his stuff."

Lee got two quick strikes on Todd before letting loose an uncharacteristic wild pitch. Jensen scored and Handley, the potential tying run, hurried to third. But Lee calmly fanned Todd, ensuring the 2–1 triumph that cut the Pirates' lead to one-half game. Only five games remained for each team, including the next two against each other.

All over America, the Great Depression was still haunting the population, especially in the big cities where unemployed men sold apples on street corners. Not many people had money to spare. But on Wednesday afternoon Wrigley Field bulged with 34,465 customers as Clay Bryant and Bob Klinger warmed up. At a lean six feet and 180 pounds, Klinger was a rare rookie, a thirty-year-old righthander who had finally made the big leagues after seasons of struggle in the minors. On the Pirate staff, he was considered the fourth starter behind Bauers, Tobin, and Cy Blanton, but he had established himself. In his twenty previous starts, he had a 12–5 record with ten complete games. And with five days' rest, he was ready.

Bryant, starting again with only two days' rest, didn't have his best fastball. In the sixth inning rookie leftfielder Johnny Rizzo hit his twenty-first homer and the Pirates added two more runs for a 4–2 lead.

In the Cub sixth, Hartnett opened with a double that centerfielder Lloyd Waner couldn't hold, then Collins was credited with a double when rightfielder Paul Waner misjudged his fly ball. Collins soon scored on pinch hitter Ken O'Dea's sacrifice fly for a 4–4 tie. But with one out in the seventh, the Waner brothers each singled. Vance Page, the Cub reliever, then committed what the Pirates claimed was a balk.

"Page stepped slightly away from the box as he pitched to Rizzo, who bounced into a double play," wrote Edward F. Balinger in the *Pittsburgh Post-Gazette*. "Todd and all the Pirates set up the claim of a balk. The kicking did no good."

According to the Pirates, first-base umpire Dolly Stark signaled a balk but backed away when Rizzo swung, hitting a grounder to shortstop for a Jurges-to-Herman-to-Collins double play. Three out. In the tradition of the time, the Cub infielders sailed their gloves onto the outfield grass and hurried into their dugout.

In the eighth the Pirates put together another rally. Vaughan walked and Suhr singled. Hartnett summoned lefthander Larry French from the bullpen. Traynor summoned his best pinch hitter, thirty-seven-year-old Heinie Manush, who had won the 1926 American League batting title with .378 for the Detroit Tigers.

Manush singled, scoring Vaughan for a 5–4 lead and prompting

Hartnett to motion to his bullpen for Bill Lee again. Obviously weary, Lee gave up a single to Handley that scored Suhr for a 6–4 lead. Todd grounded to Jurges, who cut down Manush at the plate. But with Klinger the next batter, Traynor disdained a pinch hitter, notably ignoring Woody Jensen, a thirty-one-year-old lefthanded-swinging reserve outfielder who would hit only .200 that season but who had batted .324 in 1935. Traynor, who was considered the best third baseman in history until Brooks Robinson and Mike Schmidt came along, remains a cherished figure in Pittsburgh, but his decision not to use a pinch hitter for Klinger would be remembered there as an unforgivable tactical mistake.

"Two on, only one out, a chance to put the game away, but no pinch hitter," Jensen would say more than half a century later. "That was the play that no one could understand. Klinger had a tired arm. He had struggled through seven innings. Traynor had no conception of anything. If we could've locked him up in the clubhouse, we would've won."

Cavarretta was surprised to see Klinger walking toward the batter's box. After seven hard innings, the Pirate righthander's control was erratic. With Klinger up, Lee uncorked a wild pitch. Handley scooted to third, but Todd, a slow runner, stayed at first. Klinger then bounced into a double play to end the inning and the threat. But when Ripper Collins led off the eighth for the Cubs with a single, Traynor decided to remove Klinger.

"If you let Klinger hit, let him pitch," Jensen would complain. "But when the first man up singles, Traynor takes him out. We had Ed Brandt and Red Lucas in the bullpen but Traynor put in, of all people, Bill Swift, who had never beaten the Cubs."

Traynor was hoping that in the gathering gloom Swift's fastball would appear faster. But the thirty-year-old righthander's control wasn't sharp. He walked Jurges. With runners on second and first, none out, and trailing by two runs, Hartnett didn't hesitate to do what Traynor had not done: use a pinch hitter for his pitcher. As good as Lee was, Hartnett turned to Tony Lazzeri, a future Hall of Famer who had joined the Cubs that season after more than a decade as the Yankees' second baseman. Lazzeri doubled, scoring Collins and narrowing the Pirates' lead to 6–5. Traynor stubbornly stuck with Swift, who walked third baseman Stan Hack to load the bases. When Herman's single scored Jurges for a 6–6 tie, Traynor finally brought in Mace Brown, who quickly got Frank Demaree to bounce into a double play.

That's when plate umpire George Barr met with the managers and the other umpires and assessed the approaching darkness. In those years before daylight saving time, sunset in Chicago that Wednesday would be at 5:37 P.M. Time for only one more inning.

Hartnett's new pitcher was Charlie Root, whose 605 appearances for the Cubs has endured as the club record. The husky righthander was a twenty-six-game winner in 1927 but is best remembered as the pitcher when Babe Ruth supposedly pointed to centerfield in Wrigley Field during the 1932 World Series and smashed a home run. Now, at thirty-nine, Root was primarily a relief pitcher with a 7–7 record and eight saves.

Except for Paul Waner's two-out single, Root had no trouble with the Pirates in the ninth. And with the Cubs batting in the bottom of the ninth, Mace Brown also appeared to be having no trouble.

Cavarretta, who would win the 1945 National League batting title with a .355 average and would later manage the Cubs, flied out. Centerfielder Carl Reynolds grounded out. Now, with Hartnett up, Brown's first pitch was a curveball. Called strike. Another curveball. Swinging strike.

"Hartnett didn't look good on either of 'em," Brown would recall. "I don't mean to sound egotistical, but I had a good curveball. I thought, I'm going to strike him out with another curveball. I wanted to throw it in the dirt and he probably would've chased it, but I threw it high."

And it hung.

"If I'd thrown a fastball, he'd have taken it," Brown would recall. "But as soon as he hit it, I knew it was gone."

So did Hartnett.

"I knew it the minute I hit it," the Cub manager said later. "I swung with everything I had and then I got that kind of feeling you get when the blood rushes out of your head and you get dizzy."

The ball descended into the leftfield bleachers.

"Only a row or two in," Cavarretta would recall.

By the time Hartnett approached second base, dozens of fans had hopped over the red brick wall in front of the box seats. By the time he neared third base, hundreds were on the field celebrating.

"I don't think I walked a step to the plate, I was carried in," Hartnett said. "But when I got there I saw George Barr taking a good look. He was going to make sure I touched that platter."

Out in rightfield, Paul Waner stood staring at the celebration as if transfixed.

"I should've run into the clubhouse, but I didn't," Waner later remembered. "I just stood out there and watched Hartnett circle the bases and take the lousy pennant with him. I just watched and wondered, sort of objectively, how he could ever get all the way around to touch home plate. The crowd was in an uproar, gone wild. His teammates and the crowd all were mobbing him, throwing him up in the air. I've never seen anything like it. I just stood there and stared, like I was sort of somebody else, and wondered what the chances were that he would actually make it all the way around the bases. When I finally did turn and go into the clubhouse, it was just like a funeral. Mace Brown was sitting in front of his locker, crying like a baby. I stayed with him all that night. I was afraid he was going to commit suicide. That home run took all the fight out of us."

The Cubs not only had won, 7–6, but had jumped over the Pirates into first place by one-half game.

"Mister," first baseman Ripper Collins asked Hartnett in the clubhouse, "can I have your autograph?"

Soon a fan holding what he claimed was the home run ball was ushered into the Cub manager's office. Hartnett thanked the fan for the ball, then autographed another ball and presented it to him.

"That was the shot that did it," Hartnett would say later of his homer. "That took the heart out of the Pirates."

Heart and soul. In Thursday's finale of the three-game series, Russ Bauers, with a 13–13 record, had an opportunity to return the Pirates to first place. But his control was shaky. He walked three in the first inning. When he walked another in the second, Traynor removed him. Bill Lee, pitching for the fourth straight day, started and finished a seven-hitter in a 10–1 triumph that lifted the Cubs to a one-and-one-half-game lead.

"You must be slipping, Bill," righthander Tex Carleton told his teammate. "You let 'em score a run."

Lee complained mildly of a "tight arm" after having pitched a complete game, relieved, relieved, and pitched another complete game in four consecutive victories that the Cubs needed if they were to win the pennant. Hartnett's "Homer in the Gloaming" has endured as one of Chicago's most glorious sports moments, but Lee's contribution in that final week is often forgotten, along with his 22–9 record with a 2.66 earned run average, nine shutouts and two saves in 291 innings. His best season. He pitched for another decade, mostly with glasses in order to see his catcher's signals, but he eventually needed surgery for a detached retina in each eye. Before his death in 1977, he had been blind for several years.

Gabby Hartnett's homer in the gloaming. *UPI Photo*

With Lee's victory that swept the Pirates series, the Cubs had won ten in a row and twenty of their last twenty-two games. Even so, the Pirates were still mathematically alive.

In a Friday doubleheader in Cincinnati, the Pirates lost the opener, 4–1, when Paul Derringer outpitched Jim Tobin before Bauers, trying to atone for his shaky start the previous day, won the second game, 4–1. Darkness in St. Louis created a 7–7 tie there for the Cubs, who remained one and one-half games ahead going into Saturday's doubleheader with the Cardinals.

The Cubs lost the opener of that October 1 doubleheader, but shortly after the Pirates' loss in Cincinnati was posted, the Cubs clinched the pennant with a 10–3 rout in the second game.

Charlie Root, the oldest Cub, got the final out while Dizzy Dean was perched on the dugout steps, pounding a bat against a steel post and yelling, "Pour it on" the same Cardinals for whom he had once pitched so gallantly. Two days later some 300,000 people cheered the Cubs in a downtown Chicago motorcade of open cars to city hall, where the fans continued to cheer the players, especially Hartnett.

"That homer," he often said, "was the greatest thrill of my life."

But when the Cubs were swept in four games by the Yankees in the World Series, their usually happy-go-lucky manager temporarily stashed the thrill of his pennant-turning homer into a corner of his memory.

"Coming back from New York on the train," Cavarretta remembered, "Gabby was really storming and cussing us out."

In Pittsburgh, where the Pirates' 1938 World Series press pins would be a collector's item, there was only mourning.

"I was traded over to Pittsburgh from Boston the next year," first baseman Elbie Fletcher once said. "It was sad, because all they talked about was Hartnett's home run. That home run was still on everybody's mind, haunting them like a ghost. Management knew it. That's why they were trying to shake up the club. But it didn't help. The players talked about Hartnett's home run all year and finished sixth."

Gabby Hartnett's homer in the gloaming surely haunted Mace Brown, who pitched for another decade but was never quite so effective.

"I still think about that homer," he would say more than half a century later. "Not that it bothers me, but it crosses my mind."

1940

The Crybaby Mutiny

Oscar Vitt. *AP/Wide World Photo*

B OB FELLER WAS being hit hard. Soon the Cleveland Indians' ace would be lifted for a pinch hitter. But when the Boston Red Sox were scoring some of their early runs on the cool, cloudy Tuesday afternoon of June 11, 1940, in Fenway Park, some Indians couldn't help but be aware of manager Oscar Vitt's grumbling in their dugout.

"Look at him," Vitt was heard saying. "He's supposed to be my ace. How am I supposed to win a pennant with that kind of pitching?"

In the hours after that 9–2 loss, some of Feller's teammates told him of Vitt's remarks. Feller wasn't surprised. Ever since Vitt had taken over as the Indian manager in 1938, he had been openly critical of many of his players. As a manager who was his own third-base coach, Vitt sometimes even griped to the opposing team after one of the Indians struck out or popped up.

"How," Vitt occasionally said in disgust while staring into the Indians' dugout, "am I supposed to win with a bum like that?"

When a cold rain washed out infield practice before a game at Griffith Stadium in Washington earlier on that eastern swing, first baseman Hal Trosky shivered and said, "It's all right with me. I'll probably get pneumonia if I go out in that rain."

"Why don't you?" Vitt snapped. "You're not doing us any good."

Then fifty years old, Oscar Vitt had often struck out or popped up during his decade as an infielder with the Detroit Tigers and the Red Sox. At five-ten and 150 pounds, he never batted higher than .254, with a career total of only four homers. But his reputation as a scrappy, smart player helped him become a minor league manager, notably with the 1937 Newark Bears, a New York Yankee farm team that won 109 games and the International League pennant by twenty-five and one-half games. Considered the best minor league team ever, those Bears had such future Yankee stars as second baseman Joe Gordon and outfielder Charlie Keller. Vitt's success there prompted the Indians to hire him in 1938 to succeed Steve O'Neill after a fourth-place finish. One day in spring training Feller happened to discuss his new manager with Bob (Suitcase) Seeds, the New York Giants' well-traveled outfielder who had been with the Newark Bears the previous season.

"Hell," Seeds told Feller, "if it hadn't been for Vitt, we would've won by fifty games."

The Indians finished third in both 1938 and 1939, but in 1940 they were expected to challenge the Yankees, who had won four consecutive World Series, for the American League pennant. No longer a prodigy, twenty-one-year-old Bob Feller was already baseball's premier pitcher. At age twenty the season before, he had put together a 24–9 record with a 2.85 earned run average, 246 strikeouts, and 24 complete games, justifying one of his nicknames: the Van Meter Meteor. As a youngster in Van Meter, Iowa, about twenty-five miles from Des Moines, he had been nurtured as a pitcher by his father, who installed a pitching rubber and a home plate in the yard behind their farm.

"When I was twelve," Feller once said, "Dad and I built a ballfield on our farm so we could play teams from other towns."

More than half a century before the motion picture *Field of Dreams* featured a fictional diamond next to an Iowa cornfield, young Robert William Andrew Feller was playing baseball on a real diamond surrounded by corn, cows, horses, chickens, and pigs.

"We fenced off the pasture, we even had a little grandstand behind first base," he once said. "And we charged twenty-five cents."

Signed by scout C. C. (Cy) Slapnicka, the teenager also known as "Rapid Robert" joined the Indians at age seventeen during the 1936 season. After a few relief appearances, he started eight games, posting a 5–3 record. In only sixty-two innings, he had seventy-six strikeouts, including seventeen in one game against the Philadelphia Athletics, breaking Rube Waddell's league record. When the season ended, he returned to high school for his senior year. After he left school to report to spring training in 1937, the Indians arranged for tutors to help him complete his credits toward a diploma. He had a 9–7 record in 1937 and a 17–11 record in 1938. As if to prove that his 1939 statistics weren't a fluke, on opening day in 1940 he fired a no-hitter against the Chicago White Sox in Comiskey Park.

Feller anchored the Indians' starting rotation, which included righthander Mel Harder, near the end of a consistent career in which he would win 223 games, and lefthanders Al Milnar and Al Smith.

The day after Vitt ridiculed Feller's pitching at Fenway Park, the

Red Sox raked Milnar and Harder, 9–5, the Indians' third consecutive loss and their eighth in thirteen games. Suddenly two games out, the Indians boarded a train for Cleveland, where they would oppose the Philadelphia Athletics the next day. Even though the Red Sox were in first place, the Indians feared the Yankees and the Detroit Tigers more. But mostly they feared Vitt's lack of leadership. Over their steaks in the dining car rolling through Massachusetts and into New York, about a dozen Indians decided to meet with the club president, Alva Bradley, and demand that Vitt be fired.

Most of the dissatisfied Indians were older players: first baseman Hal Trosky, third baseman Ken Keltner, catcher Rollie Hemsley, outfielders Ben Chapman and Jeff Heath, along with pitchers Mel Harder, Al Milnar, Johnny Allen, and some others. Feller was one of the few young players to join the mutiny, but two rookies, shortstop Lou Boudreau and second baseman Ray Mack, were not asked to cooperate.

In addition to Vitt's sarcastic remarks to opposing managers and players about his players' ability, they knew he had disparaged them when talking to sportswriters and fans. They knew he had compared them unfavorably to his Newark Bears team. They remembered him praising them to their faces, then criticizing them bitterly in conversations with others. In the dugout, they considered him a "wild man," storming up and down while making caustic comments that created jitters for some players. They felt that their manager's antics had made them the laughingstock of baseball, that their dignity and pride had been undermined.

Thursday morning, after their train arrived at Union Station, nearly a dozen Indians assembled in Alva Bradley's office in the Marion Building on West Third Street.

That afternoon the Indians snapped their slump, defeating the Tigers, 3–2, in eleven innings when second baseman Charlie Gehringer committed a rare double error, fumbling Chapman's grounder and then throwing wildly past Rudy York at first base as outfielder Beau Bell scored the winning run. But the next morning's Cleveland *Plain Dealer* broke the story of the mutiny on its front page.

"In an act without known parallel in baseball history," Gordon Cobbledick wrote, "the Indians yesterday presented to president Alva Bradley a demand that Oscar Vitt be removed as manager."

Many of the Indians suspected that Cobbledick, who traveled with the Indians, had been tipped off by Hemsley, who hoped to be Vitt's successor. But in the meeting, Bradley, who was in his thirteenth year as club president, informed the players that there would be no immediate successor.

"I can't fire him right now," Feller heard Bradley say of Vitt, "but I will after the season."

After the Thursday meeting, Bradley attended that afternoon's game at League Park and talked to Vitt, but the Indian president apparently never mentioned the mutiny. That evening Cobbledick sought a comment from Vitt on the meeting for his story.

"Mr. Bradley did not tell me about this affair when I saw him after the game," said Vitt, who apparently then phoned the Indian president. "When I reached him tonight, he stated that he had intended to talk to me about it tomorrow morning."

Vitt added that he had "no reason to believe that any member of the club felt any enmity" toward him.

"Nobody," he added, "can say that I have not given one hundred percent in energy to the team. I can't imagine what could have impelled them to do this. It looks as if somebody has been stirring up some trouble."

"Is there a fifth column on the team?" he was asked.

"There might be ninety-nine columns," Vitt replied.

None of the Indians was willing to be quoted by name, but one player who requested anonymity disclosed how the unrest had developed during the 1939 season. In one confrontation that year outfielder Jeff Heath was so angry at Vitt, he threatened to punch the manager. When Bradley signed Vitt for 1940, the situation subsided.

"But before this season was two weeks old," that player was quoted as saying, "Vitt had driven most of us half crazy. We simply feel now that we can't play ball for him any longer. We're a good ballclub and we've got a good chance to win the pennant, but if he manages the team all year, we'll be lucky to finish in fourth place."

Hours after Cobbledick's story appeared in Friday morning's *Plain Dealer*, Vitt told his players in a clubhouse meeting, "I'm still the manager. Let's go out and play ball." But before that afternoon's game with the Tigers he was described as "glum and silent" as he sat on the dugout steps while Bradley sat in a nearby box.

"Worse tangles than this have been straightened out," Bradley said. "I think a few disgruntled players got others to join them."

Bradley watched Johnny Allen stop the Tigers, 8–0, on a two-hitter. But on Saturday the Indians lost, 7–4, to the Philadelphia Athletics and Cleveland's fans were in full cry. Before Sunday's doubleheader, first baseman Hal Trosky, considered a mutiny ringleader, was booed on his return from his mother's funeral. When Vitt walked to the plate to meet with the umpires, he was cheered. Feller then pitched a 4–2 three-hitter with twelve strikeouts, and Milnar scattered eight hits in the 4–2 second game, the Indians' fourth victory in five games since the meeting in Bradley's office. But instead of departing to their homes after the doubleheader, the Indian players called a meeting. In a statement signed by all the players in the meeting except centerfielder Roy Weatherly, they ended their mutiny. Weatherly didn't sign what amounted to an apology because he had never been part of the protest.

"It's up to me to play baseball," Weatherly explained, "for whoever the manager is."

Vitt seemed satisfied with the players' signed statement that relieved Bradley of a decision. "My manner," Vitt said in his defense, "showed my desire to win." But the damage to the Indians' image had been done. Cleveland's players had a new nickname: Crybabies. It would follow them for the remainder of the season and into baseball lore. Whenever players on any team criticize their manager now, historians think of the 1940 Cleveland Crybabies who demanded that the club president, Alva Bradley, fire Oscar Vitt as manager.

Despite the rebellion's failure, it seemed to spark the Indians' pennant drive. Within a week after the meeting in Bradley's office, the mutineers had reclaimed first place. During the steamy weeks of July, the Indians were in and out of first place, but in August they appeared to take command.

Suddenly, the Indians floundered. They lost both games of a Labor Day doubleheader in Cleveland to the seventh-place St. Louis Browns, then lost three straight in Detroit where a Tiger fan placed a baby's glass milk bottle, complete with rubber nipple, atop the visitors' dugout. Now the Indians really had something to cry about: they were slumping and the Tigers were surging. Lynwood (Schoolboy) Rowe outpitched Feller, 7–2. Tommy Bridges and Al Benton combined for an 11–3 victory. Louis (Bobo) Newsom breezed, 10–5, for his eighteenth triumph. Those five consecutive losses narrowed the Indians' lead to only one game. After the second loss in Detroit, several Indians met that Thursday night in one of their rooms at the Book-Cadillac Hotel.

"If there was a meeting," Al Milnar told the Cleveland writers the next day, "I didn't know anything about it."

"I was out watching girls play softball," Ben Chapman said. "I was at the meeting in Washington two weeks ago and it was all right. The fellows simply got together and promised to hustle and play the game for the rest of the season, but I didn't attend any meeting in Detroit. I'm through with meetings."

Whoever was or was not there, Bradley confirmed that the players had met in the Book-Cadillac for what he described as a "pep rally."

Whatever the description, the players already had usurped Vitt's authority. Many were ignoring the manager's signs. If ordered to bunt, a batter might swing away. Or a base runner might try to steal second on his own.

"Bradley could've stood by Vitt or stood by the players," *Plain Dealer* columnist Ed Macauley wrote. "He did neither."

"It could've happened," *Detroit News* columnist H. G. Salsinger wrote, tweaking the city across Lake Erie, "only in Cleveland."

With three weeks remaining in the season, the pennant race had just begun. Returning to Cleveland on Saturday, September 7, against the Chicago White Sox, the Indians lost their sixth in a row, 5–4, narrowing their lead over the Tigers to .011 points. When the Indians lost on Monday to lefthander Thornton Lee of the Chicago White Sox, 2–1, the Tigers moved into first place by one-half game. The Yankees, who had been 51–51 in early August, were only one game back.

"All we hear from Vitt," an anonymous Indian player had grumbled during spring training, "is what a great team the Yankees are and what a great manager Joe McCarthy is."

"They want to hang me for telling the truth and frankly expressing my opinion," Vitt responded at the time. "And since I've always spoken frankly, why should I change?"

Tuesday those Yankees, with Joe DiMaggio leading the league in batting, arrived in Cleveland, only to be rained out. When Bob (Lefty) Grove of the Red Sox stifled the Tigers, 6–5, the Indians were back in first place. But only briefly. Wednesday, September 11 was a rare day in baseball. At one time or another, three teams were in first place. Before their doubleheader with the Yankees, the Indians were on top. When the Yankees won the opener, 5–3, they were leading the league. But when the Tigers routed the Red Sox, 11–7, while the Indians won the second game, 5–3, on Yankee first baseman Ellsworth (Babe) Dahlgren's error, the Tigers took a one-half-game lead into a three-game series with the Yankees.

"We're going to shoot the best we have at 'em," Tiger manager Del Baker said. "Rowe, Bridges, and Newsom."

Quiet and narrow-faced, Baker had been a minor league catcher except for three seasons with the Tigers before managing in the minors. Considered an expert sign stealer as a Tiger coach under Mickey Cochrane, he was in his third season as manager. In the spring he had supervised the decision that turned these Tigers into a contender: moving Hank Greenberg to leftfield and installing Rudy York at first base.

As a first baseman in 1938, Greenberg hit fifty-eight homers, the most serious threat to Babe Ruth's record of sixty until Roger Maris surpassed it with sixty-one in 1961.

Instead of complaining about having to move to leftfield, as some sluggers of his stature would have done, Greenberg tried to be the best leftfielder he could be. During batting practice in spring training Greenberg fielded all the grounders and fly balls hit there. After the exhibition games he had a coach throw balls over his head against the fence so he could learn how to turn, take the ricochet, and line up his throws to second base, third base, and home plate. His stature also didn't keep him from kind gestures to his teammates, especially young players. He once told catcher Birdie Tebbetts and righthander Fred Hutchinson to go to the London Chop House, then one of Detroit's best restaurants.

"Tell them you're on the Tigers," Greenberg said, "and that I suggested you go there."

That night the maitre d' led Tebbetts and Hutchinson to a corner table where they had dinner.

"They served us what the help ate, which was better than the food in almost any restaurant in town," Tebbetts would say years later. "And they only charged us a couple of bucks."

Another time Greenberg took Rudy York, a Cherokee Indian who could hardly read and write, to his tailor.

"This young man needs two suits," Greenberg said. "Measure him, make them up, and send me the bill."

For all his homers and all his kindness, Greenberg often was insulted by opposing players because of his Jewish heritage. But instead of deterring him, such treatment seemed to spur him on. In the opener of the Yankee series, his thirty-second homer lifted the Tigers to their seventh victory in eight games, 6–3. The next day Bridges's curveball spun an 8–0 shutout. When the Yankees shelled Newsom, 16–7, on Joe Gordon's two homers and DiMaggio's two doubles and two singles, the Tigers still led by one-half game because the Indians lost to Red Sox rookie lefthander Earl Johnson, 2–1. But on Sunday the Tigers lost again, 6–1, to Washington's lefthanded knuckleballer Emil (Dutch) Leonard, while the Indians swept the Athletics, 5–0 on Feller's two-hitter and 8–5.

"My control was just about perfect," said Feller, whose no-hit bid ended with first baseman Dick Siebert's bloop single with one out in the eighth. "It was only the second game I've ever pitched without giving up a base on balls."

With two weeks remaining in the pennant race, while the Luftwaffe dropped bombs on London in what would develop into the Battle of Britain, the Indians had regained first place by one game but the Yankees, losing a doubleheader to the lowly Browns in St. Louis, had dropped to three and one-half games behind, never to challenge again. When the Indians split a doubleheader with the Philadelphia A's on Monday, the Tigers edged to within one-half game with a 9–2 rout of the Senators for Newsom's nineteenth. By Thursday the Tigers had pulled into a flat-footed tie when Floyd Giebell, a thirty-year-old righthander just up from Buffalo of the International League where he had a hard-luck 15–16 record, and Paul (Dizzy) Trout swept the A's, 13–2 and 10–1. In the A's clubhouse, baseball's Grand Old Man, seventy-seven-year-old manager-owner Connie Mack, wearing his familiar high starched collar and a blue suit, smiled at what he could appreciate better than anybody else.

"This is the dizziest race in American League history," he said. "There hasn't been anything like this since 1908 when the same two teams went down to the last day."

With only eight games remaining for each team, the Indians and the Tigers each had an 85–61 record. Six of those remaining games would be against each other, beginning with a three-game series in Detroit: Harder vs. Newsom on Friday, Milnar vs. Rowe on Saturday, Feller vs. Bridges on Sunday.

But to Tiger fans, the Indians were still the Crybabies who had demanded three months earlier that their manager be fired.

When the Indians arrived in Detroit by train Thursday night, teenagers threw eggs and fruit and yelled, "Crybabies, crybabies." To protect the Indians before Friday's opener, eight Detroit policemen were stationed around their dugout. As the Indians appeared, one by one, the Briggs Stadium fans booed and chanted, "Crybabies, crybabies." During batting practice a fan pushed a doll carriage onto the field, then hurried away. At least one of the Indians was amused. With a laugh, Ben Chapman put his bats in the carriage and rolled it toward home plate as photographers surrounded him. One fan, alluding to the

Russian Revolution in 1917, held up a homemade sign: "Leon 'Hal' TroTsky vs. Oscar Vitt." When the photographers posed the two managers, Del Baker reached out and felt Vitt's pulse.

"You're actually nervous, Oscar," the Tiger manager said.

Nervous or not, the Indians jumped on Bobo Newsom for a 4–1 lead that Harder protected through seven innings. "From a standpoint of craftsmanship," Greenberg would say later, "I've never seen a better pitched game than what Harder was pitching. Yes, I said never. He never made a mistake. He never made a wrong pitch." But in the eighth Harder walked Barney McCosky, then Gehringer slashed a single. In the bullpen, Feller had thrown only a few pitches, but Vitt waved him in.

"Harder had pitched beautiful ball," Vitt later explained, "but he appeared to be losing his stuff."

Feller never found his stuff. Greenberg singled. York singled. Higgins singled. Vitt brought in Joe Dobson, but the Tigers' five-run rally snatched a 6–5 lead that righthander Al Benton preserved. Now the Tigers were in front by one game. Harder defended Vitt's move, saying, "Neither Greenberg nor York has had much success with Feller this season. I thought it was a good move to bring him in." Even so, Vitt was being second-guessed not only for Feller's failure but for using him at all.

"If the Indians fail to win the pennant," Gordon Cobbledick wrote in the *Plain Dealer*, "it will be because Feller has been worn to a frazzle by working in and out of turn."

With only two days' rest after his two-hitter the previous Sunday against the A's, Feller had won his twenty-sixth on Wednesday with a five-hitter, 2–1, in a duel with Sid Hudson of the Senators. After only one day's rest, he had been brought in by Vitt to relieve Harder, his sixth relief appearance in addition to his thirty-five starts. For the season, his twenty-one-year-old arm had already worked 302 innings.

"It would be a pity," Cobbledick wrote, "if the greatest pitching arm in baseball and one of the greatest in baseball history were ruined by overwork, as many a fine arm before it has been. No pennant is important enough to risk such a gold mine."

At least publicly, the gold mine didn't complain. "I didn't throw many balls in the bullpen," Feller said, "but I thought my arm was in shape to go. I just didn't have it." Vitt insisted, "If I had it to do over again, I'd take out Harder and use Feller." But the Indian manager had another worry: that the Tigers had somebody with binoculars in the centerfield bleachers stealing the catcher's signs to the pitcher.

"For the rest of this series," Vitt told his pitchers and catchers, "I want you to change signs every inning."

Informed of Vitt's suspicion about the binoculars in centerfield, *Detroit News* columnist H. G. Salsinger questioned the Indian manager, asking, "Do you really think it could be done?"

"Yes," Vitt said.

"How could he signal the batter?"

"With his hat?"

"One hat," Salsinger asked, "among several thousand hats?"

"Yes," Vitt said.

"You're sure?"

"Didn't I play here for years?" Vitt said. "Do you mean to tell me you don't remember the old signal station in Cherry Street behind leftfield? Maybe you've forgotten, but I haven't. It's just an old tradition at Michigan and Trumbull avenues and by that I mean it's an old tradition that won't die."

Years later, in the book *Hank Greenberg: The Story of My Life*, the Tiger slugger acknowledged the 1940 sign stealer.

"Tommy Bridges had purchased a new hunting rifle with a long-range gauge on it, a telescopic lens," Greenberg remembered. "Tommy had pitched the day before so he and Pinky Higgins, out with an injury, were sitting in the upper deck in leftfield. Tommy was pointing the rifle and looking through the telescopic lens when he looked down at the catcher. Sure enough, he was able to see the catcher's signs to the pitcher. He came down to the dugout and told us he thought he would be able to relay the pitches to the batter. The next day, he tested it. He moved over above the bullpen in left centerfield. You could look over the right shoulder of the pitcher and see the signal."

When Bridges pulled his right hand down, that meant a curveball. If he kept his right hand up, it meant a fastball.

"Only the Yankees suspected anything," Greenberg recalled. "McCarthy sent somebody out to the bullpen. We moved the spot to the upper deck. We brought one of our minor league managers to Detroit and he sat in the upper deck with binoculars. If he pulled his right hand off the binoculars, it was a fastball. If he left it up there on the binoculars, curveball. Even when the bleachers were filled, we knew exactly where he was sitting."

According to Greenberg, over a two-week span that September, he batted .458 with twenty-seven hits (thirteen homers, two triples, five doubles, seven singles), thirty-three runs batted in, and thirty runs scored.

Vitt's information had been correct, but he couldn't prove it. Saturday the Tigers won again, 5–0, on Schoolboy Rowe's five-hitter. Before the game Rowe spent time posing for a *Detroit News* photographer. In the photo that appeared in the paper, he seemed to be sitting on top of a world shaped like a baseball. Many players would have been too superstitious to do that, especially before a game, but Rowe never gave it a thought.

"I've never seen Rowe better," Trosky said. "I thought he had as much stuff as he had when he pitched Detroit to the 1934 and 1935 pennants."

By winning, the Tigers forced Vitt to make a decision on Sunday's starter. To rest Feller for Tuesday's game in Cleveland with the Browns, Vitt had hoped to start Harry Eisenstat against the Tigers in Sunday's finale. Vitt knew that the Tigers had knocked out Feller four times that season. But with the Tigers now two games ahead, Vitt had no choice.

"I've been tired lately," Feller acknowledged, "but I didn't do any throwing today and I don't see any reason why I shouldn't be pretty fast."

That Saturday the Feller family in Van Meter, Iowa, moved into a new $25,000 brick home on their 380-acre farm. It had ten rooms, musical door chimes, and a foot switch under the dining room table to summon the maid. The farmhouse where Bob was born had been sold and removed to another site. And on Sunday, with 56,771 Tiger fans chanting "Crybabies," the precocious pitcher whose fame and fortune had purchased the Feller family's new home scattered eight hits, including Greenberg's fortieth homer, in a 10–5 victory that lifted the Indians to within one game. Only five games remained for each team, with the Tigers due in Cleveland on Friday.

If the Indians could win, it would create the first all-Ohio World Series. The Cincinnati Reds had clinched the National League pennant. Their manager, Bill McKechnie, had scouted Sunday's game. "I fear Feller," he said, "more than the Tigers' slugging."

Neither team played on Monday, although the Tigers, on Baker's orders, took batting practice that morning. Thousands of their fans were planning to travel to the final weekend series in Cleveland by car, train, plane, and the steamer across Lake Erie that docked near Municipal Stadium, baseball's biggest ballpark, with a seating capacity at the time of 78,000. Because it was so big, the Indians played there only when a big crowd was expected; otherwise they used little League Park. But in early September the pennant race had prompted Alva

Bradley to schedule all the Indians' remaining games in the huge lakeside stadium. The more seats, the more customers the Indians could accommodate. Even if those customers would be Tiger fans.

"Don't be thinking about the Tigers," Vitt reminded his players. "We've got two games with the Browns before the Tigers get here."

In midseason the sixth-place Browns had lost fourteen in a row, but they had knocked the Yankees out of the race and manager Fred Haney, one of Vitt's oldest friends, had saved submarine-ball right-hander Eldon Auker and lefthander Vern Kennedy for the Indians. In the Tuesday opener Auker, who had been discarded by both the Tigers and the Red Sox, outpitched Mel Harder, 7–2, for his fifteenth victory.

"Chalk up another win for the old castoff," Haney said. "He should've had a shutout."

That loss dropped the Indians to one and one-half games behind the rained-out Tigers, who now had to play the White Sox in a Wednesday doubleheader. While the Indians were stopping the Browns, 4–2, on Al Milnar's seven-hitter, the Tigers won the first game, 10–9, in ten innings on Rudy York's double. Bobo Newsom, who worked the last two innings, picked up his twentieth victory, but that chilly, windy afternoon he had only begun to pitch. He also started the second game against Johnny Rigney, who had a 2–1 lead in the seventh with two strikes on Greenberg. As several Indians listened to the Tiger game on their clubhouse radio, Feller had some advice for Rigney.

"Throw him a fastball knee-high," Feller said.

Rigney threw a curve that Greenberg smashed into the leftfield stands for his forty-first homer and his 150th run batted in. Even though that homer only tied the score, the Indians seemed to sense that the Tigers would win. Turning to his Indian roommate, rookie out-fielder Clarence (Soup) Campbell, Feller said, "Let's get going." In the eighth, the Tigers added another run on McCosky's single, Gehringer's single, a walk to Greenberg, and York's sacrifice fly. Newsom completed the 3–2 triumph. Credited with both victories, Newsom had redeemed himself.

"I knew the fans were getting on me," he said. "After I was knocked out by the Yankees and taken out of the Cleveland game, some of 'em thought I couldn't win in the clutch. I guess I showed 'em."

In another corner of the Tiger clubhouse, equipment manager Bob Conway was packing gray road uniforms for Thursday's train ride.

"This was supposed to be the boys' last trip of the season," he said, "but I have a hunch they'll be going to Cincinnati next week." Now two games ahead, the Tigers needed to win only once in Cleveland to get to the World Series for the third time in seven years. But in Friday's opener they had to face Feller, rested and ready after not having pitched since Sunday. For the Tigers, it was Rowe's turn to pitch, but Baker wouldn't commit himself.

"I won't make up my mind about Rowe until half an hour before game time," the Tiger manager said as his players were checking into the Hotel Cleveland after their train arrived Thursday evening. "The Schoolboy has a sore arm and I'd be foolish to start him if the weather is damp and cold."

Because fans in Detroit's railroad station had thrown eggs and tomatoes at the Indians the week before, about four hundred Cleveland fans gathered at Union Station to meet the Tigers' train. Despite the presence of twenty-five policemen, when the Tiger players appeared on the platform of Track 15, fans above the stairs began hurling tomatoes, beets, and overripe apples. Seeing the fruit splattering, Gehringer warned his teammates.

"Follow me," he said, knowing their hotel was above the station. "I know the way to the freight elevator."

Perhaps the least known of those Tigers scurrying across a ramp to the freight elevator was Floyd Giebell, who had beaten the A's in his only start a week earlier. Not long after Giebell arrived in his room, the phone rang. Baker asked him to come up to the manager's suite.

"You're starting tomorrow," Baker told the rookie righthander. "I want to rest our other pitchers."

Giebell wasn't completely surprised. He had heard whispers that rather than use Rowe against Feller, the manager might choose a sacrificial lamb from among him, nineteen-year-old Hal Newhouser (9–9 that season), Dizzy Trout, and Fred Hutchinson (each 3–7). But now Baker explained the decision.

"On the train I met with our eight regulars," Giebell heard Baker say. "I told them I wanted to use one of the young pitchers against Feller to rest the other starters. You got seven of the eight votes."

According to Giebell, only Hank Greenberg didn't vote for him. Not that Giebell was offended. That was Greenberg's prerogative. The other Tiger regulars' reasoning was that, of the four candidates, Giebell had more minor league experience and had the best control. Even if the Indians hit him hard, many of their drives would be long outs.

The foul lines in Municipal Stadium then were only 320 feet, but the left-center and right-center power alleys were 435 feet, and the center-field wall was 450 feet.

When Giebell walked out to warm up on Friday near the Tigers' third-base dugout, none of the Indians even bothered to heckle him. They thought, Giebell assumed, that he would be a pigeon.

Rudy York could have told them Giebell wasn't. When he first joined the Tigers the year before, Giebell noticed that his street shoes twice were splattered by tobacco juice spit playfully by York, who had the next locker. The next time it happened, Giebell filled a bucket with water and dumped it over York's head.

York grunted, but he never spit on Giebell's shoes again.

In the clubhouse that Friday afternoon, Baker had taken New-houser aside. "I'm starting Giebell," the manager said, "but I want you to be ready from the first inning on." Newhouser was already warm-ing up as Giebell strode to the mound and Greenberg trotted to leftfield. During batting practice, Greenberg had been the target of tomatoes, assorted fruits, and lunch leftovers. With the Indians about to bat, a few more tomatoes splattered on the grass. Now, as Green-berg settled under Roy Weatherly's first-inning fly ball, more toma-toes and fruit fell around him. Baker hopped out of the Tiger dugout to protest to umpire Bill Summers, who walked over to the public-address announcer.

"Ladies and gentlemen," Summers intoned, "the management of the Detroit club will remove their team from the field if the throwing does not stop. Every time a fly ball is hit and a Detroit player is interfered with, the umpires will call the batter out."

Boos thundered from the Ladies' Day crowd of 45,553. Minutes later, in the Tiger bullpen, Birdie Tebbetts was knocked unconscious by what Schoolboy Rowe, sitting next to him, described as a half-bushel basket of green tomatoes and empty beer bottles. Tebbetts was shaking the cobwebs out of his head as he walked underneath the stands when somebody pointed to a twenty-five-year-old man who had been apprehended by police for having thrown the basket. Teb-betts, feisty as ever, turned and punched him.

Out on the field, Giebell and Feller were locked in a scoreless duel through three innings. With one out in the fourth, Gehringer walked. Greenberg struck out, but York lifted a high fly ball down the 320-foot leftfield line as Ben Chapman drifted toward the wall for what ap-peared to be a towering foul popup. But the wind was blowing from third base to first base.

The wind's got it, Feller realized. The wind's going to keep it fair.

The ball landed in the stands about a foot fair and about a foot into the first row. York's thirty-third homer had provided a 2–0 lead that Giebell would protect with a six-hit shutout. Feller fired a three-hitter but lost to this virtual unknown who wasn't even eligible for the World Series roster. The sacrificial lamb had outpitched baseball's big bad wolf. In four different innings, the Indians had two baserunners. Giebell responded by fanning one or more in each inning, including three strikeouts of Chapman in clutch situations: first and third with one out, first and second with none out, second and third with one out. But in the Tigers' clubhouse celebration, Giebell hardly raised his voice.

"It's nothing to get excited about," he said. "I think I should've been on the club all season."

Out of the West Virginia panhandle, Giebell had signed with the Tigers in 1937 after impressing their scouts in a semipro tournament in Dayton, Ohio. When his minor league seasons ended, he had returned to Holliday Cove, West Virginia, and earned an accounting degree at Salem College while also working on his father's corn and wheat farm.

"I've got to get back there for the harvest," he said.

Floyd Giebell (top left) and Tiger Manager Del Baker celebrate on the shoulders of catcher Billy Sullivan, pitcher Johnny Gorsica, and first baseman Rudy York. *UPI Photo*

125

"When your dad hears what you did," one of the writers said, "I bet he'll pick up a plow and throw it into the next county."

"With one hand," Giebell said, laughing.

Baker, meanwhile, talked about how "even if I make one hundred bad guesses before I retire, they can't take this one away from me. I had a hunch the kid would deliver, but I never dreamed he would pitch such a perfect game." When his players read that in the papers the next day, they resented their manager taking credit for a pitching choice that many of them had voted on. But now they were still whooping it up when Walter O. Briggs, the Tiger owner, arrived in the clubhouse. Sitting in a wheelchair because of his crippled legs, he congratulated Baker and then found Giebell.

"You were great, youngster," Briggs said. "I predict you are going to have a great future with the Tigers."

The previous Tuesday, in their meeting to determine World Series shares, the Tigers had voted Giebell a flat $500, a thoughtful sum considering that at the time he had contributed only one victory after having been recalled from Buffalo two weeks earlier. After the pennant clincher, the players agreed to increase Giebell's share. But before they could, Briggs acted.

"I'm assuring that young man a full World Series share," the Tiger owner said. "The club will make up the difference."

When the Tigers lost the World Series to the Reds in seven games, the losing share amounted to $3,532. In addition to his $500 check from the commissioner's office, which disburses the Series shares, Floyd Giebell, who would never win another game in the big leagues, received a $3,032 check from the Tiger owner. As for the Indians, they defended their June mutiny.

"If we hadn't done it, we wouldn't have been in the race," Feller remembered. "It brought us closer together."

The day after the Indians were eliminated, Oscar Vitt confronted Alva Bradley about his future as the manager.

"To tell the truth, Oscar, I don't know," the Indian president said. "Nothing will be done until the board of directors meeting after I come back from vacation."

When the directors met, Oscar Vitt was fired. Roger Peckinpaugh was named to succeed him. The Crybabies won their argument, but they didn't win the pennant.

1941

Whitlow Wyatt. *AP/Wide World Photo*

NNING AFTER INNING, zero after zero, the Brooklyn Dodgers and the St. Louis Cardinals were creating a memorable game that would turn a memorable pennant race. Instead of heating up in late August or September, this 1941 struggle had been boiling since May, if not the start of the season. Now, on Saturday, September 13, in the finale of a three-game series at Sportsman's Park, their endless duel had developed into a scoreless duel between each team's best pitcher: Whitlow Wyatt vs. Mort Cooper.

In the sixth Cooper's three walks had loaded the bases, but as the Cardinals' husky righthander walked to the mound for the eighth inning he had a no-hitter. In his sweat-stained gray uniform, Wyatt, a thirty-three-year-old righthander resurrected from the minors three years earlier, had pitched out of two threats.

Now, in the top of the eighth, Fred (Dixie) Walker, the popular outfielder who was known in Brooklyn as "the People's Cherce," drilled a double into the right-centerfield gap, spoiling Cooper's no-hit bid and quieting a sellout crowd of 32,691. If the Cardinals won, the two teams would be tied for first place. But a Dodger victory would drop the Cardinals two games behind, with each team having fourteen games remaining.

With an 0–2 count on him, Billy Herman, the Dodger second baseman, stared beyond Cooper to where Walker, leading off second, was peering at catcher Gus Mancuso.

"When Mancuso flashed the sign for a curveball," Walker would say later, "I relayed it to Billy, but his eyes bugged out so far I was sure the Cards would switch."

They didn't. Cooper threw his curveball. "Some batters don't want to know what pitch is coming," Dodger catcher Mickey Owen remembered, "but Billy Herman would take signs off anybody." With his firm swing, Herman lined that curveball off the rightfield fence for another double as Walker scored. After all those zeros, the Dodgers finally had put a *1* on the scoreboard. It was Wyatt's game to win. With two out in the ninth, Enos Slaughter, the Cardinal outfielder who had missed five weeks recuperating from a broken collarbone, was announced as a pinch hitter. Leo Durocher, the Dodgers' fiery manager, hurried to the mound.

"This guy," Durocher told Wyatt, "can hurt you."

As if Wyatt wasn't aware of that. In the fifth he had pitched out of a tougher situation. Second and third, none out. He struck out Mancuso. He struck out Cooper.

"Their little third baseman, Jimmy Brown, was up next," Wyatt would remember years later. "I never let him hit my fastball. I threw him a slow curve and he bounced it to Camilli."

In the sixth, with the bases loaded and two out, Cardinal shortstop Marty Marion had slashed a sharp grounder over second base, but shortstop Pee Wee Reese snatched it and flipped to Herman for a force out. Now, with the lefthanded-swinging Slaughter representing the tying run with two out in the ninth, Wyatt didn't dare risk hanging a slow curve.

"Ball one," Wyatt recalled. "Strike one, called. Strike two, swing. Strike three, swing. I threw three fastballs right by him."

With their 1–0 classic, the Dodgers were two games up. As they boarded their sleeper train for Cincinnati, anti-Nazi and guerrilla gunfire in the Netherlands, Yugoslavia, Hungary, Rumania, and Norway reflected life there under Hitler's rule. When the Japanese bombed Pearl Harbor less than three months later, World War II would erupt. But for now, America was at peace. America had only a pennant race to worry about, a pennant race punctuated by Leo Durocher's continual confrontations with umpires, a pennant race that blessed Brooklyn with baseball credibility after more than two decades without a World Series.

In those radio days, if someone in a show's audience mentioned that he or she was from Brooklyn, everybody laughed. One reason was the baseball reputation of the Dodgers over the past decade: the Daffiness Boys, three base runners on third, fly balls bouncing off Floyd (Babe) Herman's shoulders, a bird fluttering from under manager Casey Stengel's cap as he tipped it, fans who lovingly described their team as "the Bums," if not "dem Bums."

All that changed in 1938 after Larry MacPhail took command as the Dodgers' general manager. He installed lights at Ebbets Field. He hired Walter (Red) Barber to broadcast Dodger games. He signed Babe Ruth as a first-base coach. Most important, he named Leo Durocher manager. Quite simply, MacPhail assembled a better team with better players. In trades he acquired first baseman Dolf Camilli, outfielder Joe Medwick, catcher Mickey Owen, righthanders Kirby Higbe and Curt Davis. He claimed Dixie Walker on waivers. He found Whitlow Wyatt in the minors. He purchased baby-faced shortstop Harold (Pee Wee) Reese from the Boston Red Sox farm team in Louisville. He promoted centerfielder Harold (Pete) Reiser, a pheenom who had been liberated by Commissioner Kenesaw Mountain Landis from the Cardinals' farm system. He let Leo Durocher swagger and squawk.

Even though the Dodgers now were a contender, they remained "the Bums" to their fans. But as the 1941 season began, neither Walker nor Herman, who produced those back-to-back doubles in Wyatt's 1–0 victory, were in the lineup.

On Opening Day, Walker was on the bench. MacPhail had ordered Durocher to use Paul Waner, once a legendary hitter with the Pittsburgh Pirates, in rightfield. When the manager complied, he received a telegram signed by five thousand Dodger fans threatening a boycott of Ebbets Field unless Walker, the People's Cherce, was reinstated. Waner solved the problem. Then nearly thirty-eight years old, he batted .171 with no extra base hits in eleven games. MacPhail sold Waner to the Boston Braves and Walker returned to rightfield.

For all his bluster, MacPhail knew that if the Dodgers were to dethrone the Cincinnati Reds and overtake the Cardinals, they needed a better second baseman than Pete Coscarart.

Billy Herman had been a fixture with the Cubs for more than a decade—a future Hall of Famer who had been on three pennant-winning teams. But in early May, at age thirty-one and struggling with a .194 average, he was available. When the Cubs arrived in New York to play the Giants at the Polo Grounds, MacPhail pounced on Cub general manager Jimmy Gallagher and manager Jimmy Wilson.

"I brought a bottle of Napoleon brandy to their room, but I fooled 'em," MacPhail once said. "I poured myself a lot of drinks, but most of 'em went down the bathroom drain."

Eventually they shook hands on the deal: Herman for infielder Johnny Hudson, outfielder Charlie Gilbert, and $65,000. Elsewhere in the Commodore, the Dodgers' new second baseman was sleeping when his phone rang around two o'clock in the morning.

"I heard MacPhail say, 'I just bought the pennant,'" Herman recalled. "He told me to get dressed and come down to Jimmy Gallagher's room for a drink."

Herman remembers shaking hands with MacPhail, staying a few

minutes without having a drink, then returning to his room and going back to sleep. After a late breakfast, he took the subway to the Prospect Park station in Brooklyn, a short walk from Ebbets Field.

"I went to the Dodger clubhouse," he said, "put on a Dodger uniform, went four for four, and the Dodgers won."

As the Cardinals arrived in Ebbets Field the next day for a two-game series, the Dodgers trailed by one-half game. Their duel had begun. When the Dodgers took both games, they led by one and one-half games although the Cardinals still were in first place by percentage points. About three weeks later, when Wyatt outpitched Mort Cooper, 6–0, on home runs by Reiser and Camilli on June 3 in the finale of a three-game series at Ebbets Field, they were tied for first place.

"Mort Cooper was a rounder, you wouldn't call him an angel," shortstop Marty Marion would say years later. "He could throw hard. His forkball made him a great pitcher."

The next season Mort Cooper would be voted the National League's most valuable player for his 22–7 record and 1.78 earned run average. He would win twenty-one games in 1943 and twenty-two in 1944 despite an ailing arm that had him chewing aspirin on the mound. His brother Walker usually caught him, as he had since they were growing up as sons of a rural mail carrier in Atherton, Missouri, not far from Kansas City.

"Mort was bigger than most of the kids around; he could throw the ball harder," his younger brother once said. "The other kids used to hurt their hands catching him. Nobody wanted to. So my father made me catch him and it's been that way ever since."

Walker Cooper, known as "Muley" because of his square jaw, was the strong, silent type who liked to play tricks on his teammates. "When you weren't looking," Marion recalled, "he'd give you a hot foot." But in the evening after a road game during those years before most weekday games were played at night, the brothers were seldom seen together.

"One didn't want the other one," Marion would remember with a smile, "to know what he was doing."

But to baseball's most famous brother battery, blood was thicker than beanballs. Mort never hesitated to throw a knockdown pitch because Walker once assured him, "If a hitter tries to go after you, don't worry. I'll grab him before he gets to you." Beanballs were a way of life in those years. Pete Reiser was beaned twice that season, by Ike Pearson of the Philadelphia Phillies at Ebbets Field only five days after the opener and by Paul Erickson of the Chicago Cubs at Wrigley Field in August. Commissioner Kenesaw Mountain Landis, whose office was in Chicago, visited Reiser in the hospital and asked, "Do you think Erickson threw at you intentionally?"

"No, sir," Reiser said.

"You didn't hear anybody yell 'Stick it in his ear'?"

"Yes, sir."

"Then why don't you think he threw at you intentionally?"

"Because he doesn't have that kind of control. I lost the ball in the shirts in centerfield."

"Then you won't accuse Erickson of throwing at you."

"No, sir."

Reiser knew that Dodger pitchers, with or without Durocher's orders, also threw at hitters. Wyatt especially. To the twenty-two-year-old Reiser, the thirty-three-year-old Wyatt was an idol because the Georgia farmer had been "nice" to him as a rookie. But how had Wyatt been nice?

"He said 'Hello' to me," Reiser said.

Dolf Camilli also had been nice to him. As the Dodger captain he discouraged the older players from hazing their two youngest players, Reiser and Reese.

"Leave those kids alone," Camilli said. "They're going to help us win the pennant."

Camilli's teammates listened. At five-ten and 180 pounds, he wasn't that big, but this ex-boxer was physically powerful. At thirty-four, he was having his best season. He would hit thirty-four homers and drive in 120 runs as the National League's most valuable player and its smoothest first baseman.

Pistol Pete Reiser would win the batting title with .343 while Wyatt and Kirby Higbe each would lead the league with 22 games.

"Whitlow was usually in a one-run game," Camilli remembered. "He was an even better pitcher than his record because it seemed like he was always matched against the other team's ace: Mort Cooper, Carl Hubbell, Paul Derringer. Whitlow really earned his wins, but Higbe always seemed to have eight or ten runs. At the Polo Grounds early that season, Higbe came up to me in the dugout and said, 'Hit me a home run.' I'll be damned if I didn't hit a home run. After that, you know how ballplayers are superstitious, Higbe would always ask me to hit a home run for him. Two-thirds of the time it seemed like I did. I was proud of that. Sometimes they don't fall for you."

At the All-Star break, the Dodgers had jumped into a three-game lead, then increased it to four as the Cardinals arrived in Brooklyn for a two-game series against Wyatt and Higbe. But the Cardinals won both. By the end of July, the Cardinals had a two-game lead in a pennant race that was as hot as the wool uniforms of that era.

"When you came into the dugout," Cardinal centerfielder Terry Moore once said, "your shoes would squish from the sweat. Squish, squish, squish."

None of the trains or hotels were air-conditioned in those years, although the Netherlands Plaza in Cincinnati had an air-conditioned lobby.

"To stay cool in the room at night," Moore once said, "we'd order up a lot of ice, throw it in the bathtub, take our bedsheets and throw them in the tub, wring them out, throw them on the bed and lie there until they'd get hot again. Then throw them in the tub again."

Over five weeks in August and early September, the lead changed hands eight times and the two teams were never more than two games apart even though the Cardinals were riddled by injuries.

In addition to Slaughter's fractured collarbone, Mort Cooper needed bone chip surgery on his pitching elbow. His brother Walker had a broken shoulder. Moore was dizzy from a beaning. First baseman Johnny Mize had a broken finger, third baseman Jimmy Brown a broken hand, second baseman Frank Crespi a dislocated finger. Lefthander Max Lanier had an inflamed tendon on his pitching elbow, lefthander Clyde Shoun a jammed ankle.

"If we'd been healthy," Slaughter has said, "the Dodgers never would have won that year."

Maybe not, but the Dodgers weren't waiting for the Cardinals to lose. In the opener of a doubleheader with the Braves on Labor Day, Camilli hit his twenty-ninth homer off Tom Earley over the rightfield screen into Bedford Avenue to tie the score in the eighth inning, a double with two out in the tenth to keep the Dodgers alive, and a single with two out in the fifteenth to win the game, 6–5. No telling how many votes he earned that day for the Most Valuable Player award.

By the following Monday, the Dodgers were three games ahead as their train rumbled out of Grand Central Station for their final road trip, a seventeen-day journey to six cities: Chicago, St. Louis, Cincinnati, Pittsburgh, Philadelphia, and Boston.

When the Dodgers lost a Wednesday doubleheader to the Cubs while the Cardinals were sweeping a doubleheader with the Phillies, their lead suddenly shrank to one game. But as they arrived at Union Station in St. Louis late that evening, the Dodger players seemed more interested in the fact Durocher's Doberman pinscher, a present for his wife Grace, could walk on his hind legs and answer to "Butch." Durocher got off the train leading the Doberman, but soon he was talking about the Cardinal series.

"Fitzsimmons goes in the opener," he said. "It takes a breaking ball to stop the Cardinals and his knuckleball is the ideal delivery."

Two weeks earlier forty-year-old Fred Fitzsimmons had stomped around the mound at Ebbets Field after two errors by Pee Wee Reese in a 3–2 loss to the Cardinals for a split of their four-game series.

"Fred could be nasty, he was from the old school," Reese recalled. "I once told him, 'Nice pitching' and he said, 'I know it.' "

"They called him Fat Freddie," remembered Mickey Owen, "but there wasn't an ounce of fat on him. He just had a thick body."

Against the Cardinals in the Thursday opener, Fat Freddie not only stomped around the mound, he snarled at them and threw at them.

"He didn't like Johnny Mize, who earlier that season I think it was, hit a low line drive back at him," Owen said. "Freddie couldn't get his glove over in time, so he just stuck out his bare hand and deflected the ball to Pee Wee who threw Mize out. It hurts my hand now to even think about it, but Freddie never let on. He just stomped around the mound like he always did. He was an extreme competitor. He always bore down."

When the Cardinals staked lefthander Ernie White to a 2–0 lead, Fitzsimmons bore down even harder. So did Camilli, whose three-run homer put the Dodgers ahead, 4–2; then Walker's two-run single in the eleventh produced a 6–4 victory. Hot-water packs couldn't even straighten Fitzsimmons's aging arm.

But that game had been interrupted several times. Durocher, Cardinal manager Billy Southworth, and several players, notably Fitzsimmons, had argued with the umpires, especially when Durocher thought White balked in the eighth with Reiser on third. The squabbles had begun before the game when Durocher refused to pose with Southworth for photographers. Durocher pretended he was superstitious. Southworth, once a testy outfielder with the Pirates, Giants, and Cardinals, understood.

"I'm out to beat him and he's out to beat me," the Cardinal manager said. "So why pose in front of the public smiling and shaking hands when we don't feel that way at all?"

When the managers' bitterness overflowed into continual wrangling with the umpires, it annoyed Ford Frick, the National League president, who viewed the opener from the press box. Before Friday's game, Frick ordered Durocher and Southworth to meet with him and his four umpires: umpire-in-chief Bill Klem, Al Barlick, Lee Ballanfant and Ralph (Babe) Pinelli.

"This is not an argument," Frick said to the two managers. "We are telling you that we are going to run the ballgame. We are going to treat you as though you were eighth-place teams and if a man's actions call for his dismissal from the game, he will be dismissed. If it hurts either team, that's just too bad."

The managers and players were quiet as Howard Pollet, the Cardinals' stylish lefthander up from Houston of the Texas League, and lefthander Max Lanier combined to outpitch Curt Davis, 4–3.

"Wyatt pitches tomorrow," Durocher barked, "and aside from that I have nothing to say. We put men on third base twice with Medwick up and if he couldn't score them, what could we do?"

As the Cardinal leftfielder in the 1934 World Series, Joe Medwick slid hard into Tiger third baseman Marv Owen, provoking a torrent of trash from Detroit fans that resulted in Commissioner Landis removing Medwick from the seventh game. Known as "Ducky Wucky" because of his waddling walk, Medwick won the triple crown in 1937, leading the NL with a .374 average, thirty-one homers, and 154 runs batted in. Soon after being traded to the Dodgers early in the 1940 season, he was beaned by Cardinal righthander Bob Bowman at Ebbets Field. Seeing his new leftfielder unconscious, Durocher grappled with police to get at Bowman while the umpires held off several of Medwick's new teammates. When the twenty-nine-year-old Bowman, escorted by two detectives, later departed through the Dodger dugout, MacPhail swung at him from a box seat, knocking Bowman's cap off.

"Bowman," charged MacPhail, "had an argument this morning in the Commodore Hotel with Durocher and Medwick; he even threatened Medwick."

That allegation was never confirmed. Even though Medwick returned in 1941 to hit .318 with eighteen homers and eighty-eight runs batted in, he never approached his best seasons. And after Medwick had stranded those two runners at third base in Friday's game, Durocher benched him for Saturday's finale against Mort Cooper and inserted Jimmy Wasdell, a lefthanded batter.

"But the big news is, Dixie Walker's leading off," Durocher said. "When you get a hunch, you've got to go with it."

The hunch worked. In breaking up Mort Cooper's no-hitter, those eighth-inning doubles by Walker and Herman supported Wyatt's three-hitter for the memorable 1–0 triumph that opened a two-game lead.

"Leo had courage," Owen recalled. "For quick decisions, for instincts and intuition, Leo was always right."

"Leo was a good manager, fiery, and he kept the players that way," Camilli remembered. "Nobody ever dozed off."

Sunday the Cardinals moved to within one and one-half games, sweeping a doubleheader from the Giants as Lon Warneke outpitched Carl Hubbell, 1–0, and Howard Krist won in 10 innings, 6–5. That day the Cardinals announced that three farmhands were to report immediately: from New Orleans of the Southern Association righthander Johnny Beazley, from Rochester of the International League third baseman George (Whitey) Kurowski, and a twenty-year-old outfielder whose career would inspire a bigger-than-life bronze statue outside Busch Memorial Stadium a quarter of a century later, Stanley Frank Musial.

In Cincinnati that Sunday about five hundred of Reese's friends from Louisville, Kentucky, arrived by train, "The Pee Wee Reese Special." He responded with three hits in a 7–5 victory, prompting MacPhail to announce that World Series ticket applications would be accepted for the three games at Ebbets Field: $20.05 for a box seat strip, $16.75 for a reserved seat strip.

But the Dodgers' relationship with the umpires was deteriorating. Sunday evening in the lobby of the Netherlands Plaza hotel, Dixie Walker and third-base coach Charlie Dressen got into a noisy argument with Jocko Conlan. The next afternoon at Crosley Field, before stepping into the batter's box as the leadoff hitter against Red ace Paul Derringer, Walker resumed the argument, this time with plate umpire Larry Goetz. When the Dodger outfielder persisted, Goetz bristled.

"Get in there and hit," he ordered.

Walker kept yapping. Goetz signaled for Derringer to pitch. When the ball thudded into catcher Ernie Lombardi's mitt, Goetz yelled, "Strike." Walker and Durocher, who bolted out of the dugout, now had a new reason to argue. In their debate, Durocher stood on the plate, thereby preventing Derringer from throwing another pitch.

But the Dodgers, the Reds, and the umpires would remember this game for other reasons, beginning with Johnny Allen, the Dodgers' surprise starter. As a lean, mean righthander suspected of throwing the illegal spitball, Allen had a 20–10 record for the Cleveland Indians in 1936 and a dazzling 15–1 record the next year. Then he skidded. Sold to the St. Louis Browns for $20,000 before the 1941 season, he was 2–5 with a 6.58 earned run average when the Dodgers acquired him on waivers. Now, his pitching staff worn and weary, Durocher was desperate. In Allen's ten previous Dodger appearances, including three starts, he had a shaky 2–0 record.

Against Derringer, the Reds' ace, Durocher was hoping for Allen to provide maybe five good innings. But another memorable 0–0 game evolved. Allen, who nearly threw a punch at Red manager Bill McKechnie in the fourth for complaining that he was throwing a spit-ball, kept mowing the Reds down. Through nine innings, he allowed only second baseman Benny Zientara's scratch single. Through fifteen scoreless innings in his duel with Derringer, he allowed only six hits.

"Johnny changed his shirt three times," Owen remembered. "After the third inning, Durocher told him, 'I'll get you a dry shirt, just go another inning.' After a few more innings, Durocher told him, 'You're going good. How about you keep going? Get him another dry shirt.' Then around the twelfth, Durocher said, 'You think you can go one more?' Johnny looked up from where he was sitting and said, 'I can't even get off my ass.' But he kept pitching. Durocher always got the last ounce of sweat."

In the sixteenth, Durocher let Allen bat. When the thirty-five-year-old pitcher was safe on shortstop Eddie Joost's throwing error, Durocher inserted a pinch runner, Pete Coscarart, but the Dodgers couldn't score. In the Crosley Field twilight, Hugh Casey retired the Reds in the bottom of the sixteenth. When the umpires gathered to decide if the game should continue, crew chief John (Beans) Reardon ruled, "The way the pitchers are going, I think we can get in another inning." But after Pete Reiser's leadoff homer in the seventeenth, the Reds, apparently on orders from McKechnie, decided to let the Dodgers keep hitting, hoping that the umpires would be forced to call the game because of darkness. The final score then would revert to 0–0 through sixteen innings.

With Derringer appearing to throw softer pitches, Dolf Camilli singled and third baseman Lew Riggs singled. McKechnie took his time calling to the bullpen for Joe Beggs, who took his time walking in.

In the Dodger dugout, Durocher told his players, "Swing at every pitch, but don't try to get a hit." Medwick bounced a grounder to Beggs, who threw to second, but shortstop Eddie Joost fumbled the ball. Reese bunted, but catcher Dick West fumbled the ball, finally grabbed it, but didn't throw to first. On a weak swing, Owen singled.

"I was trying," he said later, "to strike out."

"Try to strike out more often," a teammate said.

With Casey the next batter, McKechnie took his time calling for another pitcher, Jim (Milkman) Turner. Casey bounced back to

Turner, who threw to third baseman Billy Werber for a force-out, but Werber didn't even try to complete a double play. Walker popped to Werber, but when Jocko Conlan invoked the infield fly rule, McKechnie beefed.

"Get back to the dugout," Larry Goetz told the Red manager, "or I'll forfeit this game."

Finally, with a feeble swing, Herman struck out, but the Reds had fallen behind, 5–0. In the stands some fans burned rolled-up newspapers and waved their impromptu torches. But the umpires were determined to complete the inning. Just as the Reds had delayed, now the Dodgers were hurrying. Pinch hitter Jimmy Gleeson popped up. But then Casey, peering at the plate in the darkness while trying to hurry, walked two batters before Ernie Koy and Joost grounded out.

In the confusion, the Dodgers had a two-game lead. But in the National League office Tuesday morning, Ford Frick labeled the seventeenth inning a "farce" and warned that any repetition would result in a forfeit along with a $1,000 fine for the club and a $100 fine for the manager.

That afternoon the Dodgers lost to the Reds, 4–3, in eleven innings. When darkness called the Cardinals' 1–1 tie with the Giants, the difference was now one and one-half games. Wednesday the Dodgers won in Pittsburgh, 6–4, behind Curt Davis while the Cardinals were playing a doubleheader with the Braves. Pollet won the opener, 6–1. Before the second game Southworth approached young Stan Musial.

"You're in the lineup," the manager said.

The raw rookie with a corkscrew batting stance had opened the season for a salary of $150 a month at Springfield, Illinois, of the Western Association, a class C minor league. When he was hitting .379 with 26 homers and 94 runs batted in after only 87 games, he was promoted to Rochester, New York, of the International League, where he hit .326 in 54 games for $450 a month. When the Red Wings were eliminated from the playoffs by the Newark Bears, he returned to his Donora, Pennsylvania, hometown. But a Western Union messenger soon handed him a telegram.

"Report to Cardinals in St. Louis immediately," it read. "Branch Rickey."

Originally signed as a lefthanded pitcher, Musial had injured his arm the previous season making a shoestring catch as an occasional outfielder for Daytona Beach of the Florida State League, where he had a 15–5 record. Now he took a late train out of Pittsburgh for St. Louis,

Stan Musial in his Rochester Red Wings uniform. *National Baseball Library and Archive, Cooperstown, N.Y.*

where his outfielder's salary would be prorated at $750 a month. He assumed he would mostly be sitting in the Cardinals' dugout during the final two weeks of this pennant race. He had batted only .238 for Rochester in the playoffs, and the Cardinals also had recalled Walter Sessi, another young lefthanded-swinging outfielder. Sessi had led the Texas League in total bases while hitting .301 with fourteen homers and ninety-eight runs batted in for the Houston Buffaloes. But now, to his surprise, Musial was in the lineup for the second game against the Braves, playing rightfield and batting third; at Rochester he had batted second. But to his consternation, Jim Tobin's knuckleball was fluttering. Musial had never faced a knuckleball pitcher before. His first at-bat, he popped up. But his second time up, Musial lashed a two-run double against the rightfield fence. He later added a single. The Cardinals won, 3–2, on Estel Crabtree's homer. The next day Musial, batting cleanup, singled off Manny Salvo, but the Cardinals lost, 4–1.

"If the Cardinals had brought me up earlier," Musial told Pee Wee Reese years later, "we'd have won the pennant."

Maybe yes, maybe no. In his twelve games, Musial would bat .426, with four doubles and a homer while driving in seven runs. Over the next two decades, he would put together a .331 career average with 3,630 hits, including 475 homers. The voice of an unknown Ebbets Field fan would nickname him. "Uh-oh," a fan was heard to say there, "here's that Man again." From then on he was "Stan the Man." But on their stormy road trip that would decide this pennant race, the Dodgers weren't about to fold. Even when it appeared they might on September 18 at Forbes Field, when Hugh Casey was trying to protect a 5–4 lead in the eighth.

Vince DiMaggio, Joe's older brother and the Pirate centerfielder, was on third with two out. With catcher Al Lopez at bat, DiMaggio suddenly feinted breaking for the plate as if he were about to steal home.

"Casey had a way of winding up and going way down," Lopez recalled. "When Casey saw DiMaggio break, I thought Casey stopped. I thought he hesitated. I jumped out of the batter's box and yelled, 'Balk.'"

Plate umpire George Magerkurth agreed. DiMaggio trotted across with the tying run. Casey, hurrying down from the mound, and Durocher, rushing out of the dugout, confronted the big beefy umpire who hated his "Meathead" nickname. When the argument ended, Casey returned to the mound and fired three high fastballs that narrowly missed Lopez and that Owen had to stretch to catch.

"Is he throwing at you or at me?" Magerkurth asked.

"I don't know," Lopez said, "but I'm ready for him."

Taking off his mask, Magerkurth warned Casey that another high inside pitch would result in his ejection. Durocher objected and was ejected. On the next pitch, Lopez walked. Alf Anderson, a twenty-seven-year-old rookie shortstop who batted .215 that season with only ten runs batted in, sliced a liner down the rightfield line for a triple as Lopez scored the winning run.

Under the Forbes Field grandstand, Durocher muttered, "Who the hell is Alf Anderson?," threw a chair through the window of the umpires' room, and broke every lightbulb within reach. On the way to their clubhouse, several Dodgers berated Magerkurth before he disappeared into the umpires' room.

Manager Leo Durocher (center) and catcher Mickey Owen argue umpire George
Magerkurth's balk call in Pittsburgh. *AP/Wide World Photo*

In the Pirates' clubhouse, Vince DiMaggio told the writers that his
break for home while Lopez was stepping out of the batter's box was a
prearranged play to create a balk. Lopez denied that, saying, "No, no,
no." But when Durocher was informed of DiMaggio's revelation, he
blew another fuse.

"How in the hell can a pitcher make a balk when the batter is out of
the batter's box?" Durocher asked. "Lopez pulled a job on us and
nobody but a chowderhead umpire would've fallen for it. I called him
everything I could think of, but my vocabulary isn't large enough to

express what I think of his incompetence. Every time we've seen him in a series this year we've had trouble. I never want to see him again."

Durocher remembered his dispute with umpire Al Barlick when the Dodgers thought Ernie White of the Cardinals had balked in St. Louis.

"We argued about that," Durocher said, "but finally young Barlick said, 'Well, maybe he did balk, but this is too important a game to lose on a technicality.' How do you like that? Now we lose one because Magerkurth was stampeded into calling a balk that didn't happen."

At the time, the Dodgers feared that Magerkurth's balk call had dropped them into a tie for first place. But the Cardinals lost to the Braves, 4–1, while also losing Johnny Mize again with a wrenched shoulder.

Still steaming, the Dodgers took a train that Thursday night to Philadelphia for a five-game series: doubleheaders Saturday and Sunday, a single game Monday afternoon. The following weekend the Dodgers would finish the season with two games against the Phillies at Ebbets Field, a rare stretch of seven games in nine days against the same team. During Friday's open date, umpire-in-chief Bill Klem arrived from New York to interrogate Durocher and several players about the Magerkurth incident. Durocher was fined $150. Camilli, Medwick, Wyatt, infielder Pete Coscarart, and catcher Herman Franks each were fined $25 for the postgame scene. MacPhail also had taken the train down from New York to comfort his team.

"You were lucky," Durocher told him. "You didn't have to watch what happened yesterday."

"What makes you think I was lucky?" MacPhail said. "Did you ever kick a $150 radio apart?"

Durocher had not yet begun to fight. In his Warwick Hotel suite, he twice brushed off telephone requests for an interview from Ted Meier, a Philadelphia-based Associated Press sportswriter. Meier waited for Durocher to come down to the lobby. That evening he saw Durocher get off an elevator and enter the cocktail lounge. He followed. After a while Meier asked, "Do you think the Dodgers will win seven straight from the Phillies?" Durocher barked an obscenity.

"Who," snapped Meier, "do you think you're talking to? Magerkurth?"

Soon the lounge was "thick with language," as Tommy Holmes of the *Brooklyn Eagle* would write. Durocher suggested, "Let's go outside and settle this." Meier, a burly 230 pounds, had played football at the University of Pittsburgh. Durocher was a willowy 173, if that.

They walked to a nearby alley, where their argument got louder. With three quick right hands, Durocher dropped Meier to his knees before John McDonald, the Dodgers' traveling secretary, and a few others broke up the brawl.

"He's fast," Meier said later. "I swung back, but the others stopped us."

Durocher returned to the hotel and went up to his suite to change his clothes. Dapper as ever, he returned to the lobby, where Meier was waiting. They shook hands.

"There was nothing to it," Durocher said. "Everything is fine now."

"Everything's O.K. now," Meier said. "I guess Leo was just on edge."

The edge was that the Cardinals were now only one-half game behind after a 3–1 win over the Cubs on Harry Gumbert's eleventh victory, his fifth in a row. Musial went three for three with a double and two singles. Terry Moore, shaking an oh-for-thirteen slump on returning from his August 21 beaning by Brave rookie lefthander Art Johnson, had two doubles. Moore's presence had the Cardinals wondering: What if he had been in centerfield instead of Johnny Hopp the day of the 1–0 loss to the Dodgers on the consecutive doubles by Walker and Herman to right center?

"I might've caught those balls," Moore said, "but Hopp made a catch in that game that I might not have made."

Musial, despite six hits in his first eleven at-bats, had not yet been fully accepted by the older Cardinal players. In the tradition of the time, a rookie had no rights in the batting cage. After one or two swings, Musial heard Walker Cooper growl, "Get your ass out of there." When the Cubs started lefthander Johnny Schmitz in Saturday's game, Southworth benched the lefthanded-hitting rookie and inserted Erv Dusak, another rookie outfielder. Dusak went hitless and the Cardinals lost, 7–3, on Bob Scheffing's pinch-hit grand slam homer in a six-run ninth-inning rally that marred righthander Howard Krist's 10–0 record. After growing up not far from St. Louis, Scheffing had been a Cardinal farmhand catcher and a minor league manager at age twenty-three before joining the Cubs that season at twenty-eight. He would hit only twenty homers in his career.

Scheffing's grand slam enabled the Dodgers to create some breathing room in their Saturday doubleheader. Casey saved the opener, 3–1, for Wyatt, who wondered, "Are we ever going to have an easy game?" Hearing that, Jimmy Wasdell said, "First easy game we have will be the World Series against the Yankees."

But the second game was relatively easy, 6–1, for Higbe, who once said, "I'm as strong as a bull and twice as smart." Now the Dodgers were two games up, but Southworth had learned his lesson: keep Musial in the lineup, no matter who's pitching. Sunday the Cardinals swept the Cubs, 6–5 and 7–0, as the rookie his teammates called "Musical" had six hits. Batting cleanup against Claude Passeau in the opener, he had two doubles, two singles, and scored the winning run in the ninth by streaking home from second, when Cub catcher Clyde McCullough forgot to cover the plate after he had fielded Coaker Triplett's topped grounder and thrown to first base. Musial's dash was typical of how the Cardinals just kept running.

"Any time you made one of those Cardinals slide," said Casey Stengel, the manager of the seventh-place Braves that season, "it was a moral victory."

When the Cubs started lefthander Vern Olsen in the second game, Musial stayed in the lineup. With two singles, he lifted his average to a dazzling .588.

"The Cardinals," wrote W. J. McGoogan in the *St. Louis Post-Dispatch*, "displayed a young outfielder who gives all indications of being a real star."

By now the older Cardinals had begun to accept the slender rookie with the boyish smile. During their train ride to Pittsburgh that night he was sitting in the club car with Moore and Mize when he asked if they remembered a game against some Cardinal farmhands the previous spring at the club's minor league camp in Columbus, Georgia.

"I hit a home run," Moore recalled.

"I was the pitcher," Musial said.

"You were the pitcher?" Moore said.

"I didn't want to pitch," Musial said. "Mr. Rickey had sent me there as an outfielder, but I was a pitcher before I hurt my arm. One of the minor league managers, Clay Hopper, asked me to pitch because I had more experience than any of the kid pitchers there."

"I hit a home run that day too," Mize said.

"I know," Musial said. "I was the pitcher."

By now Mize and many of the other older Cardinals were wondering why Musial hadn't been brought up from Rochester in August when Slaughter and Moore were out of the lineup with injuries.

"Rickey said we didn't have anybody to help us," Mize once said. "Then in September he brings up Musial. Why didn't he bring Musial up earlier? It might've won the pennant for us."

That same Sunday, in a doubleheader at Shibe Park, the Dodgers had attracted a sellout 35,909, including several thousand who had traveled from Brooklyn by car, train, and chartered buses.

"Brooklyn is here," one voice roared.

During batting practice, another loud Brooklyn voice was heard ordering the Phillies to "Git off the field. We want our Bums to git some practice." Behind the Dodgers' dugout sat one of Durocher's pals, actor George Raft, accompanied by actress Betty Grable. Not far away was Durocher's loudest loyalist, Eddie Battan, whistling between his teeth, two horseshoes hanging from his belt, and wearing a pith helmet autographed by all the Dodger players. Nearby another fan, Bill Fleischer, was yelling through a coxswain's megaphone strapped to his mouth. Between innings, and sometimes during, Shorty Laurice conducted the discord of the Dodgers Sym-Phony, often off key but never off stride.

Despite this support, the Dodgers split. Johnny Allen pitched the 8–3 opener, but the Phillies took the second game, 6–3, on outfielder Danny Litwhiler's first-inning grand slam homer off righthander Luke (Hot Potato) Hamlin.

Ted McGrew, the Dodgers' chief scout, had told Durocher that MacPhail had a hunch on Hamlin, a twenty-game winner in 1939 who now was struggling with an 8–7 record and the bad habit of allowing home runs. Perhaps afraid of being second-guessed by MacPhail if a different starter failed, Durocher agreed to use Hamlin. That night at Bookbinder's restaurant the Dodger manager was seated under an old photograph of President Abraham Lincoln and his vice president Hannibal Hamlin.

"Take me to another table," Durocher bellowed. "I cannot eat looking at that name."

Going into the season's final week, the Dodgers still had a one-game lead. With the Cardinals idle Monday, Curt Davis blanked the Phillies, 5–0, increasing the lead to one and one-half games. With the Dodgers idle Tuesday, the Cardinals lost the opener of a doubleheader in Pittsburgh, 4–0, on lefthander Ken Heintzelman's six-hitter. In the second game, Musial hit his first major league homer off Rip Sewell and added two singles in a 9–0 rout. Still a one-and-one-half-game difference.

By now the Dodgers were in Boston, where several hundred Brooklyn fans had joined them. American Airlines had added two noontime flights from La Guardia Airport.

Wednesday the Dodgers won, 4–2, for Higbe's twenty-second victory. Jim Tobin of the Braves had a 2–0 lead until the seventh when Dixie Walker lofted a three-run triple over the head of leftfielder Max

West, prompting other Dodgers to wonder why West had been playing him so shallow.

"Guess they didn't know your strength?" one teased.

"I didn't know I had any left," Walker said, smiling.

Harry Gumbert's six-hitter kept the Cardinals alive, 4–0, in Pittsburgh as Musial drove in the first run with a single off Johnny Lanning. But time was running out. Each team had only three games remaining. Thursday the Dodgers were leading, 6–0, when Whitlow Wyatt strode to the mound for the ninth inning just as the Cardinals' 3–1 loss in Pittsburgh to righthander Max Butcher was posted on the Braves scoreboard. Before the game Musial had received a traveling bag from his Donora neighbors and he had responded with two singles, but Pirates rookie shortstop Billy Cox tripled off Ernie White and scored on Arky Vaughan's sacrifice fly. First baseman Elbie Fletcher hit a two-run inside-the-park homer.

Three more outs and the Dodgers would be two and one-half games up with only two to play. Wyatt needed only nine pitches. Ground out. Fly out. Paul Waner's two-out single. Ground out.

Of all the Dodger players, Wyatt seemed to be the happiest. "After all the things that have happened to me," he said at his locker, "after being on the verge of quitting the game, I just can't believe what's happened. I bounced all over the major and minor league map for years and years and suddenly find myself pitching the game that clinches the pennant."

For all the cheers in the clubhouse, the celebration had only begun. On the train to New York, the players gulped champagne and sprayed each other with it. They cut each other's ties with scissors. They tossed mashed potatoes into the face of one of Durocher's pals, Tony Martin, the actor and singer who superstitiously had been wearing a tan gabardine suit for a week.

"Some of us got so messy," Reese recalled, "we had to change clothes before we got to Grand Central."

Trains from Boston always stopped at the 125th Street station in upper Manhattan, but Durocher requested that this train go through to Grand Central Station on 42nd Street.

"I don't want anybody getting on at 125th," he said. "There'll be enough people at Grand Central."

By eleven o'clock that evening some ten thousand fans had assembled at Grand Central, many with homemade signs such as "The Bums Done It" and "Moider Duh Yanks." One by one, Durocher and his Dodgers basked in their welcome. But the manager didn't realize that

Larry MacPhail had been waiting on the 125th Street platform to join the celebration. When MacPhail finally found Durocher that night, he asked whose idea it was not to stop at 125th Street.

"It was my idea," Durocher said.

"You're fired," MacPhail fumed.

In the sobriety of the next morning, Durocher was still the manager. After all, the World Series was yet to be played, with the Dodgers losing in five after Hugh Casey's third strike on Tommy Henrich got away from Mickey Owen for what would have been the final out of the fourth game. But on the Monday after the season ended, with half a dozen marching bands tootling and thumping, with Durocher and MacPhail sitting together, the Dodgers had waved from open cars to an estimated one million people in Brooklyn from Grand Army Plaza to Borough Hall, where thousands cheered the introductions and speeches. When it was over, Meyer Berger of *The New York Times* talked to one of the street cleaners.

"It's late and I'll miss my supper," the sanitation worker said. "But for the Bums, it's an honor. I'll tell my kids I swept up for the Bums."

The Dodgers' pennant parade winds through downtown Brooklyn. *UPI Photo*

The Browns' Only Pennant

The 1944 St. Louis Browns. (front row) Batting practice pitcher Orville Paul, Sam Zoldak, Ellis Clary, coach Fred Hofmann, manager Luke Sewell, coach Zack Taylor, Mike Chartak, Frank Mancuso, Gene Moore, Don Gutteridge, batboy Bob Scanlon (center) (middle row) Traveling secretary Charles DeWitt, George Caster, Floyd Baker, Nelson Potter, Al Zarilla, Chet Laabs, George McQuinn, Mark Christman, Milt Byrnes, Vern Stephens, trainer Bob Bauman, equipment manager Red Hanley (top row) Lefty West, Tex Shirley, Bob Muncrief, Tom Hafey, Red Hayworth, Jack Kramer, Al Hollingsworth, Denny Galehouse, Mike Kreevich, Sig Jakucki. *Allied Photocolor*

IG JAKUCKI HAD been around. Mostly around semipro baseball and bars, in the Army and elsewhere.

"He was an alcoholic," one of his St. Louis Brown teammates remembered, "but he could pitch."

On the final day of the 1944 season the Browns needed someone who could pitch. Tied for first place with the Tigers, who would be playing the Washington Senators in Detroit, the Browns were depending on Jakucki to complete a sweep of a four-game series with the Yankees at Sportsman's Park. But about eleven o'clock the night before, in the lobby of the Melbourne Hotel in St. Louis, coach Zack Taylor had spotted the thirty-five-year-old righthander carrying a brown bag. Taylor knew what was inside the bag.

"You're not taking that bottle to your room," Taylor said.

"You're not going to take it away from me," Jakucki said.

"You're not going to drink tonight," Taylor said. "Not when you're pitching for the pennant tomorrow."

"I won't drink tonight," Jakucki said.

"I don't believe you," the coach replied.

"I promise you I won't take a drink tonight, but don't try to take this bottle away or there'll be trouble."

"You promise?"

"I promise."

About an hour before the game the next day, Jakucki sat on the trainer's table in the Browns' clubhouse. While massaging Jakucki's right arm, trainer Bob Bauman couldn't help but smell the whiskey on the pitcher's breath.

"I thought you promised not to drink last night," Bauman said.

"I kept my promise. I promised Zack Taylor I wouldn't take a drink last night, but I didn't promise I wouldn't take one this morning."

Just one. Or two. Or three.

Big and blond, Sigmund (Jack) Jakucki had grown up in Camden, New Jersey, across the Delaware River from Philadelphia, joined the Army in 1927 at age eighteen, made a name for himself in Hawaii as the best pitcher and best hitter on the Schofield Army Barracks team, and stayed there to play semipro ball after his discharge. His drinking buddies passed the hat to pay his passage to the mainland in 1934 for a tryout with the San Francisco Seals of the Pacific Coast League, who sent him to Galveston of the Texas League. Two years later he joined the Browns in September.

"He'd lost nineteen games for Galveston," Bill DeWitt, then the Browns' general manager, once said, "but he had a good arm."

Not good enough to prevent an 0–3 record. Not good enough to allow manager Rogers Hornsby to ignore his drinking. The next year he was back in the minors, then he drifted to the Texas semipro circuit. In the 1940 National Semi-Pro Tournament in Wichita, Kansas, he pitched Houston Grand Prize Beer to third place. After a few drinks later that day, he dangled an umpire by the heels from an Arkansas River bridge. That enhanced his legend, but not his career.

"We'd forgotten all about him," DeWitt once said, "but when we were short on pitching in forty-four, somebody in Texas told us, 'You better sign him before another team does.' "

At that stage of World War II, with American soldiers preparing for the D Day invasion of Normandy, every major league team was short on pitching. As the 1944 season approached, the Browns led the American League in 4-F players, those deferred for military service. With the travel restrictions of the war years, major league teams weren't allowed to go spring training in Florida or Arizona. They had to stay close to home. The Browns gathered at Cape Girardeau, Missouri, using the Southeast Missouri State Teachers College gym and a nearby arena that often held cattle shows.

"The arena had a dirt floor," Don Gutteridge said. "You could take grounders there."

Gutteridge was the Browns' club pro. At thirty-two, the little second baseman had been playing in St. Louis since 1936, at first with the Cardinals and now with the franchise that had never won a pennant. Cynics joked that the Browns were "first in shoes, first in booze, and last in the American League." But not always. In 1922, with Hall of Fame first baseman George Sisler batting .420, the Browns had challenged Babe Ruth and the Yankees, only to finish second by one game. At that time the Browns owned St. Louis as well as Sportsman's

Park, but in 1926 the Cardinals won the National League pennant, the World Series, and the town. In 1936, the Browns' season attendance sagged to only 80,922.

By late 1941, the Browns' owner, Don Barnes, was hoping to move his nearly bankrupt franchise to Los Angeles. But the day before the American League owners were to vote, the Japanese attacked Pearl Harbor. Permission denied.

Stuck in St. Louis, the Browns finished a decent third in 1942, then slipped to sixth. But as Opening Day 1944 neared, the Browns realized that their war-riddled roster was as good as any of the other American League teams. Even that of the Yankees, who had won the three previous pennants.

"One day in spring training the pitchers were changing their shirts," Bob Bauman recalled. "Jakucki, Jack Kramer, Nelson Potter, George Caster, and one of them said, 'We play the Yankees the last four games at home. Wouldn't it be great if it came down to that for the pennant?' "

It had come down to that. Going into the final weekend, the Tigers were one game ahead of the Browns and three games ahead of the Yankees, who mathematically were still alive.

For the Browns, it had not been easy to stay in the race. Six months earlier in Cape Girardeau, manager Luke Sewell knew he had problems to solve as best he could. His centerfielder, thirty-five-year-old Mike Kreevich, had a reputation as a beer drinker. One night Sewell strolled into a bar where Kreevich was sitting on a stool.

"You've had enough, Mike," the manager said.

Sewell drove him back to the team hotel, took Kreevich's key, and locked him in his room. About an hour later, when Sewell decided to check the bar again, Kreevich was sitting on the same stool, having another beer. He had opened his hotel room window and crept down the fire escape. Another night righthander Alvis (Tex) Shirley, who wore a cowboy hat to hide his baldness, poured a pitcher of beer over Jakucki's head. Shirley thought it was funny. Jakucki didn't. Shirley landed in the gutter outside the bar, but somehow rolled over on his knees with his cowboy hat still on. Such antics prompted Sewell to call Bob Bauman into his office.

"We can win this year," the manager said, "but some of these guys sometimes get careless. I'd like to have you check them on the road."

In his winter job as trainer of the St. Louis University basketball team, Bauman had checked college kids' hotel rooms. But checking grizzled professional baseball players was different.

"Let me think it over," Bauman said.

The next day the trainer told Sewell that he was willing to do it, but that he wanted to talk to the entire team in a meeting. Sewell called the players together.

"Bob's got something to say to you," he said.

"Our manager," Bauman began, "thinks we can win the pennant this year, but he's aware that some of you guys tend to stay out too much. He's asked me to check all the rooms at midnight on road trips. But if I do it, I don't want any guff from anybody. If you've got anything to say to me about it, let me hear it now."

You could've heard a pin drop. If not a jaw.

None of the players hassled Bauman, although some simply tolerated him. Every so often Bauman would open the door to find Tex Shirley wearing his cowboy hat in bed. Ten minutes later the spot starter would be skipping down the back stairs of the hotel.

"I know Vern Stephens would leave after Bob checked," Gutteridge said. "I know because we were roommates, although I mostly roomed with Vern's suitcase. He loved company. If you know what I mean."

Handsome and husky, Vern (Junior) Stephens was the Browns' best player. The twenty-three-year-old shortstop led the American League that year with 109 runs batted in while hitting .293 with 20 homers. Traded later to the Red Sox, he would lead the league twice more in runs batted in, with 159 in 1949 and 144 in 1950. He would die of a heart attack at age forty-eight while playing golf. But in 1944 he formed a solid infield with George McQuinn at first, Gutteridge at second, and Mark Christman at third. Christman had attended spring training on weekends off from assembling military fire engines at a St. Louis plant. When he passed his Army physical, he was told to expect induction in two or three weeks. But suddenly he was deferred because of a new ruling exempting anybody older than twenty-six, married with kids conceived before Pearl Harbor. Two other Browns had been deferred because they had war-essential jobs: righthander Denny Galehouse and outfielder Chet Laabs.

Galehouse was working for Goodyear Aircraft in Akron, Ohio, where he determined for Selective Service officials which plant workers were essential and which were not.

But when the Browns lost righthander Steve Sundra to the military draft, they needed another starter. DeWitt wondered if the thirty-two-year-old Galehouse could be literally a "Sunday pitcher" between his six days a week on the job. Galehouse agreed to try. After work on

Saturday, he boarded a sleeper train to wherever the Browns were playing. Sunday morning he would have breakfast at the railroad station and take a taxi to the ballpark. In those years Sunday meant a doubleheader. Galehouse would always start the first game, then take a train that would get him to Akron in time for work Monday morning. As the season progressed, he realized he was wearing himself out. He checked his draft board to determine how long it would take to be inducted if he were to quit his job. When his draft board told him it had enough men to fill its quotas for several months, he joined the Browns full-time and produced a 9–10 record.

Laabs was working in a Detroit defense plant when the Browns arranged another defense plant job in St. Louis for him. That enabled him to play home games on weekends and occasional night games.

Laabs, a short but powerful righthanded hitter, had hit twenty-seven homers and driven in ninety-nine runs for the Browns two years earlier. He had been acquired during the 1939 season with Christman in a ten-player trade with the Tigers that liberated righthander Louis (Bobo) Newsom, the symbol of the Browns' frustration in those years. On the final day of the 1938 season, Newsom completed a 20–16 record. Thinking his 226 strikeouts had surpassed those of Bob Feller, who had lost to the Tigers, Newsom phoned the Indians' clubhouse.

"I'm just calling," Newsom said, "to give you a chance to congratulate the American League's new strikeout king. I fanned thirteen today."

"Congratulations on your twentieth, Bobo," Feller said, "but I've got bad news about the strikeouts. Even though I lost today, I struck out eighteen for a new American League record."

After a long silence, Newsom said, "I hope it still ain't too late to make this call collect."

Against Feller in that game, Laabs, then a young Tiger outfielder, had struck out five times, tying a major league record he still shares with many batters. Feller had exploited Laabs's weakness for the high pitch.

"But from the waist down," Gutteridge knew, "Chet could hit a ball a hundred miles."

Playing only part-time in 1944 until he quit his wartime job, Laabs never found his groove. As the Browns awaited the concluding four-game series with the Yankees that would decide the pennant, Laabs had hit only three home runs. But rain threatened to snarl the schedule. When Thursday's games in both St. Louis and Detroit were washed out, thereby creating Friday doubleheaders, a bellboy in the lobby of the Chase Hotel told Yankee manager Joe McCarthy, "It's been raining like this since the night before last. Looks like it won't ever stop."

"It always has," McCarthy said.

That was McCarthy, blunt and basic. Upon the Yankees' arrival in St. Louis, one of the writers suggested that the Yankees were really "shooting the works" by planning to start their two best pitchers, Ernie Bonham and Hank Borowy, in the first two games.

"We shoot the works in every game," McCarthy said. "It doesn't matter if it's the Browns or any other club that we're playing. The Yankees never pull any punches and never will."

When the weather cleared for Friday's doubleheader, McCarthy matched Bonham in the opener against Jack Kramer, the handsome righthander who had been medically discharged from the Navy because of asthma. To his teammates Kramer was known as "Prissy" because he was so neat, so well dressed, so well groomed.

"His clothes were always pressed just so, he hung them up just so," Gutteridge recalled. "But he was a tough guy. In the clubhouse one day Jakucki said something about Jack's clothes. Sig was a tough guy, but Jack didn't back off. We had to get between 'em."

As the inning-by-inning scores from Detroit showed the Tigers winning their first game with the Washington Senators, 5–2, behind righthander Ruffus Gentry, the Browns knew they had to win to stay one game behind. Their 4–1 victory developed in the third inning. Bonham, who had singled and stopped at third on George (Snuffy) Stirnweiss's double, tried to increase the Yankee lead to 2–0 when Kramer's wild pitch rolled several feet from the plate. Quickly retrieving the ball, catcher Myron (Red) Hayworth dove to tag Bonham in time.

His strength perhaps sapped, Bonham was strafed in the bottom of the third for two quick runs on Kramer's double, Gutteridge's bunt single, Kreevich's single, and Laabs's single. In the eighth Stephens singled and first baseman George McQuinn homered.

For the thirty-four-year-old McQuinn, that home run was sweet. Signed by the Yankees in 1930, he had languished in their farm system for seven seasons. Lou Gehrig's power and consecutive-game streak had created a dead end for any young first baseman in the Yankee organization. When the Browns drafted McQuinn, he quickly proved himself to be a dependable hitter and a flawless first baseman.

"He made our infield," Gutteridge said. "If you threw the ball anywhere near him, he caught it."

In the second game, the Browns had to beat Borowy, a lean right-hander with a 17–11 record. But the Browns had their best pitcher on the mound: Nelson Potter, a grizzled thirty-three-year-old right-hander with an 18–7 record. If not for a ten-day suspension for allegedly throwing a spitball, Potter might have already been a twenty-game winner. The spitball had been outlawed after the 1919 season except for those pitchers who were known to be throwing it. Borowy was pitching for the Yankees at Sportsman's Park in a July 20 night game, when Luke Sewell emerged from the Browns' dugout to talk to plate umpire Cal Hubbard.

"Make Borowy keep his fingers out of his mouth," the Brown manager said.

At six-five and more than 250 pounds, Hubbard would be elected to the Pro Football Hall of Fame for a legendary career as a tackle for the New York Giants and the Green Bay Packers in the early years of the National Football League. As an umpire, he commanded respect, if not a little fear. And as Hubbard told William B. Mead in *Even the Browns*, when he walked out to talk to Borowy, he didn't mince words.

"Sewell's complaining about you putting your fingers in your mouth," Hubbard said. "Let's not do it anymore."

Borowy nodded, saying, "I didn't even know I was doing it." But as Hubbard returned to the plate, Yankee third-base coach Art Fletcher asked, "What's Sewell squealing about?"

"About Borowy putting his fingers in his mouth."

"Then make Potter keep his finger out of his mouth," Fletcher said.

"All right," Hubbard said.

Before the next inning, Hubbard approached Potter and said, "Nellie, they're complaining about you putting your fingers in your mouth. Sewell complained about Borowy, so we're not going to have any more of that. Let's don't do it."

But when Potter did it again, Hubbard told him again. Sewell hurried out of the Browns' dugout.

"Luke," said Hubbard, "you're the one that started it, complaining about Borowy putting his fingers in his mouth. Potter does it all the time. I've already told him twice. You tell him now that if he does it anymore, we're going to run him the hell out. He's your baby, Luke. He's your responsibility."

Sewell talked to Potter, but after the manager left, Potter licked his fingers in an exaggerated motion, as if to taunt the umpire. Hubbard ejected him.

"I never did say he was throwing spitters," Hubbard said later. "I just said he was violating the pitching rules. I had to put Sewell out too. He was a louse anyway, that Sewell, he was always bitching about something. I made a report out to the league, and they suspended Nellie for ten days."

Potter insisted to Hubbard that, in the cool night air, he had just been "blowing" in his hand.

"Hubbard told me, 'You can't do that,' " Potter said later. "I said, 'Cal, I'm blowing on my hand.' He said, 'I know what you're doing. You're wetting your fingers.' Which I was, but he couldn't prove it. So he kept warning me to stop it. I knew that I either had to get a little moisture some way or I was going to have trouble. So I kept doing it and he just run me out of the ballgame. Did I ever throw a spitter? No, no. And Cal Hubbard never accused me of throwing a spitball."

During his suspension, Potter returned to his Mt. Morris, Illinois, home. Nine months later his wife had a baby.

"Some people thought we named the baby Cal Hubbard Potter," he said with a smile. "That's not true."

Now, in the second game of Friday's doubleheader, Potter and Borowy were pitching against each other again. In the first inning, Gutteridge led off with a double, moved to third on Borowy's wild pitch, and scored on a ground out. It never occurred to the Yankee infielders to try to throw Gutteridge out at the plate. Surely the Browns wouldn't win with just one run. Borowy allowed only one other hit, a single by Stephens in the seventh. But the Browns won, 1–0, as Potter scattered six hits. With two on and two out in the eighth, Yankee leftfielder Johnny Lindell ripped a long drive to left center that Mike Kreevich ran down. With two out in the ninth, the Yankees had the tying run at second with forty-one-year-old pinch hitter Paul Waner up. Before the doubleheader, a Sportsman's Park fan who had seen Waner perform against the Cardinals during his best years with the Pirates, yelled, "Hey, Paul, how come you're with the Yankees?"

Waner laughed. "Because Joe DiMaggio's in the Army," he yelled back.

Over his career Waner collected 3,152 hits, more than enough to ensure his Hall of Fame plaque. Now, batting against Potter with the tying run on second base in the ninth inning, he nubbed a blooper toward short right center as the tying run rounded third base. Gutteridge kept running until he caught the ball. Years later Waner would remind Gutteridge of that blooper.

"You caught the last ball," Waner said, "that I ever hit in organized baseball."

With their sweep, the Browns had mathematically eliminated the Yankees and, more important, had lifted themselves into a tie for first place with the Tigers, each with two games remaining. Going into their Friday doubleheader with the last-place Washington Senators in Detroit, the Tigers had appeared to be in the driver's seat. Two pitchers, Hal Newhouser and Paul (Dizzy) Trout, had put them there, with twenty-eight and twenty-seven victories, respectively.

The Tigers thought they had the pennant all but wrapped up. They not only had a one-game lead but had beaten the Senators in fifteen of their previous eighteen games.

In the opener of the Tigers' doubleheader, righthander Ruffus Gentry stopped the Senators, 5–2, but in the second game outfielder Stan Spence smashed a three-run homer off Trout in the third inning. The Tigers lost, 9–2, dropping into a flat-footed tie for first place. Not that the Tiger manager, Steve O'Neill, was overly concerned.

"I'd rather have our job in the next two days than theirs," O'Neill said. "We have Newhouser tomorrow and we'll bring Trout back for Sunday's game. The Browns don't figure to keep the Yankees bottled up forever."

Starting with only two days' rest, Newhouser did his job Saturday, stopping the Yankees, 7–3, but in St. Louis an hour later Denny Galehouse completed a 2–0 shutout on rightfielder Gene Moore's sixth homer, his fourth against the Yankees that season. With the Browns and Tigers still tied for first place, the season had come down to Sunday's matchups: Sig Jakucki against Mel Queen in St. Louis after Dizzy Trout, on one day's rest, had started in Detroit against another Senator knuckleballer, Emil (Dutch) Leonard.

That morning, in Leonard's room at the Book-Cadillac Hotel not far from Briggs Stadium, the phone rang. Thirty-two years later, in an interview with Milton Richman, the United Press International sports columnist, Leonard disclosed what the voice on the other end of the phone told him.

" 'You're pitching today, aren't you?' this fellow said," Leonard remembered. "I said, 'Yeah, I think so,' and he said, 'Good, you have a chance to make a lot of money.' I said, 'What do you mean?' and he said, 'I'm authorized to offer you $20,000 if you don't have a good day.' "

Realizing that he was being offered a bribe, Leonard snapped, "Go to hell" and hung up. When he told his roommate, George Case, about the phone call, the outfielder suggested he tell manager Ossie Bluege about it. Leonard instead told coach Clyde Milan, who told Bluege, who walked over to Leonard and handed him a new ball.

"You're still the pitcher," Bluege said.

The last-place Senators were twenty-five games out of first place, but Leonard, who had lost seven straight to the Tigers over two seasons, hoped to even his record at 14–14. While his knuckleball fluttered past the Tiger bats, Stan Spence's two-run homer off a weary Trout contributed to a 3–0 lead in the fourth. By the eighth Leonard had a 4–0 lead. In the bottom of the ninth, the Tigers scratched together a run but the thirty-five-year-old lefthander completed a 4–1 four-hitter, silencing the whispers about his mysterious morning phone call. Leonard later sought out Steve O'Neill.

"I just did the best I could," Leonard said.

"You did right," the Tiger manager told him.

Newhouser, with a 29–9 record and a 2.22 earned run average in 312 innings, and Trout, with a 27–14 record and a league-leading 2.12 earned run average in a league-leading 352 innings, had combined for 56 of the Tigers' 88 victories.

"They worked their hearts out for me," O'Neill said.

Hal Newhouser and Paul (Dizzy) Trout. *Detroit Tigers*

Now the Tigers' only hope was for the Browns to lose, forcing a one-game playoff Monday in Detroit. When the Yankees took an early 2–0 lead, the Browns appeared to be collapsing under the burden of the opportunity to win the first pennant in franchise history. Stephens overthrew first. Christman bobbled a grounder. Hayworth fired high to second on a steal. For the first time since their previous owner, Phil Ball, had expanded Sportsman's Park to more than 30,000 two decades earlier, the Browns had a sellout: 35,518 paid, 37,815 altogether, the largest St. Louis crowd ever to see them play. But the Browns were butchering the ball.

In Detroit, meanwhile, thousands had remained in Briggs Stadium to follow the inning-by-inning Browns–Yankees scores posted on the scoreboard there.

But in the fourth inning, shortly after the Tigers' loss appeared on the Sportsman's Park scoreboard, Mike Kreevich singled and Chet Laabs smashed a Queen fastball for a home run into the leftfield bleachers and a 2–2 tie. With two out in the fifth, Kreevich singled and Laabs homered again, this time off a Queen curveball into the left-centerfield bleachers. In the eighth Stephens lofted a homer off Borowy onto the pavilion roof in rightfield. Jakucki, meanwhile, had settled down. Those two early error-tainted runs had not disturbed his determination.

"If you went to the mound to talk to him," Gutteridge said, "Sig would glare and say, 'What the hell do you want? I'll get 'em out.' "

With the pennant at stake, Jakucki did just that. He closed out a 5–2 victory that detonated a St. Louis celebration. Fans rushed through the nearby streets. Trolleys outside Sportsman's Park stopped. For one day at least, the Browns owned the city again. But not for long. The other St. Louis team, the Cardinals, had breezed to their third consecutive National League pennant.

On October 4 the Browns and Cardinals opened what was known as the St. Louis Streetcar Series, one of a kind. Denny Galehouse outpitched Mort Cooper, 2–1, in the first game, and the Browns won the third game, 6–2, behind Jack Kramer's seven-hitter.

After that, the Cardinals took command, winning three straight. Jakucki, Galehouse, and Potter weren't quite good enough. The Browns never came close to another pennant. The next season, with a one-armed outfielder named Pete Gray symbolizing baseball's desperate search for talent in the final months of World War II, the Browns finished third. Soon they returned to the second division. After the 1952 season, the Browns franchise was moved to Baltimore, but not

Chet Laabs (second from right in bottom row) enjoys his two pennant-winning homers with (left to right) Al Hollingsworth, Vern Stephens, Sig Jakucki, and George McQuinn. Behind them (left to right) are Mike Chartak, Babe Martin, Sam Zoldak, Ellis Clary, and batboy Bob Scanlon. *AP/Wide World Photo*

before owner Bill Veeck produced baseball's most memorable stunt: midget pinch hitter Eddie Gaedel walking on four pitches from Bob Cain of the Tigers in a 1951 game. Because of Gaedel's little niche in Browns history, the pennant-winning 1944 team is often forgotten.

"Some people said, 'The Browns didn't deserve to win that pennant, the Browns didn't have a good team, the Browns were just a bunch of castoffs,' " Don Gutteridge said. "But we had the best team in the American League that year."

Lou Boudreau's Year

Satchel Paige and Bill Veeck. *AP/Wide World Photo*

NONE OF THE Boston Red Sox players liked the schedule switch, but they couldn't complain about the cause. The week before, on September 13, 1948, one of the Cleveland Indians' pitchers, Don Black, had collapsed with a brain hemorrhage while batting. The year before, his 10–12 record had included a no-hitter. This season he had skidded to 2–2, a thirty-two-year-old righthander hanging on with a history of drinking and debts. Now, as Don Black drifted in and out of a coma, doctors knew he would never pitch again. In an era before baseball pensions and medical plans, Indian owner Bill Veeck knew that one of his favorite players needed money.

"The big game with the Red Sox," Veeck announced. "We're making that Don Black Night."

By a quirk of the American League schedule, the Red Sox would be stopping in Cleveland for one game on September 22, a Wednesday afternoon. With the Red Sox, Indians, and New York Yankees fighting for first place, about 30,000 tickets had already been sold.

"Whatever our club's share is from the sale above 30,000," Veeck said, "we'll turn that over to Don and his wife."

But the Indians needed permission from the Red Sox to switch the game from afternoon to night. Veeck phoned Tom Yawkey.

"Absolutely," the Red Sox owner said. "And we'll be glad to contribute our club's share above the $30,000 advance."

"No," Veeck said. "I want Don to know that the money represents the city of Cleveland's high regard for him."

Nobody doubted Veeck's sincerity. But the Red Sox players didn't like the idea of having to hit under the Municipal Stadium lights, especially having to hit Bob Feller's fastball under those lights. They also didn't like the idea of having to listen to many more thousands rooting for the Indians in a crucial game: a total of 76,772, as it turned out, which represented $40,380 for Don Black and represented who knows how much influence in the pennant race in a game that turned in the first inning.

With one out and Indian centerfielder Thurman Tucker on first, Joe Dobson had two strikes on Indian shortstop-manager Lou Boudreau.

"Tucker was a threat to run," Red Sox catcher Birdie Tebbetts would say later, "but Boudreau hadn't struck out against us all season."

On the next pitch, Tucker broke for second. Red Sox shortstop Vern Stephens, hoping to protect his area because he knew Boudreau seldom struck out, didn't break immediately to cover the bag. But this time Boudreau swung and missed, one of only nine times he struck out all season.

"Stephens held his position a moment too long," Tebbetts said. "My throw was perfect, but Stephens's delay allowed Tucker to be safe."

Instead of executing an inning-ending double play, the Red Sox were confronted with Tucker on second and all those roaring rooters. Second baseman Joe Gordon's single scored Tucker, and then third baseman Ken Keltner's twenty-eighth homer provided the Indians with a 3–0 lead.

"All because," Tebbetts said, "none of us thought Boudreau would strike out."

Those three quick runs were all Feller needed in a 5–2 three-hitter that lifted the Indians into a tie for first place with the Red Sox, with the third-place Yankees only one-half game behind. After a shaky start, the twenty-nine-year-old Feller had not been as dominating this season as in 1946, when he had a 26–15 record with a then-record 348 strikeouts for a sixth-place team. But over his last few starts he had permitted only six earned runs in fifty innings while striking out thirty-six. Just when the Indians needed him most in bidding for their first pennant since 1920, he had regained the form that made batters blink.

"I thought Feller was as good as I've ever seen," Ted Williams said in the Red Sox clubhouse that night. "He broke off a curve against me that fairly exploded. Some of his fastballs, particularly when he had a couple of strikes on me, were just good enough to make me swing even if they were a trifle out of the strike zone."

Praise indeed for Feller's control. Williams seldom swung at pitches even a millimeter outside the strike zone. Having turned thirty three weeks earlier, the six-three leftfielder known as the "Splendid Splinter" reigned as baseball's best hitter. In compiling his .344 lifetime average with 521 homers, he had batted .406 in 1941 and would hit .369 this season. When the Red Sox won the 1946 pennant, he had been voted the first of his two Most Valuable Player awards. By 1948 he had already earned two triple crowns, leading the AL in batting, runs batted in, and homers in both 1942 and 1947, and four of his six batting titles.

"When I walk down the street," he once said, "I want people to say, 'There goes the greatest hitter that ever lived.'"

His career numbers would have been even greater had he not lost five seasons as a Marine pilot, three during World War II and the better part of two in the Korean War, where he survived his jet fighter's flaming crash landing. At age thirty-nine in 1957 he batted .388, only five hits short of another .400 season. But throughout his career he feuded openly with Boston sportswriters, dubbing them the "Knights of the Keyboard," and occasionally with the Fenway Park fans. After hitting a long homer at Fenway Park once, he looked up at the press box and spit. But he has endured as Boston's most cherished baseball player.

"Baseball has been the most wonderful thing in my life," he told the crowd before his final Fenway Park game at the end of the 1960 season. "If I were starting over again and someone asked me where is the one place I would like to play, I would want it to be in Boston, with the greatest owner in baseball and the greatest fans in America."

In the eighth inning that day, with Jack Fisher of the Baltimore Orioles pitching, the forty-two-year-old slugger known by then as Teddy Ballgame crashed a home run off the canopy of the Red Sox bullpen. As he hurried into the dugout, he heard fans chanting, "We Want Ted, We Want Ted." He never moved. When the ninth began, he trotted to leftfield, not knowing that manager Pinky Higgins had dispatched Carroll Hardy there. Realizing that Higgins had created a curtain call, he hurried off the Fenway Park field for the last time.

"That's it," he said in the clubhouse. "I'm finished."

Even though the Red Sox still had three games in Yankee Stadium, Ted Williams had ended his career with a flourish, with a home run. But strategically, his career always would be intertwined with that of Lou Boudreau, the Indians' shortstop-manager. In the opener of a July 14, 1946, doubleheader with the Indians at Fenway Park, Williams hit three homers and drove in eight runs in an 11–8 victory. His first time up in the second game, he doubled. His next time up, the bases were empty. Boudreau waved to his teammates.

"The shift," he yelled. "The shift."

Boudreau moved to the normal second-base position. Third baseman Ken Keltner moved slightly to the right of second base. First baseman Jimmy Wasdell hugged the foul line on the grass beyond the infield dirt. Second baseman Jack Conway was in short rightfield. Rightfielder Hank Edwards was deep. Centerfielder Pat Seerey was deep in right-centerfield. Only leftfielder George Case remained on the third-base side of second base.

Boudreau had been planning what would be known as the "Williams shift" for more than a week. Two of his coaches, George Susce and Oscar Melillo, had tried to talk him out of it, one saying, "It won't work." But in the Indians' clubhouse between games of the Fenway Park doubleheader, he had sketched the shift on paper and thumbtacked it to the bulletin board. As he started to explain it, some of his players smiled, some smirked.

"Don't laugh," Boudreau said. "I'm serious."

In the batter's box now, Williams, seeing the Indian players shift, turned to plate umpire Bill Summers and said, "Get those guys back in their normal positions." Summers shrugged.

"As long as they're out there, Ted," the umpire said, "they can stand anywhere they want."

In his anger, Williams was gripping the bat so hard that Indian catcher Jim Hegan would tell his teammates that "sawdust was coming out of the handle." Moments later the Red Sox slugger bounced to Boudreau, a shortstop playing second base, so to speak. Other teams soon used similar defensive alignments, but only when the bases were empty. In time, Williams sometimes swung toward leftfield. He even bunted occasionally. But he usually tried to defy the shift and succeeded often enough.

Boudreau would be remembered as much for having designed the Williams shift as for all of his Hall of Fame credentials.

Ironically, Boudreau had almost been traded by Veeck to the St. Louis Browns before the 1948 season. Veeck agreed to swap Boudreau, outfielders George Metkovich and Dick Kokos, and $100,000 for shortstop Vern Stephens, righthanders Jack Kramer and Ellis Kinder, and outfielder Paul Lehner. But when Bill DeWitt demanded another $90,000 to add to Boudreau's salary over three years, Veeck backed off.

"Best deal I never made," Veeck would often say later.

Spurned by Veeck and desperate for cash, the Browns shipped Stephens, Kramer, and Kinder to the Red Sox in two separate deals for a total of $395,000 and nine obscure players. Stephens solidified the

Red Sox infield alongside Bobby Doerr at second base, Johnny Pesky at third, and Billy Goodman at first. Kramer and Kinder joined another righthander, Joe Dobson, and lefthander Mel Parnell in the rotation for Joe McCarthy's first season as Red Sox manager. After having guided the Yankees to seven World Series titles and eight pennants, Marse Joe was aloof but always aware. On seeing his players in a card game once, he snapped, "You memorize every card in the deck, but you can't remember the bunt sign." When differences with Yankee owner Larry MacPhail developed early in the 1946 season, he resigned. But his players never ceased to respect him.

"Never a day went by," Joe DiMaggio once said, "that you didn't learn something from Joe McCarthy."

When the Red Sox hired baseball's most successful manager, cynics wondered if McCarthy and Williams would get along, but they did. Now, with the Red Sox battling the Indians and the Yankees in the final week of the 1948 season, cynics wondered if McCarthy knew how to win a tight pennant race; his Yankee teams had always coasted to first place. McCarthy's primary problem was the Red Sox pitching staff. It was nowhere near as deep as the Indian staff. After a shaky start, Feller was blazing to a 19–14 record. "For one important game," Yankee manager Bucky Harris had said two weeks earlier, "I would still take Feller over any pitcher in the league." Boudreau also had another future Hall of Famer, righthander Bob Lemon, as well as twenty-eight-year-old rookie lefthander Gene Bearden, righthander Steve Gromek, and lefthander Sam Zoldak. In the bullpen were skinny righthander Russ Christopher and the legendary Leroy (Satchel) Paige, the Indians' second black player.

In midseason the year before, Veeck had signed the American League's first black player, Larry Doby, who in 1952 and 1954 would lead the league in home runs. Doby joined the Indians only eleven weeks after Jackie Robinson of the Brooklyn Dodgers had arrived as the major leagues' first black player.

"Just because Jackie was only eleven weeks ahead of me in 1947 didn't make it any easier for me," Doby has said. "The day I joined the Indians, a few of the players wouldn't shake hands with me. Some of the players on other teams and some of the fans were rough, but coach Bill McKechnie took me under his wing. He told me, 'You're going to have to go through a lot, but you're going to have to grit your teeth. If you don't stick it out, it might take a long time before another Negro gets a chance.' "

Doby stuck it out. Moved to the outfield in 1948, he would bat .301

with fourteen homers and sixty-six runs batted in. By midseason, Bill Veeck was hoping to sign another black player.

"Can you come to the ballpark early tomorrow?" Veeck asked Boudreau. "I want you to check out a young pitcher coming in for a tryout. He might help us down the stretch."

Boudreau had often judged a young pitcher's stuff by taking a few swings himself. But this "young" pitcher turned out to be Satchel Paige, then forty-two years old according to a July 7, 1906, birth certificate or at least forty-eight years old according to Veeck's research of the Mobile, Alabama, municipal records. Whatever his age, Satch had been pitching for various Negro League teams, notably the Kansas City Monarchs, for at least two decades. In the off-season he had barnstormed with other black players against a team of major league players organized by Bob Feller, whose fastball prompted Satch to address him as "Bob Rapid." Veeck had suggested signing Paige earlier in the season, but Boudreau had resisted. Now, in early July, the owner had imported him for a secret tryout. After catching Paige's fifty warmup pitches, Boudreau stepped into the batter's box.

"Lou was leading both leagues with a batting average of almost .400, but against Paige he batted .000," Veeck told Ed Linn in his autobiography, *Veeck, as in Wreck.* "Satch threw twenty pitches. Nineteen of them were strikes. Lou swung nineteen times and he had nothing that looked like a base hit. After a final pop fly, Lou dropped his bat, came over to me and said, 'Don't let him get away, Will. We can use him.' "

Over the final three months, Satchel Paige would produce a 6–1 record with a 2.48 earned run average, including a 4–0 record with two shutouts in his seven starts. In his fourteen relief appearances, he would be 2–1 with one save. Whatever his age, he still had his control along with his sly fastball. And his sly wit. He's best remembered for saying, "Don't look back, something may be gaining on you." And shortly after his arrival, when the Indians' front office realized that a different "Mrs. Paige" was picking up the ticket he left for every game, Satch was asked to identify his wife for their records.

"Well, it's like this," he said. "I'm not married, but I'm in great demand."

Satchel Paige also helped create a great demand for Indians tickets. With a good team and good promotion, their season attendance of 2,620,627 would set a major league record. Two years earlier, Ted Williams and the Red Sox had won the pennant. The previous year Joe DiMaggio and the Yankees had prevailed. Now the upstart Indians were involved in a pennant race with two teams accustomed to the pennant grind. Darkly handsome, thirty-one-year-old shortstop Lou Boudreau had been the Indians' manager since he was twenty-four. Now he was having the time of his life as well as the season of his life: a .355 average with 18 homers, 106 runs batted in, 116 runs scored. As the Indians awaited a three-game weekend series in Detroit, he showed that he also was ready for the challenge of his life.

"I might move Wally Judnich to centerfield," he said, "and put Eddie Robinson at first base."

By benching centerfielder Thurman Tucker, Boudreau was going against the managerial philosophy that you don't break up a winning combination. Asked about that, his eyes flashed under his thick black eyebrows.

"The hell with that," he said. "We're trying to win a pennant, not bow to go along with an old-fogey superstition."

The Red Sox had gone on to New York for a three-game series. Thursday afternoon Birdie Tebbetts was standing in the lobby of the Commodore Hotel when he learned that Yankee lefthander Eddie Lopat had been beaten in Chicago by Frank Papish, a thirty-year-old lefthander with a 2–8 record.

"With Lopat out of the way," Tebbetts declared, "we have no Yankee pitcher to fear."

Friday the Red Sox knocked out Vic Raschi in the fourth inning and Williams drove in three runs with a double and a bases-loaded walk. But the Red Sox should have feared one of their own pitchers. Ellis Kinder forgot to cover first base, the Yankees scored two gift runs and went on to win, 9–6. When the Indians' seven-game winning streak was snapped in Detroit, 4–3, on righthander Fred Hutchinson's seven-hitter, the three teams suddenly were tied for first place at 91–56, each with only seven games remaining. After a coin toss in his Chicago office, AL president Will Harridge announced the playoff schedule if the season ended in a three-way tie: the Indians would play the Red Sox in Boston, with the survivor opposing the Yankees in either Cleveland or Boston.

Saturday the Red Sox knocked out Allie Reynolds in the fourth inning of a 7–2 victory on Jack Kramer's seven-hitter, and the Indians pounded the Tigers, 9–3, for Bearden's seventeenth. As a Yankee farmhand, Bearden had been optioned in 1946 to the Oakland Oaks of the Pacific Coast League. He hadn't completely recovered from World War II wounds suffered as a sailor in the sinking of the battleship USS *Helena* in the Pacific. He had an aluminum plate in his right knee that kept him in a Navy hospital for two years before he could walk properly and another aluminum plate in his head.

In search of more pitching after the 1946 season, Veeck was intrigued by Bearden's potential. He phoned Casey Stengel, the Oakland manager who had once been his manager in Milwaukee when he owned that minor league team. "If the Yankees are crazy enough to give him up," Stengel said, "grab him." Bearden spent 1947 in the minors but now he was hypnotizing batters with his knuckleball. He would never be anywhere near this good again. One theory is that Stengel, as the Yankee manager in 1949, told his hitters to lay off Bearden's knuckleball, which often dipped below the strike zone. When that information got around, Bearden kept walking too many batters. But now, having kept the Indians tied with the Red Sox for first place, he was on his way to leading the AL with a 2.43 earned run average.

"We're not out of the woods yet," Boudreau said. "Remember, the Red Sox are going home."

So were the Indians. Sunday night they returned to Cleveland all alone in first place. Feller's five-hitter had stopped the Tigers, 4–1. Yankee lefthander Tommy Byrne had stifled the Red Sox, 6–2, after Tommy Henrich nailed lefthander Mel Parnell for a two-run homer in the first inning and Joe DiMaggio drilled a two-run single in the fourth. As the Red Sox returned to Boston that Sunday night, the Braves were celebrating their first National League pennant since the "Miracle" team of 1914 that ascended from last place on July 20. Third baseman Bob Elliott's three-run homer in a 3–2 victory over the New York Giants had created an opportunity for the first all-Boston World Series. The Indians had other ideas.

"We'll win," said Veeck, "because we have the best team in the league."

"We'll win because we have the best pitching staff in the league," said vice president Hank Greenberg, the former Tiger slugger who had finished his Hall of Fame career the year before with the Pittsburgh Pirates. "Neither the Red Sox nor the Yankees can name their starting pitchers in the remaining five games and be reasonably certain they'll win."

"We'll win," said Boudreau, "because we have Bob Feller pitching for us."

"We'll win," said Satchel Paige, "because we just ain't gonna lose no more."

Boudreau had his best pitchers lined up: Bearden and Feller would face the White Sox on Tuesday and Wednesday, then Lemon, Bearden, and Feller would face the Tigers in the final weekend series. But in Cleveland the pennant race was about to be upstaged by one of Veeck's more memorable promotions. He had read a letter to the editor in the *Cleveland Press* that complained about ballclubs having a "day" or a "night" for well-paid players who didn't need money or gifts instead of for somebody like him, an Army veteran who did. The letter was signed "Good Old Joe Early." Veeck agreed.

"As a thank-you to all our fans," the Indians' owner announced, "we're going to have a 'Good Old Joe Early Night' symbolizing an average fan."

In contributing to a record major league season attendance of 2,620,629 customers, 60,405 showed up for the "night" honoring the twenty-four-year-old Chevrolet plant security guard. The first 20,000 female fans to arrive at Municipal Stadium that evening each received a Princess Aloha lavender orchid flown in from Hawaii overnight on a United Airlines DC-3. And when Joe Early walked out to home plate, the festivities began.

"We're giving Joe," the announcer blared, "a few presents."

His "new house in early American architecture" turned out to be an outhouse. His "fully equipped automobile" turned out to be a circus Model T Ford, filled with a bevy of beautiful models, which backfired while the fenders fell off. His "variety of pets" included pigs, chickens, and a sway-backed horse. But soon the real gifts arrived: a new Ford convertible with a year's supply of gas and oil, a radio-phonograph, a refrigerator, a washing machine, a wristwatch, clothing, and luggage.

"Everything," acknowledged Veeck, "we could talk the local merchants into contributing."

Even better, with the Red Sox and Yankees losing, the Indians jumped into a two-game lead. Bearden's four-hitter stopped the White Sox, 11–0, on Allie Clark's homer and three singles. The Yankees lost in Philadelphia when Carl Scheib outpitched Vic Raschi, 5–2. And the Red Sox lost to the Washington Senators, 4–2, on Ray Scarborough's six-hitter, which had the Fenway Park fans hooting Williams, who returned the fire. After he struck out in the third, Williams took another swing and let his bat fly toward the far end of the Red Sox dugout. After a good catch in the fifth, he turned to his hecklers and raised both hands high, his index fingers up.

"That's the first time this season he's acted that way," Burt Whitman wrote in the *Boston Herald*.

Williams had been frustrated by Scarborough's style. "Ray never gave you anything to hit," he would say years later. "He had a low outside sinker, a hard fastball down and in, a great curveball. He always threw it just close enough to the plate that you had to swing." Entering the clubhouse that day, Williams cursed softly, flung his glove into his locker, and barked, "Gimme a cold drink." Nearly an hour later, still in his uniform, Williams strolled into the trainer's room and stretched out on a rubbing table. When the writers left to return to the press box, he was still there, talking to manager Joe McCarthy, who was trying to get him to look ahead, not back.

"That's baseball," McCarthy had told the writers. "There's another game tomorrow. If we won today, we'd still have to win tomorrow."

But if the Red Sox had won, they would have remained only one game behind. Now they were two back after losing to Scarborough, a high school mathematics and science teacher in the off-season.

"Ray was pitching," joked Senator manager Joe Kuhel, "in the fourth dimension."

The loss to Scarborough has haunted Red Sox history. That victory gave the seventh-place Senators' best pitcher a 14–8 record in his drive to win fifteen, which he did on the final day of the season. In one of the twists of fate that always seem to affect a pennant race, he hadn't had an opportunity to pitch against the Indians during the Senators' last series in Cleveland.

"I wanted to get a crack at the Indians," he said. "But when we were in Detroit, I got word my wife and daughter and mother were in a terrible automobile accident. I got a plane out of Detroit and stayed with them four days. They're coming along fine."

Wednesday the Indians stayed two games ahead. On only two days' rest, Feller didn't have his best fastball, striking out only three and scattering ten hits, but he stopped the White Sox, 5–2, on Joe Gordon's thirty-second homer and Ken Keltner's thirty-first. Yankee rookie righthander Bob Porterfield, just up from the Newark farm, won in Philadelphia, 4–2, on a three-run homer by rookie outfielder Hank Bauer, just up from the Kansas City farm. Ellis Kinder handled the Senators, 5–1, while Fenway Park buzzed with the news from Ebbets Field in Brooklyn: Brave outfielder Jeff Heath had broken his left ankle in a slide at home plate. Not that the Red Sox players sympathized. One was overheard to mutter, "Serves the son of a bitch right." During the Braves' pennant celebration, Heath had told a radio reporter that he hoped the Indians would win the pennant, not the Red Sox.

"If we play in that big ballpark in Cleveland," Heath said, "the World Series shares will be bigger than if we played in Fenway."

With the Indians idle Thursday, the Red Sox and the Yankees each moved to within one and one-half games. Parnell curved the Senators, 7–3, for his fifteenth victory. As a steady drizzle soaked Shibe Park, the Yankees needed to use Vic Raschi in relief in the ninth to preserve a 9–7 triumph.

"At least we're not going to hand it to 'em on a platter," Bucky Harris said. "They're going to have to earn it."

With an opportunity to clinch a tie Friday by winning the opener of their three-game series with the Tigers, the Indians took a 3–2 lead into the ninth with Lemon pitching. On an oh-and-two pitch, Eddie Mayo topped a roller down the third-base line, but Lemon's throw hit the Tiger second baseman in the back. Lemon struck out pinch hitter Johnny Bero, but walked pinch hitters Johnny Groth and Joe Ginsberg, loading the bases. Boudreau called for Russ Christopher, who led the AL with seventeen saves. But the skinny righthander didn't save this game. He walked shortstop Johnny Lipon, forcing in the tying run. Neil Berry grounded to Keltner, who forced Groth at the plate, but first baseman Walter Judnich dropped catcher Jim Hegan's double-play throw. Outfielder Jimmy Outlaw singled over Gordon's head for two runs and a 5–3 victory that sliced the Indians' lead to one game.

With only two games remaining for each team, the Indians would use Bearden against Tiger righthander Lou Kretlow on Saturday, then Feller against Hal Newhouser on Sunday. For the Red Sox and Yankees, each one game behind the Indians going into their Fenway Park showdown, the matchups were Jack Kramer–Tommy Byrne and Joe Dobson–Bob Porterfield.

After the first inning Saturday, the Yankees never recovered. Byrne walked Johnny Pesky, then decided to throw Williams a fastball on a one-one count. Byrne was hoping the Red Sox slugger would foul it off, and then he would spin his best curveball. Byrne never threw that curveball. Williams deposited the fastball into the centerfield bullpen for his twenty-fifth homer.

"I think that's the first hit Williams ever got off me," Byrne would say later. "Maybe he got a single sometime, but I don't remember it."

Needing only those two quick runs, Kramer coasted to his eighteenth victory, 5–1. When Bearden blanked the Tigers, 8–0, for his nineteenth, the Indians clinched a tie, the Yankees were eliminated, but the Red Sox were still alive.

"Porterfield for them tomorrow? Not Raschi?" McCarthy said. "It doesn't make any difference. Whoever it is has to get the ball over the plate."

In those years there was no provision in the major league rules for a rained-out game to be played after the season had ended if it affected the pennant race. If the Indians were rained out Sunday in Cleveland, they would win the pennant by one-half game even if the Red Sox won their finale. The decision to start or cancel such a game because of inclement weather rested with the home club, not the umpires, as it does now.

"If I followed my own inclinations," Veeck said with a grin, "I'd call it off when the first cloud came over."

To avert any accusations, Veeck asked American League president Will Harridge to dispatch league officials to rule in case it rained. Umpire-in-chief Tommy Connolly and umpire Cal Hubbard arrived Sunday morning. But no such decision was needed. Under cool but sunny skies, 74,181 marched on huge Municipal Stadium along the Lake Erie shore, confident that Feller would clinch the pennant even though the Tigers were using Newhouser, their ace lefthander with a 20–12 record. In Fenway Park, meanwhile, the Yankees took a quick 2–0 lead. But when Dom DiMaggio singled in the third inning the public-address announcer blared, "Attention, please. Detroit has the bases loaded, one run in, and Dick Wakefield at bat." Moments later the public-address announcer turned on his microphone again.

"Attention, please," his voice blared. "Wakefield doubled and Detroit now leads, three to nothing."

As if the cheers were his cue, Ted Williams sliced a double down the leftfield line against the shift, scoring DiMaggio. Vern Stephens singled off third baseman Bobby Brown's glove. Bobby Doerr drilled a two-run double to right center. Stan Spence walked. Billy Goodman singled, prompting Bucky Harris to remove Porterfield and bring in Vic Raschi. By now the scoreboard boy behind the Wall in leftfield had put up a yellow 4 for Detroit, yellow meaning the Tigers were still hitting. Soon he replaced it with a white 4, meaning the Tigers' half-inning had ended.

As the Red Sox took a 5–2 lead and the Indians fell behind, 4–0, those Fenway Park fans with portable radios also knew something else: Feller had been knocked out.

Not that the Yankees surrendered. Joe DiMaggio's second double sparked a two-run rally in the fifth that knocked out Dobson, brought in lefthander Earl Johnson, and narrowed the Red Sox lead to 5–4.

Then in the sixth Dom DiMaggio hit his ninth homer. As he rounded the bases, he wondered if his brother Joe remembered their conversation the night before. Dom was driving Joe to the Wellesley Hills home of Dom's fiancée, Emily Frederick, for dinner with her family.

"You guys did a job on us today," Joe said. "I'll make up for that tomorrow. I'll hit my fortieth homer."

"Don't underestimate me," Dom said quietly but firmly. "The only DiMaggio home run tomorrow will be my ninth."

In the Red Sox dugout now some players were singing, "Who's better than his brother Joe? Dom-i-nic Di-Magg-i-o." And the rally had only begun. Pesky beat out a bunt. Williams popped up (after having been on base thirteen consecutive times), but Stephens hit his twenty-ninth homer. Doerr's single finished Raschi. The rout was on. The Red Sox would win, 10–5, as their fans saluted Joe DiMaggio with a long and loud ovation when he limped to the dugout in the ninth, removed for a pinch runner after his fourth hit—two doubles and two singles. By then Newhouser had finished a five-hitter that stopped the Indians, 7–1, and created the first one-game pennant playoff in major league history.

"This is the gamest team I've ever had," McCarthy said. "We were counted out as late as last Wednesday."

But the big question was: With two tired pitching staffs, who would be the starters Monday at Fenway Park?

"I had everybody working in the bullpen," Joe McCarthy said. "I'll try to dream up a starter tonight."

The best guess was that McCarthy would start either Parnell, who had a 15–8 record, or Kinder, who was 10–7. But some of the Red Sox players seemed more concerned about what Pesky would be wearing tomorrow. Knowing he would be the best man Sunday night in the wedding of a naval officer friend, he had worn his blue Navy officer's uniform to the ballpark and now he was putting it on.

"You little squirt," Earl Johnson said, "you better wear that tomorrow."

"It's what we do out there that counts," Pesky said. "Not what we wear."

"No, no, you've got to wear that uniform again tomorrow," Johnson said. "We won with it today, we'll win with it tomorrow."

"Damn right," trainer Eddie Froelich said. "You've got to wear that uniform."

"All right," Pesky finally said. "I promise I'll wear this uniform tomorrow."

Always the hitter, Ted Williams naturally was more concerned with knowing the Indians' starter. When he asked outfielder Wally Moses, the veteran outfielder said, "I guess it will be Lemon. He's been tough against us this year." Hearing that, Williams roared, "I don't give a damn if he's beaten us twenty times this year. We'll knock his brains out tomorrow." But in Cleveland, before the door to the Indians' clubhouse was opened to the sportswriters, Lou Boudreau had called a team meeting. During it, Larry Doby would remember years later, Bill McKechnie suggested that Bearden start against the Red Sox.

"This game is as important to you as it is to me," Boudreau finally said to his players. "I want to start Bearden tomorrow, but if you don't agree, let me know."

Johnny Berardino, a thirty-one-year-old utility infielder, objected, saying, "I don't know if a lefthander should start in Fenway." Joe Gordon suggested, "Let's look at the records." Boudreau agreed, asking that the pitching records be checked. He found that there wasn't much difference between the success of either righthanded pitchers or lefthanded pitchers. When the discussion continued, Gordon stood up.

"Lou, you've picked the pitchers for one hundred fifty-four games," the second baseman said. "You pick the pitcher for this game."

Berardino, later an actor for twenty-five years on the soap opera "General Hospital," nodded, saying, "I'll go along with that." Boudreau smiled, then said, "I don't want anybody telling the writers who's pitching tomorrow. I don't want the Red Sox to know. Sometimes a surprise has an effect on a team." Boudreau also didn't want Bearden to be bothered by writers and photographers. When the clubhouse was finally opened, Boudreau announced, "My starter will be Feller, Bearden, or Lemon but it won't make any difference who pitches. We're going to Boston and win the pennant, then stay there for the World Series with the Braves. We're just going to Boston a day earlier." When the Indians arrived at Union Terminal for their 9:00 P.M. train, more than a thousand fans had gathered to see them off. As the train rumbled along Lake Erie toward Buffalo, several Indian veterans had a few drinks before climbing into their Pullman berths. Tomorrow's starter would remain a secret, but Joe Gordon defended Boudreau to the writers.

"There's no better manager and no better player," Gordon said. "It makes me sick the way he's second-guessed. And I'll tell you another thing: he's picked the pitcher for this game and he's picked the right one. You wait and see."

Joe McCarthy, meanwhile, was keeping everybody guessing. As the Red Sox relaxed after Sunday's game, he called Birdie Tebbetts into his office. Tebbetts wasn't surprised. McCarthy had often confided in him. Maybe because both were Irish. Maybe because McCarthy knew his catcher always covered for him when he "rode the White Horse," as the Red Sox players phrased it when their manager drank a little too much of that Scotch whisky. But this time McCarthy had a question for Tebbetts.

"Have you got a pitcher for tomorrow?"

Tebbetts nodded and said, "Hughson."

Then thirty-two, Cecil (Tex) Hughson had been the Red Sox' ace righthander in 1946 with a 20–11 record before skidding to a 12–11 the next year. This season, bothered by arm trouble, he had been strictly a relief pitcher, with a 3–1 record in fifteen games, but Tebbetts knew he had been throwing well lately.

"No, Birdie," McCarthy said. "We're at the point of winning or losing the pennant. Hughson's been in the minors. He's had a bad arm. If we lose with him, he'd be blamed and that would be unfair to him. I can't do it. Go out and see who wants to pitch tomorrow, but I've got somebody in mind."

Tebbetts watched as McCarthy picked up a small piece of paper, scribbled on it, and placed it upside down on his desk.

One by one, Tebbetts went around the clubhouse and talked to the possible candidates: Mel Parnell, Jack Kramer, Ellis Kinder, Tex Hughson, Denny Galehouse, Dave (Boo) Ferriss, Mickey Harris, even Joe Dobson, who had started Sunday's game. All the pitchers, except lefthanded reliever Earl Johnson, who had worked in Sunday's game and would be in the bullpen again tomorrow, had the same response.

"Everybody wants the ball," Tebbetts reported.

At his desk, McCarthy turned over the piece of paper and showed it to his catcher. On it was scribbled "Galehouse." Tebbetts was surprised. Galehouse had an 8–7 record, but the thirty-six-year-old righthander had been at his best in relief: 4–1 with three saves, in contrast to 4–6 as a starter. But throughout his career Galehouse had been considered a tough competitor. He had helped pitch the 1944 St. Louis Browns to the pennant, winning a crucial game against McCarthy's Yankees on the final weekend. In that year's World Series opener he had prevailed in a 2–1 duel with Mort Cooper, the Cardinal ace. McCarthy hadn't forgotten that Galehouse had won big games. And the husky righthander was rested. Tebbetts left McCarthy's office,

Denny Galehouse. *AP/Wide World Photo*

showered, and strolled toward his car in the players' parking lot. Galehouse happened to be there.

"Who's starting tomorrow?" Galehouse asked.

"I've got a hunch it's you," Tebbetts said.

Parnell was assuming he would start. He had three days' rest. He had a 15–8 record, including 3–2 against the Indians. After the twenty-six-year-old lefthander from New Orleans arrived at Fenway Park for Monday's playoff, he took his time getting dressed, as the starting pitcher always does. His teammates were out on the field, the hitters taking batting practice, the pitchers shagging balls in the outfield. Parnell was sitting alone at his locker when McCarthy approached him.

"Son, I've changed my mind," McCarthy said. "I'm going with the righthander. The elements are against the lefthander because the wind is blowing out."

Parnell looked around the clubhouse. The righthander? Which righthander? Kinder? Kramer? All the other pitchers were out on the field. But then he heard McCarthy tell batboy Don Fitzpatrick, "Go outside and tell Galehouse to come in." Galehouse soon appeared. "He was as white as a ghost," Parnell would say years later.

"I wasn't nervous, I knew I was pitching," Galehouse would remember. "When I got to the ballpark that morning, a new ball was on the upper shelf of my locker. That meant I was starting. Then I was told to shag balls, to keep the Indians guessing."

When his teammates learned that Galehouse was starting, most were stunned. Dom DiMaggio wondered if McCarthy remembered how Connie Mack started Howard Ehmke against McCarthy's Cubs in the 1929 World Series opener. Ehmke had a 7–2 record for the Philadelphia A's that season, but he had started only eight games, completing only two. Then thirty-five years old, the lanky right-hander had pitched only fifty-four and two-thirds innings before Mack assigned him to scout the Cubs, who had mostly righthanded hitters. Ehmke struck out thirteen, then a World Series record, in a 3–1 eight-hitter. Galehouse fell into the Ehmke mold. He hadn't started since September 18 in St. Louis when the Browns knocked him out in a four-run fourth. In his previous start against the Indians, on August 25 at Fenway, he had been knocked out in a four-run second. He hadn't won since August 11 when he stopped the A's in Fenway. Now he had been selected by McCarthy to pitch the Red Sox to the pennant. But at his locker, Ted Williams had accepted McCarthy's choice. "I didn't give managing a thought," he would say years later. "I didn't think about our pitcher. I was only thinking about who the Indians' pitcher would be." The Red Sox still didn't know the Indians' starter. McCarthy had dispatched clubhouse man Johnny Orlando to the Indians' clubhouse as a spy. Orlando knew that Indian trainer Lefty Weisman always put a ball under the cap in the starting pitcher's locker. But in the hours before today's playoff, on Boudreau's orders, Weisman had put a ball under several pitchers' caps.

"Are you starting?" Orlando asked Bob Lemon.

"I got a ball under my cap, don't I?" Lemon said.

"No, I'm starting," Bob Feller said.

"How can you both be starting?" Orlando asked.

"There's a ball under my cap too," Feller said.

The Red Sox didn't know Bearden was starting until the lean lefthander began to warm up. But when the Indians saw Galehouse warming up, Boudreau thought McCarthy was trying to fool him into stacking his lineup with lefthanded hitters, then, after the first Indians' batter, McCarthy would bring in Parnell.

"Go under the stands," Boudreau told traveling secretary Spud Goldstein. "See if Parnell's warming up somewhere."

Goldstein searched, but none of the other Red Sox pitchers were warming up under the stands. Galehouse was really the starter. His success would depend on his control. He wasn't sharp. With a two-and-one count on Boudreau in the first, he tried to clip the outside corner with a curve that hung. Boudreau lifted it to leftfield. Williams took a few steps in, realized that the wind was blowing the ball toward the Wall, then watched it drop into the net for a home run. After the Red Sox retaliated with a run, Boudreau led off the fourth with a single. Gordon singled. Keltner slammed his thirty-first homer into the net above the Wall for a 4–1 lead.

"Keltner liked to lean over the plate," Galehouse remembered. "I threw inside. Not at him, just to straighten him up. But he had a quick bat and he got around on it. That was my last pitch."

McCarthy called for Kinder, who was stung for another run on Larry Doby's double, Bob Kennedy's bunt, and Jim Hegan's ground out. In the fifth Boudreau hit Kinder's change-up into the screen. Boudreau would add another single as Bearden's knuckleball kept the Red Sox off balance for his twentieth victory, 6–3, a five-hitter with six strikeouts. At the final out, the Indians lifted Bearden onto their shoulders and carried him to the dugout. Although his teammates had known that Bearden would start, he had been almost as much of a surprise as Galehouse.

"I didn't tell anybody Bearden would pitch because I didn't want him to be bothered," Boudreau said. "I should have known better. He could have posed all night for photographers and still won."

Joining in the Indians' clubhouse celebration was Brave outfielder

Gene Bearden's eyes reflect the Indians' pennant joy with manager Lou Boudreau (center) and third baseman Ken Keltner. *AP/Wide World Photo*

Jeff Heath, hobbling around on crutches as his ex-teammates autographed the cast on his left leg. "Now that we won," said Berardino, his onetime Indians roommate, "your World Series share will be bigger." As the Indians celebrated into the night at the Kenmore Hotel, nobody was enjoying the pennant more than Boudreau's dugout guru, sixty-two-year-old coach Bill McKechnie.

"It never gets old," he said. "It never gets old."

But the Deacon, like the other Indian coaches, was already looking ahead to Wednesday's opener of the World Series, which the Indians would win in six games.

"Let's get out of here," McKechnie said. "Let's go over and take a look at that other ballpark."

In the Red Sox clubhouse, Johnny Pesky was staring at his Navy officer's uniform. "Yesterday they said it brought us luck, today it didn't," he said. "All those superstitions are the bunk." Galehouse looked up to see Tom Yawkey, the Red Sox owner, who was shaking hands with each of his players. "I'm sorry I let you down," Galehouse said.

"All anybody can do is their best," Yawkey said. "I know you always do that, Denny."

In the manager's office, McCarthy wouldn't explain why he had chosen Galehouse rather than Parnell, Kinder, or Kramer as his starting pitcher. When one of the writers suggested that the Red Sox players had a history of not rising to the occasion in a big game, McCarthy looked up.

"Please don't say that," he snapped. "Say that I didn't have a good day if you want to. But don't say anything about our players. They gave their best as they always do."

Their best wasn't quite good enough. Yes, the Red Sox had been two games behind with only three to play and had won them all to force the first one-game pennant playoff in major league history. But now they had lost the playoff. Now their fans would be wondering for decades why Joe McCarthy had started Denny Galehouse.

"There's only one way to prevent a playoff," Tom Yawkey was saying now in the clubhouse. "That's to win by twenty games. The way I hope we do next year."

The Joe DiMaggio Theater

After his fourth homer against the Red Sox, Joe DiMaggio is greeted by Tommy Henrich (15) and George Stirnweiss (1).
AP/Wide World Photo

JOE DiMaggio had signed baseball's first $100,000 contract in 1949, but ten weeks into the schedule he had not earned a penny. Even before the Yankees assembled in St. Petersburg, Florida, for spring training, he complained that his right heel felt "like it had a nail" in it. During a Dallas exhibition game about a week before the opener, he limped to the dugout.

"The pain's unbearable," he said.

Dr. George Bennett, the Baltimore orthopedist who had performed bone spur surgery on the heel several months earlier, recommended X-ray treatments and salt injections to dissolve calcium deposits. But the season had begun with DiMaggio on crutches, wearing a camel's hair coat instead of his pin-striped uniform. The healing process had continued to be slow. Now, in the Yankee clubhouse at Fenway Park before a June 28 night game, manager Casey Stengel, surrounded by New York and Boston sportswriters, was waiting to learn if his thirty-four-year-old centerfielder was finally ready to play.

"If he tells me he can play, he'll play," Stengel said.

"Why didn't he come up today on the train with the team?"

"He stayed in New York this morning to see if he could find a trick shoe to take some of the strain off his heel. He took an afternoon plane."

"How's he looked in batting practice?"

"He's been working out now about a week and a half and he says it feels pretty good," Stengel said. "We told him from the first to do it his way. You don't have to worry about a man like him. He'll give it to you when he's got it. The real trouble with a man like him is keeping him from trying to do too much too soon."

Joe DiMaggio had not yet earned any of his $100,000 salary, but he had earned Casey Stengel's description as "a man like him."

Over his Hall of Fame career, the stately slugger known as the

Yankee Clipper would hit .325 with 361 homers and 1,537 runs batted in despite Yankee Stadium's vast valley in left-centerfield, despite losing three seasons during World War II to Army service. In 1941 he had hit safely in a record fifty-six consecutive games. One of eight children of an Italian immigrant fisherman, he had a sixty-one-game streak with his hometown San Francisco Seals of the Pacific Coast League in 1933 as an eighteen-year-old rookie. But the true measure of his importance to the Yankees was their success. In his thirteen seasons, the Yankees would win nine World Series and ten American League pennants. With his dignified manner and dignified dark suits, white shirts, silk ties, and glossy black shoes, he popularized the word *class* in baseball.

"When he walked into the clubhouse," Yankee clubhouse man Pete Sheehy once said, "the lights flickered."

Now, with Casey Stengel talking to the writers in the Fenway Park clubhouse, Joe DiMaggio arrived. As he changed into his uniform, he realized that the manager was peering at him through a gap in the writers. Peering back, DiMaggio caught Stengel's gaze and nodded. As if on cue, Stengel looked around at the writers.

"I've just been told the man can play," he said. "So he's in the lineup, batting fourth."

Not that anybody was expecting much. The night before, after more than a week of batting practice mostly against Al Schacht, the former major league pitcher and baseball clown who owned a midtown Manhattan restaurant, DiMaggio had popped up four times against Kirby Higbe's knuckleball in a mayor's charity exhibition game with the New York Giants at Yankee Stadium. And tonight he would be facing the flaming fastball of Mickey McDermott, a rookie lefthander with a 2–0 record who had blanked the St. Louis Browns on three hits in his previous start.

"Not the ideal pitcher to come back against," DiMaggio told teammate Tommy Henrich. "I haven't faced a lefthander since spring training."

But on his flight to Boston, he had explained to a friend, Dick Allen, a Boston businessman, that he intended to play because of Fenway Park's nearby leftfield wall, alias the Green Monster, alias the Wall.

"You don't get a chance to swing at that wall too often," DiMaggio said. "I've already missed three of our eleven games in Fenway this year."

Even without DiMaggio, the Yankees were in first place with a 41–

24 start, four and one-half games ahead of the Philadelphia Athletics, five games ahead of the Red Sox. But with ten victories in their last eleven games, if this Red Sox team managed by Joe McCarthy, whose Yankees had won seven World Series and eight pennants, could sweep the three-game series, the race would be on. That hope had attracted 36,228 customers, a Fenway Park record for a night game. Quietly, all those Red Sox rooters were hoping that if DiMaggio was rusty, the Yankees might slump. But when he walked up to the plate to lead off the second inning, he received a standing ovation from the Red Sox fans, who always seemed to admire him as much as Yankee fans did.

"McDermott kept throwing his fastball and I kept fouling them off, swinging late," he would say years later. "I must've fouled off six or seven pitches."

On the next swing, DiMaggio drilled a single into leftfield and scored on Hank Bauer's three-run homer. The next inning, he slammed a two-run homer into the net atop the Wall for a 5–4 lead. But with two out in the ninth, Ted Williams was up.

"Joe would appreciate it," catcher Yogi Berra said to Williams, "if you would end this game by hitting a nice easy fly."

Williams did just that, lifting a fly ball to center that DiMaggio caught. "That fly was hit just right to catch," DiMaggio said later. "Ted sometimes hits sinkers which are tough, but this one had a nice loft to it." And the Yankee slugger's voice had a nice lilt to it. "My legs tightened up on me in the late innings. The heel doesn't bother me now, but it probably will in the morning." If it did, it didn't affect him in Wednesday afternoon's game. After the Red Sox knocked out left-hander Tommy Byrne in the first and took a 7–1 lead, DiMaggio hit a three-run homer in the fifth off righthander Ellis Kinder just over the top of the Wall into the screen.

"Flukiest homer I've ever hit," DiMaggio would remember. "He threw me a pitch that broke on the outside. I was fooled, but with two strikes I was protecting the plate. I just tried to get a piece of it. If a bird had been perched on the fence above the 379-foot sign, the ball would've hit it."

Usually stoic, DiMaggio was smiling as he approached home plate, maybe because of that "flukiest" homer. Charlie Silvera, the next batter, greeted him at the plate. So did base runners Phil Rizzuto and Tommy Henrich, who draped their arms around him as they trotted to the dugout. Gene Woodling's three-run double in the seventh created a 7–7 tie, then DiMaggio hit another homer in the eighth off lefthander Earl Johnson.

"That was off a curveball," DiMaggio remembered. "It hung there waiting to be smacked."

After that 9–7 victory, one of the Yankees welcomed the Boston writers with "Here come the undertakers from the Red Sox burial." And the Red Sox would lose again Thursday, 6–3, when DiMaggio hit another three-run homer, a towering shot in the seventh off lefthander Mel Parnell that clanged against a metal light tower in left-centerfield above his youngest brother, Red Sox centerfielder Dom DiMaggio.

"On that one," DiMaggio recalled, "I really caught all of it."

Over the three games, DiMaggio hit four homers and a single, scored five runs, and knocked in nine. All this after having missed the first ten weeks of the season. All this against the rival Red Sox in their own ballpark.

"I really surprised myself," DiMaggio would say years later. "We shocked 'em. They didn't say a word. Not even my brother."

Suddenly the Yankees had opened an eight-game lead on the third-place Red Sox, and Joe DiMaggio had opened Williams's old wounds.

"The Red Sox," *Boston Herald* sports columnist Bill Cunningham wrote after the second game, "have no one great dynamic personality who can lift them bodily by his very presence and his tremendous performance. In short, they have no Joe DiMaggio. He's a pressure player, a money player and a clutch player. Anytime he walks up to the plate, the game walks up there with him. The Red Sox counterpart is Ted Williams and the record is beginning to say in disturbing repetition that Mr. Williams does not come through in the clutch. Not against major opposition. Not when the blow means the lead or the game. He didn't do it in the 1946 World Series. He didn't do it in the all-important playoff game with Cleveland last year. He didn't do it [in this series]. This is no attempt to ride Mr. Williams. His batting average is always beautiful. His r.b.i.'s are impressive. He hits magnificent home runs. He generally gets on and he usually scores. But we're talking in terms of the prime Power Man who, even if crippled, can limp up there as New York's famed Yankee Clipper did and turn the contest around with a mighty swing of his mace. We're furthermore talking about the type of nonpareil who is expected to do it, who can be depended upon to do it. The Yankees have one, and they now have him back."

Williams was accustomed to being roasted by Dave Egan, the Boston *American*'s vitriolic sports columnist. But now, with Cunningham's words stuck in their slugger's craw, the Red Sox took a midnight train to Philadelphia where the loss of a July 4 doubleheader dropped them twelve games behind the Yankees.

Most people in Boston had surrendered, but Joe McCarthy hadn't. After those two losses in Philadelphia, the Red Sox manager said, "We can still win the pennant. I'm not saying we're going to, but we can." Even though his pennant-winning Yankee teams with Babe Ruth, Lou Gehrig, and Joe DiMaggio had usually torn the American League apart by September, cigar-smoking Marse Joe had always been too successful to surrender. He knew he had a team good enough to win, virtually the same team that had lost a pennant playoff to the Cleveland Indians the year before. Williams, Dom DiMaggio, and Al Zarilla in the outfield. Billy Goodman at first base, future Hall of Famer Bobby Doerr at second, slugger Vern Stephens at shortstop, Johnny Pesky at third. Birdie Tebbetts catching Mel Parnell, Ellis Kinder, Joe Dobson, and Chuck Stobbs. And soon McCarthy's patience was rewarded; the Red Sox surged. Even when they lost a September 11 doubleheader in Philadelphia, McCarthy wasn't discouraged.

"Whether we won or lost today didn't make much difference," he said. "We'd still have to beat the Yankees in those five games at the end of the season."

Those five games: two in Boston on September 24 and 25, a makeup game in New York the next day, and the final two in New York on October 2 and 3. But if those five games were to mean anything, the Red Sox had to be within striking distance by then. Although the Yankees' spirits had been lifted by DiMaggio, relief lefthander Joe Page and shortstop Phil Rizzuto had kept them atop the standings.

"The Yankees have pitching, and they have Joe Page," said Zack Taylor, the St. Louis Browns' manager. "If Joe McCarthy had Page, the Red Sox would be ten games in front."

Joe Page had emerged in 1947 after a scolding by DiMaggio for his nocturnal habits. Pitching poorly, Page appeared on his way back to the minors. To console himself after a bad game, he stayed out long after midnight before returning to the hotel room he shared with DiMaggio.

"What the hell are you doing?" DiMaggio had snapped. "The way you live, you're letting the team down and you're letting yourself down."

Page's world turned. That season he produced a 14–8 record with a 2.48 earned run average and seventeen saves. In the 1947 World Series against the Brooklyn Dodgers, he was credited with the victory in the decisive seventh game after having saved another triumph. In 1948 he skidded to 7–8 with a 4.26 earned run average, creating the since disproved theory that a relief pitcher cannot be effective two years in a row. But in 1949, when Americans hummed the songs from Rodgers and Hammerstein's *South Pacific*, he would have a 13–8 record with a 2.59 earned run average and twenty-seven saves. He would never be this good again, but now, as the Yankees moved through September, he was the man coming out of the bullpen whenever starters Vic Raschi, Allie Reynolds, Ed Lopat, or Tommy Byrne faltered.

"Joe Page," said Casey Stengel, "is a relief pitcher who provides relief."

Phil Rizzuto provided other elements: sure hands on a ground ball, an accurate arm, an underrated bat, deft bunts, and flawless base running. At five-six and 150 pounds, he had grown up in Brooklyn but was dismissed as too small at Dodger and Giant tryouts. Casey Stengel, then the Dodger manager, told him, "Go get a shoeshine box." But a Yankee scout, Paul Krichell, signed Rizzuto and now, ironically, Stengel was the Yankee manager.

"I wouldn't want you to repeat this to my owners," Stengel told the writers, "but I'd gladly pay my way around the circuit following this team just to watch my shortstop perform. He can do everything. He makes unbelievable plays. He can hit a long ball when he wants to. He can beat out bunts to both sides of the plate. One or two shortstops may beat him in the RBI column, but that's all. He leads in every other department."

Rizzuto would bat .275 and score 110 runs as a leadoff man for the first time in his career, one of Stengel's many moves in showing that he was more manager than comedian.

When the Yankees finished third in 1948, general manager George Weiss fired Bucky Harris and hired Stengel, who would be the most famous manager in this famous franchise's history: seven World Series titles (including a record five straight) and ten pennants in his twelve seasons. But the choice surprised most baseball people. In nine seasons directing the Dodgers and the Boston Braves, his teams had finished as high as fifth only twice. In his twelve seasons as a minor league manager, his teams had won only two pennants, twenty years apart. At the Yankee news conference announcing his hiring, fifty-eight-year-old Charles Dillon Stengel justified his reputation.

"I want first of all," he began, "to thank Mr. Bob Topping for this opportunity."

Dan Topping was the Yankee co-owner, not his brother Bob, but the mix-up was understandable. Bob was in the headlines then for his marital problems with Arlene Judge, the film actress who had once been Dan's wife. Not that Dan Topping was annoyed. He laughed along with everybody else. Laughter was to become the most common reaction to the Yankee manager over the next twelve seasons. Laughter at his syntax. Laughter at his philosophy. And his laughter on his way to the bank with all those World Series shares. But in 1949 he had not yet convinced anybody that he was a shrewd manager.

"There'll be some changes, but we'll go slow," he said. "You can tear down a club a lot quicker than you can build it up."

Stengel's primary change was installing a platoon system, notably with Bobby Brown and Billy Johnson at third base, with Hank Bauer and Gene Woodling in the outfield. Stengel believed that righthanded batters hit better against lefthanded pitchers, and lefthanded batters against righthanded pitchers. The players didn't agree, but they couldn't disagree with the results: the Yankees were in first place. And sometimes even the players agreed that Stengel had a mystic touch.

"In the middle of one game," Bauer remembered, "the old man put Cliff Mapes in rightfield, moved me to leftfield, and we both threw a guy out at the plate. But he never told us who was playing and who wasn't. We had to check the lineup card every day."

Stengel's lineup card also had future Hall of Fame catcher Yogi Berra, whose throwing had been polished by coach Bill Dickey, a Hall of Fame catcher himself. In one of his first inspired one-liners, Berra acknowledged, "Bill Dickey learned me his experience." Nobody had to learn Berra how to hit. He would wallop twenty homers and drive in ninety-one runs. Tommy Henrich, moved to first base from right-field after DiMaggio's return, would whack twenty-four homers and knock in eighty-five runs. Henrich had been impressed with Stengel early in the season on a train about to leave Philadelphia after a loss. Even before the train pulled out, four Yankees were sitting around playing "Twenty Questions," then a popular radio game show. But when Stengel realized what the four players were doing, he glared.

"I got a question for you guys," the new manager snapped. "Which one of you ain't going to be here tomorrow?"

But on September 18, with the Red Sox now only two and one-half games behind, the Yankees had gathered for a Sunday afternoon game with the Indians when they learned that DiMaggio was ill. He remained in his Elysee Hotel suite that he shared with his good friend George Solotaire, a New York ticket broker. Up in Boston that afternoon the Red Sox routed the Chicago White Sox, 11–5. Williams hit his thirty-ninth and fortieth homers and drove in 6 runs for a total of 153, Vern Stephens hit his fortieth homer for 150 runs batted in, and Ellis Kinder coasted to his twenty-first victory. But the Yankees also won, 7–3, with Joe Page pitching the last three innings.

"DiMaggio is running a high fever," Yankee publicist Arthur (Red) Patterson told the writers. "He might miss tomorrow's game too."

It was more than a high fever. Soon the diagnosis was changed to the flu, then to viral pneumonia. "I'd flood the sheets with perspiration," DiMaggio would say years later. "The chambermaid had to redo the bed every few hours." Monday, with the Red Sox idle, lefthander Ed Lopat, who relied on junk-ball pitches, stopped the Indians, 6–0, on a five-hitter. The Yankees were three games up. Tuesday the Yankees won again, 3–1, as Page preserved Allie Reynolds's 17–5 record. The Red Sox won, 5–3, after Joe McCarthy disrupted Bob Lemon's no-hit bid by complaining to plate umpire Cal Hubbard that the Indian righthander was fingering the peak of his cap between pitches.

"Look at his cap," McCarthy demanded.

Soon after Hubbard ordered Lemon to discard his sweat-stained cap for a new one, Mel Parnell's sixth-inning single spoiled Lemon's no-hitter and sparked a five-run rally. Parnell's twenty-fourth victory tied the Red Sox record for a lefthander set by Babe Ruth, who was 24–13 in 1917 before switching to the outfield. At dinner that night in a Boston restaurant, Lemon noticed a gray fedora behind the bar.

"Who's hat is that?" Lemon asked.

"Tom Yawkey left it here one night," the bartender said.

"Let me borrow it for a day."

When the next day's game was about to start, Lemon, wearing the gray fedora instead of his Indian cap, sauntered behind home plate and stared at Hubbard.

"This cap all right?" Lemon asked.

"Fine," the umpire said, smiling.

That afternoon the Red Sox, after trailing 3–1, rallied to win, 9–6, on Williams's forty-first homer into their bullpen off Steve Gromek. When the Boston writers arrived in the Red Sox clubhouse, Williams stared at Bill Cunningham.

"Can't hit in the clutch?" Williams said with a sneer.

That afternoon in New York the Yankees had taken an early 8–1 lead. All the Red Sox players had left their clubhouse by the time equipment manager Johnny Orlando hurried into McCarthy's office.

"The White Sox beat the Yanks, nine to eight," Orlando said. "Gus Zernial hit a three-run homer off Page in the ninth."

Calmly flicking the ashes off his cigar, McCarthy looked up and said, "What am I supposed to do? Jump out of my chair?" Even though Page had failed, for a change, McCarthy knew that he had nobody in his bullpen like the Yankee lefthander. To preserve that afternoon's victory, McCarthy had used his ace righthander and legendary drinker, Ellis Kinder, for the last three innings. Credited with the victory, Kinder was now 22–5. Since the Red Sox were not scheduled Thursday and Friday, he was still McCarthy's choice to start Saturday against the Yankees in the first of those five games that presumably would decide the pennant.

"I'll be ready Saturday," he had said. "This was just a workout. The arm feels great. I only threw fifteen pitches in the bullpen."

Thursday the Yankees were rained out in Washington, creating a doubleheader Friday afternoon. They lost the opener, 9–8, in the tenth inning when righthander Sid Hudson's pop fly off Page fell between Henrich, who had backed off the ball, and second baseman George Stirnweiss, who lunged too late for it. The Yankees won the second game, 7–1, behind righthander Fred Sanford, so they remained two games up. But when they arrived in Boston the next morning they were still without Joe DiMaggio.

"His temperature is nearly normal and his appetite is good," Dr. Jacques Fischl reported. "He's better, but he's not ready to play."

True to his word, Kinder was ready to pitch. His six-hitter blanked the Yankees, 3–0, as Williams slammed his forty-second homer twenty-six rows deep into the wing of the rightfield grandstand. With his curveball creating four called third strikes in his thirteenth consecutive victory, Kinder was now 23–5, including 4–0 against the Yankees, whose lead had been sliced to one game. But when McCarthy was congratulated, he shrugged.

"What for?" the Red Sox manager said. "It's just another game. There's another tomorrow."

Sunday's game produced another Red Sox victory, their ninth straight, and a tie for first place. Johnny Pesky slashed a double in the first, knocked in two runs with a single in the second, and his seventh-inning single off Allie Reynolds preceded Williams's forty-third homer. Parnell spun a four-hitter, 4–1, for a 25–7 record.

"You pitched a great game, boy," McCarthy said.

"Thank you, Mr. McCarthy," the lefthander said.

Up in the press box, Bill Cunningham began typing an apology to Ted Williams for what the *Herald* sports columnist had written

Ted Williams and Ellis Kinder. *UPI Photo*

about him during DiMaggio's midseason return. In the clubhouse, the photographers were asking Williams to pose with Parnell and Pesky.

"Just one shot," the slugger told them.

After the first flashbulb popped, Williams turned and strode to his locker. Soon the Red Sox were boarding a train at the Back Bay station for Monday's makeup game at Yankee Stadium, the start of the season's final week. When the Red Sox went on to Washington for three games, the Yankees would remain at the Stadium for three against Philadelphia. Then they would finish the season Saturday and Sunday in New York against each other. But now, with the two teams tied for first place, Monday's game attracted 66,156 to the House That Ruth Built, the Babe Ruth the Red Sox had sold to the Yankees in 1920, the Babe Ruth whose departure from Boston created the title of Dan Shaughnessy's 1990 book about the Red Sox' frustrations, *The Curse of the Bambino*.

With first place at stake, Monday's pitchers were Mickey McDermott and Tommy Byrne, two wild lefthanders, in what developed into a wild game.

To protect a 6–3 lead, Stengel called for Page in the fifth, but by the eighth the lefthander had lost his fastball. Tebbetts led off with a single, and pinch hitter Lou Stringer walked. Dom DiMaggio singled off Rizzuto's glove for one run. When Stirnweiss muffed Pesky's grounder, another run scored. Williams's grounder was ruled a hit when Page forgot to cover first. Stephens's sacrifice fly drove in the tying run. Doerr dropped a squeeze-play bunt toward Henrich, who threw to catcher Ralph Houk, but plate umpire Bill Grieve ruled Pesky safe. Houk and Stengel protested so vigorously that umpire Cal Hubbard had to push them away.

After the 7–6 loss dropped the Yankees a game behind, outfielder Cliff Mapes yelled at Grieve, "How much did you have on the game?"

Grieve whirled. "There's never been an umpire found guilty of anything like the ballplayers, throwing games and like that," he shouted, alluding to the Black Sox scandal. "You . . . ," but Cal Hubbard and Charley Berry moved him toward the umpires' room.

Mapes would be fined $200 by American League president Will Harridge and ordered to apologize to Grieve, which he did. Houk and Stengel each were fined $150 for their outbursts. Houk kept insisting that he had blocked Pesky from the plate. Pesky disagreed.

"Houk seemed to have frozen for an instant," the Red Sox third baseman said. "When he did tag me, it was on the hip after my feet had touched the plate."

Virtually forgotten were rightfielder Al Zarilla's two sensational catches. With two on in the second, he leaped high above the 344-foot sign on the low rightfield wall to snatch Johnny Lindell's slicing drive. In the ninth he made a diving, toppling catch of Henrich's low liner to help Kinder preserve the victory. The day before, Zarilla had nailed Henrich at the plate with a perfect on-the-fly throw to Tebbetts. With what would be a .277 average and ten homers, Zarilla had more than justified McCarthy's appraisal of him as a "hustling, lively type of player who can run and throw" after his May 5 arrival from the Browns in a trade for outfielder Stan Spence and $100,000.

Tuesday afternoon Vic Raschi dominated the A's, 3–1, for his twentieth win. That night the Red Sox, prevented from taking batting practice by a steady drizzle in Griffith Stadium, strafed the Senators with twelve hits, 6–4.

Wednesday the Yankees won again, 7–5, on Rizzuto's squeeze bunt off lefthander Alex Kellner for the go-ahead run. Before that game, Joe DiMaggio, pale and drawn after losing eighteen pounds in his slow recovery from viral pneumonia, took batting practice. He was hoping to be ready for the two weekend games with the Red Sox at the Stadium, especially the Saturday opener, which would be "Joe DiMaggio Day." Still weak, he took only fifteen swings, hitting only one ball into the leftfield stands. He hurried to the clubhouse.

"I'm going right back to my hotel and rest, but I'll be out again tomorrow," he said. "At the end of that workout, it felt as if the bat was swinging me."

In Washington, the Red Sox had put together a run against right-hander Ray Scarborough, their 1948 nemesis. They were hoping to protect that 1–0 lead as Chuck Stobbs went to the mound for the ninth, but singles by Roberto Ortiz, Eddie Robinson, and Al Kozar tied the score. McCarthy waved to his bullpen for Kinder as Parnell continued to warm up. Sam Dente's single loaded the bases, then Senator manager Joe Kuhel sent up Buddy Lewis, a lefthanded batter, as a pinch hitter. McCarthy called for Parnell.

With a one-one count, Tebbetts suspected a squeeze play, signaled for a pitchout, and tagged Robinson for the second out as Kozar moved to third. With a ball and two strikes on Lewis, Parnell's curve-ball bounced away from Tebbetts for a wild pitch as Kozar scored. The Red Sox had lost, 2–1.

On hearing that score, Tommy Henrich knew the Yankees had a chance. Not only had the Red Sox dropped into a tie for first place again, but two Senators involved in that rally, outfielder Al Kozar and shortstop Sam Dente, had once been Red Sox teammates, along with two other Senators, outfielder Sam Mele and lefthander Mickey Harris. "Tomorrow," Harris promised, "I'll beat 'em myself." Thursday it rained in both Washington and New York, postponing Harris's opportunity until Friday and altering the Athletics' pitching.

When the A's assistant manager, fifty-nine-year-old Earle Mack, the son of owner-manager Connie Mack, received several telegrams and letters criticizing his naming Phil Marchildon as Friday's pitcher, he announced that Dick Fowler would start.

"They aren't going to point any fingers at us," Earle Mack said. "Look at all these letters and telegrams. They even accuse us of lying down. It's damned nasty terrible stuff. We'll try to keep these letters from Dad, but I think he did see some of them."

Still wearing the high starched collar popular at the turn of the century, eighty-six-year-old Connie Mack had returned to Philadelphia with an upset stomach. Although Earle Mack had played only five major league games as a catcher–first baseman–third baseman, all for his father's team, he had been an A's coach for decades.

"Some of these letters," Earle Mack said, "even say we're not trying because Dad gave out a story one day picking the Yankees to win."

Marchildon had a 19–9 record in 1947 for the A's, but a sore arm had contributed to his 0–3 record for the fifth-place A's in 1949, provoking the telegrams and letters. He hadn't pitched for nearly three months before returning in late August. In his second start, he didn't last the first inning as the Red Sox scored five quick runs. Fowler had been knocked out by the Yankees in the third inning of Tuesday's game but he had a respectable 14–11 record.

"If Fowler can't do the job," Earle Mack said, "Carl Scheib will be next. And if Fowler and Scheib can't stop them, we'll come in with Bobby Shantz, Lou Brissie, and Joe Coleman."

Fowler did the job. He completed a four-hitter, 4–1, after first baseman Ferris Fain hit a three-run homer off Lopat in the third. "That shows 'em," Earle Mack said. "I just tore up a telegram that said, 'Don't pitch tired Fowler. Use your ace, Kellner.' " In Washington, meanwhile, McCarthy had to use his ace, Ellis Kinder, in relief to assure an 11–9 victory after Mickey Harris and the other Senator pitchers had issued fourteen walks. In the ninth Kinder was strafed for two doubles and a single before he walked two to load the bases with one out, but he got Sam Mele to bounce into a game-ending double play.

As the Red Sox hurried for their train to New York, they again had a one-game lead. All they needed was a victory either Saturday or Sunday out of these pitching matchups: Parnell-Reynolds, Kinder-Raschi.

But the question the Yankees couldn't answer yet was: Would Joe DiMaggio play and if he did, how well would he play? Before Thursday's game had been rained out, he reported, "I feel much better." Friday he took batting practice again and announced, "I might be able to play." Not long after DiMaggio arrived for Saturday's game, Stengel asked, "Can you take one turn at bat?"

"Sure," he said. "I'll try to play three innings."

DiMaggio took batting practice. To stay warm in the cloudy chill during the Joe DiMaggio Day ceremonies, he wore his navy blue Yankee jacket as he stood with his seven-year-old son, Joe, Jr., near home plate for nearly an hour. Two of his brothers, Dom in his Red Sox uniform and Tom, stood behind him. When their mother, Rosalie, was introduced, she walked past Joe and hugged Dom.

"I saw Joseph yesterday," she explained later. "I hadn't seen Dominic."

With his words booming out of the scoreboard loudspeakers, the Yankee Clipper acknowledged the gifts: an automobile for himself and another for his mother, a twenty-two-foot Chris Craft powerboat, and dozens of other presents. He would donate nearly $50,000 in cash gifts to the Damon Runyon Cancer Fund and the New York Heart Fund. Then he looked around at the 69,551 spectators.

"When I was in San Francisco," he said, "Lefty O'Doul told me, 'Joe, don't let the big city scare you. New York is the friendliest town in the world.' This day proves it. I want to thank the fans, my friends, my manager Casey Stengel and my teammates, the gamest fightingest bunch that ever lived. And I want to thank the good Lord for making me a Yankee."

He turned toward Joe McCarthy, who had presented him with a scroll signed by the Red Sox.

"They're a grand bunch too," he said. "If we don't win the pennant, I'm happy that they will."

Soon the game was on. The Red Sox jumped on Reynolds for a quick 1–0 lead. Dom DiMaggio singled. Williams singled. DiMaggio moved to third on a wild pitch and scored on Stephens's fly to left. With one out in the third, Reynolds, overthrowing in his determination, walked Pesky, Williams, and Stephens before Bobby Doerr sliced a single past second baseman Jerry Coleman for a 2–0 lead. Stengel didn't hesitate. He waved to the bullpen for Page even though it was only the third inning. At the mound Stengel stared at him.

"How far can you go?"

"A long way," Page said.

"Then get going."

Page walked Zarilla, forcing in a run. He also walked Goodman, forcing in another run. But the husky lefthander's rising fastball struck out Tebbetts and Parnell. With the Yankees trailing, 4–0, DiMaggio trotted in from centerfield, caught Stengel's eye in the dugout, held up his right hand, and waved five fingers: he would play through the fifth inning.

As the Red Sox moved to their positions with a four-run lead and Parnell pitching, they could almost taste the champagne stored in a Stadium Club refrigerator. Especially the talkative Tebbetts.

When Rizzuto fouled off a pitch in the bottom of the third, he heard Tebbetts say, "Tonight we'll be drinking champagne and tomorrow we'll pitch the Yale kid. Think you can hit a kid from Yale, Rizzuto?" During the season the Red Sox had signed righthander Frank Quinn off the Yale campus. In eight appearances, Quinn had worked a total of only twenty-two innings, all after games had been decided. Deterred by arm trouble, Quinn would never win a game in the majors (or lose one, for that matter), but the Yankees were angered by the wisecrack they remember although Tebbetts doesn't.

In the dugout, Rizzuto grumbled, "That Tebbetts, you know what he told me: that their Yale kid will be pitching tomorrow." His teammates had never seen him so furious.

"It wasn't like Phil created a pep rally," Henrich would say years later. "But it was something that annoyed us, it maybe helped us put some runs together against Parnell."

In the fourth, Joe DiMaggio, who had fanned in the first, sliced a ground-rule double into the rightfield stands. Johnson struck out, but Bauer singled, and the Yankees finally had a run. Bauer moved to third on Lindell's long single and scored on Coleman's fly ball to Dom DiMaggio to make it 4–2. In the fifth Rizzuto opened with a single. Henrich bounced a grounder toward the mound. Another pitcher might have turned it into a double play, but the ball skidded through Parnell for an infield hit. Berra's single scored Rizzuto and, with Joe DiMaggio up, McCarthy called for righthander Joe Dobson.

DiMaggio slashed the ball back at Dobson. Again, another pitcher might have turned the hot grounder into a double play, but the ball skidded off Dobson's glove and rolled onto the grass behind the mound. DiMaggio beat it out. With the bases loaded, McCarthy preferred to keep his infielders in their normal position. Johnson bounced into a double play as Henrich hurried across the plate, tying the score at 4–4. When the inning ended, DiMaggio's five innings supposedly were up but he never even looked at Stengel in the dugout. He hopped up the concrete steps and trotted to centerfield.

Page and Dobson maintained the 4–4 tie into the eighth. Hoping that lefthanded pinch hitters might have better success against Dobson's curveball, Stengel had Bobby Brown bat for Johnson and Cliff Mapes bat for Bauer, but the Red Sox righthander got them out.

With Johnny Lindell the next batter, Stengel had another lefthanded pinch hitter available, Charlie Keller, but the manager decided to let Lindell swing. As a righthanded batter, Lindell was in the lineup only because Parnell had been the Red Sox starter. Over the season the thirty-three-year-old leftfielder hadn't done much except annoy general manager George Weiss with his nocturnal adventures as the club rogue.

"I wish," Lindell often said, "that Weiss would give me all the money he spends to have detectives follow me around."

For all his size and strength at six-four and 217 pounds, Lindell was batting only .238 with only five homers and only twenty-six runs batted in. Once a successful righthanded knuckleball pitcher in the Yankee farm system (23–4 at Newark in 1941), he had been transferred to the outfield two years later by Joe McCarthy, then the Yankee manager. In 1944 he hit .300 for the Yankees with eighteen homers and 103 runs batted in, but in Stengel's platoon system, he was only a part-time player. This was only his seventy-eighth game of the season, only his sixty-fifth in the outfield. Now, as Lindell dug into the batter's box, Tebbetts called for a high fastball.

Dobson pitched. Lindell swung. The ball rose higher and higher, soared over Williams's head and landed in the lower leftfield stands. Home run.

"It's all McCarthy's fault," Lindell later told the Boston writers. "When I came up to the Yankees, he switched me to the outfield."

The Yankees were ahead, 5–4, and after Joe Page mowed down the Red Sox in the ninth, the two teams were tied for first place. Despite their disappointment, the Red Sox knew that they could still win the pennant by taking tomorrow's season finale. And for all of the Yankees' elation in their clubhouse, they knew that they still had to win tomorrow.

"It's not done yet," Joe DiMaggio kept telling his teammates. "Don't forget that. It's not done yet. We've got to win tomorrow."

DiMaggio was smiling. His double and single had generated the pair of two-run innings that erased the 4–0 deficit, and he had remained in centerfield for all nine innings. But he was weary. "I was just playing from inning to inning," he told the writers. "The last few outs my shinbones were getting cramped. My legs feel hard and swollen." In his small office off the clubhouse, Stengel, wearing only his gray sweatshirt, said, "That DiMaggio is a wonder. How about him playing the whole game?" But now the writers were asking questions.

"Who's your starter tomorrow?"

"It'll be Raschi tomorrow, and it'll be Reynolds tomorrow, and it'll be Page tomorrow."

"Who's your starter in the World Series opener?"

With an exaggerated wink, Stengel said, "There will be a slight delay on that one." In the Red Sox clubhouse, nobody was joking with Joe McCarthy about his World Series starter. At his locker Williams looked up when he realized some of the Boston writers had just walked over from the Yankee clubhouse.

"Who's pitching for them?" Williams asked.

Reading from his notebook, one of the writers said, "Stengel told us, 'It'll be Raschi tomorrow, and it'll be Reynolds tomorrow, and it'll be Page tomorrow.' " Hearing that, Pesky smiled.

"How about Lopat?" he said.

Vic Raschi, known as the Springfield Rifle because he grew up in that western Massachusetts city, didn't throw quite as hard as Reynolds, but hard enough. Swarthy and often silent, the thirty-year-old righthander was a tough competitor. Asked once by pitching coach Jim Turner how he intended to pitch to a certain hitter, he replied, "Hard." Although never so hard as to throw at a hitter's head. As a youngster, his brother Eugene had been blinded when beaned in a sandlot game. That memory haunted the Yankee righthander. But for him Sunday's showdown had a hard meaning. The year before, he had been bypassed by manager Bucky Harris during the final crucial weekend in Boston after having lost all four of his starts against the Red Sox that season. Ignoring Raschi's 19–8 record, Harris had used rookie Bob Porterfield, who didn't survive the third inning as the Yankees were eliminated.

With the 1949 pennant at stake, Stengel never thought about not starting Raschi, just as McCarthy never thought about not starting Ellis Kinder.

Coincidentally, in that final series with the Yankees the year before, Kinder had been bypassed when McCarthy chose Joe Dobson to start the Saturday game. But now Kinder was the American League's best pitcher, and its most surprising success story. Out of the hills around Jackson, Tennessee, he spent World War II in the Army and didn't get to the big leagues with the Browns until 1946, when he was thirty-one. Traded to the Red Sox, he put together an ordinary 10–7 record in 1948. But as he took the subway downtown to the Commodore Hotel after Saturday's game, he had a 23–5 record, six shutouts, and a streak of thirteen victories. He was 7–2 against the Yankees over his career and 4–0 this season, including a 3–0 six-hitter in his previous start eight days earlier and two innings of shutout relief in Monday's makeup game. In his thirteen relief appearances, he had earned four saves. But his teammates knew he was their most devoted drinker. Devoted mostly to bourbon.

"Take him out tonight," Vern Stephens, who knew Kinder from the Browns, told Arthur Richman, a New York *Daily Mirror* sportswriter. "We don't want Ol' Folks doing anything different."

Around eleven o'clock that Saturday night, when Red Sox batboy Johnny Donovan checked the Commodore room that Kinder was sharing with Dobson, both pitchers were there. By midnight Dobson was alone. Kinder had departed to meet his friend Arthur Richman in one of the nearby Lexington Avenue bars close to the *Mirror* office.

"He didn't talk much about Sunday's game," Richman, later an executive with both the Mets and Yankees, would remember. "He hadn't lost in months. He had every confidence. We stayed out until the bars closed at four in the morning."

Kinder returned to the hotel with a female companion, got a few hours' sleep, phoned room service, and grunted, "Get some coffee up here." He took the Lexington Avenue subway to the 161st Street station with some of the early arrivals in the crowd of 68,055, then walked around to the players' entrance of Yankee Stadium, where he would be pitching the game that would decide the pennant. When his teammates saw him, they smiled. Ol' Folks looked perfectly natural: a little hung over, a little sleepy. Just like he had looked before every other start in his sensational streak. But in the Yankee first, leadoff man Phil Rizzuto slashed a liner down the leftfield line. The ball, hugging the base of the box seats, rolled into the rain gutter.

Running toward second base, Rizzuto realized that the ball had squirted out of the gutter past Williams. He hurried to third for a triple.

With the Red Sox infielders back in their normal positions on McCarthy's orders, Rizzuto knew he could score on an infield out. Henrich knew it too. He always had trouble hitting Kinder, whose pitches seemed to travel at nine different speeds. His plan was not to swing hard, to stay flat-footed, get in front of the pitch, and hit it to the right side. He bounced a grounder to Bobby Doerr who threw to Billy Goodman as Rizzuto raced across the plate for a 1–0 lead. With two out, Joe DiMaggio tripled, chugging into third base on his sore and swollen legs.

"I was puffing like a steam engine," he would say later.

Now, with Kinder about to pitch, DiMaggio started to take a short lead when he heard third-base umpire Bill Summers yell, "Time." DiMaggio retreated to the bag, wondering why time had been called and why Summers had taken a few steps toward him.

"I thought I'd give you a breather, Joe," the umpire said.

DiMaggio nodded his appreciation. Summers waved his arms. The game resumed. Through seven innings Rizzuto's run would be the only run as Kinder dueled Raschi for the pennant. With one out in the eighth and Kinder due to bat, McCarthy sent up Tom Wright as a pinch hitter. Wright, just up from the minors, had appeared in only four games, three others late in the 1948 season. In his six major league at-bats, he had two hits, a double and a triple. When he walked, the tying run was on first, but Dom DiMaggio bounced into a double play.

Without a dependable relief pitcher, McCarthy had been forced to use Kinder and Parnell out of the bullpen down the stretch. With the first two Yankee batters in the eighth, Henrich and Berra, both left-handed, McCarthy waved for Parnell, but the twenty-five-game winner was weary. He hadn't lasted six innings as Saturday's starter after his ninth-inning wild pitch in Wednesday's loss in Washington had wasted eight shutout innings. Now he threw to Henrich, who swung and missed. He had been trying to hit to leftfield, away from his power. Behind him, he heard Joe DiMaggio's voice.

"Go for it," DiMaggio was yelling to him.

Henrich went for it, swatting a curveball into the rightfield stands for his twenty-fourth homer.

Now it was 2–0, a big difference from 1–0.

When Berra singled, McCarthy changed pitchers again. With Di-Maggio coming up, the Red Sox manager called for Cecil (Tex) Hughson, a thirty-three-year-old righthander who hadn't pitched for three weeks. Hughson had once been the ace of the Red Sox staff. He had a 22–6 record in 1942 and after returning from military service, a 20–11 record in 1946. Arm trouble limited him to a 3–1 record in 1948 and, after surgery in the off-season, he started only twice in 1949 before being relegated to McCarthy's doghouse, an afterthought in the bullpen. Summoned now to keep the Red Sox alive, he was even more surprised than his teammates were. Quickly, he got DiMaggio to bounce into a double play.

One more out and maybe the Red Sox, down by only 2–0, could do something in the ninth. But the Yankees weren't through with Hughson, who would be pitching in the big leagues for the last time. Yesterday's hero, Lindell, singled. Billy Johnson singled and when Williams bobbled the ball, Hank Bauer, who was running for Lindell, hurried to third. With second base open, McCarthy decided to walk Cliff Mapes, a lefthanded hitter, so that Hughson could pitch to Jerry Coleman, the skinny second baseman.

As the eighth hitter in the batting order, Coleman, a rookie who got his chance when George Stirnweiss suffered a severely spiked hand on opening day, had a .274 average, but not much power: twenty doubles, five triples, only two homers. Having grown up in

San Francisco, where Joe DiMaggio was an idol, Coleman once glanced out to centerfield and realized he was playing second base with Joe DiMaggio out there behind him. Now, with the bases loaded and the pennant at stake, Coleman didn't even look back to see if a pinch hitter was behind him. He knew that with the Yankees ahead, Stengel would stay with his best defensive players.

On a high inside fastball, Coleman looped the ball toward right-field. Doerr ran out. Zarilla ran in and dove, but couldn't quite catch it.

"He only hit it with half his bat," Zarilla said later. "The ball didn't go quite high enough. I didn't touch it. Missed it by inches."

Bauer and Johnson scored easily. When third-base coach Frank Crosetti noticed that Zarilla had landed hard in diving for the ball and couldn't retrieve it, he waved Mapes home for the third run and a 5–0 lead before Doerr's throw cut down Coleman at third.

"I just kept going," Coleman would say later. "Anytime another runner was trying to score, Casey wanted you to draw the throw."

But the Red Sox didn't go quietly. Pesky fouled out, but Williams walked and Stephens singled. Doerr lifted a long fly that Joe DiMaggio chased but, in his weariness, couldn't run down. Williams and Stephens scored on the triple. Now it was 5–2 with a runner on third. Out in centerfield DiMaggio had to make a decision.

"I should've had Doerr's ball in my hip pocket," he would say years later. "My legs felt like lead. In the best interests of the Yankees, I knew I had to take myself out."

Seeing DiMaggio trotting toward the dugout, Stengel waved Cliff Mapes to centerfield from rightfield, moved Hank Bauer from leftfield to rightfield, and inserted Gene Woodling in leftfield. Zarilla flied to Mapes but with two out, Goodman singled. Now it was 5–3 with a runner on first and Birdie Tebbetts, the potential tying run, at bat. Henrich walked toward the mound with the ball, but Raschi glared at him.

"Give me the goddamn ball," Raschi snapped, "and get the hell out of here."

Turning away, Henrich smiled. Same ol' Raschi, tough as nails. Moments later Tebbetts lifted a pop foul along the first-base line. Henrich caught it. The Yankees had won the pennant with a 97–57 record. They would win the World Series from the Brooklyn Dodgers, four games to one. But the Red Sox, for the second straight season, had produced a 96–58 regular-season record, which would win most pennants. And for the second straight season they had lost the pennant in their final game, the only major league team ever to do that. Some of their loyalists second-guessed McCarthy's decision to remove Kinder for a pinch hitter, but in the Red Sox clubhouse Tebbetts defended his manager.

"He had to," Tebbetts said. "You're one run behind in the eighth. You've got one out and your pitcher's coming up. You've got to use a pinch hitter."

That basic baseball strategy did not appease Ellis Kinder. At his locker he looked up at his friend Arthur Richman, clutched his throat, and growled, "Shit in the neck again," his way of saying that for all their statistics, the Red Sox again had been unable to win the biggest game of the season. Williams had led the league with forty-three homers and 159 runs batted in, losing the triple crown when George Kell, the Tiger third baseman, edged him for the batting title, .3429 to .3427. Parnell won twenty-five games, Kinder twenty-three. The Red Sox had a 61–16 record at Fenway Park (only 35–42 on the road). Despite the two losses in Yankee Stadium, the Red Sox had a 61–22 finish.

"Two exasperating endings in two years," Ted Williams would say years later, referring to the 1948 and 1949 seasons. "We should've won both of 'em."

But over the last four games in Washington and New York, three of which the Red Sox lost, Bobby Doerr was their only player to get a hit in each game. Williams had one hit in twelve at-bats, Pesky none in fifteen, Tebbetts none in twelve, Stephens two in ten, Dom DiMaggio three in seventeen. Even so, Kinder blamed McCarthy more than anyone else for the game that meant the pennant. He believed he would have blanked the Yankees in the eighth and ninth while those three Red Sox runs in the ninth would have meant a 3–1 victory. Not that the Yankees agreed. To them, if Vic Raschi had needed to pitch a 1–0 shutout, he would have done just that.

"In my mind," Tommy Henrich told the writers, "nobody was going to beat Raschi in this game."

When the Red Sox were returning to Boston by train, Kinder, fortified by bourbon, stormed into Joe McCarthy's compartment and derided the manager. But more than anyone else, Red Sox owner Tom Yawkey understood why the Red Sox lost.

"Two teams," he said, "can't win the same pennant."

1951

The Giants' 37-7 Finish

In the double play that turned the 1951 pennant race, Giant third baseman Bobby Thomson whirls and throws to first after tagging Jackie Robinson of the Dodgers. *AP/Wide World Photo*

IS FACE ONLY inches from his glove, his lean body in a crouch at third base, Bobby Thomson was staring at Andy Pafko in the batter's box as Jackie Robinson danced just outside the chalked baseline. In the sunny glow of Sunday afternoon, September 9, 1951, at Ebbets Field, the New York Giants were leading the Brooklyn Dodgers, 2–1, in the eighth inning of what would create a two-game swing in the pennant race.

Monte Irvin, the Giants' cleanup hitter and leftfielder, had smashed a two-run homer in the fourth off Ralph Branca, the Dodgers' twenty-five-year-old righthander. With one out in the eighth, Duke Snider had doubled off the scoreboard in rightfield and Robinson had tripled off the centerfield exit gate. Hopping out of the Giants' dugout in his jaunty stride, Leo Durocher had hurried to the mound to talk to Sal Maglie, the Giant ace with a shadowy stubble of beard. Shortly after Maglie's return from the Mexican League in 1949, Durocher had said, "He looks like the barber at the third chair." The nickname stuck, but soon the Barber stood for his ability to shave batters' chins with high inside fastballs before spinning his curveball over the outside corner. Now, with Durocher talking to Maglie, the Dodger fans hooted and waved their white handkerchiefs.

As soon as Durocher returned to the dugout, public-address announcer Tex Rickard blared, "Please do not wave handkerchiefs from the stands." That only provoked more handkerchiefs.

While the crowd was wondering if Robinson would try to steal home, Pafko slashed a grounder inside the third-base line. With a backhanded stab, Thomson caught the ball. Robinson, desperate to get back to third, spun and slid. Thomson lunged, tagged him, straightened, and threw to Whitey Lockman at first base. Thomson had turned a double into a double play. Trotting to the dugout, he felt a pat on his shoulder and heard Maglie's voice.

"Great play," the Giant righthander said.

Durocher, going out to coach in the top of the ninth, shook hands with the third baseman he had molded from a centerfielder only two months earlier.

"That's the greatest play," Durocher would say later, "I've ever seen a third baseman make."

The hooting had been silenced, the handkerchiefs stuffed into pockets. In the Dodger dugout, Ralph Branca, who had been removed for a pinch hitter in the seventh, shook his head at Thomson's reflex play. If that ball got through, Robinson would have scored for 2–2, Pafko would be on second with a double, and maybe Maglie would be out of the game. When the Giants completed their 2–1 victory, Thomson moved through their dugout to the dirt runway used by both teams leading to the adjacent clubhouses underneath the steel-girder skeleton of the grandstand.

"You were lucky, Thomson," he heard a Brooklyn voice yell from the ramps above. "Lucky, lucky, lucky."

Thomson smiled. The raging rivalry between the Giants and the Dodgers had settled in his psyche. Even in that dirt runway he never spoke to any of the Dodgers except for an occasional "Hello" to Gil Hodges, their huge first baseman. Now, still relishing having turned Pafko's double into a double play, Thomson tossed his glove into his locker in the old clubhouse used by the visiting team. Branca was toweling himself after a shower in the Dodgers' clubhouse.

Neither had any reason to suspect that in three weeks and three days they would be handcuffed in history.

Ten years earlier, as a teenager living on Staten Island across New York Bay from Brooklyn, Thomson had spent the summer playing shortstop for the Dodger Rookies, a sandlot team sponsored by the Dodger organization. He had been told not to sign with a major league team without checking with the Dodgers, but when the Giants offered him a minor league contract for $100 a month after his 1942 graduation from Curtis High School, the Dodgers weren't interested in matching the money. When he hit a game-winning homer one night for the Giants' farm team at Rocky Mount of the Bi-State League, the fans passed the hat for him.

"How much did you get?" a teammate asked.

"About twelve dollars," Thomson said, smiling.

Had he signed with the Dodgers, maybe Thomson would have developed into the dependable leftfielder the Dodger teams of his era never had. Instead, after learning to be a bombardier in the Army Air Corps during World War II, he advanced quickly through the Giants' farm system to the big leagues. As a rookie centerfielder in 1947, he hit 29 homers and drove in 85 runs. Two years later, he batted .309 with 27 homers while driving in 109 runs. Known as the Staten Island Scot, swift and strong at 6–2 and 180, he had been born in Glasgow, Scotland, in 1923 five days after his father boarded a ship to seek work in America as a cabinetmaker. Three years later the family was reunited. During his bachelor years with the Giants, he continued to live with his mother in their Staten Island home. To go to work, he drove to the ferry terminal, floated across New York Bay past the Statue of Liberty, then drove up the West Side Highway to the Polo Grounds.

"It takes me an hour and a half to get here," Thomson would tell his teammates, "but Staten Island's worth it."

As another local boy who made good, Ralph Branca was living with his parents in Mount Vernon, just north of the Bronx border. Husky and darkly handsome at six-three and 220 pounds, he had gentle eyes, a gentle smile, and a Roman nose that inspired his Dodger teammates to call him "Honker." He had grown up as a Giants fan at A. B. Davis High School, where his older brother John was the ace pitcher while he mostly played second base or rightfield. He was only sixteen when he tagged along with his brother to a tryout camp at the Polo Grounds, but the Giants didn't even let him throw. The next week they went to a Yankee Stadium tryout camp where his fastball impressed the scouts.

"Too young," the card in the Yankee office read. "Get in touch with him next year."

By then the Dodgers had signed him after he and his brother rode the subway for more than two hours to a tryout camp in the Sheepshead Bay area of Brooklyn. Following his freshman year at New York University, he joined the Olean (New York) Dodgers of the Pennsylvania–Ontario–New York League, the Pony League. Near the end of the 1944 season he was in the big leagues. At age twenty-one in 1947, he was a twenty-one game winner. He never regained that form, but he had been a dependable starter: 14–9 in 1948 and 13–5 in 1949 before skidding to 7–9. Now, with the Dodgers moving toward the 1951 pennant, he knew that despite this Sunday afternoon's 2–1 loss to the Giants, his record was a solid 13–7. He knew that the Dodgers, having finished their season series against the Giants with a 13–9 edge, had a solid five and one-half game lead with three weeks remaining. He didn't expect to see the Giants again until next year.

Waiting for Branca now outside the clubhouse was his blond fiancée, Ann Mulvey, the daughter of one of the Dodger owners.

Shortly after the World Series, they would be married on October 20 at St. Francis of Assisi Church in Flatbush.

In the visitors' clubhouse, Thomson was dressing near newly cemented bricks across what had been a wide wooden door. Although locked and bolted, that door had led to the Dodgers' clubhouse. The bricks had been put there on orders from the National League office. When the Dodgers swept a three-game series at Ebbets Field on August 9 for what appeared to be an insurmountable twelve-game lead, the Giants heard Dodger voices on the other side of that door.

"Roll out the barrel," the voices were singing. "We got the Giants on the run . . ."

Some of the Giants believed they heard Branca's baritone among those voices, but when Charlie Dressen, the Dodger manager, organized the chorus, Branca declined.

"I don't want to do that," he said.

Knowing that taunting could only backfire, several Dodgers pleaded with their teammates to "Shut up" or "Leave 'em alone." But that didn't deter the singers or Jackie Robinson, who was yelling, "Eat your heart out, Leo." Robinson also was slamming a bat against that wooden door as if beating a drum at what he thought was the Giants' funeral. As his Giant teammates seethed silently, second baseman Eddie Stanky couldn't take any more of the bat drumming from his onetime Dodger teammate.

"Shove that bat up your ass," Stanky yelled.

At his locker, thirty-two-year-old Monte Irvin was watching Durocher, who dressed alongside his coaches and players. Irvin was expecting Durocher to explode, but the Giant manager, whose philosophy was to let sleeping dogs lie, reacted quietly.

"I don't have to make any speeches," Durocher told his players. "If that doesn't wake you up, nothing will."

By the time the writers covering the Giants arrived in the clubhouse, the taunting had stopped. But with the Giants twelve games behind, one of the writers asked if Durocher was planning any lineup changes.

"No changes," he barked. "If they go down, I go down with them. If they go up, I go up too. This is my team and I'm going to stick with it."

Durocher had been building "my kind of team" since taking command of the Giants during the 1948 season in one of baseball's most startling switches. Brash and brazen, once the St. Louis Cardinal shortstop in their Gashouse Gang era, he had been named the Dodgers' manager in 1939. Hailed when the Dodgers won the 1941 pennant, he was suspended for the 1947 season by Commissioner A. B. (Happy) Chandler for what was vaguely described as an "accumulation of unpleasant incidents" that were "detrimental to baseball." After his return in 1948, the Dodgers skidded into the second division. Branch Rickey, their pious president, was becoming more and more disenchanted with Durocher, now married to Laraine Day, a Hollywood actress. Rickey asked traveling secretary Harold Parrott to suggest to Durocher that he resign.

"If he wants me to resign," Durocher growled, "let him tell me himself. Eyeball to eyeball."

That season the Giants also were stumbling. Their owner, Horace Stoneham, had decided to replace Mel Ott, who in 1946 had been identified by Durocher as the reason "nice guys finish last." Stoneham sought permission from Rickey to talk to Burt Shotton, who had guided the Dodgers to the 1947 pennant as Durocher's stand-in.

"No," said Rickey. "I may need Burt myself."

"Does that mean," Stoneham asked, "that Durocher might be available?"

"You may talk to him," Rickey said.

The news shook New York to its National League roots. Giants fans felt belittled, Dodger fans felt betrayed. The night Durocher returned to Ebbets Field wearing "New York" in black-and-orange lettering across his gray uniform, he was treated as a traitor. By then Durocher already was telling Stoneham that he needed to create "my kind of team," meaning swift and smart with good pitchers and good gloves. The year before, the Giants had finished a distant fourth despite a record 221 homers. First baseman Johnny Mize led the league with 51 homers and 138 runs batted in. Outfielder Willard Marshall hit 36, catcher Walker Cooper hit 35. Even with Durocher's arrival, basically the same Giant team finished a distant fifth in 1948 as Mize hit 40 homers and third baseman Sid Gordon hit 30.

"With this team, I can't steal, I can't bunt, I can't hit and run," Durocher told Stoneham. "All I can do is wait for a home run."

Stoneham was stubborn. He enjoyed all those home runs. He also enjoyed a drink. But he didn't like to drink alone. If his manager or one of his front office employees thought it was time to go home, Stoneham would say, "Sitsee," meaning sit and have another drink.

"You work for me," Stoneham would say. "Sitsee."

When the fifth-place Giants were finishing twenty-four games out with a 73–81 record in 1949, Stoneham finally agreed that Durocher needed "my kind of team." Mize was sold to the Yankees in a September waiver deal. At the baseball meetings Marshall, Gordon, shortstop John (Buddy) Kerr, and righthander Red Webb were traded to the Boston Braves for shortstop Alvin Dark, who had been the 1948 Rookie of the Year, and Stanky, a scrappy second baseman who had played for Durocher in Brooklyn.

"He can't hit, he can't run, and he can't field," Durocher often said of Stanky. "But he's my kind of player. He comes to kill you."

In 1950 the Giants were coming together. Monte Irvin, who had languished in the Negro Leagues before Jackie Robinson emerged as baseball's first black major leaguer in 1947, hit fifteen homers and drove in sixty-six runs as a first baseman–outfielder. Don Mueller, who swung a bat as if it were a wand, was installed in rightfield next to Thomson and leftfielder Carroll (Whitey) Lockman. Sal Maglie, finally absolved from having jumped to the Mexican League in 1945, posted a stunning 18–4 record, joining Larry Jansen, Sheldon Jones, and lefthander Dave Koslo in the rotation. Another starter was Jim Hearn, a young righthander obtained from the Cardinals early that season. Wes Westrum had developed into a wise catcher. In 1950 the Philadelphia Phillies, after losing eight of ten games, held on to win the pennant on the final day. Dick Sisler hit a three-run homer off Don Newcombe in the tenth inning at Ebbets Field for a 4–1 victory after Phillies centerfielder Richie Ashburn had thrown out Cal Abrams at the plate in the ninth to avert a one-game pennant playoff. After rising to third place with an 86–68 record, only five games out, the Giants were rated a serious contender as the 1951 season approached.

"I got my kind of team now," Durocher bragged at spring training in St. Petersburg, Florida, the Giants having swapped their traditional Phoenix, Arizona, site with the Yankees for that one year. "We're going to win it."

When the bell rang, the Giants were left in the gate. They thudded into last place with a 2–12 start that included an eleven-game losing streak. In their Polo Grounds opener, hours after New York City had welcomed General of the Army Douglas MacArthur home from Korea with a City Hall ticker-tape parade, Durocher was upstaged by Charlie Dressen, the peppery new Dodger manager. During the off-season Walter O'Malley, a Brooklyn attorney, had organized the purchase of Rickey's twenty-five percent stock for $1 million. As the new Dodger president, O'Malley hired Dressen, once a popular Dodger third-base coach under Durocher, to succeed Shotton.

"Just stay close," Dressen would tell his Dodger players in a tight game. "I'll think of something."

Dressen wanted to prove that he was smarter than Durocher and now he jumped at the first chance. With the Giants losing, 7–3, in the seventh inning of the their home opener, Durocher sent up thirty-year-old infielder Artie Wilson as a pinch hitter against Newcombe with the bases loaded. In the Dodgers' dugout the beady-eyed Dressen whistled shrilly through his teeth. The umpires turned.

"Time out," Dressen yelled.

Wilson was a rookie up from the Pacific Coast League, where Dressen had managed Oakland the previous season. As if using semaphore flags, Dressen waved in rightfielder Carl Furillo to where second baseman Jackie Robinson usually was stationed, moved Robinson to the shortstop side of second base, positioned shortstop Pee Wee Reese closer to third base, put third baseman Billy Cox near the foul line, waved centerfielder Duke Snider to straightaway leftfield and put leftfielder Don Thompson near the foul line.

Wilson stepped into the batter's box. Newcombe wound up and pitched. Wilson tapped a one-hopper to Newcombe.

Dressen never had it so good. He also never had so many good players. As a cleanup hitter who didn't hit that many home runs, as a base runner who rattled opposing pitchers, Jackie Robinson played as if a bonfire were blazing inside him. Roy Campanella hit home runs while catching and cajoling Don Newcombe, lefthander Elwin (Preacher) Roe, Carl Erskine, Branca, and Clyde King, a bespectacled relief pitcher. Pee Wee Reese was the club pro at shortstop, Billy Cox a vacuum cleaner at third base, Gil Hodges a slugger and a smoothie at first base. As the only lefthanded hitter in the day-to-day lineup, centerfielder Edwin (Duke) Snider feasted on the righthanded pitchers that opponents invariably started. Carl Furillo, with an arm that nicknamed him the Reading Rifle, protected the "Hit Sign, Win Suit" Abe Stark sign at the base of the Ebbets Field scoreboard in rightfield. Only in leftfield were the Dodgers groping for a regular. Around noon on June 15 the Dodgers were about to take batting practice before the opener of a three-game series in Chicago when Newcombe spotted Andy Pafko, the Cub centerfielder.

"Hey, Pafko," he yelled. "You're going to be a Dodger tomorrow."

Pafko laughed. Players often teased each other about being traded. But that evening at his Chicago home Pafko's phone rang. Hours before the trade deadline Emil (Buzzie) Bavasi, the Dodgers' new general manager in the O'Malley regime, had swung a blockbuster. He obtained Pafko, catcher Al (Rube) Walker, infielder Wayne Terwilliger

Charlie Dressen and Jackie Robinson. *National Baseball Library and Archive,*
Cooperstown, N.Y.

and lefthander Johnny Schmitz from the Cubs for outfielder Gene
Hermanski, catcher Bruce Edwards, infielder Eddie Miksis, and lefthander Joe Hatten.

In the thirty-year-old Pafko, the Dodgers had not only assured
themselves of an established leftfielder, they apparently had assured
themselves of the pennant.

The year before, Pafko, a righthanded-swinging slugger, had hit
thirty-six homers and driven in ninety-two runs while batting .304. In

their new uniforms near the batting cage at Wrigley Field the next day, Pafko turned to Hermanski and said, "It's like handing me $5,000," meaning the approximate amount of a winning team's World Series share in those years.

"Yeah," Hermanski snapped. "My $5,000."

Durocher also was annoyed. He threatened never to speak to Frank Frisch, his onetime Gashouse Gang manager who as the Cub manager had approved the deal. According to some newspaper reports, Durocher had been willing to trade Thomson to the Cubs for Pafko. But quietly Durocher had been making moves. When the Giants were 16–17 on May 21 before a getaway game in St. Louis, he tossed Monte Irvin's first baseman's glove to Whitey Lockman.

"Whitey, you're playing first base today," Durocher said. "Monte's in leftfield."

Irvin was delighted; he had been uncomfortable at first base. Lockman was stunned. Unlike many outfielders, he often took grounders during batting practice, usually at shortstop. But at first base he was a stranger. He found the footwork tricky. Every so often, in shifting his feet to take a throw, one of his feet would be across too much of the bag, in danger of being spiked by a runner. About a month later, Lockman was on first base after a single when Brave first baseman Earl Torgeson turned to him.

"Whitey," said Torgeson, "you're going to get one of your feet cut off. Don't worry about shifting your feet. Just put your right foot against the bag and stretch for the throw."

Three days after the Irvin-Lockman switch, Durocher made another move. He finally persuaded Stoneham to bring up twenty-year-old centerfielder Willie Mays, who was hitting .477 with eight homers for the Minneapolis Millers in the American Association. Durocher had seen Mays play only once, in a Florida exhibition game, but that was enough. For an update, he phoned Tommy Heath, the Millers' manager.

"What should I know about this kid?" Durocher said.

"Keep him in centerfield," Heath said. "It's the only position he's ever played. He can cover it like a tent."

Mays joined the Giants as they were about to finish batting practice before a Friday night game in Philadelphia.

"Let the kid hit," Durocher yelled.

The first few pitches, Mays stubbed grounders, popped up, lofted soft fly balls. But he smashed the next pitch into Shibe Park's upper leftfield stands. He rattled the seats in centerfield. He dented the scoreboard in rightfield. By now the Phillies, about to take infield practice, were staring at the rookie in the batting cage. So were his Giant teammates.

"Now you know," Durocher told the writers, "why I wanted this kid."

During that three-game weekend series, Mays, batting third, was hitless in twelve at-bats: 0 for 5 against Bubba Church, 0 for 3 against Robin Roberts, 0 for 4 against Russ Meyer. But on Monday night, his first time up at the Polo Grounds against Warren Spahn, a thirty-year-old Brave lefthander who would win 363 games, he hit a home run onto the leftfield roof, the first of his career total of 660 homers, third behind Henry Aaron's 755 and Babe Ruth's 714.

"Watch this kid go now," Durocher said.

Mays slumped again, going one for twenty-five before justifying Durocher's faith. He would hit .274 with twenty homers and drive in sixty-eight runs. His arrival moved Thomson to leftfield, with Irvin transferring to right. Thomson's average kept falling. Durocher restored Mueller to right, with Irvin returning to left. But when third baseman Henry Thompson slumped, Durocher remembered that Thomson had played third briefly in 1946 after being brought up from the Jersey City farm team in the International League.

"I want you to take some grounders at third," Durocher said. "You played the infield before. You can handle it."

Thomson wasn't so sure. He considered himself a centerfielder, and a good one. But he knew he wasn't hitting. He knew Mays was now the centerfielder. He knew playing third base was maybe his last chance of staying in the lineup. To his surprise, he gracefully fielded the grounders Durocher hit him.

"You'll be great there," Durocher told him.

Installed at third base on July 20, Thomson enjoyed being on his toes for every pitch, exhorting the pitchers to "Bend your back" or "Let 'er rip." And he began to hit. Instead of his usual straight-up stance, he accepted a batting tip from Durocher to crouch more.

"Spring out of that crouch," Durocher told him.

With a new position and a new batting stance, Thomson had a new life. But the Dodgers were still running away with the pennant. With that three-game sweep at Ebbets Field that provoked the taunting serenade through the clubhouse door on August 9, the Dodgers had a twelve and one-half game lead. Two days later Robin Roberts blanked the Giants, 4–0, while Branca was stopping the Braves, 10–3, in the opener of a doubleheader. Between games the Dodgers had a thirteen and one-half game lead, the number that would be chiseled onto their tombstone. Although the Dodgers lost the second game, 8–4, they were still thirteen ahead.

With the Dodgers having forty-eight games remaining on Sunday morning, August 12, they had a 70–36 record, a remarkable .660 percentage. With forty-four games left, the Giants were struggling at 59–51, a shaky .536.

When the Giants swept a doubleheader from the Phillies that Sunday, the Dodgers didn't even look over their shoulders. Tuesday night, in the last of fourteen night games at the Polo Grounds that season, Charlie Dressen opened with Erv Palica, a righthander he had labeled as having "no guts" only a few weeks earlier. Palica lost to righthander George Spencer, 4–2. The next afternoon, the Dodgers lost again, 3–1, when Branca surrendered a two-run homer to Wes Westrum in the eighth after Mays had singled. But the talk was all about Mays's dazzling double play. With Cox on third, Branca on first, Furillo up, and one out in the eighth, Mays remembered Durocher's order: because of Mueller's weaker arm, if a hard throw was needed, the rookie centerfielder was to catch any fly ball between them.

"If the ball's high enough," Mays reminded Mueller, "I'll take it."

Furillo lifted a fly ball into right center. Sprinting across the grass, Mays stretched and snared it. Cox tagged up and raced for the plate. As if he were a whirling dervish, Mays spun completely around, spotted Lockman in the cutoff position between first base and the mound, aimed at Lockman's chest, and threw. The ball hummed past Lockman to Westrum, who tagged Cox, ending the inning.

"That's the perfectest throw I ever made," Mays said later.

Furillo labelled it "Luck, that was the luckiest throw I've ever seen." When the writers asked Dressen about Mays's play, the Dodger manager scoffed.

"I'd like to see him do it again," Dressen snapped.

To some Dodger players, Cox, never an aggressive base runner, had made two mistakes. On Branca's humpback single, they thought Cox should have scored from second, not stopped at third. On Mays's throw, Cox tried to hook-slide instead of sliding straight in. Cox's feet had stopped short of the plate when Westrum tagged him.

Thursday afternoon Sal Maglie outpitched Don Newcombe, 2–1. The Dodgers' lead was down to nine and one-half games and the Giants suddenly had won six straight. Not that the Giants thought they had a real chance. Don Mueller had already phoned his brother

LeRoy in St. Louis to plan their annual October fishing trip to Minnesota.

"The pike and the bass will be waiting for us," Don said.

Without realizing it, the Giants had begun to put together a sixteen-game winning streak. But not even Durocher was taking it too seriously. Against the lesser teams such as the Cubs and the Pirates, he was letting Dark and Stanky manage. In a way.

"I'll change pitchers," Durocher told them, "but you can tell me when to bunt, steal, and hit and run."

Dark and Stanky enjoyed thinking like a manager, which each would be later on. Their teammates, in that era of mostly one-year contracts, were enjoying the streak, hustling for their 1952 salaries. But as the streak continued, Durocher wore the same blue blazer and gray slacks every day.

"Maybe we ought to lose," Dark joked, "so Leo can get his clothes cleaned."

The streak finally ended on August 28 at the Polo Grounds when Cardinal lefthander Howard Pollet fired a 2–0 six-hitter. But the Dodgers were still in command, especially Branca. The previous Friday night he had outpitched Paul Minner of the Cubs, 1–0, on a three-hitter with ten strikeouts. Now he was asked by Dressen to pitch the opener of Monday's twi-night doubleheader against the Pirates on only two days' rest. He couldn't resist. In the minors, Branca remembered, "I always pitched the second game of a twi-night doubleheader, the nine-inning game. If they had let me pitch the seven-inning opener in the dusk, I would've pitched a no-hitter." Against the Pirates, he almost did. In his 5–0 triumph he had a no-hitter until the ninth when shortstop Pete Castiglione of the Pirates looped a single just out of Pee Wee Reese's reach. But on what appeared to be a one-hop line single to right in the third, Furillo had thrown out pitcher Mel Queen at first base to keep the no-hitter alive.

"First time I ever did that," Furillo said.

But having worked eighteen innings over four days, Branca's arm tightened in the area of the triceps muscle. He could throw but his fastball didn't have that extra zip. He never mentioned it to Dressen.

It'll work itself out, Branca assumed. He wouldn't start again until Saturday.

With their winning streak, the Giants had moved to within five games. Dressen didn't seem concerned. Especially when the Giants' rooters mentioned that if only there hadn't been that eleven-game losing streak early in the season.

"What kind of logic is that?" Dressen said. "Don't they realize we beat 'em in six of those eleven games?"

As the Dodgers arrived at the Polo Grounds on Saturday, September 1 for two weekend games, they were again seven games ahead. Their statistics almost jumped out of statistician Alan Roth's bulging brown leather briefcase. Robinson was batting .342 with 16 homers and 73 runs batted in, Campanella was at .316 with 28 homers and 89 runs batted in, Hodges had 36 homers and 88 runs batted in, Snider 28 homers and 92 runs batted in, Furillo 14 homers and 83 runs batted in, Reese 10 homers and 77 runs batted in. Roe was 18–2, Newcombe 17–7, Erskine 14–9, Branca 13–9, Clyde King 14–6, mostly in relief. Dressen was strutting, but only in his bathrobe in his Granada Hotel suite. Ill with the flu, he had designated coaches Harry (Cookie) Lavagetto and Clyde Sukeforth to share the strategy during the Giants series. Branca, with four days' rest following his two consecutive shutouts, would open against Maglie, but Durocher sounded brave.

"Don't count us out," he warned. "Baseballs can bounce just as funny as footballs."

That gloomy Saturday afternoon, no funny bounces were necessary. Durocher had been telling Don Mueller, "You got to hump up and crank a few out." His rightfielder had hit only nine homers all season. Now he ended Branca's shutout streak with a first-inning blast into the upper rightfield stands. In the second Thomson hit a two-run homer into the upper leftfield deck. With the bases loaded in the top of the third, Maglie's first pitch, high and inside, clipped Robinson on the left wrist, forcing in a run. Plate umpire Lee Ballanfant waved for Durocher and Lavagetto.

"No more of this," Ballanfant ordered.

Durocher argued that, with the bases loaded, Maglie surely was not trying to hit Robinson. Others remembered that earlier in the season, Robinson, annoyed at Maglie's inside pitches, had bunted down the first-base line to draw Maglie over and had deliberately run into him. Now, as the inning ended with Hodges striking out, Robinson and Maglie traded words. In the bottom of the third Mueller hit a two-run homer. Mueller hit another two-run homer off righthander Phil Haugstad in the seventh. The Giants won, 8–1, on Maglie's seven-hitter. In their clubhouse Mueller put aside the "little bat" he had used to hit three homers.

"I don't want to break it," he explained. "It's a Musial model. Thirty-one inches. Thirty-four and a half ounces. I'll use a new bat tomorrow, but it's the same model. Same length, same weight."

Sunday afternoon Dressen returned to the Dodger dugout, but righthander Jim Hearn enjoyed an 11–2 rout. Thomson hit his twenty-fifth homer. In the sixth Mueller, using his new bat, crashed a three-run homer off Newcombe, who had been fuming over Maglie's bench-jockeying that he was "choking." In the eighth Mueller, after taking Phil Haugstad's first pitch, heard his teammates calling to him from the dugout. Stepping out, he glanced at Irvin in the on-deck circle.

"Your wife just had a baby boy," Irvin said.

Genevieve Mueller had been a week overdue with their first of three sons. Her husband hit Haugstad's next pitch for a two-run homer. Rounding third, he yelled to Durocher, "It's a boy! It's a boy!" His five homers in two games tied a major league record shared by Cap Anson, Ty Cobb, Tony Lazzeri, and Ralph Kiner. Haugstad's reaction to Mueller's feat was to deck Thomson and plunk Mays.

"One more like that," plate umpire Al Barlick yelled at Haugstad, "and you're gone too."

In the fifth Barlick had thumbed Branca and Dick Williams off the bench. In the sixth he ejected Newcombe for objecting to a call. When he also ejected Robinson and Clem Labine, a crew-cut righthander recalled on July 17 from the St. Paul farm, Dressen whistled. Barlick spun.

"I'm clearing my bench," Dressen said.

In two earlier games the Dodger manager had sent his players to the clubhouse, ostensibly to protect them from the umpires' wrath. Now, in twos and threes, the remaining Dodgers trudged across centerfield to the visitors' clubhouse where Dressen knew they would be safe from Barlick's thumb. But the Dodgers were no longer safe from the Giants, suddenly five games behind. According to whispers that surfaced later, the signs by the other team's catcher at the Polo Grounds also were no longer safe. On a World War II veteran's midseason suggestion, the Giants had installed a powerful naval telescope at one of the windows in Durocher's office in the centerfield clubhouse. Electricians hooked up a buzzer system from the spotter behind the telescope. The buzzer was connected to both the Giants' first-base dugout and to their rightfield bullpen, where catcher Sal Yvars sat at the far end of the bench. No buzz meant the spotter behind the telescope had stolen the sign for a fastball. One buzz meant a breaking ball.

"Watch me in the bullpen," Yvars told his teammates. "I'll have a baseball in my hand. If I hold on to the ball, it's a fastball. If I toss the ball in the air, it's a breaking ball."

Some batters preferred not to know what the next pitch would be; they didn't want to expect a curve and get skulled by a fastball. Others feasted on the buzzer system. But the telescope couldn't always beat a tough pitcher. In a Labor Day doubleheader with the Phillies at the Polo Grounds, the Giants lost the opener to Robin Roberts, 6–3, before Dave Koslo won, 3–1. At Ebbets Field, the Dodgers swept the Braves, 7–2 and 7–2, on Roy Campanella's six hits, including his thirtieth and thirty-first homers. With twenty-three games remaining, the Dodgers had an 84–47 record; with twenty-one games left, the Giants were 79–54, having won twenty of their last twenty-three games. But the Dodgers again had a six-game lead. Enough for Dressen to shrug off his $100 fine by NL president Ford Frick for "failure to control his players on the bench" in Sunday's game. Enough for Newcombe to ask Buzzie Bavasi for a $5,000 advance against his World Series check.

"What for?" Bavasi asked.

"I want to buy a Cadillac."

"You don't need five thousand dollars."

"I do for the one I want," Newcombe said. "It's a Cadillac Sedan de Ville, sky blue. My first Cadillac."

"When do I get it back?" Bavasi asked.

"Keep my Series share," Newcombe said.

Wednesday afternoon the Giants kept the pressure on, sweeping a doubleheader at Braves Field, 3–2 and 9–1. That night, despite the twinges in his arm, Branca preserved a five-and-one-half-game lead by stopping the Phillies, 5–2, on Gil Hodges's grand slam, his thirty-seventh homer, a Dodger record. After a Thursday rainout, thirty-six-year-old Preacher Roe, whose skinny left arm had ached a week earlier, walked six and let loose a rare wild pitch but improved his record to an amazing 19–2 as the Dodgers pounded the Phillies, 11–6, while Larry Jansen scattered ten hits in a 7–3 victory over the Braves.

Now it was the Giants' turn to go to Ebbets Field for two weekend games. Saturday afternoon Newcombe fired a 9–0 two-hitter while Robinson had three hits and rattled both Hearn and Spencer with his jitterbug leads off third base. Up in the press box Dick Young of the *Daily News* wrote that "the Brooks virtually wrapped up the flag." With twenty games remaining, the Dodgers were six and one-half games ahead.

Sunday afternoon most of those in the sellout crowd of 34,004 were hoping to gloat at the Giants' funeral, but they left muttering. Irvin jolted Branca with that two-run homer, Thomson turned his lunging stop of Pafko's hard grounder into a dazzling double play after Robinson had taken a long lead off third, and Maglie emerged as a twenty-game winner who had three different curveballs. One acted like a slider. Another was slow and sweeping, almost as if it were a change-up. The third broke quickly. With that 2–1 victory, the Giants kept themselves alive, only five and one-half games out.

"We're through playing the Dodgers, we can't do ourselves any good worrying about them anymore," Durocher told the writers. "We'll just have to try to win 'em all the rest of the way."

In the Dodgers' clubhouse, Dressen had a problem. Campanella had suffered a bruised right hip in a slide. But when the Dodgers opened a western trip in Cincinnati Tuesday night, Campy's name was in the lineup.

"It hurts a little when I swing and run," the chubby catcher said. "But what's a little pain?"

Knowing that Dave Koslo had won the opener of the Giants' twi-night doubleheader in St. Louis, 10–5, Labine used his sinker and curveball to blank the Reds, 7–0, on a two-hitter. When the Giants lost the second game, the Dodgers were six ahead.

The magic number had been reduced to eleven: any combination of Dodger victories and Giant losses adding up to eleven would end the race.

"We could clinch on this trip," Furillo said in the lobby of the Netherlands Plaza the next morning. "We can win every game. Well, maybe we'll lose one, but we could do that and still clinch before we get home. Then I'm going to go to the skipper and say, 'Little Charlie, I'd like to go fishing for a few days. How about it?' "

Campanella cringed. "Now just a second, let's win some ballgames first," he said. "The thing ain't over yet, so forget about the celebration and concentrate on baseball."

That afternoon the Reds won, 6–3, on outfielder Lloyd Merriman's bases-loaded triple off Erskine in the seventh. Merriman had been batting .058 against the Dodgers until then. Newcombe had suddenly departed during a three-run first inning. The big righthander had what was described as a "slight muscle pull" in his throwing elbow.

"I don't think it's bad, I should be able to take my regular turn," he said. "I felt it warming up, but I didn't say anything because I thought it would work itself out."

Wednesday night the Giants were rained out in St. Louis, creating a rare doubleheader Thursday: the Cardinals would play the Giants in the afternoon, then play the Boston Braves at night. Stunned by a six-run burst against Maglie in the second inning, the Giants lost, 6–4. Again the Dodgers were six ahead. With only thirteen games remaining, the Giants trailed in the loss column by eight. Durocher knew he had to do something different. Ever since July 20, the day he signed his 1952 contract, he had coached at third base. But at Wrigley Field on Friday afternoon, coach Herman Franks was in the third-base box.

"Maybe it'll change our luck," Durocher said.

Jim Hearn stopped the Cubs, 7–2, for his fifteenth victory, but the Dodgers hardly noticed. Before their Friday night game in Pittsburgh, they were looking to their World Series opponent. In the American League the Cleveland Indians had a one-half-game lead on the Yankees, but several Dodgers were hoping the Yankees would win. They wanted another crack at their World Series conquerors in 1947 and 1949. Jackie Robinson wasn't so sure.

"The Yankees would be tougher than Cleveland," he said. "The Yankees have a way of rising to the occasion. They can depend on good pitching from Vic Raschi and Allie Reynolds."

In a 3–1 victory that night, the Dodgers again got good pitching from Roe, now 20–2, and Pafko hit his fourteenth homer. Before Saturday's game, Branch Rickey, who had assembled this Dodger team but now was operating the Pirates, chatted with Campanella.

"You have the pennant," Rickey said. "But now I want the World Series."

That afternoon the seventh-place Pirates won, 11–2, raking Branca, Bud Podbielan, Clyde King, and Johnny Schmitz for fifteen hits. Jack Merson, an obscure second baseman up from the minors, drove in six runs with a triple, a double, and two singles. When the Giants won, 5–2, on homers by Thomson, Mays, and Mueller, the lead was five games, but Westrum had been suspended for three days and fined $50 for having "pushed" umpire Al Barlick after a disputed tag. Westrum needed the rest. He had been playing with a hairline fracture of his right forefinger for three weeks.

"Put a piece a tape on it and rub it in the dirt," Durocher had told him. "Nobody'll notice."

Sunday the Dodgers won in Chicago, 6–1. Labine's fourth victory enhanced the appraisal of Phillie manager Eddie Sawyer that the rookie righthander was "now the best pitcher in the league." But in Pittsburgh the Giants swept a doubleheader, 7–1 and 6–4, for Jansen's nineteenth win and Maglie's twenty-first. Thomson hit his twenty-eighth and twenty-ninth homers. The lead had shrunk to four and one-half games, the smallest margin since July 4.

"We can catch 'em," Thomson said.

Monday afternoon Newcombe, his elbow given an extra day's rest, had a two-run lead in the seventh but the Cubs won, 5–3, with a four-run rally featuring Gene Hermanski's pinch-hit homer off King, whose arm had tired. As Hermanski trotted to leftfield, he passed Snider coming in from centerfield.

"You're not going anywhere," Snider said. "What did you hit that homer for?"

Hermanski smiled. "That's what you get," he said, "for trading me."

As the Dodgers boarded a train for St. Louis late that afternoon, their lead had narrowed to four games and Campanella was in Illinois Masonic Hospital. Beaned low on the left ear by a sailing fastball thrown by Turk Lown, once a Dodger farmhand, Campy had been taken from the field on a stretcher. Buzzie Bavasi accompanied him to the hospital.

"You don't need to stay with me, Buzzie," Campy said. "You know I'm all right."

"If I don't stay," the general manager said, "you'll walk out of here tonight."

The next morning Campy was discharged. "I ate a big breakfast," he said. "What more proof do they need that I'm all right?" He wanted to rejoin the Dodgers in St. Louis, but doctors ordered him to rest at his St. Albans, Queens, home until the Dodgers returned to Ebbets Field on Friday night. In those years before batting helmets, Dressen was hoping that Campy's beaning would prompt a sporting goods company to devise one.

"There should be more protection on the side of the head that faces the pitcher," Dressen said. "I know it would look funny, but what's so important about how it looks. Keeping the players healthy and in the game is what's important."

Dressen was worried. Not merely about Campanella, but about how Campy's absence would affect the pennant race. Tuesday night the scoreboard in Sportsman's Park showed the Giants winning in Cincinnati, 6–5. When the Cardinals shelled Branca, 7–1, for the Dodgers' fourth defeat in seven games on the road trip, the lead was down to three games. Dressen was beginning to fret. Durocher, with the Giants off Wednesday, played golf.

"I shot seventy-seven," he announced, "and I missed five short putts."

With lefthander Max Lanier starting for the Cardinals that Wednesday night, Dressen benched Snider, moved Pafko to centerfield, and inserted Dick Williams in left field.

"In Duke's last twenty-four at-bats against Lanier," said Dressen, "he got only four hits."

Roe's neighbors in the Ozarks presented him with a sky-blue Cadillac sedan, then he pitched a 3–0 five-hitter. He now was 21–2 and the Dodgers had a three-and-one-half-game lead. Thursday afternoon the Giants lost, 3–1, in Cincinnati when Ewell (The Whip) Blackwell struck out Westrum and Hank Thompson in the ninth with the tying runs on base. About an hour later, Erskine slid a called third strike past Cardinals pinch hitter Harry (Peanuts) Lowrey in the ninth. The 4–3 victory had the Dodgers smiling. Their lead was four and one-half games. After salvaging a 5–4 record on the road trip, they were going home. They dressed quickly to board their bus to the airport, where a chartered Constellation was waiting. All except Roe, Cox, and Cal Abrams, who took a train out of Union Station that night.

"In forty-eight the Dodgers were flying from Vero Beach to Mobile coming out of spring training," Roe once said in explaining his aversion to air travel. "They had to land in Tallahassee to let me off. My heart couldn't stand it. The doctor told me never to fly again."

Their train was still somewhere in Pennsylvania when Dressen watched Campanella take batting practice before Friday night's opener against the Phillies. Despite three days' rest after his beaning, Campy kept fouling off pitches. Dressen took him aside.

"Stand here," Dressen said. "Now look up quick and run like you were going after a pop foul."

Campy pretended to circle under a high foul ball, but wobbled slightly. With a sad smile, he told the manager, "I felt a little dizzy, Skip." When the writers questioned Dressen, he said, "Campy's still woozy. No reason to play him now. I want him ready for the World Series." That night Labine, without realizing it, did something that would put him in Dressen's doghouse. With the bases loaded, most pitchers prefer to take a full windup. But when the Phillies loaded the bases in the first inning, Labine threw from the stretch position. Dressen hurried to the mound.

"What the hell are you doing?" Dressen asked.

"I think I can throw a better curveball if I go into a stretch," Labine said.

"Use your full windup."

Ignoring his manager's order, Labine went into a stretch and threw his curveball. Willie (Puddin' Head) Jones, the Phillie third baseman, smashed it into the leftfield stands. Grand slam. On his return to the dugout, Labine felt Dressen's eyes on him.

"Fresh kid," the manager snapped.

After a run-scoring single by Dick Sisler in the second, Labine was out of the game and in Dressen's doghouse. He wouldn't pitch again until Dressen was desperate on the final Sunday of the season. With the Giants idle, the Dodgers' 9–6 loss to the Phillies cut their lead to four games. Saturday afternoon Jansen stifled the Braves, 4–1, at the Polo Grounds for his twentieth win.

"We can still catch 'em," Whitey Lockman said.

"You and Bobby have been saying that for a month," Jansen said.

"And look how far we've come," Thomson said.

"But the Dodgers have to lose," Jansen said.

Dressen was awaiting his "night" at Ebbets Field. Smug and smiling, he stood at home plate accepting a $5,000 savings bond, a cream-colored Dodge station wagon, a floral horseshoe, and an oil portrait identifying him as the manager of the "National League Champions 1951." He had other reasons to smile. Campy was no longer woozy and Newcombe would be starting against Karl Drews, an ex-Yankee and Brown righthander just up from Baltimore of the International League. But Newcombe allowed ten hits by the sixth inning, Campy went hitless, and the Dodgers lost, 7–3. The lead was three.

Sunday both the Dodgers and Giants won. Campy homered off Bubba Church in the first and added three singles in a 6–3 victory as Roe increased his record to 22–2 with a six-hitter. Maglie's neighbors in Niagara Falls presented him with a car, then he scattered thirteen hits to win, 4–1, his twenty-second victory. The Giants had now won seven of their last eight, thirty-two of their last thirty-nine. Not that it seemed to matter much. With only a week to go, the Dodgers' magic number had been reduced to four.

Monday afternoon Giant second baseman Eddie Stanky's error let the Braves get an early run, but with two out in the ninth Stanky singled off third baseman Sibby Sisti's glove, scoring pinch runner Davey Williams for a 4–3 victory. The lead was now two and one-half games. And the Giants were beginning to think that "destiny" was on their side. In the eighth Braves third baseman Bob Elliott had pulled up lame running out a grounder, forcing Brave manager Tommy Holmes to move Sisti from second base to third. Some of the Giants believed that if Elliott had been at third, he would have handled Stanky's hot grounder.

"The worst we'll get is a tie," Durocher barked. "We'll win all our games. They've got to lose. They may even lose enough to be moved right out of there."

With only four games to go, Durocher had his starters lined up: Hearn and Jansen on Tuesday night and Wednesday night in Philadelphia, off Thursday and Friday, Maglie and Jansen on Saturday and Sunday in Boston. Dressen, with seven games to go, was planning to rest Roe until the World Series in order to protect the 22–2 lefthander's .917 percentage, which would set an NL record.

"You don't have to do that for me, Charlie," Roe told him. "I'll take my chances."

"If I need you Friday night in Philly, you start," Dressen said. "Otherwise, no."

Tuesday night Hearn had a 2–0 lead in the fourth inning at Shibe Park when the scoreboard showed that the Dodgers had lost, 6–3, in the opener of their twi-night doubleheader in Boston. In the fifth Mueller's single and Irwin's double added another run off Robin Roberts, the Phillies' ace with a 21–13 record. But when Puddin' Head Jones hit Hearn's first pitch in the seventh into the leftfield seats, Durocher jumped out of the dugout and trotted toward the bullpen where Maglie was sitting.

"Sal, Sal," he barked. "Get ready."

Dave Koslo and George Spencer had been throwing. Maglie wasn't due to start until Saturday in Boston but with the scoreboard showing the Braves ahead 7–0 in the second game, Durocher wanted his ace. Hearn got shortstop Granny Hamner on a pop-up, but first baseman Eddie Waitkus and catcher Del Wilber each singled. Knowing that Del Ennis would pinch-hit for Roberts, Durocher waved to the bullpen. Maglie spun a curveball. Ennis bounced into a double play. Maglie went on to ensure a 5–1 victory. With the Dodgers also losing the second game in Boston, 14–2, the lead was down to one.

"It couldn't happen," Durocher said with a smirk, "to a nicer bunch of guys."

Labine had been listed among the "probable pitchers" as the starter for the first game of that twi-night doubleheader in Boston, but he remained in Dressen's doghouse. Branca had started instead. In the first inning Bob Addis singled, Sam Jethroe homered, Earl Torgeson singled, and Sid Gordon walked. After only seventeen pitches, Branca was gone. King wasn't much better. He walked in another run, then

Brave shortstop Buddy Kerr hit a three-run triple. Johnny Schmitz, the lefthander obtained in the Pafko deal but seldom used, blanked the Braves over the next five innings, but the loss to Warren Spahn was Branca's fourth straight. In the second game Erskine was rapped for six runs in the second, Reese booted a routine grounder, and Furillo threw wildly in a loss to righthander Jim Wilson.

In their Braves Field clubhouse, the Dodgers still didn't seem worried, which is why Buzzie Bavasi was worried. The general manager feared his team was counting on the Giants losing.

But all along Reese, the calm captain, had told his teammates, "Don't worry about anybody else, just win our game." Wednesday afternoon the Dodgers did. Campanella's three-run double off Max Surkont sparked a four-run first inning and Newcombe coasted to a 15–5 win, his nineteenth. But the Braves were steaming. With a 13–3 lead in the eighth, Robinson stole home on rookie righthander Lew Burdette. To get to their clubhouse, the Dodgers had to go through the Braves' dugout, where several players were waiting.

"Stealing home in that situation is bush baseball," one of the Braves muttered. "We'll get you bastards tomorrow."

That night Monte Irvin crashed a three-run homer off Phillie righthander Andy Hansen in the first, and Jansen breezed to a 10–1 win, his twenty-first. With the Dodgers' lead still only one game, a coin toss to determine the schedule of a two-of-three playoff was held Thursday morning in New York at the National League office. With a telephone to his ear in his Kenmore Hotel suite, Dressen heard Horace Stoneham call "Heads." The coin came up tails. Over the phone Jack Collins, the Dodger business manager, told Dressen, "It's our choice." The Dodgers could play either the first game at Ebbets Field or the second and third games there. Dressen never even glanced at Buzzie Bavasi, who was sitting with him.

"First game in Brooklyn," Dressen blurted.

Bavasi was shocked. With the Dodgers' power and pitching tailored to Ebbets Field, the general manager had assumed that Dressen would prefer the second game and, if necessary, the third game there. But Dressen remembered the 1946 playoff between the Dodgers and the Cardinals. When the Cardinals lost owner Sam Breadon's coin-toss call, Durocher, then the Dodger manager, chose St. Louis as the site of the first game, with Brooklyn the site of the second and third games. When the Cardinals swept the first two games, Dressen, then the Dodger third-base coach, was convinced that Durocher had outsmarted himself.

"The big game is the first game," Dressen was saying now in his Kenmore suite. "That's the one you want at home."

Against the Braves that afternoon, Dressen suddenly switched to Roe as his starter. Labine, who hadn't pitched for five days, was still being punished for having thrown that home run ball to Jones from the stretch position.

"Don't go to the bullpen," Dressen told Labine. "Stay in the dugout."

In a duel with lefthander Chet Nichols, who would lead the league with a 2.88 earned run average, Roe wasn't sharp. With the score 3–3 in the eighth, he had already allowed eight hits before the strafing continued. Addis led off with a single. Jethroe singled, Addis hurrying to third. With the infield in to cut off the go-ahead run at the plate, Torgeson bounced to Robinson, who threw to Campanella, who had the plate blocked. Campy thought he tagged Addis in time. Photos later appeared to support him, although some people thought Addis had slid safely between Campy's legs.

Whatever happened, umpire Frank Dascoli signaled Addis safe.

Campy whirled in protest, slamming his glove into the dirt. Dascoli ejected him. Dressen, Roe, and several other Dodgers rushed the umpire. In a wild scene, coach Cookie Lavagetto was ejected, his only ejection in all his years as a player and coach. To prevent more problems, Dascoli cleared the Dodger dugout, ordering all the extra players to the clubhouse.

The Braves were ahead, 4–3. To protect that lead in the ninth, Braves manager Tommy Holmes moved Sid Gordon from third base to leftfield and installed Bob Elliott at third.

Hearing Holmes's strategy, Durocher yelled, "Good move." In the Giant offices on West 42nd Street, just down the block from Times Square, Durocher, along with farm director Carl Hubbell and other Giant employees, were listening to Red Barber's broadcast on a portable radio perched on a window ledge. With almost every pitch, Durocher had been talking about how to pitch to certain hitters or where the fielders should play them. He agreed with the Gordon-Elliott moves.

"Got to have that arm in leftfield," Durocher was saying now. "Got to have a man at third can watch out for that squeeze. They go for a scoring fly, or they go for the squeeze."

In the ninth Reese led off with a double and took third on Robinson's ground out. Only a sacrifice fly was needed to tie. In two of his previous at-bats, Campy had produced fly balls deep enough to score a runner from third base. But now, with Campy ejected, Rube Walker was the cleanup hitter. Against the lefthanded Nichols, Dressen preferred to call to the clubhouse for a righthanded batter, Wayne Terwilliger, a utility infielder with a .227 average, no homers, and only fourteen runs batted in. Terwilliger bounced to Elliott, who held Reese at third and threw to first. Two out. Nichols then fanned Pafko, and the Dodgers suddenly were only one-half game ahead. In the Giant offices Durocher beamed.

"That kid's a pitcher, huh, Carl?" Durocher yelled. "He ain't scared."

The Dodgers had lost three out of four at Braves Field, but the fireworks had only begun. Campanella, his voice shrill and his arms outstretched, was waiting for Dascoli to arrive at the door to the umpires' room only a few steps from the door to the visiting team's clubhouse. Robinson, Roe, and a few of their teammates also were waiting.

In the commotion, the panels on the umpires' door splintered, prompting a security guard to call for reinforcements: six Boston policemen.

When the Dodgers finally clumped into their clubhouse, Dressen told them, "Dascoli took that one away from you. Now you've just got to fight harder." Campanella was inconsolable. "I didn't cuss him," he squeaked. "I never cussed an umpire in my life. I just said, 'How can you call him safe when I had the plate blocked?' Before I said another word, he threw me out. I didn't cuss him and I didn't push him." Dascoli explained that when the Dodger catcher slammed down his glove in protest, it resulted in an automatic ejection.

"Dascoli's just not competent," Dressen told the writers. "We've had five incidents with him this season."

In the Giant offices on West 42nd Street now, the writers asked Durocher to look to the weekend.

"If we win our two in Boston, and we will, the Dodgers must win their three in Philadelphia to clinch it," he said. "I don't think they can do it. They're screaming at the umpires. Pretty soon they'll be screaming at each other. Pennant pressure can give the steadiest of pros the yips. Look at the won-lost percentage for the last thirty days. That tells the story. We're the solid club."

As the Dodgers awaited Friday night's game in Philadelphia, they learned of their minimal fines: Campanella and Robinson $100 each for the incidents outside the umpires' room "in the presence of fans and opposing players," and Roe $50 for not leaving the field immediately when ordered by the umpires. According to the newspapers, Robinson had kicked the umpires' room door, splintering it.

"I know who did it, but it wasn't me," Robinson told the writers. "But I won't tell who did it."

"I know who did it too," Roe told the writers on Robinson's behalf. "But it wasn't Jackie."

Roe, in yelling at Dascoli, had planted his feet inside the umpires' room door. "He slammed the door in my face so hard, it broke the panels against my legs," Roe would say years later. "That's how it splintered." Roe suggested that he tell the writers what happened to take the heat off Robinson, but Dressen told Roe to drop the subject.

"Let's forget it," Dressen said. "The club's paying the fines anyway."

In what seemed to be lenient discipline, Ford Frick acknowledged lecturing Dascoli for being "too hasty" in ejecting Campanella in the heat of a pennant race. Frick had not even considered suspensions, saying, "I wouldn't think of depriving the Dodgers of player strength at a time like this." Durocher agreed, saying, "We don't want any stigma on our pennant." That night Campy's thirty-third homer helped stake Carl Erskine to a 3-0 lead against Karl Drews, but the Phillies tied the score in the eighth on catcher Andy Seminick's two-run homer, his first in seven weeks. Richie Ashburn led off the ninth with a pop-fly single near the leftfield line. After a bunt by Dick Sisler and an intentional walk to Bill (Swish) Nicholson, Jones drilled a single under Cox's glove, scoring Ashburn.

"The kid should've won, three to one," Dressen said, referring to Erskine. "One mistake, Seminick's homer, and the game is lost."

The 4-3 loss, their sixth in the last eight games, dropped the Dodgers into a tie with the Giants, each with a 94-58 record, each with two games remaining. In his Kenmore Hotel suite, Durocher sat in a stuffed chair as if glued to it.

"I can't get up," he said. "If I make a move, I'll explode with happiness."

Saturday afternoon Maglie outpitched Spahn, 3-0, for his twenty-third victory and a temporary one-half-game lead. That night Campanella and Pafko homered as Newcombe outpitched Roberts with a 5-0 seven-hitter for his twentieth, restoring the first-place tie. Sunday morning Chub Feeney, the Giant vice president, was riding in a cab with Mary Ann Hearn to Braves Field for the season finale.

"I sure hope we win and the Dodgers lose," she said. "Jim doesn't like to pitch in Ebbets Field. Too much noise. He can't hear Westrum."

The Braves took a quick 1–0 lead. Minutes later, in the Shibe Park press box, a Western Union telegrapher deciphered the dots and dashes of a Morse code message and blurted, "Thomson hit one." His thirtieth homer had created a 1–1 tie in the second. Singles by Jansen, Stanky, and Mueller in the third made it 2–1. In the fifth Dark singled, stole second, and scored on Irvin's single for 3–1 as the Braves Field scoreboard showed the Dodgers losing to the Phillies, 6–1.

"Forget the scoreboard," Durocher barked in the Giants' dugout. "Just win our game."

In the Brave ninth, Addis led off with a double. Jethroe beat out a grounder. On a force play at second, Jethroe spiked Stanky as Addis scored. Walker Cooper, heavy and slow, beat out a high chopper. In the batter's box now, Willard Marshall, once Jansen's teammate, expected the righthander's curveball. But on Jansen's first pitch, a curveball, the ex-Giant outfielder lifted a routine fly ball to left. By the Shibe Park clock, it was 3:35 and the Dodgers were losing, 8–5, when the slots in the scoreboard for the Giants–Braves game opened and a hush fell over the 31,755 spectators. With the bottom of the sixth about to begin, Jackie Robinson, his hands on his hips, turned toward right-field, waiting for the Giants–Braves score to be posted.

In front of the scoreboard, Furillo kept staring toward the mound. Reese scooped the infield ball bounced to him by Hodges, glanced at it, then fired it to the first baseman. In the dugout, Dressen bent over the water cooler.

Of all the Dodgers, only Robinson seemed willing to look at the scoreboard. Suddenly a 3 dropped alongside NY, then a 2 alongside BOST. The Giants had won. Now the Dodgers had to win. But with the score 8–5 in the sixth, they were three runs behind with three innings left. Still ignoring Labine, Dressen had started Roe on two days' rest. In the second, a homer by first baseman Tommy Brown, once a Dodger at age sixteen during World War II, ignited a four-run rally that finished Roe.

"I guess I didn't have anything," Roe would confess later.

Branca didn't have much either. The Phillies added two runs off him in the third, then two in the fifth off King and Labine, pitching for the first time in more than a week, for their 8–5 lead. More than anybody else, Robinson felt responsible. In the second he had let Richie Ashburn's hot grounder roll off his arm as two runs scored. His first two times up, Robinson had bounced into a double play and struck out, looking. In the fifth his triple had knocked out Bubba Church, then he scored on Pafko's single off Karl Drews, narrowing the score to 6–5. But the Phillies had opened their 8–5 lead before Erskine, the Dodgers' fifth pitcher, blanked them in the sixth and seventh.

With one out in the eighth, Hodges beat out a grounder off shortstop Granny Hamner's glove. Cox singled. Rube Walker, pinchhitting for Erskine, doubled off the left-centerfield wall for 8–7, knocking out Drews and bringing in Roberts.

Furillo slashed a single and Don Thompson, running for Walker, slid headfirst across the plate with the tying run. On Reese's long fly to left, Furillo assumed it would land in the stands. He had rounded second when Sisler caught it. Furillo was doubled off first. Newcombe had been throwing in the Dodger bullpen and in the bottom of the eighth he strode to the mound. Now it was Newcombe vs. Roberts for the second time in about sixteen hours. Through the ninth, through the tenth when the lights were turned on. With two out in the eleventh, Hamner walked. Seminick pulled a long liner down the leftfield line. Newcombe and all the other Dodgers on the field and in the dugout held their breath before Pafko grabbed it for the third out.

"If that ball gets by Pafko," Dressen would say later, "it's all over."

Newcombe was weary. The night before he had pitched nine innings and won on only two days' rest. Now he was pitching again on about sixteen hours' rest. In the twelfth, his fifth inning in relief, he committed a pitcher's unpardonable sin: walking the other pitcher. Even more unpardonable, Roberts, representing the run that would knock the Dodgers out of the pennant race, was on first base with none out.

Second baseman Eddie Pellagrini bunted. Newcombe fielded it. Trying for the force on the slow-running Roberts, he threw wide to Reese at second. Hoping to advance both runners, Asburn bunted, but Hodges pounced on it and threw to Reese, forcing Pellagrini as Roberts chugged into third.

With the Dodgers' nemesis, Puddin' Head Jones, up next, Dressen signaled for an intentional walk, loading the bases and creating a force play at home. The next batter was Del Ennis, a threat to hit a sacrifice fly. Newcombe needed a strikeout. He knew how to pitch to Ennis: keep the fastball outside, keep the curveball down. Ennis looked at a third strike. Two out. The next batter was Eddie Waitkus, the thirty-two-year-old first baseman who had been shot in the chest by nineteen-year-old Ruth Ann Steinhagen during the 1949 season in a Chicago hotel room. He had recovered to help the Phillies win the 1950 pennant. Hitting .258 now, he had only one homer but he seldom struck out. With a quick swing, he lashed a low liner between Robinson and second base. Robinson dove, snaring the ball backhanded. Face first, he skidded across the infield's hard dirt, his right elbow knifing into his solar plexus. As umpire Lon Warneke signaled the third out, Robinson, thinking the ball might fall out of his glove, flipped it toward Reese, then collapsed. Reese rushed to him. So did Newcombe, who wondered if Jackie was faking because he never got hurt. Soon trainer Harold (Doc) Wendler was bending over him.

"He'll be all right," Wendler told Dressen. "He just knocked the wind out of himself."

Robinson tottered to his feet and wobbled to the dugout. The pennant was still there to be won. But with two out in the thirteenth, the Dodgers were in jeopardy again. Newcombe walked Seminick, then he walked Roberts for the second straight time. In less than twenty-four hours, Big Newk had not allowed a run over fifteen and one-third innings. Now he was simply worn out. Bud Podbielan, the Dodgers' seventh pitcher, got Pellagrini to lift a harmless fly ball for the third out. In the fourteenth, Roberts, pitching his fifteenth inning in less than twenty-four hours, still appeared strong when Reese and Snider lifted pop fouls. But on a one-one count he threw a fastball to Robinson, who hit it into the upper deck in leftfield. Asked later if he had been "shooting for the stands," Robinson grinned.

"I sure was," he said.

The Dodgers led, 9–8. Dressen had his last two pitchers, Haugstad and Schmitz, warming up when Ashburn opened the bottom of the fourteenth with a single. To the Dodgers' relief, Jones bunted. With Ashburn on second, Ennis popped to Hodges and Waitkus lofted a fly ball to Pafko. The Dodgers had survived. Their hitters had rallied from a 6–1 deficit. Newcombe had pitched gallantly, Pafko had made a saving catch. But more than anybody else, Robinson had kept the Dodgers alive with his diving catch in the twelfth inning and with his home run in the fourteenth. In the clubhouse, popping flashbulbs momentarily blinded him.

"I can't see," Robinson said.

"You could see," somebody joked, "when you hit that home run?"

"Greatest home run I ever hit."

The Dodgers were more relieved than happy. Relieved that they had battled back to win in fourteen innings after having trailed 6–1 and 8–5, relieved that they still had the opportunity to win the pennant in a playoff that would start tomorrow at Ebbets Field.

"We showed 'em we ain't a choke-up ballclub," Dressen chirped.

"Even if we lose to the Giants, everyone will know this team has no quitters."

As the Dodgers hurried to catch a train for Penn Station, the Giants were eating steaks in the dining car on their train to Grand Central, six cases of champagne still unopened. Chub Feeney arranged a telephone hookup with a New York radio station to get the play-by-play of the Dodger game. When the Dodgers finally won, Stanky was annoyed.

"Two weeks ago we'd have been happy to settle for this tie," he said. "But to think we'd already won and then have this happen."

Like all his teammates, Stanky was consoled by the Dodgers having to use seven pitchers. But despite their dazzling 37–7 finish while the Dodgers were 26–22, the Giants had nothing to celebrate.

"We'll get 'em tomorrow," Durocher said.

"You've told us that every day for a month," Dark said with a smile. "How long can we keep this up?"

"Just two out of three," Durocher said.

Around midnight Dodger president Walter O'Malley sold the television rights to the playoff opener at Ebbets Field to CBS for what would be major league baseball's first coast-to-coast telecast.

Monday morning Jim Hearn stopped at the Riverview Apartments in upper Manhattan overlooking the Hudson River to pick up Wes Westrum. On the drive to Ebbets Field they went over the Dodger hitters.

"Furillo?" Hearn said.

"First-ball hitter and a high-ball hitter. Keep it down."

"Reese?"

"Good hit-and-run man. He'll go to rightfield."

"Snider?"

"Likes the ball on the inner half of the plate. Keep it outside. Defy him to pull it."

"Robinson?"

"Keep the ball on top of him, then make him reach for it."

"Campanella?"

"Good fastball hitter. Keep the ball down."

"Pafko?"

"High-ball hitter. Anything above the belt, he'll kill it."

"Hodges?"

"Keep the ball away. He'll give you the outer third of the plate."

"Cox?"

"Another first-ball hitter and high-ball hitter."

"Branca?"

"Curve him."

At noon the Dodgers were taking batting practice when the Giants hopped up the steps of the third-base dugout. With a sly smile, infielder Bill Rigney strolled behind the cage where Robinson was hitting.

"Hey, Jackie, look around," the Giant infielder said, loud enough for the other Dodgers to hear. "You'll never guess who's here."

Robinson didn't need to look around; he knew. He also knew that, after using seven pitchers in Sunday's game, Dressen had told his staff, "Everybody's available except Roe; he'll open the World Series." He also knew that Campanella could just about walk, much less run. Campy had pulled a hamstring muscle Sunday in Philadelphia while running out a fourth-inning triple. With his right thigh tightly taped, he had hobbled through the fourteen innings. Now, his thigh injected with novocaine, he assured Dressen he could catch.

"Don't worry, Skip," he said. "I can run if I have to."

With the weather warm and hazy, Pafko's second-inning homer got the Dodgers off to a 1–0 lead. In the fourth, Branca plunked Irvin on the left forearm and Thomson smashed a fastball into the left-centerfield stands. In the eighth Irvin whacked a curve into the leftfield stands. Hearn scattered five hits. With a 3–1 victory, their eighth straight, the Giants had wrecked Dressen's master plan. The Dodger manager had counted on winning the opener at Ebbets Field before going to the Polo Grounds for the Tuesday game and, if necessary, the Wednesday game.

"Branca pitched great," the Dodger manager told the writers, "but he made two mistakes. The home run pitch to Irvin was the same one he threw him to cost us that 2–1 game just before the last road trip. It was a waist-high curve, the kind Irvin hits. Thomson hit a fastball, also waist high. I know what those guys can't hit, but I can't guide the ball for my pitchers, can I?"

Branca, who had thrown 133 pitches, wandered about the clubhouse, every so often slamming his right fist into the wall and muttering, "One pitch. Just one pitch," meaning Thomson's homer. Now that the Giants were returning to the Polo Grounds one game up, some of the Dodgers were questioning Dressen's decision to play the first game at Ebbets Field rather than the second and, if necessary, the third. But as disappointed as Dressen was, he seemed more concerned about Campanella's thigh. With one out in the fourth, Snider had singled, then raced to third on Robinson's single. Campy limped into the batter's box. With his pulled hamstring, he had not backed up throws to first base and had ignored foul pops unless they were near the plate. In the Giants' dugout, Durocher had waved his infielders back. Dark retreated onto the leftfield grass. Swinging awkwardly, Campy bounced a grounder directly to Dark, who tossed to Stanky, whose throw to Lockman was wide of the bag. But with Campy hobbling, Lockman had time to move to get the throw and tag Campy. Double play.

If he were healthy, Campy might have beaten Stanky's wide throw, allowing Snider to score for a 2–1 lead. But when Campy had to run, he couldn't.

"Roy can't run and they get a gift double play that costs us a run," Dressen growled. "Unless he's much better tomorrow, he won't catch."

Dressen wouldn't announce his Tuesday starter, saying he would choose either Erskine or Labine, but he insisted that Durocher would pitch Maglie even though the Giant manager had mentioned right-hander Sheldon Jones.

"I don't believe any of that stuff about Jones," Dressen said. "Jones was in the bullpen when today's game started, wasn't he?"

Behind the bricked-up door in the Giants' clubhouse, Durocher declined to pose for the photographers. "I'm superstitious," he said, his voice hoarse from yelling in the third-base coach's box. "I didn't pose for pictures for two weeks until I finally gave up in Boston after Saturday's game and look what happened. There'll be no pictures of me while this is on." Sitting on an equipment trunk, Hearn, once characterized by some of his ex-Cardinal teammates as "a guy who couldn't pitch for a pennant contender," posed proudly.

"I wasn't tired, not in the sense of weariness," Hearn said. "But in a game like that, something affects you, something comes over you. You're strong, yet you feel it. Maybe it's the pressure of the respon-sibility."

Tuesday afternoon Clem Labine and Sheldon Jones had that re-sponsibility. In his desperation, knowing that another loss would eliminate his team that had once been thirteen and one-half games ahead, Dressen had removed his rookie righthander from the dog-house.

"The Polo Grounds is a park for the overhand curve; the strong hitters won't pull it," Dressen told him. "Don't throw that sidearm stuff."

In the Giants' clubhouse Durocher had called Maglie and Jansen into his office, up a short flight of steps from where the players dressed.

"I want your opinion," Durocher said, staring at Maglie. "I can pitch you today on two days' rest and if you get beat, I can pitch Larry tomorrow on two days' rest."

"I'll pitch today if you want me to," Maglie said, "but I'll be better tomorrow on three days' rest."

"I'll be better with my rest too," said Jansen, superstitious enough to keep the same ink-stained bedspread in his Henry Hudson Hotel room ever since the Giants had begun closing the gap. "But I'll do whatever you want. I'll be in the bullpen if you need me."

"Sal," said Durocher, "if there's a game tomorrow, you're it."

During batting practice some of the writers surrounded another manager. With the Yankees waiting for the World Series opener on Thursday, Casey Stengel was asked which team he would rather play.

"Well," he snorted. "It's like I always say, 'If you can play a team with a one-legged catcher, you got a big edge.' "

Stengel was talking about Campanella, who still couldn't run. For this game that the Dodgers had to win, Rube Walker was Dressen's catcher. And the Dodger manager was using all his tricks. When Snider struck out in the first, Dressen whistled at plate umpire Larry Goetz.

"Spitter, spitter," Dressen yelled. "Jones is spitting on his fingers and not wiping it off."

Maybe that disturbed Jones, maybe not. The next batter, Jackie Robinson, hit a two-run homer. Nothing disturbed Labine, not even a forty-one-minute rain delay during the top of the sixth.

"I've had these in the minors," Labine told his teammates. "I'll be all right."

Minutes before the rain delay Hodges had jarred George Spencer with a homer. Pafko and Rube Walker added homers off Al Corwin in the eighth and ninth for a 10–0 rout. Labine's smooth six-hitter had only one uneasy moment: with two out in the third, Thomson was up with the bases loaded. As much as Labine liked to pitch from the stretch position, he knew he better not. On a three-two count, Thomson swung and missed at a low sweeping outside curveball that Labine had thrown with a full windup.

"I called for the curve," Dressen told the writers. "You think I'm going to have him throw a fastball there? If Labine doesn't get it over, or if Thomson doesn't swing, one run is better than four. That guy wasn't going to get the chance to hit one in the seats."

Now it was early Wednesday afternoon, October 3, gray and gloomy but warm. On the subways and highways, 34,320 Giant and Dodger fans were arriving to sit among the old steel girders of the Polo Grounds with its short foul lines: 257 feet in rightfield, 280 in leftfield. Maglie would be going against Newcombe with the pennant to be decided in each team's 157th game. Thomson had driven up the West Side Highway in his blue Mercury, thinking, If I can go three for four, we can beat 'em. In the Dodgers' clubhouse, Branca was sitting at his locker when Robinson caught his eye.

"You got to have butterflies today," Robinson said.

Branca was about to have Doc Wendler rub warm oil on his right arm. "You," Dressen had told him, "are my number one man in the bullpen." But now Dressen was confronted by Roy Campanella near the manager's locker. Sunday afternoon in Philadelphia, Campy had joked, "Just think, we win and they win, now we got to face Maglie again. If I could, I'd put on a football helmet against him." But with the pennant at stake and Maglie pitching, Dressen kept Rube Walker in the lineup. Campy was growling.

"You got to let me play, Charlie," he said.

"You can't run, Roy," the manager said.

"I'll get an injection," insisted the catcher, who would be voted the NL's most valuable player that season. "I'll be able to run then."

"You told me that Monday," the manager said.

Sal (The Barber) Maglie had beaten the Dodgers five times. His fastball shaved their chins. His three different curveballs had them flailing. But in the first inning, the Barber's razor wasn't sharp. Reese walked. Snider walked. Robinson bounced a hard single to left for a 1–0 lead. In the second the Giants erupted. Lockman singled. Thomson extended his hitting streak to fifteen consecutive games, lashing Newcombe's fastball down the leftfield line. Pafko fielded it quickly, Lockman stopping at second. Thomson, thinking he had a double, didn't look up until he was approaching second, where Lockman was waiting. Thomson tried to retreat to first, but Hodges tagged him.

Another player might have thought, If we lose, I'll be the goat. But as Thomson trotted to the dugout, he felt as free as a wild horse who couldn't be roped. He knew he would get another chance.

In the cloudy grayness of the third inning, the lights were turned on. "Maybe Thomson can see Lockman on second now," somebody in the press box joked. "Maybe the Giants can see Newcombe's fastball now," somebody else snorted. Through six innings, Newcombe kept mowing the Giants down. On only two days' rest, he had extended his shutout streak to twenty and two-thirds innings over three games in five days of pennant pressure competition. But in the seventh Irvin doubled off the leftfield wall. Lockman bunted. Walker, trying to nail Irvin at third, threw too late. Cox walked over to Newcombe, who pretended to take the ball as Cox returned to third.

"Time, time," Lockman yelled from first base. "Hey, Leo, Cox has the ball. Cox has the ball."

The hidden ball trick had been detected. Thomson lifted a long fly to Snider, deep enough for Irvin to score. When each previous inning ended, Newcombe had heard Durocher yelling, "If we stay close, we'll get you." Now, as Newcombe came off the mound with the score 1–1, he heard Durocher's raspy voice again.

"You're losing it," Durocher barked at him.

"You're running out of time," Newk growled.

For all his bravado, Newk knew he was running out of gas. In the dugout he wondered aloud if he could get through another inning. Reese and Robinson exhorted him.

"Give us one more inning," Reese said.

With one out in the top of the eighth, Maglie suddenly was strafed. Reese singled. Snider singled. With Robinson up, Maglie's wide curve bounced past Westrum for a wild pitch that allowed Reese to score. With first base open, Durocher ordered Robinson walked intentionally. Pafko singled off Thomson's glove, scoring Snider for 3–1. Hodges popped up, but Cox singled for a 4–1 lead going into the bottom of the eighth.

"Rig, Hank," Durocher yelled to Bill Rigney and Hank Thompson. "You're hitting for Westrum and Maglie."

Rigney was yanking a bat out of the rack when he heard Stanky say, "The big guy's losing it," meaning Newcombe. "We'll get him. He's losing it." Buoyed by the three-run rally, Newcombe hummed a first-pitch fastball that appeared to Rigney to be no larger than a pea. Strike one. Rigney turned to Stanky in the on-deck circle.

"Yeah, Eddie," he said. "He's really losing it."

Rigney struck out. Hank Thompson bounced to Hodges. Stanky popped to Reese. Now it was the ninth inning. Larry Jansen walked in from the Giant bullpen to face Newcombe, whose spirits had been boosted by his easy inning. In the on-deck circle, Furillo turned to Stan Strull, the Dodger batboy.

"Anybody calls me in the clubhouse for World Series tickets, I'm gone," Furillo said.

When the Dodgers went out one-two-three in the ninth and the Giants trotted to their dugout, Thomson thought the Giants just weren't good enough. Then he realized that in their 157th game, nothing had been decided yet, that the Giants still had a chance. On his way to the third-base coaching box, Durocher stopped, turned, and stared into his dugout.

"You guys have come this far," he said. "Let's give 'em a finish."

With two strikes, Dark slapped a ground single off the tip of Hodges's outstretched glove, the ball dribbling just out of Robinson's reach. In the bullpen in deep left-centerfield, Branca and Erskine had been throwing since the fifth inning. Since the seventh Dressen had been phoning bullpen coach Clyde Sukeforth every few minutes.

"Who's ready? Who's ready?" Dressen kept asking.

In the dugout Clyde King, his arm so sore he literally couldn't raise it to comb his hair, had never seen Dressen this jumpy. The manager was looking to make moves before the moves were necessary. But now, in the crisis of the ninth inning, forty-nine-year-old coach Clyde Sukeforth, once a catcher with the Reds and the Dodgers, was warming up Branca while glancing between pitches at Erskine.

"Knowing the competitor Erskine was," Sukeforth would say later, "to get one or two guys out, if I'd seen him throwing his good curveball, I'd have told Charlie that. But I didn't see his curveball and I respected Branca's fastball."

Branca, bothered throughout September by his sore shoulder, had thrown 133 pitches in Monday's 3–1 loss but had allowed only five hits, including homers by Thomson and Irvin, over eight tense innings. He had given up two hits and two runs Sunday in Philadelphia over one and one-third innings. His arm was more tight than tired. His first toss in the bullpen during the fifth inning had landed weakly in front of the plate. He had needed more time than usual to get loose. In the dugout now, as much as Dressen understandably was concerned about Newcombe's effectiveness, he seemed strangely concerned about Dark being on first base. With a 4–1 lead and a leadoff batter on first, most managers usually kept their first baseman in his normal fielding position to narrow the hole between him and the second baseman. Dressen instead signaled Hodges to hold Dark on the bag, widening the area between Robinson and the foul line.

"I remember," Dark would say years later, "Hodges being close to the bag, but not on it."

To Mueller, whose bat was more wand than weapon, it appeared that Hodges was on the bag. Mueller's gift was his ability to hit the ball through the gaps between the fielders.

"The hardest part of hitting," he often said, "isn't hitting the ball. It's hitting the ball where you want to hit it."

Mueller ripped Newcombe's fastball for a single through the wide gap between Hodges and Robinson as Dark hurried to third.

Swinging two bats, Irvin moved out of the on-deck circle but Dressen bustled to the mound. Dressen wasn't thinking about changing pitchers so much as changing catchers. He knew Campanella always got the last ounce of strength out of Newcombe, but he also knew that foul ground in the Polo Grounds was vast. What if Irvin hits a foul ball behind the plate, the Dodger manager realized, and Campy can't run well enough to get under it? The writers would second-guess him. Dressen reminded Newcombe to keep the ball away from Irvin, then trotted back to the dugout. Irvin led the NL with 121 runs batted in. He prided himself on hitting in the clutch. If you can't perform in key situations, he always told himself, don't bother to perform. But now he lifted a high foul to Hodges near first base. Returning to the dugout, he couldn't look at his teammates.

"I was trying too hard to pull the ball," he mumbled.

In the Dodgers' dugout, Dressen and the others took a deep breath. Irvin was a big out. Watching that pop-up, Lockman felt his heart sink. In the press box hanging from the upper deck behind home plate, a voice announced: "Attention, press. World Series credentials for Ebbets Field can be picked up at six o'clock tonight at the Biltmore Hotel." Settling into the batter's box, Lockman was hoping to hit a home run. Newcombe knew what Lockman was thinking. To prevent the lefthanded-swinging Lockman from pulling the ball toward the 254-foot marker on the rightfield foul line, Newcombe kept his fastball outside. Lockman swung. The ball sailed into the leftfield corner for a standup double as Dark scored for 4–2 while Mueller moved to third. Bobby Thomson was the next Giant hitter. Dressen phoned the bullpen where Branca and Erskine were throwing.

"Who's ready?" he yipped. "Who's ready?"

"Erskine just bounced his curveball," Erskine heard Sukeforth tell the manager. "Branca's ready. Branca's throwing hard."

"That's all I want to know," Dressen said.

When his curveball bounced in the dirt, Erskine was elated. When his curveball bounced, it usually meant it had dropped suddenly after dipping through the strike zone. Campanella was accustomed to

246

blocking that overhand curveball. With runners on second and third, maybe Dressen wasn't sure that Rube Walker would be able to block that curveball. Dressen didn't want a wild pitch or a passed ball. But in the third-base coach's box Durocher was frantic.

"Time, time," he was yelling.

Mueller was stretched out, writhing in pain. As the Giant right-fielder steamed into third on Lockman's double, he had glanced over his shoulder to check Pafko's throw to Reese; if that throw were mishandled, Mueller had planned to try to score. In taking his eyes off the bag, he had stumbled into it, twisting his right ankle. Durocher bent over him. Doc Bowman, the Giants' trainer, examined him.

"What did I do?" Mueller asked Bowman.

"I think you broke a bone in your foot."

X-rays would show that Mueller had torn tendons; his ankle would be in a cast for three months. Near the plate Thomson was walking in small circles. Out at second base Lockman was talking to Freddie Fitzsimmons, who had come over from the first-base coach's box.

"Say a prayer that Don's all right and that Bobby hits one," Fitz said. "Don't forget to watch yourself."

Fitzsimmons reminded Lockman of two base-running fundamentals: don't get doubled off and if the ball is hit in front of you, be careful. By now most people were staring at the mound where Dressen and Newcombe were surrounded by Reese, Robinson, Hodges, Cox, and Walker.

"What do you want to do?" Dressen asked. "It's your money as well as mine."

His players stared at each other. At second base Lockman represented the tying run. At the plate Thomson represented the winning run. The Dodger players, especially Reese, the man they addressed as "Captain," couldn't believe that Dressen, who always had all the answers, was asking them to make the decision that would win or lose the pennant. Reese finally spoke up.

"Newk's given us all he's got for the last week," the Dodger captain said. "Why don't you get somebody fresh in here?"

Dressen waved for Branca in the bullpen. At third base Clint Hartung, once a spring training pheenom who never lived up to his billing as either an outfielder or a righthanded pitcher, was running for Mueller, about to be taken on a stretcher to the Giants' clubhouse where owner Horace Stoneham was making a rare appearance.

"No matter what happens," Stoneham would tell Mueller and the others there, "I'm going to have a drink with everybody on this ballclub."

Leaving the bullpen, Branca, who had appeared fourteen times in relief this season, was thinking he could be a hero. When he heard Duke Snider yell, "Go get 'em, Honker," he smiled. Walking across the infield dirt, Branca realized that his arm not only was loose but suddenly felt stronger than it had at any time since his two consecutive shutouts more than five weeks ago. Remembering what Robinson had mentioned in the clubhouse, Branca glanced at Robinson and Reese and said, "Anybody got any butterflies?" Without a word, Robinson turned away. At the mound Branca smiled at Newcombe and said, "Don't worry about it, big fella. I'll take care of everything." Dressen tossed the ball to Branca and blurted, "Get him out." Turning quickly, Dressen marched to the dugout.

Out in centerfield, Snider realized that Dressen was really uptight.

Snider remembered how the Dodger pitchers had told him that when they arrived on the mound from the bullpen, Dressen always reminded them who and where the base runners were, how many were out, and how to pitch to the next batter. But in this crisis Dressen had all but deserted Branca.

Not that Branca noticed. He knew that Dressen knew that he knew how to pitch to Thomson.

By now Thomson, who had walked over to comfort Mueller at third base, was aware that Branca was the new pitcher. In the on-deck circle, Willie Mays was worrying. The twenty-year-old rookie assumed the Dodgers would walk Thomson intentionally, loading the bases. Mays didn't know that the intentional walk had seldom been one of Dressen's tactics. Especially when it meant putting the winning run on base, in this case the pennant-winning run. But as Mays worried, over between third and home Durocher put his arms on Thomson's shoulders.

"If you ever hit one," Durocher said, "hit one now."

Settling into the batter's box now, Thomson told himself to wait and watch, give himself a chance to hit. Wait and watch. Sixty feet, six inches away, Branca remembered that in Monday's playoff opener Thomson had homered off a fastball. This time, Branca hoped to get him to hit a curveball. But to set Thomson up for a curveball, Branca needed to get ahead in the count with some good mustard. He fired a fastball across the middle of the plate. Thomson took it but knew he should not have taken it. His body sagged slightly. In the Giants' dugout his teammates groaned. In the Dodger bullpen, Erskine and

The trajectory of Bobby Thomson's home run into the lower leftfield stands at the Polo Grounds. *AP/Wide World Photo*

Clem Labine, who was throwing now, had stopped to watch Branca's first pitch. Each gasped.

"Not there," Erskine said.

On the mound, Branca planned to waste a fastball up and inside that Thomson wouldn't swing at. Then he would spin a curveball down on the outside corner.

The fastball was up and inside.

Not wanting to risk another called strike, Thomson swung. Hit solidly, the ball rose on a low line toward the lower leftfield stands. Get down, get down, Branca thought, meaning hit the wall so Pafko could retrieve it. Seeing the ball's low trajectory, Pafko thought, I might get it, I might get it. His wife, Ellen, was praying he would. Most of the Dodger wives were at the Polo Grounds but Ellen Pafko had returned to their Chicago home at 4507 West Parker while the Dodgers were on their road trip. Minutes earlier, a taxicab driver had honked. The taxi had arrived to take her to the LaSalle Street station for the train to New York for the World Series.

"Can you wait a minute, please," she told the driver. "The game's almost over."

Now, knowing the ball had sailed into the stands, knowing the Giants had won the pennant the Dodgers thought they had won weeks earlier, the pennant her husband presumably had assured, Ellen Pafko's eyes misted. She went out and told the driver, "I'm sorry, I don't need you." By then the Polo Grounds had all but exploded. So had the New York Stock Exchange, the roar echoing across the Wall Street caverns. In homes and offices all over the New York area, people were shouting or sobbing. In the bay, fog horns on tugboats and ferryboats were blowing. Thomson, whose first thought at 3:57 P.M. had been, We beat Brooklyn, we beat Brooklyn, bounded around the bases and leaped into the arms of his teammates at home plate. Near third base, Stanky, who had been Branca's roommate when they were Dodger teammates, was rolling on the grass with Durocher, their arms around each other. In the radio booth, play-by-play announcer Russ Hodges had hollered to the rest of the world:

"The Giants win the pennant! The Giants win the pennant! The Giants win the pennant! The Giants win the pennant! Bobby Thomson hits it into the lower deck of the leftfield stands! The Giants

Jackie Robinson watches from behind second base and Ralph Branca turns from the mound as Bobby Thomson scores in the jubilation of his pennant-winning home run. *National Baseball Library and Archive, Cooperstown, N.Y.*

win the pennant and they're going crazy, they're going crazy. Ooooohhhheeee."

On the outfield grass behind second base, Jackie Robinson, his hands on his hips, had carefully watched Thomson round the bases. As soon as Thomson jumped onto home plate, Robinson turned toward the old green wooden clubhouses beyond centerfield. Branca had noticed Stanky celebrating with Durocher, but now, his head down, he turned away. Grabbing their blue Dodger jackets off the bullpen bench, Erskine and Labine looked at each other.

"I didn't see a ball go into the stands," Labine said. "I saw my wallet go into the stands with $5,000 in it."

In the box seats near the Dodgers' dugout, a blond teenager burst into tears. Noticing her sobs, Walter Winchell, the *Daily Mirror*'s syndicated gossip columnist, turned to Dodger general manager Buzzie Bavasi and said, "That kid's sure taking this pretty hard."

"You would too," Bavasi said, nodding toward Terry O'Malley, "if you were Walter O'Malley's daughter."

As the Dodgers plodded across the centerfield grass, the Giants surged across it. Surrounded by hundreds of fans who had hopped over the box seat railings, the Giants clambered up the wooden steps into the chaos of their clubhouse while the Dodgers quietly hurried into the gloom of theirs. The writers, photographers, and television cameramen who had begun gathering there in the eighth inning had already scampered to the Giants' clubhouse. Now, one by one, the Dodgers arrived. As he always did, Hodges folded his first baseman's mitt and put it in the top shelf of his locker. Robinson flung his glove into the rear of his locker. Dressen ripped his uniform shirt off, the buttons bouncing across the old wooden floor. Branca sat on the wooden stairs of the two-level clubhouse, his head bowed, his shoulders hunched, a blue *13* on the back of his uniform shirt. Barney Stein, a *New York Post* photographer, snapped the scene.

"Why me?" Duke Snider could hear Branca murmuring. "Why me?"

When some of the writers and photographers arrived, Branca, his uniform shirt off by now, was stretched out face down on the stairs, next to coach Cookie Lavagetto, who was scratching his head as if in shock.

Is this what baseball does to people? Newcombe thought.

With the hiss of the showers the only sound in the clubhouse, Branca eventually got up from the stairs, then walked up and down in front of the lockers. Soon a few writers approached him.

Ralph Branca in the Dodgers' clubhouse. *Barney Stein*

"I guess we weren't meant to win it," he told them. "The ball was high and inside. Not a good pitch."

Dressen disagreed, saying, "It was a good pitch. It would've been a strike. I thought it was just about the same pitch as the one Thomson hit in Brooklyn in Monday's game." Branca had been tagged for eleven homers by the Giants this season: Irvin five, Thomson three, Mueller two, Westrum one.

"If I had it to do over," he would say years later, "I would make the waste pitch low and outside."

In the hours to come, Branca would think of two other moments that turned the pennant race: Thomson's lunging double play on Pafko's grounder at Ebbets Field nearly a month earlier and umpire Frank Dascoli's call in Boston a week earlier. But at his locker now, Branca was being comforted by some of his teammates.

"I threw thirty of those gopher balls," Roe whispered to him.

Outside, the Dodgers could hear Giants fans chanting, "We want Thomson! We want Thomson!" Soon he appeared on the steps, still wearing his uniform with 23 on the back, smiling and waving as the crowd roared. One by one, several other Giants came out to wave and take a bow, but Lockman was stretched out in the trainer's room. His neck hurt.

Bobby Thomson waves to the multitude outside the Giants' clubhouse at the Polo Grounds. *National Baseball Library and Archive, Cooperstown, N.Y.*

"I tried to pick up Bobby and carry him off," he explained. "I got him up on my shoulders, then we got crushed by the fans."

Lockman's neck was sprained. He would bat .240 in the World Series, which the Yankees would win in six games. But now, as Lockman rubbed his neck, Irvin walked over to him. Still annoyed at having popped up in the clutch, Irvin said, "Thanks for picking me up."

"You picked us up all season," Lockman said. "You should be the MVP this year."

Thomson's homer had provided Jansen with his twenty-third victory, matching Maglie's total. At his locker Jansen was laughing. "Hey, Sal, remember when you were nine and two and I was four and four?" Jansen said. "I told you, 'I'll catch you' and you said, 'If you catch me, we'll win the pennant.' " By now Walter O'Malley, Dressen, and several Dodger players had arrived in the Giants' clubhouse. Dressen shook hands with Durocher, reminding him of their conversation on the train from California to spring training in Florida.

"You said we'd finish one-two," Dressen said. "I didn't think I'd be two."

Pee Wee Reese wished the Giant players good luck in the World Series. Preacher Roe stared at several Giants, shrugged, and said, "You all got to be shittin' me." Jackie Robinson tapped Bill Rigney on the shoulder.

"I want you to know one thing," Robinson said. "We didn't lose it. You won it."

Clem Labine stopped at Thomson's locker to shake hands. Looking up, Thomson asked, "Who are you?" In the confusion, he hadn't recognized the righthander who struck him out the day before with the bases loaded. Soon somebody introduced himself to Thomson as a representative of the Perry Como television show.

"Can you stop by the show tonight?" the stranger said. "We'll give you five hundred dollars."

"That's really nice," Thomson said, "but I want to get back to Staten Island to see my family. My mother and my sisters didn't come to the game."

"How about if we give you a thousand dollars?"

"For a thou, I guess my family can wait."

Thomson agreed, joking later that he had surrendered to his Scottish heritage. After the show at CBS television's midtown Studio 52, having asked his friend Al Corbin to drive his car home, Thomson took a cab to the Battery, dropped a nickel in the turnstile for the Staten Island ferry, rode across New York Bay, then took a cab to his older brother Jim's firehouse.

"Do you realize what you did today?" his brother said. "Do you realize something like this may never happen again?"

To celebrate, Bobby Thomson and his family had dinner at the Tavern on the Green, a popular Staten Island restaurant. Ralph Branca and his fiancée, Ann Mulvey, had planned to have dinner with Rube Walker and his wife, Millie, at Paul Daube's steakhouse in the Bronx, and they went there anyway. In the Polo Grounds parking lot Ann had been waiting in Ralph's sky-blue Oldsmobile sedan with their friend Father Pat Rowley, a Jesuit at Fordham University. Seeing the priest, Ralph asked him the question he had been asking himself.

"Why me, Father?" he asked. "Why me?"

"God chose you, Ralph," the priest said, "because He knew you'd be strong enough to bear this cross."

1964

The Phillies' Phlop

Manager Gene Mauch mulls the situation in the Phillies' dugout. *National Baseball Library and Archive, Cooperstown, N.Y.*

OST OF PHILADELPHIA was sleeping peacefully. The pennant seemed assured. As the first-place Phillies arrived at Philadelphia International Airport in the early morning darkness of Monday, September 21, 1964, about two thousand faithful fans, including Mayor James Tate, had gathered to welcome manager Gene Mauch and his players. Several days earlier the Phillies had announced World Series ticket prices for a four-game strip: $25 for a box seat, $17 for a reserved seat, $9 for a bleacher seat. Ruben Amaro, one of the Phillies' shortstops, had ordered $1,800 worth of tickets and now his wife, Judy, watched the chartered jetliner roll up to the gate.

"Ruben's mother, father, and one of his sisters," she said, "are coming up from Mexico for the World Series."

The Phillies were six and one-half games ahead with only twelve games remaining. Both the Reds and the Cardinals were struggling to finish second. Sunday afternoon Jim Bunning, the Phillies' ace righthander, had stopped a two-game losing streak, preserving a 3–2 victory in Los Angeles by striking out John Roseboro, the Dodger catcher, in the ninth inning as Tommy Davis broke for second base.

"I didn't even know he was running," Bunning said. "I was thinking of Roseboro, nothing else."

With a seven-game home stand to begin that Monday night at Connie Mack Stadium, the Phillies were thinking about the World Series, nothing else. Saturday night the Phillies were about to take batting practice in Dodger Stadium when they learned that the Reds had stunned the Cardinals, 7–5, in the opener of a twi-night doubleheader on Frank Robinson's three-run homer in the ninth inning off Bob Gibson, the Cardinals' best righthander. Told about Robinson's homer, Bunning smiled.

"That's another World Series share we've got to vote," he said.

Bunning, a lanky lumbering righthander, had an 18–5 record. In his last ten decisions, he had lost only once, a 6–5 defeat in Houston the previous Wednesday when he had started with only two days' rest after having worked ten innings in San Francisco. But that Wednesday night the second-place Cardinals had remained six and one-half games behind, losing in Milwaukee, 3–2, on second baseman Denis Menke's three-run homer off righthander Ron Taylor.

"It almost seems like the rest of the league is playing for us," said Art Mahaffey, a Phillie righthander. "We lose, they lose. That's why there's no pressure. I guess if the lead got down to one or two games, it would be different."

But the Phillies were breezing to the pennant. Bunning, obtained from the Detroit Tigers during the off-season, had pitched a perfect game against the Mets at Shea Stadium on Father's Day, befitting a future congressman from Kentucky who would sire nine children. As the Phillies batted in the top of the eighth that sweltering afternoon, Bunning changed his sweatshirt for the third time and ignored the superstition not to discuss a no-hitter, much less a perfect game.

"We're getting close; only six outs to go," he exhorted his teammates. "Start diving for the ball."

Bunning was the horse of the Phillies' staff, their answer to Don Drysdale of the Los Angeles Dodgers and Bob Gibson of the Cardinals. Like them, Bunning didn't have to be told to retaliate if one of his Phillies was plunked by an opposing pitcher. But his teammates cherished him for more than his prowess on the mound. When the Phillies' front office told the team that each player's usual two free tickets would not be available because the game was a sellout, Bunning objected.

"That's against the rules," he said.

The players got their tickets. Bunning also took charge of how his fielders should play opposing hitters. Because his fallaway follow-through seldom left him in position to stop a ball hit through the middle, he wanted his shortstop to play closer to second base against lefthanded hitters.

"If they hit the ball through the hole," he said, "it's my fault."

The Phillies' best lefthander, Chris Short, depended more on his natural ability than his dedication. He once was only one out away from a victory in Wrigley Field when he stood on the mound staring at a paper plane as it glided to the grass.

"Lefty Gomez used to do it with real airplanes," Mauch said that day, thinking of the Yankees' Hall of Fame lefthander. "Shorty does it with paper planes."

Jim Bunning warms up as Chris Short looks on. *UPI Photo*

Dennis Bennett, Art Mahaffey, Ray Culp, and rookie Rick Wise were the other starters. Jack Baldschun, Ed Roebuck, and Bobby Shantz were in the bullpen. Johnny Callison, the rightfielder whose three-run homer off Dick Radatz had won the All-Star Game at Shea Stadium, would hit 31 homers and drive in 104 runs. Richie Allen, the rookie third baseman from Wampum, Pennsylvania, would hit 29 homers and drive in 91 runs. Tony Taylor was a smooth second baseman. Bobby Wine and Ruben Amaro shared shortstop. Tony Gonzalez was the centerfielder, Wes Covington the leftfielder. Vic Power and John Herrnstein were platooning at first base ever since Frank Thomas, who had hit 7 homers and driven in 26 runs in 32 games after being acquired from the Mets in early August, broke his right thumb September 6 sliding back to second base on a pickoff play. Clay Dalrymple and Gus Triandos were the catchers.

Not exactly a great team. None of these Phillies is in the Hall of Fame. But going into the last two weeks of the season, this was a good team having a great year.

Talking to Larry Merchant of the Philadelphia *Daily News* after one of the Phillies' more fortunate victories, Gus Triandos had said, "This is the Year of the Blue Snow." Triandos remembered Jim Bunning using that phrase when they were on the Tigers together. It meant a rare year when, whatever happened, things seemed to work out for the best. Such a rare year that the snow was blue.

More than anybody else on the Phillies, the best and the brightest of baseball's young managers, Gene Mauch, recognized the blue snow.

Always in command, a relentless tactician, Mauch had been voted the NL manager of the year in 1962 even though the Phillies finished seventh. His 1961 Phillies had a record twenty-three-game losing streak in a 47–107 season, but now his 1964 Phillies surely would be the first of his many pennant-winning teams. Not that Mauch was taking the pennant for granted. He didn't like to hear his players joke, "Don't worry, Gene will think of something." He knew players won games, not the manager. Hoping to strengthen his bullpen, he had mentioned to general manager John Quinn that Hoyt Wilhelm, the knuckleball righthander then with the Chicago White Sox, was available for $50,000.

"I'm not paying $50,000," Quinn replied, "for a forty-one-year-old knuckleball pitcher."

Quinn assumed that Wilhelm's career was about over. But with the White Sox that season he would have a 12–9 record with twenty-seven saves and a 1.99 earned run average. With the White Sox, Angels, Braves, Cubs, Braves, and Dodgers, he would pitch six more seasons and part of another until age forty-eight, appearing in 316 more games with a 37–30 record and eighty-one more saves.

In Mauch's eagerness to clinch the pennant, he had begun to juggle his pitching rotation, with Mahaffey the odd man out. Mahaffey had been a nineteen-game winner for Mauch in 1962 and he had a 12–8 record now, but he had been bypassed that Wednesday night in Houston when Mauch asked Bunning to start on only two days' rest. In his six previous starts, Mahaffey had failed to survive the first inning three times. After allowing two runs in the first inning of another start, he was about to bat in the third when he heard a whistle: Mauch was sending up Danny Cater as a pinch hitter. In struggling through his other recent starts, Mahaffey had heard the sound of a ball thudding into a bullpen catcher's glove.

"If you've never pitched," he said, "you don't know what it's like to hear that pop of leather as soon as a man gets on base. I never heard it before. The next time I pitch will probably be after we clinch the pennant."

That Wednesday night in Houston, before one of the last games at Colt Stadium, where the concession stands sold mosquito spray as well as hot dogs, Mauch seemed unusually irritable. Maybe the manager thought his players had begun spending their World Series shares too soon. That afternoon his ace lefthander, Chris Short, had purchased two expensive shotguns. Ruben Amaro had bought a pistol. In the clubhouse now, Wes Covington was fondling a hunting rifle he had slid out of its hand-tooled leather case.

"This one," Covington said, squinting through the rifle's sight, "is for a sportswriter."

But maybe Mauch was concerned about starting Bunning on only two days' rest, even though the ace righthander had beaten the Colt .45's four times that season. Or maybe Mauch was concerned about another starter, Dennis Bennett, whose left shoulder had stiffened Tuesday night after six innings of a 1–0 victory that righthander Jack Baldschun finished.

"It's the first time in my life," Bennett said, "I ever picked up a ball and it hurt to throw it."

By Saturday night Bennett's arm felt well enough for him to start at Dodger Stadium and to boldly predict that he would extend his hitting streak to four consecutive games.

"Joe DiMaggio's record," he was told, "is fifty-six games."

Bennett laughed and said, "So maybe it'll take me five years."

He got a single but he didn't last three innings. The game lasted sixteen innings. The Dodgers would win, 4–3, when their speedy centerfielder, Willie Davis, took advantage of Morrie Steevens, a rookie lefthander. Steevens had just joined the Phillies in Los Angeles after being called up from the Little Rock, Arkansas, farm team that was in San Diego in the midst of the Pacific Coast League play-offs.

"What they do in Little Rock doesn't mean anything," Mauch explained. "He might get three hitters out for us that'll mean more than fifteen PCL playoffs."

With two out in the sixteenth inning that Saturday night, Jack Baldschun was pitching for the Phillies when Willie Davis singled. Davis stole second and kept going to third on Baldschun's wild pitch. Mauch waved to the bullpen for Steevens, who didn't pay enough attention to the Dodger centerfielder. With two out and two strikes on first baseman Ron Fairly, third-base coach Leo Durocher told Davis, "This kid is winding up, he's not watching you. I know you can steal home on this kid." When the rookie wound up again, Davis went. Steevens didn't realize Davis was running until it was too late. Davis stole home.

"There's a kid out there," Davis said later. "You always try to do something to shake up a kid."

"Are the Phillies in?" he was asked. "Their lead is down to five and a half with thirteen left."

"Are you kidding?" Davis said. "If things get a little tight, you watch what happens. Look at last year. We were one ahead of the Cardinals, went into St. Louis, and won three in a row. You know why? Because the pressure got them. Now the Cardinals have been through it. Like we went through it the year before."

Walter Alston didn't agree. After Bunning struck out Roseboro on Sunday afternoon to open a six-and-one-half-game lead, the Dodger manager rated the Phillies as a better team than his 1963 World Series champions that had swept the Yankees in four games.

"We had an edge in top pitching," Alston said, thinking of Sandy Koufax and Don Drysdale, "but the Phillies appear to have better speed, better defense, and more power. They also have good pitching for a short series with their four starters."

The Phillies were going home to Philadelphia, to be greeted by the mayor and about two thousand fans, to presumably clinch the pennant there. They would be playing three with the Reds and four with the Milwaukee Braves before going on the road for three in St. Louis and two in Cincinnati during the final week of the season. By then the pennant race might be over. Of the Cardinals' remaining thirteen games, seven were on the road; of the Reds' thirteen, eight were on the road, beginning Monday night at Connie Mack Stadium, the grand old ballpark named after baseball's Grand Old Man, only a few blocks from the North Philadelphia railroad station. To balance the World Series talk with reality, Mauch addressed his players.

"Just remember," the manager said, "the 1950 Phillies had a seven-and-a-half game lead with only eleven games to play. But they lost eight of their next ten and had to win the last game to save the pennant."

To his surprise, Art Mahaffey started against John Tsitouris, the Red righthander who had a reputation as a Phillie nemesis despite a 7–11 record. With one out in the sixth inning of a scoreless duel, Chico Ruiz, the Reds' rookie third baseman, singled to right. Vada Pinson's line drive off Mahaffey's glove squirted past second baseman Tony Taylor, but when Pinson tried to stretch his single into a double, rightfielder Johnny Callison nailed him. Two out, Ruiz on third, Frank Robinson up. In his concentration on the Reds' cleanup slugger, Mahaffey took a big slow windup and threw a fastball. Swinging strike. On the next pitch, Ruiz took off for home.

"It just came in my mind," the Red rookie said later. "In this game, you do or you don't."

Mahaffey didn't realize Ruiz was trying to steal home until, coming out of his windup, he saw the flash of the red-sleeved gray uniform. In the shock, Mahaffey's arm slowed, and the ball veered to the left. In the Reds' dugout, Dick Sisler, the interim manager with Fred Hutchinson dying of cancer, was stunned. In the batter's box, Robinson, never expecting Ruiz to steal home, watched Mahaffey's pitch sail wide and catcher Clay Dalrymple leap to stop it. Ruiz scored standing up.

"If it had been a strike, I think Chico would've been out," Robinson said later. "I can't ever remember anybody trying to steal home with me up."

That run turned out to be the difference in Tsitouris's first shutout of the season, 1–0. In his clubhouse office, Mauch, ever the strategist, was shaking his head over Ruiz's steal of home.

"If you're thrown out on that play," the Phillie manager said, "you're on your way back to the minors."

The lead had been sliced to five and one-half games, but the Phillies' fans hardly noticed. More than 60,000 World Series ticket applications were being filled out. Fewer than 20,000 would be accepted; the other 15,000 seats had already been allocated to ticket-plan subscribers, the commissioner's office, other major league clubs, the news media, and the players of the competing teams. While the fans were signing their checks and money orders for World Series tickets, the Sportsman's Park switchboard in St. Louis was lighting up.

Milton Richman, the United Press International baseball writer, had reported that Cardinal manager Johnny Keane would be fired and that Leo Durocher "most likely" would be hired for the 1965 season.

Three weeks earlier, with the Cardinals struggling to finish second, August (Gussie) Busch, their beer-baron owner, had secretly met with Durocher at his Grant's Farm mansion in the St. Louis suburbs. In his autobiography, *Nice Guys Finish Last*, written in collaboration with Ed Linn, Durocher remembered Busch saying, "You're the manager of the ballclub. Don't worry about the salary." Busch, who had fired general manager Bing Devine on August 17 after twenty-five years in the Cardinal organization, had asked Harry Caray, the Cardinals' announcer, to drive Durocher to Grant's Farm after hearing a radio interview in which the Dodger third-base coach told Caray of his interest in managing again.

At the time Durocher denied Richman's story, saying, "I haven't approached anybody and nobody's approached me." But when Busch was confronted with Richman's story that he had conferred with Durocher, he blanched.

"I have great admiration for Durocher and I heard that recent radio interview in which he made a pitch for a managerial job," Busch told Ed Wilks of the *St. Louis Post-Dispatch*, "but I don't know if we will make a change or not. It was hard enough to let Bing go. I consider Bing to be one of the finest fellows I've ever met, and it was a tough move to make. It would be another tough move to let Keane go."

"Has Keane done an adequate job this season?" Wilks asked.

"I have no comment on that," Busch said. "I haven't talked to anyone about our managerial situation. I haven't talked to our new general manager, Bob Howsam, or our board of directors, and we won't make any decision until after the season."

At his typewriter in the *Post-Dispatch* sports department, Wilks wrote that Busch "left Johnny Keane hanging by his thumbs today."

Signed off the St. Louis sandlots in 1930, Keane had been in the Cardinal organization for thirty-five years as a minor league infielder, coach, and manager before being promoted to succeed Solly Hemus as the Cardinal manager midway in the 1961 season. He was as quiet as Durocher was noisy, as gentlemanly as Durocher was rowdy. Keane's players admired him. He wasn't what players called "an I guy"; he stayed in the background. He knew players, not the manager, won games. When first baseman Bill White once dove for a foul ball, damaging his right shoulder, Keane took him aside.

"Don't dive for any more balls," Keane told him. "Don't try to take out anybody at second base. One play and I lose you. I can't afford that. I need you to play 162 games."

As conservative as that sounds, Keane was also aggressive. In those years not many managers were willing to risk having their pitchers throw breaking balls when behind in the count, but Keane kept reminding his rookie catcher, Tim McCarver, to call for breaking balls in those situations.

"He was one of the first managers," McCarver would say later, "to believe in doing that."

Through all the Durocher rumors, Keane had "no comment." When the story broke, he was in New York where the Cardinals, still six games out, were opening a two-game series with the last-place Mets, baseball's bad joke with a 50–98 record, not much better than their deplorable 40–120 debut as Casey Stengel's expansion clowns

Johnny Keane. *AP/Wide World Photo*

two years earlier. When the Phillies lost again Tuesday night, 9–2, to lefthander Jim O'Toole's eight-hitter while thirty-five-year-old lefthander Curt Simmons was stopping the Mets on a six-hitter, 2–1, the Reds suddenly were only four and one-half out, the Cardinals only five.

"The Phillies are slipping a little and that gives us a chance," Keane said. "We play them three more times, all at home. Then they must play their last two in Cincinnati. They're not in yet."

Wednesday the Cardinals lost to the lowly Mets, 3–1, as Galen Cisco outpitched Roger Craig. On their bus to La Guardia Airport for the short flight to Pittsburgh, shortstop Dick Groat slid into the seat next to his roommate, outfielder Bob Skinner.

"Hey, roomie," Skinner said, "we thought we needed four in Pittsburgh, but now we need five in Pittsburgh."

The Reds had beaten the Phillies again, 6–4, moving to within three and one-half games. Centerfielder Vada Pinson hit two homers and twenty-three-year-old rookie righthander Sammy Ellis, the little bull of their bullpen, preserved Billy McCool's victory in that twenty-year-old rookie lefthander's first major league start. In the seventh Ellis had walked the bases loaded with one out, but Sisler let him face Johnny Callison, the Phillies' most dangerous lefthanded batter. On a 3–2 pitch, Callison fanned. Ellis then struck out second baseman Tony Taylor.

"Sammy's my stopper," Sisler said. "He's been my good luck piece ever since I've been managing."

Sisler had taken command as acting manager on August 12 when Fred Hutchinson, coughing with lung cancer since January, had stepped down in his sixth season as Red manager. His 1961 team had won the National League pennant. In 1963 he had benched one of the Reds' most popular players, Don Blasingame, and installed a raw rookie named Pete Rose at second base. Hutch had a temper that his players respected. When the Reds once lost a doubleheader to the Mets at the Polo Grounds, he was so angry he turned to Sisler, his batting coach.

"I'm going to stay in the dugout for a few minutes," Hutch said. "By the time I get to the clubhouse, I want everybody out of there."

As the Reds trooped into their clubhouse beyond centerfield, Sisler announced, "I want all you guys to shower and get out of here before Hutch gets here." Perhaps never has an entire team showered and dressed so quickly. By the time Hutch arrived, the clubhouse was empty. But his players loved and respected this big bear of a man. Until the cancer drained him, Hutch kept managing.

"After a while, looking at Hutch was like looking at a skeleton," Rose told Roger Kahn for their book *Pete Rose: My Story*, "but I'll tell you this: that skeleton was in charge."

Now, with the Reds making their run, Dick Sisler was in charge. But only a few Reds were having big seasons. Rightfielder Frank Robinson would hit .306 with 29 homers and drive in 96 runs. Centerfielder Vada Pinson would hit 23 homers and drive in 84 runs, first baseman Deron Johnson would hit 21 homers and drive in 79 runs. Jim O'Toole would be 17–7, Jim Maloney 15–10, Bob Purkey 11–9, Joey

Jay 11–11. Sisler's roster was not as impressive as his heritage. His father, George Sisler, batted .420 in 1922 and .407 in 1920 as the St. Louis Browns' first baseman. But as the Phillies' first baseman in 1950, Dick hit a pennant-winning three-run homer off Don Newcombe of the Dodgers at Ebbets Field in the tenth inning of the season's final game. As the Reds' interim manager, a title that politely deferred to Hutch's illness, he was trying to win another pennant by overtaking, ironically, the Phillies.

Thursday the Reds, enjoying an off day in New York before a weekend series with the Mets, moved to within three games. Losing their fourth straight and their seventh in nine games, the Phillies were stifled, 5–3, by Wade Blasingame, a twenty-year-old rookie lefthander up from the Milwaukee Braves' farm at Denver of the Pacific Coast League.

Through six innings, Blasingame had a one-hit shutout, but his adventures had only begun. With one out in the seventh, Richie Allen, the Phillies' rookie third baseman, singled. Alex Johnson bounced back to Blasingame, whose throw pulled shortstop Sandy Alomar off second base, but Allen, in trying to break up the double play, overslid the bag. Alomar tagged him. Vic Power bounced to third baseman Eddie Mathews, who juggled the ball. Realizing that Johnson had rounded second, Mathews threw to second baseman Denis Menke for the third out. Asked later about those "base-running blunders," Mauch answered in a measured voice.

"If Mathews fielded it cleanly and threw it away, Johnson scores. Then it's no blunder," he said. "Allen takes a guy out of a double play so hard, he's caught off. That's no blunder."

But the Phillies' scouting report apparently had blundered on Blasingame's effectiveness against Johnson and centerfielder Adolfo Phillips when those two Phillies batted against him in the minors. Mauch insisted, "They tell me Phillips and Johnson tore him apart when they were with Little Rock." Told of this, Blasingame shrugged.

"I only pitched one inning of relief against Little Rock," he said. "I don't think I ever faced Phillips before."

When the Cardinals swept a twi-night doubleheader in Pittsburgh that Thursday, they were only three and one-half games out. In the 4–2 opener, centerfielder Curt Flood had four hits and Bob Gibson, now 17–11, struck out eleven. Ray Sadecki, now 19–10, struck out Willie Stargell four times in a 4–0 five hitter.

"But we'd feel better," Dick Groat said, "if we had won Wednesday in New York."

All season the Cardinals had been saying "If . . ." They had a solid team: third baseman Ken Boyer, first baseman Bill White, shortstop Dick Groat, centerfielder Curt Flood, leftfielder Lou Brock, catcher Tim McCarver, second baseman Julian Javier, and rookie rightfielder Mike Shannon along with their three top starters: Gibson, Sadecki, and Simmons. But if only White (who would become the National League president in 1989) had started to hit sooner after being bothered with a sore shoulder. If only Shannon had been brought up sooner. If only Barney Schultz had been in the bullpen sooner.

More than any other *if*, the Cardinals wondered if only Brock had arrived sooner than the June 15 trading deadline in that deal with the Cubs for righthander Ernie Broglio that Bing Devine, then the general manager, had finally put together.

Devine had begun pursuing Brock the year before, but the Cubs kept resisting. But on June 13, both teams were struggling. That Saturday afternoon in Los Angeles the Cardinals had lost, 3–2, their ninth defeat in their last twelve games. With a 28–29 record they were tied for seventh place with the Cubs, who had a 26–28 record. The Cardinals were packing for a flight to Houston when Devine was handed a message: call John Holland, the Cubs' general manager. Devine found a pay phone in Dodger Stadium and dialed the Cubs' office.

"What's up?" Devine asked.

"How's it going?" Holland said.

"Badly."

"We're going bad too," Holland said. "If you're still interested in Brock, we'll talk about him but we need a top pitcher."

"Who?" Devine said.

"Broglio, but we'd need an outfielder and we'll throw in a pitcher."

"We can work that out."

They mentioned a few other players, then Devine said, "Let me talk to my manager."

"When you get to Houston, call me," Holland said.

On the flight, Devine told Keane the names that had been discussed: Brock, lefthander Jack Spring and righthander Paul Toth for Broglio, aging lefthander Bobby Shantz (who would be sold to the Phillies two months later), and outfielder Doug Clemens.

"What are we waiting for?" Keane asked.

"For the plane to land," Devine said.

Nearly twenty-nine, Broglio had been struggling with a 3–5 record, far from the form that won twenty-one games for the Cardinals in

1960 and eighteen in 1963. Brock, who would be only twenty-five in a few days, was batting .251 with the Cubs, but Devine coveted his power and speed. By hitting .348 with the Cardinals the rest of the season, he would lift his overall average to .315 with fourteen homers. With Keane allowing him to steal on his own, he would have forty-three stolen bases, a prelude to his career total of 938, the major league record until Rickey Henderson surpassed it during the 1991 season. Broglio would never pitch well for the Cubs, with records of 4–7 the rest of the 1964 season, 1–6 in 1965, and 2–6 in 1966, before his career ended.

For all of Brock's immediate impact, Devine had been fired and Keane was about to be. But after Friday night's games, the Cardinals suddenly had closed to within two and one-half games, the Reds to only one and one-half.

The Cardinals had beaten the Pirates again, 5–3, knocking out righthander Don Cardwell with a three-run first inning. The Reds had swept a twi-night doubleheader from the Mets, 3–0 on Jim Maloney's one-hitter (Joe Christopher's second-inning single) and 4–1 on a Purkey-Ellis three-hitter. The Phillies lost to the Braves again, 7–5, in 12 innings. Over the days, weeks, months, years, and decades to come in Philadelphia, this defeat would be forgotten, but Gene Mauch's decision would not be forgotten. Instead of starting Art Mahaffey with three days' rest, he used Chris Short with only two days' rest. Short pitched well, allowing only one earned run and six hits until removed with one out in the seventh. Callison hit a two-run homer in the eighth for a 3–3 tie, Allen a two-run homer in the tenth for a 5–5 tie. In the twelfth Eddie Mathews knocked in the go-ahead run with a single off John Boozer that deflected off first baseman Frank Thomas's glove just past second baseman Tony Taylor. After the 7–5 loss, Mauch absolved Thomas.

"Every time somebody goes for a ball, more power to him," the manager said.

Thomas had been trying. Too hard. In his sixteen seasons in organized baseball, Frank Thomas spent twelve with teams that finished in last place, including 1962 with the Mets, the worst team in major league history. Liberated by the Phillies, he celebrated with seven homers and twenty-six runs batted in until his injury.

"I felt great, so great," he said. "It was like fifty-eight and sixty-two when I was having good years. Everything was wonderful."

Now everything was not so wonderful. The Phillies had lost five straight, and eight of their last ten games. Saturday they lost again.

Mauch started Mahaffey, who had four days' rest. In the sixth, Mahaffey had a 4–2 lead when the Braves loaded the bases with one out. Mahaffey heard leather popping in the bullpen but his manager stuck with him. He fanned Gene Oliver on three pitches. He grabbed Felipe Alou's dribbler and flipped to Triandos for an inning-ending force out. But when Joe Torre and Rico Carty opened the eighth with singles, Mahaffey was lifted. His successor, Jack Baldschun, turned Denis Menke's bunt into a force play at third. Mike de la Hoz's topped grounder skidded off Allen's glove for a single. With the bases loaded and lefthanded-swinging Ed Bailey about to pinch-hit for Chi Chi Olivo, Mauch waved for lefthander Bobby Shantz. As the Braves' rally developed, coach Harry (Peanuts) Lowrey had turned to Mauch. "Do you want to get Dalrymple in the game?" Lowrey said, knowing Dalrymple was the better defensive catcher.

"No," said Mauch, "my daughter could catch Shantz."

Now, with Bailey up, Shantz's fourth pitch, a high change-up, skidded off Triandos's glove for a passed ball that allowed Carty to score. Shantz struck out Bailey, walked Alou intentionally, and got Lee Maye on a pop-up for the third out. But the passed ball had allowed the Braves to narrow the Phillies' lead to 4–3. Mauch was mumbling to himself over having dismissed Peanuts Lowrey's suggestion.

More than ever, the Phillie manager realized that his decisions, unlike earlier in the season, were no longer infallible.

In the ninth, Henry Aaron led off with a single. Eddie Mathews singled. Frank Bolling, batting for Blasingame, fouled off two bunt attempts, then grounded to Amaro, but Taylor muffed the shortstop's throw, loading the bases. Carty crashed Shantz's first pitch off the centerfield wall for a triple. The Phillies lost again, 6–4.

"Carty hits up the middle a lot," Mauch explained later. "That's right up Bobby's alley. Only he hit it too high and too far."

Mauch's faith in Shantz seemed to translate to a loss of faith in both Baldschun and Roebuck just when the Phillies needed a dependable bullpen. In the decisive twelfth inning of Friday night's loss, seldom-used John Boozer had been the Phillies' pitcher.

"Why did you go with Boozer?" Frank Dolson of the *Philadelphia Inquirer* asked Mauch.

Mauch smiled and said, "You haven't missed too many games lately, have you?" Mauch had twice removed Baldschun in the middle of a scoreless inning and he remembered Pinson's homer off Roebuck on Wednesday night. With their sixth straight loss and their ninth in eleven games, the Phillies' lead had been sliced to only one-half game over the Reds, who stopped the Mets, 6–1, when McCool, relieving Tsitouris, fanned five of eight batters. Only one and one-half games out were the Cardinals, who stopped the Pirates, 6–3, with a frantic four-run fourth. On Mike Shannon's bases-loaded pop-fly single, Ken Boyer ran through third-base coach Vern Benson's stop sign and upended rookie catcher Jerry May as Roberto Clemente's throw skidded to the screen behind home plate. Tim McCarver bounced to first baseman Donn Clendenon, but when lefthander Bob Veale was late covering the bag and kept his back to the plate, Shannon broke for home and beat the throw. With the race tighter than ever late Saturday night, Bunning walked into Mauch's office.

"I'll take the ball tomorrow," he told the manager.

Mauch had begun to notice a different look in the eyes of some of his pitchers. During the losing streak, their cockiness had disappeared. But he had no worries about Bunning and Short. Even before Bunning volunteered, Mauch had considered asking him to start. But with only two days' rest, Bunning didn't have his best stuff. In only three innings, he was rapped for ten hits and seven runs, five earned. The Phillies lost again, a 14–8 rout. In the Braves' four-game sweep, Joe Torre had eleven hits, including two homers and two triples, and drove in seven runs. When the Reds took another doubleheader from the Mets, 4–1 behind Jim O'Toole and 3–1 behind Joey Jay, for a five-game sweep and a seven-game winning streak, the Phillies had fallen into second place. With the Cardinals completing a five-game sweep of the Pirates, 5–0, behind Roger Craig, this was the situation with a week to go:

The Reds were one game ahead of the Phillies, who were one-half game ahead of the third-place Cardinals.

High in the Connie Mack Stadium press box, Allen Lewis of the *Philadelphia Inquirer* branded the Phillies' seven-game losing streak "the blackest seven days in Philadelphia baseball history." Seven straight losses in seven straight days after the Phillies appeared to have all but clinched the pennant. Downstairs in Gene Mauch's office, a writer mentioned that some of the Braves thought the Phillies had appeared to be "tight." Mauch bristled.

"Tight?" he said. "When did they notice that? After the score reached twelve to three? Did we look tight when we went ahead, three to two? No, we came back. Then they went into that pop-fly act of theirs. Now we've got to do in five days what Cincinnati took five and a half months to do. There's a good chance we're better going after something than holding on to something."

When the Braves had a 12–3 lead that Sunday afternoon, Johnny Callison was desperate. Before going to the on-deck circle in the sixth, he turned to coach Bob Oldis and said, "Give me some chaw." Two years earlier Callison's wife had persuaded him to stop chewing tobacco, but now he knew he had to do something, anything, to try to change his team's luck and his luck. Shifting that chaw of tobacco from cheek to cheek in the sixth, he hit Tony Cloninger's fastball over the rightfield wall. In the eighth he hit Chi Chi Olivo's screwball over the rightfield wall. In the ninth he hit Olivo's fastball off the light tower to the left of the scoreboard.

"The chaw doesn't taste that bad. I mix it with bubble gum," the Phillies rightfielder said. "It got me three home runs, I'm going to keep chewing from here on in. It's a good thing we're going on the road. My wife won't know."

The Phillies were happy to be finishing the season on the road. During their final home game, boos from most of the 20,569 customers had rumbled through Connie Mack Stadium's old steel girders. Philadelphia fans were known to be among the most brutal in baseball. Several years earlier, as Gus Zernial, one of Connie Mack's outfielders on the Philadelphia Athletics, lay sprawled with a broken leg, he was booed. And after having been in first place since July 16, the Phillies were being booed.

"I've never heard ballplayers booed," Frank Thomas said, "like they're booed here."

Booed from deep in the throat, deep in the heart. Clay Dalrymple had heard those boos before.

"I don't pay any attention anymore," he said. "I figure the next night is a different game, a different group of people. There are a lot of good fans up there. I know, I've got good friends in the stands. Their hearts are breaking along with ours. It's the people who do the screaming that we hear. The people who are really for us, they're reserved. They suffer in silence. What hurts more than anything is the individual who leans into the dugout and says nasty personal things. This happens in Philadelphia. I've never seen so many individuals walk up, look you in the face, and say, 'You no-good so and so.' "

Maybe that's why Dalrymple disagreed with the school of thought that ballplayers owe more than hustle to the fans for buying tickets.

"I don't feel we owe those people anything," he said. "Winning the pennant means eight or ten thousand dollars to us, not to them."

In trying to win the pennant that Sunday afternoon, Ruben Amaro just missed Denis Menke's ground single. Then he just missed Tony

Cloninger's windblown pop fly. When he easily handled Joe Torre's routine grounder, he was jeered.

"I suppose if we win this thing, the boos would start in the World Series the first time somebody popped up," Amaro said. "The nice thing is, we're getting away."

Both the Reds and the Cardinals were going home: the Reds for three with the Pirates and two with the Phillies, the Cardinals for three with the Phillies and three with the Mets. After about four thousand fans had swarmed around the Reds' charter DC-7B at the Greater Cincinnati Airport in northern Kentucky that Sunday evening, Dick Sisler stopped at a pay phone and dialed Fred Hutchinson's home.

"I'm not saying we're going to win it," he told Hutch, "but I guarantee you this club won't choke."

Monday morning's Cincinnati *Enquirer* had two eight-column headlines across the top of its front page. "Reds Home, Leading League by Game" was above "Warren Report: Oswald Acted Alone." The Reds had won nine straight. Sisler was counting on those who had been on the Reds' pennant-winning 1961 team—Robinson, Pinson, O'Toole, Purkey, and Jay—but he had lost catcher Johnny Edwards, whose middle finger on his throwing hand had been smashed by a foul tip in Sunday's doubleheader. In contrast, the Phillies hadn't won a pennant since 1950, the Cardinals since 1946. On the Phillies, only Covington, Roebuck, Shantz, and Triandos had been on other pennant winners. On the Cardinals, only Simmons and Groat, but both had been indispensable. Simmons was a seventeen-game winner for the 1950 Phillies. Groat was not only the shortstop on the 1960 Pirate team that won the World Series on Bill Mazeroski's ninth-inning seventh-game homer off Ralph Terry of the Yankees, but he also was voted the NL's most valuable player that year. Now, the closer the Cardinals moved to first place, the firmer Groat's voice.

"We had to win all five in Pittsburgh to stay in it, and we did," he said. "Now we've got to win all three against the Phillies."

Mauch, meanwhile, was hoping it would rain. If the opener with the Cardinals was postponed until Tuesday night, Short and Bunning would be pitching with their usual three days' rest. But the St. Louis weather forecast was for clear weather all week.

"You know what I would have given," Mauch would say later, "for just one day of rain?"

In the Cardinals' clubhouse before Monday night's game, player representative Ken Boyer conducted a meeting on the postseason player shares. When the voting ended, Boyer asked, "Anything else anybody wants to talk about?" Roger Craig stood up. "I know we all have a lot of respect for Bing Devine, who put this club together," Craig said. "If we win this thing, I think Bing would be insulted if we voted him a World Series share, but we ought to make sure to give him a ring."

"I'll call him," Bob Uecker, the third-string catcher, said with a straight face.

Craig had meant a World Series ring, but long before his career as a baseball comedian, actor, and Milwaukee Brewer broadcaster, Uecker's sense of humor was always sharper than his career .200 batting average. In the laughter, the meeting broke up. Over in the Phillies' clubhouse, Mauch, somewhat desperate now, suggested that "somebody start a fight" with one of the Cardinals that night. Something, anything to jolt the team. Soon, as the Phillies trudged onto the field as the Cardinals were completing batting practice, Bill White stared at Callison and Covington.

They're really dragging, White decided. They're tired. They're finished. They're a beaten bunch.

In the Phillies' dugout, Mauch was trying to be upbeat, comparing a pennant race to an eighteen-hole round of golf.

"You bogey the first hole," he said, "and everybody says, 'You just got off to a bad start.' You bogey the eleventh hole, in the month of July, say, and nobody says anything. You bogey the seventeenth hole and everybody says, 'Oh, oh, nerves.' But all we have to do now is birdie the eighteenth hole."

Instead, so to speak, the Phillies sliced their tee shot out of bounds.

Hoping that another twenty-four hours would strengthen Dennis Bennett's sore shoulder, Mauch again started Chris Short with only two days' rest. Short was chased with one out in the sixth, charged with three runs, all earned, and seven hits as Bob Gibson and Barney Schultz combined on a five-hitter, 5–1. With their eighth straight loss, the Phillies skidded to third place, one and one-half games out while the Cardinals jumped into second place, one game behind the Reds, whose three-game series with the Pirates wouldn't start until Tuesday night. Keane didn't criticize Mauch's use of Short on two days' rest, saying, "I can't recall when we last hit Short hard," but Ken Boyer thought that the twenty-seven-year-old lefthander had been weakened by his third start in seven days.

"He didn't have that real good live explosive fastball this time," Boyer said.

Mauch defended his choice, saying, "Short's done it before. Do you think he pitched a bad game?" At his locker Dennis Bennett stared at the black-and-blue area on his left shoulder. "It's internal bleeding," he said. "They're a little concerned about it. But no sweat, I'll beat 'em tomorrow night and Jim will beat 'em the next night. We're a long way from dead. We're a looonnnggg way from dead." The next night, Bennett warmed up, then walked over to Mauch and smiled.

"I don't know how long I'll last," he said, "but I've got it. I'll give you five, six, seven good innings."

Bennett didn't last two, giving up five hits and three runs, one earned. In the first, Flood's single and Groat's double produced a run before Bennett was saved by a line-drive double play. In the second, Javier's double, Shannon's single, and McCarver's infield single convinced Mauch to bring in Roebuck, but the Cardinals already had enough runs. Barney Schultz saved Ray Sadecki's twentieth victory. With the 4–2 win, the Cardinals jumped into a first-place tie with the Reds, who were blanked, 2–0, by Bob Friend on Bill Mazeroski's two-run ninth-inning single off McCool just out of shortstop Leo Cardeñas's reach. But the Reds also seemed to be deflated by the sparse crowd of 10,858 at Crosley Field.

"You'd think that after the trip we had and the excitement we created, we'd come home and sell the place out," Sisler said. "To come home in first place and draw just ten thousand the first night, it's terrible. Just terrible."

All those empty seats at Crosley Field had the Reds' president, Bill DeWitt, wondering if Cincinnati would win the pennant but lose the franchise. Fans were complaining of parking and traffic problems at little Crosley Field, with a capacity of only 29,603, a steep grassy incline in front of the outfield fences and the Superior Towel and Linen Service laundry beyond leftfield.

"It's very disheartening, very discouraging," DeWitt said. "I just don't understand it. Some people say the sixteen thousand people who attended Barry Goldwater's rally downtown hurt us, but I can't buy that. They're not the same people. They're politicians."

The Reds had finally lost after winning nine straight, but in this pennant race of streaks, the Cardinals had now won seven straight and the third-place Phillies had lost nine straight. Wednesday night Jim Bunning again would be starting with two days' rest against the Cardinals.

"We're not choking up," Bennett insisted. "I don't think choking up means trying too hard. I think it means scared. We may be trying too hard, but I don't think there's a guy on this club who's scared."

Maybe not, but the more Bennett talked, the more scared the twenty-four-year-old lefthander sounded. Scared for his career. As a rookie in 1962, he was 9–9. The next year he improved to 9–5, but this loss had dropped him to 12–14 and labeled him a sore-arm pitcher.

"The doctor says I've aggravated it so much already, pitching some more won't make any difference," Bennett said. "Next year, I'll let them shoot me from head to foot, cut me up, anything as long as I can pitch. This game gets in your blood."

The game had been in Johnny Keane's blood for decades. Blood that bubbles in a pennant race.

"Imagine, tied for first," Keane was saying. "Somebody used the word last night. Incredible."

The Cardinals also were in Keane's blood, but the word for his future in the organization was inconclusive, if not inconsiderate. His team was tied for first place in the last week of the season, but he was still hanging by his thumbs. He was still being asked questions that Gussie Busch should have answered by now.

"Howsam told me," Keane said, "that we won't go into it until after the season."

"If you're not the manager," one of the writers asked, "would you accept another job in the organization?"

"I would not," he said.

Johnny Keane preferred to talk about George Warren (Barney) Schultz, the thirty-eight-year-old righthander resurrected on August 1 from the Jacksonville, Florida, farm in the International League when the Cardinals were 53–50, eight games out. In thirty appearances, Schultz and his knuckleball would produce 14 saves, a 1–3 record with a 1.64 earned run average, and twenty-nine strikeouts against only eleven bases on balls. With two on and two out in the eighth inning Sunday in Pittsburgh he struck out Roberto Clemente, whose .339 average would win the NL batting title. With two on and none out in the ninth inning Monday night, he got Clay Dalrymple to bounce into a double play and John Herrnstein to pop up.

"When I went out there to get Sadecki in the seventh," Keane was saying now after Tuesday night's victory, "I didn't know whether it would be Ron Taylor or Schultz."

Johnny Callison, shivering with a mysterious virus, had stroked a pinch single. Standing on first base, he called for his warmup jacket, but his fingers were shaking so badly that Bill White had to snap it up for him. With two out, Sadecki walked Tony Taylor and Keane strode to the mound.

"By the time I got there," the Cardinal manager said, "I figured if I needed one more out, Barney was the man to do it."

Schultz arrived at the mound not only with his glove, but with the old floppy oversized "knuckleball" catcher's glove that he had brought from Jacksonville with him. In the bullpen Bob Uecker had worn that glove while warming up Schultz, and now Schultz handed it to Mc-Carver, who handed his usual catcher's glove to Sadecki, who carried it to the dugout. McCarver hated catching Schultz's knuckleball, especially with runners on base, when a passed ball would be costly.

"Barney's knuckleball fluttered more because it was slower than most," McCarver often said. "It might break sideways, or down, or up, or stay on the same plane. I never knew."

Neither did the hitter. Now, with runners on first and second, Barney Schultz's knuckleball fluttered. Richie Allen swung and popped up. As much as anybody else, this knockaround knuckleball pitcher whom the Phillies originally signed in 1944 had lifted the Cardinals into the pennant race. In his minor league travels he had pitched for Wilmington, Bradford, Terre Haute, Schenectady, Hagerstown, Rock Hill, Macon, Des Moines, Denver, Hollywood, Omaha, Columbus, Houston, and Charlestown. He had pitched for the Cardinals briefly in 1955, was up with the Tigers in 1959, and returned with the Cubs in 1961 before moving to the Cardinals in 1963, but in spring training this year he was farmed out again.

"Did you consider quitting then?" a writer asked him.

"No, I believed in myself," he said. "I didn't agree in my heart that some pitchers who had been in the majors for ten years were better than I was. I felt my opportunity would come with a club that needed a veteran pitcher down the stretch."

Schultz's opportunity coincided with a manager who knew him and had faith in him. He had pitched for Keane at Omaha and Columbus.

"I think we've got a chance to do something here," Keane told Schultz when the righthander joined the Cardinals. "Just keep pitching like you did at Jacksonville."

"What took you so long to bring me up?" Schultz said, smiling. "My ERA was under one until Rochester got a couple runs off me."

As a twelve-year-old, Schultz had learned to throw a knuckleball from an older Beverly, New Jersey, neighbor, Walt Atzert. But for all of Schultz's sudden success, other pitchers understood the toll of his recent workload. After Tuesday night's game, Ray Sadecki turned to Curt Simmons, who would start Wednesday night.

"You've got to give Barney a night's rest," Sadecki said.

With his control and his change-up curveball, Simmons had a simple philosophy of how he wanted his fielders to position themselves for opposing hitters. Just play everybody straightaway except for Henry Aaron, the Braves' slugger, who should be played one step to pull.

"Why straightaway?" McCarver once asked Simmons.

"Doubleday put 'em there for a reason," he said.

With his fielders playing straightaway Wednesday night Simmons had a no-hitter until Allen singled with two out in the seventh. By then Bunning had been battered. In only three innings, he had given up six hits and six runs, five earned. McCarver hit a two-run homer in the second. Flood's double, Taylor's fumble of Brock's grounder, White's double, and Boyer's single added three in the third. But with an 8–5 lead in the ninth, Keane knew Schultz needed a night off. He brought in Gordon Richardson, who disposed of Thomas and Wine for the Phillies' tenth straight loss. Of those ten, Bunning and Short each had lost twice with two days' rest.

"I felt very good," Bunning insisted. "No excuses at all."

Flood disagreed, saying, "He wasn't ripping the ball in there. He wasn't real strong." Simmons, now 18–9, joked that "I was trying to get Phillies' World Series tickets a month ago; hell, I was trying to get them a week ago." But when asked if he enjoyed defeating the Phillies, who had released him early in the 1960 season, he shook his head.

"No, no, no," he said. "That story's four years old. They just wanted to get rid of old guys."

John Quinn, the Phillies' general manager, talked to the Cubs, the Orioles, and the Yankees about Simmons, with no takers. Then the Cardinals signed him. Since then, he compiled a 59–42 record, including 16–2 against the Phillies.

"I feel for them a little bit," Simmons said. "I just hope it never happens to us like that. It would stay with you the rest of your life."

With their eighth straight victory, the Cardinals had put together a 27–9 burst. In that span, Gibson was 8–1, Simmons 5–0, Sadecki 5–1. But now many of the Cardinals sat in their clubhouse to listen to a Cincinnati radio station's broadcast of the Reds–Pirates game. It had attracted another small crowd, only 8,168, and some had even deserted a compelling scoreless duel in extra innings. Jim Maloney had struck out thirteen in his eleven innings before Sammy Ellis arrived. Now, in the thirteenth inning, Frank Robinson walked, stole second, then stole third as Deron Johnson struck out. Bob Veale, the Pirates' ace left-hander, who had struck out sixteen, walked Tommy Harper. With a 2–0 count on Steven Boros, Harper stole second.

"You're liable to see an intentional walk here," the radio voice suggested.

"Pitch to him," McCarver yelled. "You can get him out. Pitch to him."

On a 3–2 pitch, Boros also walked. Knowing that Pirate manager Danny Murtaugh had Alvin McBean warming up in the Pirate bull-pen, Cardinal outfielder Carl Warwick said, "He's got to bring Mc-Bean in now." Murtaugh did.

"C'mon, little Alvin," said Groat, once his teammate, "throw the curve."

Leo Cardeñas popped to Mazeroski. Marty Keough, batting for Sammy Ellis, popped to Gene Freese.

"That's my man," Groat yelled. "Li'l Alvin."

In the top of the fourteenth, Johnny Keane left the clubhouse, saying, "Lela will leave me if I don't get out of here." With runners on third and first in the bottom of the fourteenth, Frank Robinson settled into the batter's box.

"How can he be up again?" Shannon asked. "He's up every inning."

Robinson walked, loading the bases, but McBean struck out Deron Johnson, and Jim Coker grounded to Dick Schofield. One by one, the Cardinals drifted out to the parking lot. On the way home, they listened to the Reds' game on their car radios. Leading off the top of the sixteenth Donn Clendenon doubled off the centerfield corner of the scoreboard and moved to third on Mazeroski's sacrifice bunt. Now the batter was Jerry May, a twenty-year-old catcher up from Asheville to replace Jim Pagliaroni, out with a chip fracture of his throwing thumb.

"Be alive, be alive," some of the Reds were shouting from the dugout. "Be alive."

Clendenon broke for the plate, but third baseman Chico Ruiz didn't anticipate a suicide-squeeze play. May bunted and Clendenon sprinted across the plate as John Tsitouris watched the ball roll to a stop near the mound. In the Reds' dugout Dick Sisler was steaming at Ruiz.

"He backed up," the Red manager would say later. "Clendenon was running and he should have followed him. He wasn't alive."

In the bottom of the sixteenth McBean retired the Reds in order and the Cardinals were in first place, one game ahead of the Reds, two and one-half games ahead of the Phillies. In the Pirates' clubhouse, manager Danny Murtaugh was making an announcement. He was resigning because of poor health. In later years, he would return to manage the Pirates, including their 1971 World Series champions, but now he was concerned about his heart problems.

"I'll handle the club here tomorrow night," he said, "but I don't think I'll go to Milwaukee."

Thursday afternoon Leo Durocher resigned from the Dodger coaching staff. Even though the Cardinals were in first place, that prompted questions for Johnny Keane about his future.

"Bob Howsam asked my indulgence on a decision until after the season is over," the Cardinal manager said. "I understood his position."

That night at Crosley Field catcher Johnny Edwards pleaded with Sisler to let him play despite his mashed finger and bruised catching hand. "I'll take novocaine, codeine, anything," Edwards said.

"I don't care what you take," Sisler said. "You're not catching."

Sisler's catcher was twenty-eight-year-old journeyman Jim Coker, who had been sold by the Phillies two years earlier because they didn't like his arm. But when two Pirate base runners tried to steal second, Coker nailed them. His homer off Steve Blass in the sixth put the Reds ahead, 4–3.

"Don't wake me up," he joked in the dugout after the homer. "Just let me sleep."

The Reds won, 5–4, with Coker also hitting a double and a single. They had sliced the Cardinals' lead to one-half game going into the final weekend. The Reds presumably would start Jim O'Toole and Jim Maloney against Short and Bunning, each finally working with three days' rest, on Friday night and Sunday afternoon. The Cardinals had Gibson, Sadecki, and Simmons rested and ready for the last-place Mets on Friday night, Saturday afternoon, and Sunday afternoon. Earlier that season the Mets had routed the Cubs, 19–1, prompting a New Yorker in a weekly run pool to phone a local radio station.

"How many runs did the Mets score today?" the man asked.

"Nineteen," he was told.

"Did they win?" he asked.

Now the Reds needed the Mets to win at least one game. If the Reds won their final two games with the Phillies while the Mets won once in St. Louis, the Reds and Cardinals would open a two-of-three playoff Monday afternoon in Cincinnati. But the Phillies, despite their ten-game losing streak, were still alive. If they won twice in Cincinnati and the Mets somehow swept the Cardinals, a three-team playoff would be necessary. Hoping to break his ten-game losing streak, Gene Mauch was near the batting cage at Crosley Field on Friday night when Fred Hutchinson approached him.

"I wish there was something I could say to help," Hutch said.

Mauch was stunned. Here was the cancer-stricken manager of a pennant race rival thinking about him. By the bottom of the seventh, the Phillies appeared doomed to their eleventh straight loss and a lively crowd of 25,228 was buzzing with Reds pennant fever. With the Reds ahead, 3–0, Deron Johnson led off with a single and moved to second on Tommy Harper's bunt. Leo Cardeñas, the Reds' slender shortstop, was up next. Mauch hurried out to talk to Chris Short.

"Don't give him a good pitch," Mauch said.

Short's next pitch, a curveball, plunked Cardeñas behind the left shoulder. As catcher Clay Dalrymple walked over to retrieve the ball, Cardeñas stood and glared at Short, who had turned his back to the plate. Waving his bat, the Red shortstop started to step toward the mound when Dalrymple heard him yell, "You sonuvabitch, I'm going to hit you with a bat." Dalrymple grabbed Cardeñas from behind.

"You're not going to hit anybody," the Phillies catcher said.

By then Jim Coker, who had been on deck as the next Red batter, and Frank Robinson had grabbed Cardeñas and taken his bat away. Order was restored, but Mauch was smiling. Short wasn't giving up and he didn't want any of his teammates to give up. In the commotion, the Phillies had been awakened, but Cardeñas would fall asleep. With one out in the top of the eighth, the Phillies' rally off Jim O'Toole began with a bloop pinch single by Frank Thomas that landed on the infield dirt behind second base when both Cardeñas and Rose hesitated.

"I was scared to hit Pete, I think he was scared to hit me," Cardeñas said later. "He don't say nothing. I don't say nothing."

Dick Sisler and many of Cardeñas's teammates believed that he was still thinking about his scene with Short instead of thinking about playing shortstop. Annoyed at Cardeñas's mistake, O'Toole walked Cookie Rojas, then Tony Taylor's single scored Thomas. Sisler brought in McCool, who got Callison out, but with righthander Sammy Ellis warming up, Sisler let McCool, a lefthander, pitch to

Richie Allen and Alex Johnson, the Phillies' two best righthanded hitters. Allen's two-run triple tied the score. Johnson's single scored Allen with the go-ahead run. The Phillies won, 4–3.

"McCool had struck out Allen more than half the times he faced him and last week Allen doubled off Ellis," Sisler was telling the writers now in his office. "As for Johnson, I knew that if I brought in Ellis, they'd send up Covington. I have great respect for Covington's bat."

Just then, angry yelling was heard in the Reds' clubhouse beyond the door to Sisler's office. Suddenly the door swung open. Reggie Otero, the third-base coach, leaned into the manager's office. Staring at Sisler, he said, "Will you come out here a minute." Glancing at the writers, Otero added, "I'm sure you gentlemen will excuse him." Hurrying into the clubhouse, Sisler slammed the door behind him, then turned to Ray (Chesty) Evans, the Reds' clubhouse man.

"Keep that door closed, Chesty," the manager said.

When the game ended, Jim O'Toole, still furious at Cardeñas for not catching Thomas's blooper, had waited for the shortstop to arrive, confronted him, and flung him across the clubhouse.

"Leo grabbed an ice pick," Frank Robinson would say later.

Robinson, Joey Jay, and others grabbed Cardeñas, then Robinson led him away. Sisler scolded Cardeñas for having awakened the Phillies by threatening Short with a bat, berated O'Toole for the scuffle, then returned to his office where the writers were waiting.

"What was that all about?" one asked.

"In a pennant race like this," Sisler said, "some players say things before they think."

"Why did Cardeñas blow up at Short?"

"Why would the Phillies want to throw at Leo then?" Sisler said. "For Leo to think that, that was bad thinking. Then he took that bad thinking out to his position. Somebody should have caught that blooper that Thomas hit."

When the writers asked Cardeñas, he said, "I was wrong." But what annoyed Sisler and the Reds even more was that they had wasted the Cardinals' loss to the Mets.

Al Jackson, the Mets' little lefthander, had outpitched Bob Gibson, 1–0 to finish his season with an 11–16 record. In the third, George Altman singled, stole second, took third on an infield out, and scored on Ed Kranepool's single to left. But with the bases loaded in the eighth, Dick Groat sliced a liner toward the rightfield foul line. It appeared to be a sure two-run double until Joe Christopher, who had positioned himself close to the line, caught it on the run.

"I played with Groat," said Christopher, remembering when they were Pirate teammates for parts of three seasons. "When he needs a hit, he goes to rightfield."

In the Cardinals' resurgence to first place, Gussie Busch had changed his mind about hiring Leo Durocher as next season's manager. Busch offered Keane a one-year contract at a substantial raise, but Keane, annoyed at all the talk that Durocher was Busch's choice, wouldn't commit himself.

"I'd rather wait until after the season to decide what I want to do," he said.

Saturday, with the Reds and Phillies idle, Sisler called a workout. Still annoyed by Cardeñas's mistake, the manager reminded his players not to allow personal grudges to disrupt their concentration on tomorrow's game. Then he talked to his pitching coach, Jim Turner, about his starter. Jim Maloney would have three days' rest, but he had pitched eleven hard innings in Wednesday night's 1–0 loss in sixteen innings; he also had a chronic although not serious problem with a shoulder muscle. Except for two and one-third innings in Wednesday night's game, John Tsitouris hadn't pitched since last Saturday.

"I like Tsitouris," Sisler said.

"It's your decision," Turner said.

"I know that," Sisler said. "Tsitouris has the rest, he has that screwball. If it goes good, fine. If it doesn't, I'll take the blame. I'd rather take the blame than have Maloney hurt his arm."

After the workout Sisler told the writers that Tsitouris would start Sunday and that Maloney would be available if the Reds were in a playoff Monday afternoon.

"It would've been Maloney, but Jim had a tough game last time," Sisler said. "John always pitches well against the Phillies. He beat them one to nothing last time."

Tsitouris had a 9–12 record, but against the Phillies he was 2–2 that season and 5–3 over his career. He was well rested. He also seemed relaxed. When the writers told him he was pitching Sunday's finale, he shook his head.

"I'm not pitching tomorrow," he said.

"You are according to the man in there."

"It doesn't matter what he says," Tsitouris said, trying not to smile. "It's what I say and I'm not pitching such an important game unless they give me $2,000 extra."

At the next locker, relief pitcher Ryne Duren said, "You'll pitch it because you're a great pitcher."

"All right then," Tsitouris said, going along with the gag. "As long as you put it that way."

That afternoon the Cardinals lost again. The Mets jumped on Sadecki for a 4–0 lead in the first. Kranepool hit a two-run homer off Craig for 8–3 in the third. Joe Christopher, Charley Smith, Bobby Klaus, and George Altman also homered in a 15–5 rout that had Casey Stengel glowing.

"We got fellas who can hit home runs too," the Met manager said. "It's tough to catch those balls in the bleachers."

Stunned by two losses to the Mets, the Cardinals had dropped into a tie with the Reds, with the Phillies only one game back. Sunday morning, Tim McCarver left his room at the Bel Air East Hotel and walked down Lindell Boulevard to the St. Louis University church for the nine o'clock mass.

"Please, God," he prayed, "I might not ever be on another team with a chance to win the pennant. Please let me play well today."

For the first time in major league history, a three-way first-place playoff was a possibility. If the Reds lost to the Phillies again on Sunday while the Cardinals lost to the Mets again, a three-way tie would be created. The round-robin playoff schedule had already been determined, with two losses eliminating a team.

Monday: Cincinnati at Philadelphia.

Tuesday: St. Louis at Cincinnati.

Wednesday: Philadelphia at St. Louis.

After those three games, if one of the teams had lost twice, that team would be eliminated. Another draw for the two surviving teams then would be held, with the teams playing until one had lost a second game. If each of the three teams was 1–1, another draw would be held to determine which two teams played next, with the third team drawing a bye. The loser of that game would be eliminated, then the winner of that game and the team that had drawn the bye would play one game for the pennant.

"The situation is still in our hands," Keane said. "We've bounced back from shellackings all year. Baseball is a game of bounces. The clubs that couldn't or wouldn't bounce are not in the position we are."

After blowing Friday night's game, the Reds needed to bounce if they hoped to win, or at least tie. Some of their players quietly disagreed with Sisler's decision to start Tsitouris instead of Maloney, especially because Maloney hadn't allowed a run in twenty innings since a virus prevented him from facing the Cardinals two weeks earlier. Maloney was the Reds' ace. The year before he had been a twenty-three-game winner with 265 strikeouts. It wasn't as if he had only one or two days' rest. Even though he had pitched eleven hard innings Wednesday night, he had three days' rest. Start him and let him go as far as he can. But if Fred Hutchinson disagreed with Sisler's choice, the ailing manager never let on.

"Not once has Hutch second-guessed me on any of my moves, and a number of them backfired," Sisler had said earlier in the week. "Hutch rarely offers advice, never criticism. Once he asked me my thinking behind a move I made. I explained and he said, 'I'll buy that.' It was a sound move, even if it did backfire."

Sisler had phoned Hutchinson in August when the acting manager benched Rose for "not carrying out his responsibilities as a leadoff hitter." As much as Hutch liked Rose, he told Sisler, "That's up to you, Dick. If you think it's the right move, go ahead." Now, with the pennant at stake, Sisler thought that starting Tsitouris was the right move.

"It's our turn today," Frank Thomas had said when the Phillies were taking batting practice. "The Reds started us on our ten-game skid that dropped us out of first place. We're due to reciprocate."

With one out in the third, Tony Gonzalez drew a walk from Tsitouris, and Richie Allen doubled off the centerfield fence. Sisler ordered Johnny Callison walked intentionally, loading the bases. Wes Covington drilled a two-run single to right. Sisler called for lefthander Joe Nuxhall, but Tony Taylor clunked a broken-bat single for a 3–0 lead.

In the fifth Allen crashed a homer to center off Billy McCool. In the sixth Allen crashed a three-run homer to right off Joey Jay.

In the Phillies' dugout Ruben Amaro was praying, "Please, God, give us one more game." But for that to happen, the Mets had to beat the Cardinals again. When the Sportsman's Park scoreboard showed that the Phillies had scored a total of five runs in the sixth for a 9–0 lead, Ken Boyer took a deep breath.

"That took the pressure off," the Cardinal third baseman would say later. "After that, we figured we've only got our game to worry about."

By then the Cardinals didn't have to worry. Keane had removed Simmons and brought in Bob Gibson when the Mets went ahead, 3–2, in the fifth. But the Cardinals rallied for three in the bottom of the fifth on singles by White, Boyer, and second baseman Dal Maxvill, filling in for the ailing Julian Javier. They added three in the sixth on Brock's double, White's homer, and McCarver's double. In the eighth they scored three more on Flood's leadoff homer, Groat's double, and McCarver's single. But with one out in the ninth, Gibson walked two. Despite an 11–4 lead, Keane waved to the bullpen for Barney Schultz.

"How's your arm?" Keane had asked him earlier. "Are you too tired to give me an inning?"

"If you need me to win this game," Schultz said, "how my arm feels isn't important."

Now, as Schultz walked past Boyer on his way to the mound, the Cardinal captain said, "C'mon, Barn, let's wrap 'er up." With a seven-run lead, Schultz smiled.

"I won't lose this one," he said.

Schultz fluttered his knuckleball past Charley Smith for the second out. But with Rod Kanehl up, that knuckleball fluttered past Mc-Carver for a passed ball, the runners moving up. Kanehl's single made it 11–5, but Kranepool lifted a pop foul that McCarver caught near the Cardinals' dugout.

"That's when I realized," Schultz would say later, "the load that had been on my shoulders during the last weeks of the race. Everybody was banking on me."

Some of the 30,146 fans hopped over the box seat railings to celebrate the Cardinals' first pennant since 1946, their tenth since 1926 when Johnny Keane, then a fourteen-year-old St. Louis youngster, got up at five o'clock to get on line for a World Series bleacher seat. Now he was the manager of a pennant-winning Cardinal team.

"The turning point," Keane was saying in his office, "was the day in June when Bing Devine traded for Lou Brock."

Gussie Busch, who had been drinking champagne in the clubhouse, burst into Keane's office with a glass of champagne in one hand, a beer in the other. "This is the happiest day of my life," the Cardinal owner said.

"Can you pose with Johnny?" a photographer asked.

"Let me put my arm around him," Busch suggested.

As flashbulbs popped, fans outside the ballpark could be heard chanting, "We want Keane, we want Keane."

The Yankees, it would develop, also wanted Keane.

Only a few weeks later, after the Cardinals won the World Series from the Yankees in seven games, Yogi Berra was fired as the Yankee manager and Keane was hired to succeed him. Some baseball people insisted that Yankee general manager Ralph Houk, having decided before the team's surge to the pennant that Berra would not be retained, had assigned an emissary to contact Keane when the Cardinals were struggling and that Keane had secretly agreed to be the next Yankee manager. Houk and front office aide Bill Bergesch, who was called on the carpet by commissioner Ford Frick, denied having done so. But whatever Keane did or did not know about his future that final Sunday, he knew that at Crosley Field the Reds had lost to the Phillies, 10–0, before a turnout of 28,535, who finally realized there was a pennant race. Before the game Jim Bunning was on the rubbing table in the Phillies' clubhouse when Fred Hutchinson, stooped and drawn, peered in.

"Where is that little bastard?" Hutch asked.

"You just missed him," Bunning said, knowing he was looking for Mauch. "He's out on the field."

"I just want to say goodbye," Hutch said.

The cancer-stricken manager had watched the game in the warmth of Bill DeWitt's rooftop box but now, the race over, he had entered Sisler's office as the manager talked to the writers.

"The boys and myself," Sisler said, "are sorry we couldn't win it for that gentleman over there."

Sisler glanced beyond the group of writers to where Hutch was leaning against the wall. Not that Hutch wanted any sympathy.

"I'm sorry they didn't win it for themselves," he said.

Since moving into first place a week earlier, the Reds had lost four of their last five games, including three shutouts. Always a realist, Frank Robinson had no excuses.

"We've got nobody to blame but ourselves," he said.

Pete Rose had a different theory. "I think we all got pennant fever," the young second baseman said. "I think the guys tried too hard. I wish we could've had another week on the road." Vada Pinson shook his head and shrugged.

"Think how the Phillies must feel," the Red centerfielder said. "It's got to be worse for them."

In the Phillies' clubhouse, Mauch had spun the dial on a portable radio to listen to the last few innings of the Cardinals–Mets game. When he heard that Bill White's homer off Jack Fisher had opened a 7–4 lead in the sixth, he turned off the radio. Except for the clack of bats being packed by equipment men, the only sound now was the hissing spray in the showers. All that blue snow had melted.

"I didn't want to spray the champagne, I didn't want to gulp the champagne," Gus Triandos, who would never play in a World Series, was saying. "I just wanted to sip the champagne."

Only two weeks ago the Phillies had left Los Angeles with a lead of six and one-half games with only twelve games remaining. If only they hadn't lost ten straight before winning their last two games when Short and Bunning each started with their normal three days' rest. If only they had won four of those twelve, they would have won the pennant. If only Frank Thomas hadn't been hurt. If only Mauch hadn't juggled the rotation.

In the years to come, some of the Phillies would blame Mauch, but others would defend him.

With the pennant lost and the season over, Mauch felt bad for all his players, especially for Johnny Callison. He knew that had the Phillies won the pennant, Callison would almost certainly be voted most valuable player; Ken Boyer was chosen instead. Now, sitting at his locker, Mauch took a long drag on a cigarette and looked up at the writers.

"I just wore the pitching out," he said.

"Would you have done anything differently?"

"If I knew how it was going to come out, I might've done a couple of things different. When you manage the way I want to manage, you don't miss something by a game or two. All I can say is that I wish I did as well as the players did. They did a great job. That's all I've got to say."

"Are you implying you did something wrong?"

"I'm implying nothing," the manager said.

Several hours later, as the Phillies' chartered jet arrived at Philadelphia International Airport, two thousand fans had gathered. To cheer, not to boo. In the decades to come, the phlop of the '64 Phillies would be remembered more emotionally in Philadelphia than the World Series victory of the '80 team. And for all his strategic skills, Gene Mauch would never manage a World Series team. Now, as the Phillies' jet stopped at the gate, their manager stood and turned to his players.

"I want to be the first one off," he told them. "You guys didn't lose it. I did."

1967

Four for the Money

Eddie Stanky. *Chicago White Sox*

OUTSIDE FENWAY PARK, most of the Boston Red Sox were boarding chartered buses to Logan Airport on Sunday, September 17, 1967, for the flight to Detroit and the start of an eight-game road trip. But inside, having endured the embarrassment of being swept by the eighth-place Baltimore Orioles in a three-game weekend series, Carl Yastrzemski was knotting his tie and grumbling.

"I'm glad to get out of this park," he said.

"You mean Friendly Fenway?" a writer asked.

"It's not very friendly when the wind's blowing in your face," the Red Sox slugger said. "For seven days that wind was blowing in from right field. There's no way for a lefthanded hitter to hit one out against that wind."

"Boog Powell found a way."

"He really crunched that ball," Yaz said, referring to the Orioles' huge first baseman. "I thought it would land in Copley Square but it just about fell into the Orioles' bullpen because of the wind."

With their 5–2 loss, the Red Sox had found a way to drop into a third-place tie in the frantic four-team American League pennant race.

Entering the final two weeks of the season, the Detroit Tigers were in first place with an 85–65 record, with the Chicago White Sox at 85–66, only one-half game behind. The Red Sox and the Minnesota Twins, each 84–66, were only one game out. But looking to the Red Sox' two games in Detroit after having been embarrassed by the Orioles, manager Dick Williams decided on a shakeup.

"Jose Tartabull will be in rightfield, Russ Gibson will catch, and Dalton Jones will play third base," Williams said. "We need some lefthanded hitters in Detroit."

The Tigers had rolled into first place with a four-game winning streak, but it ended that Sunday in Detroit when Washington Senator lefthander Frank Bertaina spun a 5–0 seven-hitter. In his office, Tiger manager Mayo Smith surveyed the situation.

"Whoever wins," Smith predicted, "will need a 10–2 finish."

Before the Twins' game at Comiskey Park that Sunday afternoon, manager Cal Ermer told his players, "This thing is far from over." But after White Sox lefthander Gary Peters had fired a 4–0 four-hitter for a three-game sweep that knocked the Twins out of a share of first place, Eddie Stanky was crowing.

"We did it all," the White Sox manager said. "We played every phase of the game. We came from behind. We played defense. We used the bullpen. We moved the runners around. We even hit the home run. You can't ask for more than that."

Of the four teams, the White Sox had been the most resilient. On Saturday, September 9, at Comiskey Park, they took a 3–0 lead into the ninth against the Tigers with Peters pitching. Six singles, three walks, and three more pitchers later, the Tigers had rallied for a 7–3 victory. "We've had big innings before, but never in the ninth inning," Tiger rightfielder Al Kaline said. "These are the kinds of games we used to lose." And if not for outfielder Ken Berry's taunting from the White Sox dugout, maybe the Tigers would have lost. Kaline had led off the ninth with a single. With a hard wind blowing in from leftfield, Willie Horton was up.

"Hey, Willie," Berry yelled. "Let's see you hit one today. Go ahead, hit one."

Horton tried. Without the wind, his high fly ball probably would have soared into the leftfield stands. Instead, it landed several feet short, in Walt (No-Neck) Williams's glove.

"What's the matter, Willie?" Berry taunted. "Can't you hit 'em anymore?"

The other Tigers were annoyed. Some attributed their seven-run rally as answering Berry's jibes. Until then, the Tigers had only been annoyed with Eddie Stanky for spouting that the Tigers should win the pennant by ten games, for grabbing his throat in a chokeup gesture when Tiger righthander Joe Sparma pitched, for telling the umpires to order Wally Moses to stay inside the first-base coach's box. But with that seven-run rally that kept them in first-place with the Twins, the Tigers had answered Stanky too.

"I'm not going to resign," the White Sox manager said before walking his tiny brown poodle, Go-Go, in the darkening outfield. "We'll show up for tomorrow's doubleheader."

The White Sox swept the Tigers, 6–0 and 4–0, with righthander

Joel Horlen pitching a no-hitter in the opener. In his previous seasons, Horlen often had trouble getting through the early innings. But this year he decided to use a split warmup: throw for ten minutes, rest for five minutes, throw for eight more minutes. In his no-hitter the White Sox–Tiger rivalry flared briefly after one of Horlen's pitches clipped catcher Bill Freehan on the left elbow. The next time Horlen batted, righthander Dave Wickersham plunked the thirty-year-old White Sox righthander on the left thigh.

"I wasn't trying to hurt Horlen," Wickersham would say later. "but I don't like guys throwing at Freehan. Stanky himself says Bill is our most valuable player. You got to protect your own guys."

Horlen, meanwhile, was explaining to the writers the secret to his no-hitter: chewing two sheets of Scotties facial tissues. The slender Texan had tried chewing gum or tobacco, but neither agreed with him. In addition to keeping his no-hitter game ball, Horlen planned to put the White Sox lineup card and Western Union's inning-by-inning ticker tape in his scrapbook.

"Maybe," he said, "I ought to save this wad of tissue too."

In any pennant race, the managers are always central characters. But more than most, these four managers' different personalities would reflect the day-to-day struggle. Eddie Stanky, smug and sarcastic, who had stolen a 5–4 victory over the Twins by using four pinch runners in a hectic ninth inning, another example of his finding a way to win for a White Sox team without that much talent. Dick Williams, fiery and demanding, trying to win a pennant for Red Sox owner Tom Yawkey and make a name for himself in his first season as a major league manager after a shoulder injury clouded his career as a touted young Brooklyn Dodger outfielder. Mayo Smith, calm and controlled, hoping his patience would help his Tiger bullpen pitchers develop faith in themselves. Cal Ermer, careful and cool, hired to succeed the fired Sam Mele on June 9 after two decades as a minor league manager, willing to let his Twin players do it their way.

Of the four teams, the Red Sox had to survive the darkest hour: the tragic beaning of Tony Conigliaro, their twenty-two-year-old righthanded-swinging slugger.

For tall, dark, and handsome Tony C., out of nearby Revere, Massachusetts, it was as if the Wall in leftfield at Fenway Park, the thirty-seven-foot-high Green Monster, had been built in 1912 with him in mind. On the first pitch of his first at-bat there as a nineteen-year-old rookie outfielder in 1964, he hit a home run over the net above the Wall. On that Fenway Park Opening Day the Red Sox were donating the net proceeds to the John F. Kennedy Memorial Library, in honor of the president who had been assassinated five months earlier. Among the dignitaries at the game were former Attorney General Bobby Kennedy, Senator Ted Kennedy, and Governor Endicott (Chub) Peabody.

"Hitting a homer was the least I could do," Tony C. said later with a smile, "after they all showed up for my home debut."

As a rookie that year, Tony C. hit twenty-four homers. With thirty-two the next year, he was the youngest player ever to lead the American League in homers. He added twenty-eight in 1966. Earlier in the 1967 season he had emerged, at twenty-two, as the youngest player ever to accumulate one hundred major league homers. He was on his way to Cooperstown, a threat to surpass Babe Ruth's total of 714 homers. Maybe even Henry Aaron's eventual record of 755 homers. When he stepped into the batter's box in the fourth inning on August 18 at Fenway Park, he already had twenty homers. With a .287 average, he had already driven in sixty-seven runs.

On the mound now at Fenway Park that Friday night, Jack Hamilton, a California Angel righthander, fired a fastball. High and inside.

Throwing up his hands and jerking his head, Conigliaro somehow knocked off his batting helmet. The pitch sailed even more inside and smashed into his left cheekbone just below the eye socket.

"I never hit a guy that hard in my life," Hamilton would say years later. "He went right down. He just collapsed."

Darting from the Red Sox dugout, Dick Williams and trainer Buddy LeRoux rushed to him. Rico Petrocelli, who had been on deck, knelt over him and tried to comfort him.

"You'll be all right, Tony," the Red Sox shortstop whispered. "You'll be all right."

Other teammates stood nearby and stared. Tony C.'s left eye was already completely shut, the skin swollen and discolored, as if a purple veil had been drawn across it. Blood trickled from his nose. Jim Lonborg, Joe Foy, and Mike Ryan slid him onto the stretcher. Carefully lifting the stretcher, Lonborg, Ryan, LeRoux, and Angel trainer Fred Federico carried him into the Red Sox dugout and through the tunnel to the clubhouse, where Dr. Thomas Tierney was waiting.

"It hurts like hell," Conigliaro told the Red Sox physician. "I heard a hissing sound and that was all."

The pitch that struck him had been hissing—some Red Sox suspected it to have been an illegal spitball. Now in his sixth major league season after having been with the Philadelphia Phillies, Detroit Tigers, and New York Mets before being traded to the Angels two months earlier, Hamilton had occasionally confided to teammates that he threw a spitball.

"But the pitch that hit Tony was a fastball, believe me," Hamilton would say years later. "He'd been hit a lot of times. He crowded the plate. I know in my heart I wasn't trying to hit him."

Tony C. had been hounded by other injuries from pitched balls: a fractured arm as a rookie, a cracked wrist in 1965, and a hairline arm fracture during spring training five months earlier. This time X-rays showed a shattered cheekbone, but his doctors were more concerned about his vision. Nearly a month later, with the swelling down, his eyes were examined. In his healthy right eye, he still had enviable 20/10 vision. But with cloudy 20/100 vision in his damaged left eye, his depth perception had been affected. His season was over. He also would miss the 1968 season. But he would hit twenty homers in 1969 and lead the league with thirty-six in 1970 while driving in 116 runs. Traded, ironically, to the Angels the next year when his vision began blurring, he hit only four homers. He drifted into singing and broadcasting. He was scheduled to audition for a Red Sox broadcasting job in 1982 when his brother Billy was driving him to Logan Airport.

"I glanced over at Tony," his brother would say years later. "He seemed to be making a face, but he was having a heart attack. I turned around and drove to Mass. General as fast as I could. About a mile from the hospital, he slumped over and his eyes rolled up. By the time we got to the hospital, he had no pulse. That's when the brain damage occurred."

Tony C., then thirty-seven, was in a coma for nearly five weeks before he spoke. Following complications from pneumonia, he needed surgery to remove part of his left lung. He never recovered. He died in 1990 at age forty-five after having required around-the-clock nursing since his heart attack. The youngest slugger to hit one hundred homers had never really been the same since his 1967 beaning. To replace him that year, the Red Sox signed Ken (Hawk) Harrelson, who had been released by the Kansas City Athletics on August 21 after criticizing owner Charles O. Finley for firing Alvin Dark as manager.

Harrelson was quoted as having described Finley as a "menace to baseball," a phrase the outfielder denied saying. Whatever he did or did not say, his release had put him on the open market as a free agent nearly a decade before an arbitrator, Peter Seitz, liberated baseball players from the reserve clause. Available to the highest bidder in a pennant race, Harrelson preferred to join the Red Sox for a reported $75,000 bonus even though the White Sox had offered $100,000.

But with Harrelson in a slump, Dick Williams juggled his lineup for Monday night's resumption of the pennant race. Yaz slashed a double and a single, walked, and struck out. The Red Sox were trailing the Tigers, 5–4, when Yaz silently said a Hail Mary before facing righthanded reliever Fred Lasher with one out in the ninth. With a two balls–no strikes count, catcher Bill Freehan, who considered Yaz a good breaking-ball hitter, signaled for Lasher's best pitch, a fastball. Yaz deposited it in the upper rightfield deck at Tiger Stadium for his fortieth homer, joining Jimmie Foxx, Ted Williams, and Dick Stuart as the only Red Sox sluggers to attain that plateau. In the top of the tenth, righthander Mike Marshall was pitching to Dalton Jones, a surprise starter at third base who already had three singles. This time Jones crashed a homer off a steel girder in the upper rightfield stands. Red Sox, 6–5.

"This had to be the best game of baseball I've ever played in the big leagues," Jones was saying now. "There's something about this ballpark. I just feel better coming to the plate here than I do anywhere else."

Tom Yawkey phoned Dick Williams to say "I'll buy the beer" for what the manager described as "our biggest win of the year." Suddenly the Red Sox, the Tigers, and the Twins, who had won in Kansas City on Jim Kaat's 2–0 six-hitter, each had the same record: 85–66.

"Do you think there'll be a playoff?" a writer asked Williams.

"We're in a playoff every night," the Red Sox manager replied.

With an opportunity in Anaheim to move into first place by one-half game, the White Sox flubbed it. They lost to the Angels, 3–2, on Rick Reichardt's ninth-inning single off reliever Bob Locker. That dropped the White Sox into fourth place, one-half game back to the three leaders. By then Tiger rookie lefthander Mickey Lolich was sleeping soundly. Tuesday night he would be pitching against the Red Sox with first place at stake, but before he left the clubhouse one of the writers had questioned him about the burden of pitching that game.

"I'm not worrying about it," Lolich said.

"But how will you cope with the pressure?"

"I'll relax by riding my bike for about two hours before I come to the ballpark," he said, meaning his 250-cc Kawasaki motorcycle. "That's relaxing to me. Why worry? Too many people worry."

"You're the giant-killer now?" a writer said.

"Not the Giants, the Red Sox," Lolich said with a laugh. "Get the right team."

And the right league.

Hours later, Denny McLain, the Tiger righthander with a 17–16 record, was lying on the couch in the family room of his Farmington Hills ranch home, watching "The Untouchables" on television. Starting against the Red Sox that Monday night, he had been strafed for four runs in only two innings. Annoyed at himself, he had kicked his locker with his left foot, but thought nothing of it. Now, as he watched Robert Stack portray Elliot Ness, he heard a noise in his garage. Alarmed, he jumped up, not realizing that his left foot was asleep. He toppled to the floor, his left ankle severely sprained.

He never found out what the noise had been. Maybe a squirrel knocking over a rake.

Tuesday night McLain was on crutches. He wouldn't pitch again until the season's final game. Mickey Lolich throttled the Red Sox for eight innings, allowing only four singles. He struck out thirteen and had a 2–1 lead on centerfielder Jim Northrup's two-run homer off righthander Lee Stange in the sixth. But in the Red Sox ninth second baseman Jerry Adair led off with a single. Yaz walked on four pitches. First baseman George Scott twice tried to bunt but missed the ball, then singled to center, scoring Adair with the tying run. Mayo Smith took Lolich out and used righthander Earl Wilson in relief for the first time all season. Rookie centerfielder Reggie Smith bunted, Yaz moving to third and Scott to second. Wilson's first pitch to leftfielder Norm Siebern skidded off Bill Freehan's glove, Yaz scoring on what the official scorer called a wild pitch. Scott then scored on Russ Gibson's sacrifice fly for a 4–2 lead. In the bottom of the ninth the Tigers had two on when Dick Williams brought in Bill Landis, a little-used lefthander. At the mound Williams pointed to the pitching rubber.

"You know what this is?" the manager asked Landis.

With a laugh, Landis nodded. Williams pointed to Eddie Mathews, the future Hall of Famer who had already hit more than five hundred homers.

"All I want you to do," Williams said, "is get him out."

Mathews struck out, then Williams brought in Gary Bell to pitch to Al Kaline, who lined to Smith for the final out. With that 4–2 triumph, the Red Sox shared first place with the Twins, who won, 8–2, in Kansas City on righthander Dave Boswell's two-hitter. When the

White Sox stopped the Angels, 3–0, on Joel Horlen's six-hitter for his eighteenth victory, they were in third place, one-half game behind the co-leaders. The Tigers were fourth, one game out. Mayo Smith was concerned about his hitters' tendency to leave too many runners on base. Over the season the Tigers already had left 130 more runners on base than the Red Sox had.

"This has been going on in Detroit long before I got here," Smith said. "We don't have enough hitters who put the bat on the ball. The strikeout figures show that."

Eleven stranded base runners had sabotaged Lolich's performance, but when one of the writers told the rookie lefthander how well he had pitched for eight innings, he disagreed.

"Pitched good?" he grumbled. "Why do you say that? I lost. I'd rather give up seven runs and fifteen hits and win. If I had my bike here now, I'd go drive into a guardrail."

Wednesday night in Cleveland the Red Sox were losing, 2–0, to Sudden Sam McDowell until Yaz hit his forty-first homer and Rico Petrocelli hit a two-run homer. In the ninth Yaz added his third single, took second on a wild pitch, and scored on Reggie Smith's single for the tie-breaking run in a 5–4 victory. Yaz had been seething ever since June when Eddie Stanky had called him "an All-Star from the neck down." With his four hits, Yaz now loomed as a triple crown candidate. His .316 average led Frank Robinson of the Orioles by four percentage points. He also was leading the league in homers and runs batted in.

"Of course I feel there's a lot riding on every pitch these days, but it's not just on me," Yaz said. "It's the same for everybody on the team. Whatever I feel up there in a tight spot, it doesn't bother me. I know they're trying hard to get me out and that makes me try harder to get a hit."

The son of a Bridgehampton, New York, potato farmer, Carl Yastrzemski had grown up wanting to play for the Yankees because of Yankee Stadium's short rightfield stands. When his father demanded a $100,000 bonus from the Yankees, scout Ray Garland, who was offering $60,000, tossed a pencil that hit the ceiling of the Yastrzemski's kitchen.

"Nobody throws a pencil in my house," his father yelled. "Get the hell out and don't ever come back."

Scouts from other teams came instead: the Phillies, the Reds, the Tigers as well as the Dodgers and the Giants, who had just moved to Los Angeles and San Francisco. During the Depression the Brooklyn

Dodgers had wanted to sign the elder Carl Yastrzemski, but he preferred the financial stability of the potato farm he shared with his brother Tom.

"If only you were still in Brooklyn," the father told the Dodger scout.

Eventually the Red Sox signed Yaz for a $108,000 bonus although he was a skinny five-eleven and 160 pounds at the time. In 1961 at age twenty-one, after only two minor league seasons, he joined the Red Sox to stay. Over his Hall of Fame career he would bat .285 with 452 homers, but 1967 was his best year by far. His 44 homers would share the American League lead with Harmon Killebrew's. He would lead the league in five other categories: .326 average, .622 slugging average, 189 hits, 112 runs scored, 121 runs batted in.

Yaz had never driven in one hundred runs before. The most homers he had hit before were twenty in 1965. But now, in his first pennant race, he was never better.

When the Twins, the Tigers, and the White Sox also won Wednesday, the four teams were still separated by only one game. Dean Chance struck out thirteen and fired a four-hitter at the Kansas City Athletics for his eighteenth victory as the Twins won, 6–2, in Minnesota. The Tigers routed the Yankees, 10–1, with Al Kaline hitting his twenty-fifth homer. White Sox centerfielder Tommy Agee drove in

Harmon Killebrew and Tony Oliva. *UPI Photo*

three runs in a 6–4 victory over the Angels, but Early Wynn, the 300-game winner who was now the Twins' pitching coach, established the potential World Series value of the ten games that remained on each contender's schedules.

"I want the word passed along to these guys," Wynn said. "The last ten games are worth $1,000 per game per man."

Thursday the Twins stopped the Athletics, 4–0, on lefthander Jim Merritt's two-hitter and back-to-back homers in the sixth by Harmon Killebrew, his fortieth, and Tony Oliva, his seventeenth. As the afternoon game ended, the Metropolitan Stadium organist played "Meet Me in St. Louis," where the Cardinals had already clinched the National League pennant.

"I hope that guy playing the organ is right," Cal Ermer said.

Now forty-three years old with steel-gray hair, Calvin Coolidge Ermer had played only one game in the major leagues. As a Washington Senator second baseman in 1947, he was hitless in three at-bats. But after gravitating to the minors as a manager, he was inspired by Walter Alston's success as the Dodger manager in Brooklyn and Los Angeles after having had only one big-league at-bat as a St. Louis Cardinal first baseman.

"Alston gave me hope," Ermer said. "Like him, I played one game in the big leagues. Like him, I was an organization man, managing in the minors and hoping one day to get the call from the big team."

Ermer had three minor league pennant winners at Orlando of the Florida State League, Charlotte of the Tri-State League, and Birmingham of the Southern Association before joining the Twins organization. When the phone call came on June 9, the plane carrying his Denver Bears of the American Association was bouncing through the fringe of a tornado above Denver. When the plane landed he was paged.

"You have a message, Mr. Ermer," he was told. "The message is, 'Don't go home, go to the ballpark.' "

There he received the real message: the Twins owner, Calvin Griffith, was hiring him to succeed Sam Mele as manager. Now the Twins had the opportunity to be the first team ever to win a pennant after changing managers in midseason.

"I like winning in the afternoon," Cal Ermer was saying now, "then listening for those other clubs at night."

That night the Tigers and the White Sox were not scheduled, but the Red Sox retained their share of first place, winning again, 6–5.

Gary Bell stifled the Indians, the team that had traded him to the Red Sox three months earlier. Bell's leadoff double in the seventh sparked the winning rally. But to Dick Williams, the significance of this fourth straight victory was that his players now had won forty games on the road, the league's best road record. In contrast, the 1966 Red Sox had won only thirty-two road games.

"This team," Williams said, "was built to win in all parks. We play eighty-one games on the road and to stress Fenway's dimensions would be wrong."

Friday afternoon the Twins dominated the Yankees, 8–2. Cesar Tovar hit his fifth and sixth homers in lefthander Jim Kaat's sixth consecutive victory. When the Red Sox split a twi-night doubleheader in Baltimore, the Twins were in first place. Williams had bragged a little too soon about the Red Sox' road record. They were routed, 10–0, in the opener, but righthander Jose Santiago scattered nine hits to win the second game, 10–3, as Ken Harrelson and Joe Foy each had four hits. That night the Tigers swept the Washington Senators, 8–3 for righthander Earl Wilson's twenty-second victory and 4–0 for Mickey Lolich's twelfth on only two days' rest, while the White Sox were losing in Cleveland, 2–1, in thirteen innings. Now the Twins were in first place with an 89–66 record. The Red Sox were one-half game back, the Tigers one game back, the White Sox two games back.

Saturday the Twins lost to the Yankees, 6–2. Tom Shopay, a virtually unknown outfielder who had hit only nine homers at Syracuse of the International League, hit his first major league homer, a three-run shot off Dave Boswell in the third. But why was Shopay even in the lineup?

"I know the contenders expect you to stay away from rookies against the top clubs in a pennant race, but I had no choice," Yankee manager Ralph Houk explained. "I was forced to use Shopay because of injuries to Tom Tresh and Bill Robinson and the military service call of Steve Whitaker."

The other contenders weren't complaining. The fourth-place White Sox moved to within one game of the Twins on Joel Horlen's 8–0 three-hitter in Cleveland. The Red Sox remained one-half game out, but dropped to third place with a 7–5 loss on Oriole third baseman Brooks Robinson's eighth-inning homer. Yaz's forty-second homer had helped the Red Sox rally for a 5–4 lead in the fifth, but later he sat at his locker and stared at the clubhouse floor for nearly ten minutes. Joe Foy patted Yaz and said, "We're still only a half-game out, buddy." Yaz didn't look up. "All we got to do," Foy said, "is win the five we got left and we can win it, buddy." With a deep breath, Yaz finally lifted his head.

"I suppose this is the toughest loss of the year," Yaz said. "They jumped out to that four-nothing lead and beat us, then we came back and beat them. Then to give it back to them . . ."

The Tigers, now one-half game back in second place, weren't scheduled Saturday, but manager Mayo Smith set his rotation for the next week: righthander Joe Sparma would pitch Sunday in Washington, Wilson would come back Monday in New York on only two days' rest, and Lolich would start there Tuesday on three days' rest. After an off day Wednesday, Wilson would start Thursday against the Angels in Detroit on only two days' rest, and Lolich would start Friday, also with only two days' rest.

"I don't know yet about Saturday and Sunday," the Tiger manager said. "Let's see what happens between now and then."

Smith's reliance on Wilson and Lolich reminded writers of the 1948 Boston Braves' slogan: "Spahn, Sain, and a day of rain." Warren Spahn had continued to pitch into the 1965 season, winning a total of 363 games, the most of any lefthander in major league history. Johnny Sain was now the Tigers' pitching coach.

"How do Wilson and Lolich rate," Sain was asked, "with 'Spahn, Sain, and a day of rain'?"

Mickey Lolich. *Detroit Tigers*

"These two are tougher and they have an off day Wednesday to give 'em some rest," Sain said. "It's great that they want to do it. Pitching with two days' rest won't hurt here and there. In 1948 with the Braves I pitched nine complete games in twenty-nine days. That was a little too much."

But on Sunday afternoon in District of Columbia Stadium the Tigers blew another game that would haunt them.

Going into the bottom of the ninth the Tigers led, 4–2, with Fred Lasher pitching. Senator first baseman Mike Epstein led off with a single. Second baseman Frank Coggins bounced a grounder to Dick McAuliffe near second base. McAuliffe lunged to tag Epstein, but missed him, slipped, and fell. Desperate to get Coggins at first, he threw weakly and late.

"I thought I could get them both," McAuliffe said later. "Epstein was right in front of me. He might have run out of the line, but the umpires never called it. Anyway, that's when I slipped and fell down. I couldn't get much on the throw to first."

Third baseman Ken McMullen bunted, moving Epstein to third and Coggins to second. Catcher Paul Casanova singled, making it 4–3. Gil Hodges, the Senator manager, sent up lefthanded-swinging Dick Nen as a pinch hitter for shortstop Tim Cullen, prompting Mayo Smith to wave for lefthander John Hiller. Hodges countered with righthanded batter Cap Peterson, who lifted a fly ball. Two out. Up now was Senator catcher Doug Camilli, batting .173 with only fourteen hits. He fouled off three pitches, then took ball one. Another foul. Ball two. Ball three. Two more foul balls. On the tenth pitch, Camilli lined a single over second base, scoring Coggins, making it 4–4. Knowing that the Senators' next batter, outfielder Fred Valentine, was a switch hitter, Smith stayed with Hiller. After two foul balls, Valentine singled, Casanova scored, and the Tigers had lost, 5–4. As in every pennant race, one team, in this year the Senators, always emerges as a spoiler.

"We didn't spoil them," one of the Senators said later. "McAuliffe spoiled himself."

In the Tigers' clubhouse, Mayo Smith calmly explained his thinking. "I couldn't let Lasher pitch to Nen," the manager said. "Lasher keeps the ball down and Nen's a low-ball hitter." But the loss had his players furious. When their chartered bus started to pull away from D.C. Stadium, one of the players yelled, "Hold it, bussy. Two more." Joe Sparma and bullpen righthander Dave Wickersham had almost been left behind. When the bus driver opened the door, a voice in the rear growled, "Get on the bus. Get on the bus."

The Tigers were feeling the pain of the pennant race. They had dropped into fourth place, one and one-half games out, while the three other contenders were winning.

That afternoon Bob Allison's three-run homer off Yankee left-hander Steve Barber launched the first-place Twins to a 9–2 victory. Dean Chance scattered nine hits for his twentieth victory, then proclaimed his availability as the starter against the Angels on Wednesday in Metropolitan Stadium on two days' rest.

"If the man wants me," he said, meaning Ermer, "I'll be ready. I didn't try to blow the ball by the Yankees until the ninth.' "

In Baltimore the Red Sox had eighteen hits in an 11–7 rout. Dalton Jones drove in five runs with a triple and three singles. George Scott hit his eighteenth homer and three singles. Jerry Adair had a double and three singles. But the pennant race ploy occurred when Dick Williams removed Jim Lonborg after six innings to rest the Red Sox ace.

"He'll start Wednesday against the Indians," Williams said. "After only six innings, two days' rest should be enough."

The White Sox, with righthander Don McMahon pitching five perfect innings of relief, had held off the Indians, 3–1.

Entering the final week, the first-place Twins were one-half game ahead of the Red Sox, one game ahead of the White Sox, and one and one-half games ahead of the Tigers. The Twins would be home for three with the Angels before going to Boston for two weekend games after the Red Sox had played the sixth-place Indians there twice. The Tigers would play two in New York, then return to Detroit for four with the Angels. The White Sox would go to Kansas City for two with the last-place A's before returning to Chicago for three with the Senators, who were battling for fifth place.

"The White Sox will win because they finish against Kansas City and Washington," Angel manager Bill Rigney predicted. "I like Gary Peters and Joel Horlen pitching the final games for the White Sox."

The Angels would finish fifth with a respectable 84–77 record, halfway down the ten-team American League standings. But over the final week the Angels would be the only team opposing two of the contenders. Rigney's decisions would be as much a part of the pennant race as any of the main managers'. He would use his three best starting pitchers (George Brunet, Jim McGlothlin, and Rickey Clark) against the Twins and the Tigers, just as he had against the White Sox in Anaheim the previous week. And with his frisky manner, Rigney would be heard from, beginning late Monday afternoon after Twin shortstop Zoilo Versalles griped about Rigney's strategy in the Angels' 9–2 triumph in chilly Metropolitan Stadium.

"Rigney picked the White Sox to win the pennant, so he's trying to beat us," Versalles said. "He didn't need to do what he did in the seventh inning. Both moves were hotdog baseball."

With the Angels leading, 7–2, and runners on first and second, Rigney had catcher Bob (Buck) Rodgers bunt. Rigney sent up Bill Skowron to pinch-hit for lefthander Steve Hamilton, prompting Cal Ermer to walk Skowron intentionally, loading the bases. Third baseman Aurelio Rodriguez singled for two more runs. The two moves that annoyed Versalles were the bunt and taking out a pitcher for a pinch hitter in a 7–2 game. When the Twin shortstop's complaint was relayed to Rigney by the writers, the Angel manager exploded.

"What's he want us to do: play seven men?" Rigney snapped. "Does he want us to give in just because we aren't in the top four? Does he want us to go home? I'll tell you something: Versalles went home six weeks ago."

When the Twins won the 1965 pennant, Versalles had been voted the American League's most valuable player. With a .273 average, he had led the league with forty-five doubles, twelve triples, and 126 runs scored. But this season the twenty-seven-year-old Cuban shortstop was batting only .202.

"Did he ever think," Rigney stormed, "that if he hit .270, the Twins would be ahead by ten games? We're not trying to spoil it for anybody. We're just trying to win as many games as we can."

Seeing the writers scribbling Rigney's angry words into their notebooks, Angel shortstop Jim Fregosi stopped on his way to the shower and said, "Gee, Skip, you're going to be as famous as Eddie Stanky." The White Sox manager, in one of his almost daily pronouncements, had declared recently that the Tigers should have already clinched the pennant by ten games, a comment that Mayo Smith shrugged off.

"Anybody who knows Eddie well pays no attention to him," the Tiger manager said. "Eddie enjoys irritating people. He's a great little agitator, a wonderful actor. If he were in Hollywood, he'd win an Oscar every year."

But in a pennant race, the idea is not to win an Oscar, but to win games. For not only the contenders, but for all the other teams in the league. Upstairs in Metropolitan Stadium now, when Twins owner Calvin Griffith heard that Zoilo Versalles had complained about Rigney's seventh-inning strategy with a five-run lead, he agreed with the Angel manager.

"Win is the name of the game," Griffith said. "Rigney is playing it to the hilt. This is exactly what I'd want my manager to do. I know he'll do the same in their four games in Detroit this weekend."

Not all Twins fans were as understanding as the Twins owner. That evening Rigney and his coaches went to dinner at Harry's restaurant in downtown Minneapolis. The maitre d' led them to a quiet table. When their waiter arrived, he recognized the Angel manager.

"How come you pulled your pitcher so fast with a five-run lead?" he asked.

Rigney didn't even look up. "Just shut up and pour the water," he said.

With the Twins losing, the Red Sox, who were not scheduled, moved into a first-place tie. The White Sox, who had an intrasquad game in Kansas City to stay as sharp as possible on their off day, were now only one-half game behind. Not that everybody had been holding their breath. When one of the Chicago writers told White Sox centerfielder Tommy Agee that the Twins had lost that afternoon, he shrugged.

"I didn't know they were playing," he said.

The Tigers knew. In the hours before their night game at Yankee Stadium, they realized that a victory would pull them to within one game of first place. Starting on only two days' rest, Earl Wilson pitched well, but not well enough. He lost, 2–0, to lefthander Al Downing's four-hitter. Just as Tom Shopay had stabbed the Twins with his homer the previous Friday, another Yankee rookie just up from the minors, twenty-two-year-old shortstop Jerry Kenney, drove in Monday night's winning run with a single. When one of the writers suggested to Mayo Smith that his players had been "flat," the Tiger manager shook his head.

"Why should they be flat?" he said. "Having the Twins lose in the afternoon was a real tonic."

The Twins' loss had been a real opportunity for the Tigers, but it turned out to be just another wasted opportunity. Tuesday afternoon the Twins won, 7–3, as utility infielder Jackie Hernandez and outfielder Sandy Valdespino rode Rigney and the Angels from the dugout. Jim Kaat struck out thirteen in a five-hitter. Harmon Killebrew crashed two moon-shot homers that had Cal Ermer smiling.

"Like I've said all along," the Twins manager joked, "this is a game of inches."

To be exact, 10,380 inches, the combined distance of Killebrew's 435-foot homer off Jim McGlothlin over the centerfield screen and his

430-foot homer off Pete Cimino into the left-centerfield pavilion. According to Twins historians, Killebrew had never hit two homers that far in the same game. But in his mild manner, the husky slugger known as "Killer" minimized the measurements.

"Winning games and the pennant," the Twins first baseman said, "is the most important thing now."

Killebrew's homers were the talk of the Twins' clubhouse. "When he hits the ball," centerfielder Ted Uhlaender said, "if he takes two steps, stops, then starts to run again, it's gone." Third-base coach Billy Martin, whose checkered career as a manager would begin with the Twins in 1969, remembered Killebrew's concentration in the batter's box.

"He had the same strained look on his face in a clutch situation that Mickey Mantle did," Martin said. "You just knew he was going to hit a home run."

Killebrew, who would hit 573 homers over his Hall of Fame career, now had forty-three this season. Yaz hit his forty-third a few hours later, but the Red Sox lost to the Indians, 6–3, on twenty-six-year-old Cuban righthander Luis Tiant's eight-hitter. Yaz's average was up to .319 with 115 runs batted in. As early as the first inning, with Jose Tartabull on second with one out, Indian manager Joe Adcock had ordered Tiant to walk Yaz intentionally.

"I don't think Yaz knows what pressure is," Adcock explained later. "He hit five smashes against us in Cleveland last week and I decided he had beaten us often enough. We walked him to try somebody else."

That night Mickey Lolich blanked the Yankees in a 1–0 duel with Mel Stottlemyre, his second straight shutout. The Tigers were still fourth, but the Twins were all alone in first place, one game ahead of both the Red Sox and the White Sox, who had been rained out in Kansas City.

"I'm the most disappointed guy in the world," Eddie Stanky said. "I hate these postponements. It tears up everything, but I'm going to stick to my pitching plans."

Gary Peters and Joel Horlen would be pitching Wednesday's twi-night doubleheader against the last-place A's, but by the time it started, both the Red Sox and the Twins had lost. The week before, the Indians remembered, Jim Lonborg had been quoted as saying, "You only have to throw close to Vic Davalillo and you can forget him." Starting on only two days' rest, Lonborg buzzed his first pitch under the chin of the Indian centerfielder. Davalillo twisted out of the way, the ball careened off the backstop, and 18,415 cheered Lonborg's purpose pitch. The next inning Davalillo stroked a two-run single. Luis Tiant spun a 6–0 shutout. The Red Sox had lost five consecutive games in Not-So-Friendly Fenway, three to the eighth-place Orioles nearly two weeks earlier and now two to the sixth-place Indians. Joe Adcock had a theory.

"That first pitch of the game may have beaten Lonborg," the Indian manager said. "He may have done us a favor."

In the Red Sox clubhouse, Yaz and many of his teammates knew the reality of the situation: we're probably out of it now. Outside, several writers had assembled. They wouldn't be allowed to enter until the security guard got the word. Through a crack in the door, one of the writers was trying to see how the players were reacting to the two-game sweep that appeared to wreck their pennant chances.

"Anybody throw anything?" another writer asked.

"Not yet."

"Anybody slug anybody?"

"Not yet."

"Then what are they doing?"

"They're eating."

"They're what?"

In the Fenway Park press box later, *Boston Herald* columnist Tim Horgan would write, "The Sox did not go out with a bang and they did not go out with a whimper. They went out with a ham on rye." When the clubhouse door finally opened, Dick Williams, munching a ham and cheese sandwich and holding a bottle of beer, was surrounded by writers.

"Is the club running scared?" one asked.

"We're not running scared," the Red Sox manager said. "We've been playing ball under pressure since the All-Star break. I believe we're just trying too hard. This is as poor as the club has played all year. The pitchers are pitching high and the hitters aren't hitting. Maybe they've been pressing, but I can't fault them."

By then the Twins knew the Red Sox had lost. Opportunity was knocking, but the Twins couldn't answer.

Early in their Wednesday afternoon game Angel rightfielder Jimmie Hall had returned to the dugout and told his teammates, "Chance isn't throwing hard at all." Dean Chance, the Twins' ace, had started on only two days' rest. In the Angels' four-run fourth, first baseman Don Mincher, who had been traded by the Twins with Hall and righthander Pete Cimino for Chance, crashed a homer into the rightfield bullpen.

Now the Angels were shouting at Hernandez and Valdespino, their Tuesday tormentors. In the seventh, with two out, two on, and Killebrew awaiting a three-nothing pitch, Ermer flashed the hit sign. One swing, the manager thought, and it's a tie game. On a fastball, Killebrew lifted a harmless fly to center. The Angels would win, 5–1, as righthander Minnie Rojas preserved righthander Rickey Clark's twelfth victory. Chance was disconsolate.

"I wasn't tired," the Twins' ace said. "I was just getting the ball up too high and they hit it. If anything, I was too loose because I was so confident of winning. I just picked a real bad time not to have my good stuff. I might have cost us everything."

For the White Sox, everything now was attainable. If they were to win their twi-night doubleheader in Kansas City, they would jump into first place by one-half game. If they then were to sweep their three-game series with the Senators at Comiskey Park on the final weekend, they would win the pennant with a 94–70 record. The best the Twins and the Tigers could do was 93–69, the best the Red Sox could do was 92–70. Of the four teams, only the White Sox controlled their own destiny. Their pitching staff would have a 2.45 earned run average, the major leagues' lowest since the 1919 Chicago Cubs' 2.19. And tonight their two aces, Peters (16–10) and Horlen (19–7), were pitching. But stunningly, the White Sox lost both games to the last-place A's, 5–2 to twenty-three-year-old righthander Chuck Dobson in the opener and 4–0 to twenty-one-year-old righthander Jim (Catfish) Hunter's three-hitter. Across the top of the front page, the eight-column headline in Thursday morning's *Chicago Tribune* summed up the situation:

GOOD GRIEF! SOX DROP TWO.

During the doubleheader, Dick Williams listened alone to the games on his car radio outside his Peabody, Massachusetts, apartment while drinking a few beers. When he went to bed, his Red Sox still had a chance. In wasting their opportunity to lead by one-half game, the White Sox had dropped into fourth place, one and one-half games behind the Twins, who remained one game ahead of both the Red Sox and the Tigers. In his misery Eddie Stanky was drinking milk late Wednesday night in old Municipal Stadium when he finally took questions from the writers.

"Do you still have a chance?" one asked.

"Still have a chance? Still have a chance?" the White Sox manager snapped, his voice rising. "I've been in baseball thirty years. I've seen seven runs scored against us in the ninth inning this year. I've seen ten-game winning streaks. I've seen us in first place. I've seen us in fifth place. I've seen us in sixth place. We win our last three, we're happy. I'm paid to manage the White Sox for one hundred sixty-two games. Or more, if necessary."

"What about your pitching for the three games with Washington?"

"Our pitching rotation was assured a week ago. Where were you?"

"How about a picture of you?" a newspaper photographer asked.

"Take me, but no pictures of my players when they're dejected."

Thursday only the Tigers were dejected. When a chilly drizzle turned the opener of their four-game series with the Angels at Tiger Stadium into a Friday doubleheader, Bill Rigney said, "It really hurt Detroit psychologically. It's always tougher to win a doubleheader than two games in two days. Besides, I didn't have my big man, Rich Reichardt, in the lineup. He's got a sore left wrist. But he might be able to play all the way now." In the Tigers' clubhouse Mayo Smith was still stunned by Wednesday's results.

"Lonborg lost, Chance lost, Peters lost, Horlen lost," Smith was saying at his desk.

"What kind of odds," one of the writers wondered, "would you get on that parlay?"

"The same kind you'd get on the Tigers beating the Orioles fifteen out of eighteen."

Friday the Tigers and Angels were rained out again, creating Saturday and Sunday doubleheaders. In Boston the Twins and Red Sox each had workouts, awaiting Saturday's showdown between Jim Kaat and Jose Santiago in the opener of their two-game series. Mathematically, the White Sox still had a chance to create a playoff if they could sweep three from the Senators. Leading off the first inning, Senator shortstop Tom Cullen bounced a grounder to third baseman Ken Boyer, whose throw skidded off Tom McCraw's glove. McCraw scolded himself for not using two hands. Hank Allen grounded to shortstop Ron Hansen, who tossed to Don Buford for the force, but trying for the double play Buford threw wild. Allen scurried to second. Stanky ordered Frank Howard walked intentionally. On a three-one pitch, Fred Valentine lifted a high foul. McCraw drifted under it, but the ball landed just out of the first baseman's reach, beyond a new railing around a two-foot-deep ditch that had been dug for a World Series television camera platform.

McCraw stared at the ditch. Where had it come from?

On the next pitch, Valentine singled, scoring Allen for a 1–0 lead that righthander Phil Ortega protected. The White Sox had been mathematically eliminated. Maybe as much by that ditch for a television camera platform as by Ortega's four-hitter and Valentine's single. During batting practice McCraw had seen a similar railing and ditch, about ten feet long and six feet wide, over near the White Sox' dugout behind third base, but he hadn't noticed the ditch near the Senators' dugout. Until it was too late.

Now it was too late for the White Sox.

All season their theme song on the clubhouse juke box had been Merle Haggard's "Branded Man," but now they sat at their lockers in the silence of elimination. After a few minutes, Eddie Stanky emerged from his office.

"The mouse," the manager told his players, "had the elephant on the chair."

When the writers were finally allowed into Stanky's office, he was calm.

"Gentlemen," he said, "I didn't mean to keep you waiting so long, but I wanted to talk to my players. I wanted to make sure these guys weren't depressed. I told them how proud I was of them. I told them how tough it was this week. There was one man responsible for losing more games than any of them. Me, the manager. For one hundred fifty-five games, they were the talk of the earth, the talk of the earth. But now Detroit, Minnesota, and Boston, they're relieved now because the laughingstock of the American League is not a contender anymore. The elephants were fearful of the mouse, but now they can sigh with relief. My boys don't have to bow their heads. I don't give a shit who wins. One of my last statements to my men is that some of us will ride again."

"Will the Cardinals be too good for the American League team in the World Series?"

"The Series? We're supposed to root for the American League team, but I don't give a damn who wins. I'm going to the Instructional League. I couldn't care less about the Series. Money isn't everything, but to play in a World Series is so thrilling. And for us the thrill is gone. They say, 'You had a taste of three of them.' I did, but I would've traded all three for this one."

"You sound sentimental."

"Sentimental? I'm very sentimental. That's what makes me a poor manager. I'm too sentimental."

"What about the pop foul McCraw couldn't reach because of that ditch near the first-base dugout?"

"That had nothing to do with it."

Jerry Green of the *Detroit News* had noticed a book on a shelf behind Stanky's desk: Cornelius Ryan's best-seller *The Last Battle*. For the White Sox, this 1–0 loss indeed had been the last battle. But for the Twins, the Red Sox, and the Tigers, the battle was just beginning.

Entering the last two days of the season, the Twins had a one-game lead on both the Tigers and the Red Sox.

Before leaving Minnesota, the Twins had argued among themselves in voting World Series shares. Some didn't want to award former manager Sam Mele a dime, prompting others to argue that if Mele didn't get any money, Cal Ermer shouldn't get any. In the end, Mele got nothing and Ermer got a full share. But now the Twins were trying to forget that mean-spirited meeting. In the Sheraton Boston coffee shop Saturday morning, Jim Kaat had his usual game-day breakfast: scrambled eggs, buttered toast, and black coffee. No milk. No ham, bacon, or sausage. As he checked the standings in the *Boston Globe*, he knew this was the game the Twins had to win, this was the game he had to win. But he was more confident than at any time in his career. In winning seven straight starts, he had never pitched better.

If the Twins won today, the Red Sox would be eliminated and the Tigers would need to win three out of four to create a two-of-three playoff even if the Twins were to lose Sunday's game. Should the Twins also win Sunday's game, the Tigers would need to sweep four to tie.

If the Red Sox were to stay alive after having lost eleven of their previous sixteen games with the Twins this season, Jose Santiago had to justify his emergence as an effective starter after having been in the bullpen most of his career. But this twenty-seven-year-old righthander out of Juana Diaz, Puerto Rico, was confident.

"I promise you, Yaz," he said, "Killebrew isn't going to hit any homers off me today, O.K.?"

"Jose, you stop him," the Red Sox slugger said, "and I'll make sure to hit a homer for you."

With his Lynnfield home filled with his family up from Long Island for the weekend, Yaz had checked into the Colonial Hilton hotel in nearby Wakefield on Friday night to assure himself a good night's sleep. But he awoke at five o'clock and walked the Colonial golf course. Driving to Fenway Park, he realized he had never been in anything like this pennant race. For the last month, it seemed to him as if every pitch was an at-bat. But he had thrived on the concentration. For all the tension, after batting practice he napped for fifteen minutes in the trainer's room. With the national governors' convention about to open in Boston, this Saturday afternoon game had attracted several politicians, notably Vice President Hubert H. Humphrey, once a senator from Minnesota, and Massachusetts Senator Ted Kennedy.

"We're really up against it," Humphrey told Tom Yawkey. "We've got to beat Cardinal Cushing, Senator Ed Brooke, Governor Volpe, and the entire Kennedy family as well as the Red Sox."

Hearing that, Ted Kennedy laughed. "We're happy to have the vice president with us," he said. "We'll give him every bit of hospitality possible, but not enough runs to win the game."

For the Red Sox, winning both games was mandatory. One loss and they would be eliminated. Now, as Kaat and Santiago finished warming up, as teenagers hung from the billboards across Lansdowne Street behind leftfield, Vice President Humphrey prepared to throw out the first ball from a box near the Red Sox dugout. But he didn't have every politician's baseball prop. He didn't have a glove. Quickly a Secret Service agent stepped down into the Red Sox dugout and grabbed a glove off the bench. Rico Petrocelli's glove.

As soon as the vice president tossed the ceremonial ball, Dick Williams didn't take his eyes off the glove until the agent returned it to the Red Sox shortstop.

Williams soon had another worry. Santiago was shaky. Leading off the first inning, Versalles singled. Tovar flied out, but Killebrew walked. Oliva singled, Versalles scoring. Bob Allison singled, loading the bases. Rookie second baseman Rod Carew lined to Adair at third, but Santiago was still struggling. One run in, bases loaded, two out, and a three-one count on Uhlaender as baseballs could be heard thudding into catchers' mitts in the Red Sox bullpen. Peering from the dugout, Williams decided if Santiago walked Uhlaender or gave up a hit to the Twin outfielder, he was out of there. On the next pitch, Uhlaender slapped a grounder to second baseman Mike Andrews for the third out. Santiago strode into the dugout.

"That's all they're going to get," he told his teammates. "Just get me some runs."

It wouldn't be easy. Jim Kaat had his best stuff. He struck out four of the first eight batters. In the third, with a one-two count on Santiago, the Twins' big lefthander wanted to keep his fastball low and away. Leaning back toward third base to get a little extra on the pitch as he threw, he heard a pop in his left elbow. Santiago fanned. One out.

But on the mound, Kaat felt a numb vibration in his elbow, as if his funnybone had been struck. In a way, it had. Struck by the wear and tear on his elbow during those seven straight victories.

"Time," he yelled. "Time out."

Cal Ermer hurried to the mound. Wringing his left arm, Kaat stared at the manager.

"I don't think I can pitch."

Ermer waved for Jim Perry to start warming up. Over his career Perry, the older brother of Gaylord Perry, would win 215 games. He would be 20–6 in 1969 and 24–12 the next year. But in 1967, his 8–7 record included only eleven starts. Now, after a hurried ten-minute warmup, he had to protect a 1–0 lead. He got the last two outs in the third and moved through the fourth. In the fifth Reggie Smith opened with a double. Next up was catcher Russ Gibson, but needing a run, Williams didn't want to entrust the situation to a .206 hitter.

"Dalton," the Red Sox manager yelled.

Pinch hitter Dalton Jones tapped a roller to Carew, an apparently easy out. But the ball took a bad hop off the second baseman's shoulder. Third and first, nobody out. Perry struck out Santiago and Andrews, but Jerry Adair lined a single to right, tying the score. On Yaz's bouncer past Killebrew's glove, Carew snatched the ball and turned to throw to first, but Perry wasn't covering the bag. Perry had moved off the mound but when he saw the ball get past Killebrew, he hesitated. Instead of three out, Jones scored for a 2–1 lead.

The Twins didn't fold. In the sixth, Allison walked, Uhlaender singled, and pinch hitter Rich Reese singled, tying the score before Perry was yanked for a pinch hitter. But in the bottom of the sixth, George Scott slammed righthander Ron Kline's first pitch into the centerfield stands. The Red Sox led, 3–2.

With one out in the seventh, Andrews beat out a check-swing tap near the mound. Adair's grounder to Kline appeared to be an inning-ending double play, but Versalles dropped the throw. With Yaz up, Ermer waved for lefthander Jim Merritt. With the count three and one, Yaz was looking for a fastball. Merritt threw a fastball. Yaz whacked it into the Twins' bullpen, his forty-fourth homer. As he trotted home, the crowd of 32,909 celebrated the 6–2 lead, all but Vice President Humphrey. Now, as Yaz moved out to leftfield for the eighth, a husky fan hopped the railing and ran to him.

"I don't care if it costs me fifty dollars," the fan told him. "You just won me more money than I ever made in my life."

When security guards dragged the fan away, Yaz smiled, but he knew the fan's money wasn't safe yet. Just before Yaz's homer, Santiago had confided in trainer Buddy LeRoux in the dugout.

"I'm tired," Santiago said, "but don't tell Dick."

As soon as Santiago opened the eighth by walking Allison, Williams called for Gary Bell, who got through the rest of the inning. In the ninth, the Twins were down to their last out when Tovar doubled. With a four-run lead and Killebrew up, Williams signaled for Bell to throw a fastball. Williams knew the risk: Killebrew might hit it out to tie Yaz for the homer lead, but he didn't want Bell walking him. The risk materialized. Killebrew hit his forty-fourth homer, but Bell got Oliva to close a 6–4 victory that many Twins blamed on Jim Perry for not covering first base.

"The pitcher's got to be there," Ermer said.

"Are you going to fine him?" a writer asked.

"There's no punishment to fit the crime."

Had the Twins won, the Red Sox would have been eliminated. But now the two teams were tied for first place. In tomorrow's season finale, Jim Lonborg would go against Dean Chance, with the winner the possible pennant winner, depending on the outcome of the Tigers' games. In the Red Sox clubhouse, Yaz turned to clubhouse man Don Fitzpatrick.

"Hey, Fitzie," he yelled. "If California beats Detroit two games, it's champagne for everybody on me." Turning to the writers, he added, "The least I can do is buy the champagne."

The champagne stayed on ice. That morning Mickey Lolich had hopped on his motorcycle for the forty-mile trip to Tiger Stadium, where he would oppose the Angels in the opener of their doubleheader. As usual, he didn't ride the freeways. Too dangerous. At a red light about three miles from his home he noticed a car carrying friends coming down from Jackson, Michigan, for the weekend. Making a U-turn, he led them back to his house. After driving all of them to Tiger Stadium in his car, he spun his third straight shutout, 5–0, a three-hitter with eleven strikeouts. Angel starter George Brunet lasted only two innings.

"You're number one now," Lolich would be told later.

"Not me," he said. "Earl Wilson is still number one."

Whatever the ranking of the Tiger aces, for the moment the Tigers themselves were number one, precisely .001 ahead of both the Red Sox and the Twins. If the Tigers could sweep their two doubleheaders, they would win the pennant. In their second game Saturday at Tiger Stadium, they appeared about to open a one-half-game lead on this cool, cloudy, sometimes drizzly day. Earl Wilson had a 4–2 lead, but when he walked Jimmie Hall to open the seventh, Fred Lasher relieved. Dick McAuliffe's two-run homer provided a 6–2 lead, but in the eighth the Angels rallied. Jim Fregosi led off with a single. Jimmie Hall walked. Don Mincher singled for 6–3, then Rick Reichardt singled for 6–4 as Mincher moved to third. Smith called for Hank Aguirre, a thirty-five-year-old lanky lefthander with an 0–0 record and no saves over only forty innings in twenty-nine relief appearances. Roger Repoz was due to bat, but Rigney sent up Bubba Morton, a righthanded pinch hitter.

Morton tapped to Aguirre, who threw to first as Mayo Smith and other Tiger voices were yelling, "Mincher, Mincher." Aguirre had forgotten about Mincher, who raced across the plate. Now it was 6–5.

Annoyed at his mistake, Aguirre walked Bob Rodgers, then walked to the dugout as Smith called Fred Gladding from the bullpen. Bobby Knoop scratched a single off Gladding's glove, loading the bases. Smith waved for lefthander John Hiller, but Tom Satriano's single made it 6–6. Bob (Hawk) Taylor struck out, but on a two-two pitch Fregosi singled to center for two runs. It would end that way, 8–6 for the Angels, another disaster for the Tiger bullpen and a memorable mistake by Hank Aguirre.

"I asked Hank what happened," Mayo Smith reported. "He told me, 'I didn't look for Mincher and I didn't hear Freehan call for the ball.' "

Even so, the Tigers were still alive. No matter which team won Sunday in Boston, the Tigers would create a best-two-of-three pennant playoff if Joe Sparma and Denny McLain could sweep the Angels in their Sunday doubleheader. McLain hadn't pitched since severely spraining his left ankle nearly two weeks earlier but during Saturday's doubleheader he had been injected with cortisone and Xylocaine. In Sunday morning's newspapers, the standings looked like this:

Red Sox	91–70	.565	—
Twins	91–70	.565	—
Tigers	90–70	.563	½

For the Red Sox, the pitching matchup was ominous. Jim Lonborg's lifetime record against the Twins was 0–6, this season 0–3. Since joining the Twins this season, Dean Chance was 4–0 against the Red Sox. Now the two righthanders would be pitching for the pennant, or at least for a pennant playoff.

"This is the first big game I've ever pitched," Lonborg had said after Saturday's game. "I've never even seen a game this big."

Sitting in the trainer's room late that afternoon, Lonborg told Ken Harrelson how, in his 21–9 record, he had been much more effective on the road (14–4) than at Fenway Park (7–5).

"Then stay on the 'road' tonight," Harrelson said. "Take my room at the Sheraton. I've got another place to stay."

Good idea. Lonborg knew his apartment would be a zoo that night. Tomorrow's starter returned to the Charles River Park pad that he shared with restaurateur Neil McNerney, who owned two of Boston's most popular bars, Mother's and Smoky Joe's. He grabbed his shaving kit and his friend William Craig's best-seller *The Fall of Japan*. Soon he was moving through the Sheraton Boston lobby as if the Red Sox were on a road trip. He settled into bed early, began reading his book, but soon fell asleep.

In the morning, glancing through the *Boston Globe*, he noticed his comfortable lead on Sam McDowell for the strikeout crown, 241 to 229. He knew he didn't have to worry about strikeouts. Leaving the hotel for Fenway Park, he felt as if he were on the road.

But no matter where he had slept, Lonborg soon knew he was in Fenway. With two out in the first, he walked Killebrew, then Oliva drilled a double to left, the ball skipping off the wet grass past Yaz's glove. Hurrying to third, Killebrew was stunned to see Billy Martin waving him on. Killer was known for his power, not his speed. By now first baseman George Scott had moved across the infield to cut off Reggie Smith's throw. Puffing around third, Killebrew appeared to be an easy out until Scott flung the ball high over catcher Russ Gibson's head.

With two out in the third, Lonborg walked Tovar and Killebrew singled to left. When the ball skipped past Yaz for an error, Tovar scored. Now it was 2–0 on two unearned runs.

On the mound, Lonborg wondered if this was going to be one of those days when nothing went right and his teammates weren't going to get many runs. But then he told himself, I've never lost two games in a row this season and I'm not going to start now. Just bear down. We'll get some runs in the sixth or the seventh. He also was completely comfortable being caught by thirty-eight-year-old Elston Howard, signed in midseason after the Yankees had released him. In the past, Lonborg occasionally had been indecisive about what pitch to throw, not always agreeing with the catcher's call. But he never questioned

Howard's calls. Now, after the Twins' early runs, his fastball was moving more and more.

"We'll keep working the fastball," Howard told him after the fourth. "It's really moving."

Through five innings, Chance appeared to be breezing, but Rod Carew, who would be voted the American League Rookie of the Year, thought otherwise. Chance had been jumpy right from the start. His face was drawn, he was sweating more than usual, and he wasn't joking with his teammates. With the Red Sox still trailing, 2–0, and with Lonborg due to lead off the sixth, many of the 35,770 Red Sox loyalists wondered if Williams might remove him for a pinch hitter who would spark a rally. Not that Lonborg was looking over his shoulder. More than most pitchers, he took batting practice seriously.

"You'll keep yourself in a ballgame," coach Bobby Doerr always told the Red Sox pitchers, "if the manager knows you can hit."

With his right arm in his Red Sox jacket, Lonborg clacked up the steps of the dugout with a bat, then slipped his jacket to the batboy. His first time up, he had singled on Chance's first pitch, a fastball down the middle. He expected another fastball. As he moved out of the on-deck circle, he noticed that third baseman Cesar Tovar was back on the dirt. Lonborg considered himself fast enough to beat out a bunt. In batting practice, he took bunting seriously, if only because Dick Williams took it seriously. Chance threw his fastball. Lonborg bunted. Tovar hurried in but bobbled the ball. Lonborg sprinted across first base. Bunt single.

Putting on his jacket at first base, Lonborg knew he wasn't on the road now; he knew he didn't want to be on the road now. His bunt had Fenway Park roaring. For him. And for the next batter, Jerry Adair, who responded by lining a single.

With runners on second and first, Dalton Jones got the bunt sign but fouled off the pitch. Swinging away, the Red Sox third baseman slashed a single past Tovar into leftfield, loading the bases. In the on-deck circle, Yaz tossed away the weighted bat as the Fenway Park roar surrounded him. Yaz dug in. Chance fired. Yaz swung, scorching a line drive to center that scored Lonborg and Adair with the tying runs.

Now the roar surrounded Ken Harrelson, who slapped a hard grounder to Zoilo Versalles, who threw to the plate. Too late as Jones slid across. The Red Sox were ahead, 3–2, and Cal Ermer waved to the bullpen for Al Worthington.

With Scott up, Worthington uncorked two wild pitches, permitting Yaz to score and Jose Tartabull, who was running for Harrelson, to go to third. "I didn't feel good out there," Worthington would say later. "I didn't have much coordination." He fanned Scott, but Petrocelli walked. Reggie Smith bounced a grounder off Killebrew's knee, and Tartabull scored the fifth run on the error. When the inning finally ended with the Red Sox ahead, 5–2, the roar accompanied Lonborg to the mound as organist John Kiley played "The Night They Invented Champagne." But in the Red Sox clubhouse nobody dared to open a bottle.

With one out in the eighth, Twin pinch hitter Rich Reese singled. Tovar grounded to Adair, who tagged Reese and flipped to Scott for a dazzling double play. But the Red Sox second baseman had been severely spiked by Reese on his left leg. Adair limped to the dugout, Mike Andrews replacing him.

Two out, none on. Lonborg seemed secure. But with Killebrew up, Red Sox pitching coach Sal Maglie walked to the mound. "He'll be looking for the long ball," Maglie advised. "Pitch him tough." Lonborg pitched tough, but Killebrew singled. Oliva singled. Allison suddenly represented the tying run. The tension was too much for Carol Yastrzemski, who left her seat holding her rosary beads. Yaz's wife walked under the stands. She didn't see Allison's liner into the leftfield corner, which appeared to be a certain double. She didn't see her husband snatch the ball and whip it to Andrews who tagged Allison for the third out. Killebrew had scored to lift the Twins to within 5–3, but the inning was over.

"I didn't care if Oliva scored too," Yaz would say later. "I wanted to keep Allison from being the tying run at second. I knew a good throw would get him."

In the ninth Uhlaender opened with a bad-hop single off Petrocelli's face. Carew bounced to Andrews, who tagged Uhlaender and flipped to Scott, a carbon copy of Adair's double play. Down to his last out, Ermer went against the book. Instead of letting lefthanded-swinging catcher Russ Nixon bat, he sent up righthanded Rich Rollins as a pinch hitter. Pop up. Petrocelli squeezed it. Red Sox, 5–3. Now the roar and his teammates surrounded Lonborg as hundreds of fans swarmed across the grass. The other Red Sox ducked into the dugout but Lonborg, perched atop fans' shoulders, was swept out to rightfield. Some hugged and kissed him. Others tore his uniform, tore his sweatshirt, stole his cap. When police finally rescued him, he wobbled into the Red Sox clubhouse.

"I was scared to death," he said.

Jim Lonborg floats atop the Fenway fans. *AP/Wide World Photo*

Tom Yawkey hugged Lonborg, then the Red Sox owner hugged Yaz and Dick Williams and the others. With a double and three singles, Yaz had gone seven for eight in the two games to earn the triple crown: a .326 average, 121 runs batted in, and 44 homers, sharing the homer title with Harmon Killebrew.

"I've never seen a perfect player," Williams told Yaz, "but you were one for us. I've never seen a player have a season like that."

For all the celebration, the Red Sox had only clinched a tie. The Tigers had won their opener, 6–4, with Willie Horton hitting a two-run homer off Clyde Wright in the first. If the Tigers won the second game, the best-two-of-three playoff would begin at Fenway Park tomorrow. In the Red Sox clubhouse, the champagne had not been opened, but Williams noticed righthander Lee Stange raising a beer.

"Take it easy with that stuff, Stinger," the manager said. "If there's a game tomorrow, you're going."

No matter what, the Twins were going home. Dean Chance, embarrassed at losing the big one, had showered and departed before the game ended. Some of his teammates griped that their ace righthander didn't have the guts to stay around, but Rod Carew knew that Chance felt just awful; he didn't want to face his teammates. Chance never heard Cal Ermer tell his players, "You have nothing to be ashamed of. You gave it your best shot." When the writers entered, the Twins manager told them, "The game turned on Lonborg's bunt and it wasn't that good a bunt." Asked about Tovar being back too far, Ermer agreed that "a third baseman should be looking for a bunt like that all the time." Asked about Versalles's late throw to the plate, he said, "I don't think he should've gone home."

Versalles defended his decision, saying, "The man, he's running home for the money. I'm playing for the money too. It was the only choice I had. Somebody has to win. Somebody has to lose."

Now, in Detroit, somebody had to win and somebody had to lose. The Tigers had presented Denny McLain with a quick 3–1 lead, but he had limped to the mound on his sore ankle and in the third inning he would limp off. "I can't land on it," he told Smith, meaning the ankle couldn't support his weight as he came down on it out of his windup. Now, with John Hiller pitching in the third, Angel first baseman Don Mincher crashed his twenty-fifth homer, his third in the doubleheader, for a 4–3 lead. The Angels extended their lead to 8–3 before McAuliffe's two-run single in the seventh pulled the Tigers to within 8–5.

Desperate to keep the Tigers within striking distance, Mayo Smith had used almost his entire staff: McLain, Hiller, Mike Marshall, Dave Wickersham, Hank Aguirre, Fred Lasher, Pat Dobson, and now Mickey Lolich, who struck out three of five batters in the eighth and ninth to extend his scoreless streak to twenty-eight and two-thirds innings.

Over the two doubleheaders, Rigney had already used twelve pitchers, including six twice and one three times. Minnie Rojas had finished the eighth but Rigney walked over to George Brunet, whose record had dipped to 11–19 with his loss in Saturday's opener. Rigney knew Brunet's reputation for celebrating a victory with a few drinks and for lamenting a loss with a few drinks. Now the Angel manager, looking ahead to lefthanded-swinging Dick McAuliffe being the potential tying run in the bottom of the ninth, stared into the eyes of the thirty-two-year-old lefthander.

"How bad were you last night?"

"Not bad," Brunet replied. "Not bad."

"How bad?" Rigney repeated.

"Not real bad."

"Think you can get one hitter?"

"Sure, I can."

"Go warm up."

Rigney now had three pitchers throwing in the bullpen. Leading off the Tiger ninth, Bill Freehan, who had caught all thirty-six innings over the last two days, doubled off Rojas down the leftfield line. Originally the Tigers–Angels game was to have been shown on television, but the NBC network switched to the Oakland Raiders–Kansas City Chiefs football game instead. Near the radio in the Red Sox clubhouse, Yaz, surrounded by his teammates, was listening to Tiger broadcaster Ernie Harwell and sipping a beer.

"C'mon, Minnie, bear down," Yaz said.

Don Wert walked. The Tigers had the tying run at the plate in the final inning of their final game with the pennant still at stake. As soon as Lenny Green, a lefthanded-swinging outfielder, was announced as a pinch hitter for Lolich, Rigney called for Brunet, who now was risking the embarrassment of being a twenty-game loser.

"You get out of this, George," Red Sox third baseman Joe Foy mumbled, "and we'll send you a case of champagne."

Seeing the lefthander, Mayo Smith called Green back and sent up Jim Price, a righthanded-swinging catcher. Price lifted a harmless fly ball. One out. McAuliffe up. In his previous 673 plate appearances, he had grounded into only one double play. Brunet threw. McAuliffe swung, bouncing the ball to Knoop, who flipped it to Fregosi, who fired it to Mincher at first base. Double play. The Tigers had lost, 8–5. In the Red Sox clubhouse, Dick Williams whooped.

"It's over!" he yelled. "It's over!"

At last, the champagne bottles were uncorked. Hoisted onto a table, Yaz told his teammates, "Thanks for not quitting. Thanks for giving me the thrill of my life." In the manager's office, Tom Yawkey lifted a paper cup of champagne and said, "I want to have a toast with you, Dick." Williams lifted his cup.

"Here's to you, sir," the thirty-nine-year-old manager said, "for giving me the opportunity."

"And here's to you, Dick, for making the best of it," the often frustrated Red Sox owner said. "This is the happiest moment of my life."

For the Tigers, tied with the Twins for second place, it was one of their unhappiest moments.

"We came up a little short," Mayo Smith was saying now in his office. "But these guys didn't quit. You're not quitting when you've got eight runs against you and you have the tying run at the plate in the ninth."

In the Angels' clubhouse, George Brunet all but apologized for eliminating the Tigers.

"I hated to do it against them, Detroit is my favorite team," the lefthander out of Houghton, Michigan, said. "They're a nice bunch of guys. They came a long way in the race. I'm sorry I had to end it."

The phone rang on Bill Rigney's desk. Jim Campbell, the Tigers' general manager, was calling.

"I'm sitting here with Mr. Fetzer," Campbell said, referring to John Fetzer, the Tigers' owner. "We want you to come up and have a drink with us."

"You don't want to see me," Rigney said.

"The hell we don't," Campbell told him.

When the manager of the team that had just knocked the Tigers out of a pennant playoff walked into Fetzer's office, the Tigers' owner poured him a Scotch.

"You did everything you should've done to win," Fetzer said.

Oddly enough, the Angels had won more games, four, in the final week than any of the contenders. With the pennant at stake over the last seven days of the season, the four top teams had a combined 6–12 record. The Red Sox had the lowest winning percentage of a pennant winner, .568, in American League history. Back in their clubhouse, Dick Williams told Jose Santiago that he would open the World Series, which the Red Sox would lose to the Cardinals in seven games. In a quiet corner, away from the celebration, Tony Conigliaro's eyes misted. Nearly seven weeks earlier one of those eyes had been clouded by a fastball. One of those eyes eventually would prevent him from fulfilling a career with so much promise. But now, after having watched the game from the dugout, Tony C. stared at his teammates.

"We're number one," he said softly. "You guys are fabulous."

Dent in the Red Sox Armor

Ron Guidry and Rich (Goose) Gossage. *UPI Photo*

WHEN THE VOICE of public-address announcer Bob Sheppard pierced his concentration in the Yankees' dugout, Bob Lemon grumped, "What the hell is that all about!"

In his glass booth on Yankee Stadium's press box level, Sheppard had never before announced out-of-town scores. But now, on the evening of Tuesday, September 5, 1978, he had not waited for the scoreboard to post what was happening in Baltimore. He was informing 24,452 spectators that the first-place Boston Red Sox were losing to the Orioles after seven innings, 2–1. As the Yankees' manager, Lemon was annoyed.

"It bothered me. It bothered the players," he would say after the Yankees' 4–2 victory over the Detroit Tigers. "It's a distraction. We've got our own game going on."

More important, the Yankees and the Red Sox had their own pennant race going on. That night Red Sox manager Don Zimmer had started twenty-two-year-old rookie lefthander Bobby Sprowl, just up from Pawtucket of the International League. Sprowl had been inserted into the rotation instead of Bill Lee, who had objected to the June 15 trade of outfielder Bernie Carbo, had called Zimmer a "gerbil, a cute puffy-cheeked creature," and had lost seven straight starts. To many of the Red Sox, it would be one of the decisions that turned the pennant race. In Seattle two weeks earlier, Lee, assuming he would open a home stand against the California Angels on August 25, walked into Zimmer's office.

"Do you want me to fly home a day ahead of the club?" Lee asked.

"No," the manager said. "You're not starting Friday night. You'll be in the bullpen."

"Thank you," Lee said, glaring. "That answers my question."

After a 10–3 start, Lee had slumped. While losing his last seven starts, he had a 5.49 earned run average. Haywood Sullivan, the Red

Sox general manager, had been trying, without success, to trade this outspoken thirty-one-year-old lefthander known as "Spaceman" because he often sounded as if he were from another planet. When the writers learned of Zimmer's decision, they sought Lee's reaction.

"I'll go out there and work hard," he said. "They needed me before to bail this club out and maybe they'll need me again. I'll do it. I'll do it for my teammates and for baseball, but I won't do it for those two guys. Zimmer didn't make this decision by himself. Sullivan helped him."

Others wondered if Zimmer wasn't tying Lee to his doghouse for the "gerbil" remark, but the manager insisted, "I don't have anything against the man. Don't think I don't wish he were fifteen and six, but if I told him that, he'd say, 'Winning isn't everything.' Well, winning is everything. I know Lee believes it. That's what this is all about. The man's not getting people out. Look at the record."

At first Zimmer used Jim Wright as Lee's replacement, but Sprowl was called up on September 1 from Pawtucket where he had a 7–4 record after going 9–2 at Bristol of the Eastern League earlier in the season. Over his two minor league seasons he had been 24–8. But his Pawtucket manager, Joe Morgan, who a decade later would manage the Red Sox, was skeptical because of the six-two, 190-pound left-hander's 4.71 earned run average.

"I don't know if he's ready," Morgan said. "His problem is trying to throw the ball by too many guys."

Not that Sprowl doubted himself. "When I'm throwing my slider right," he said, "there's not a lefty who can hit me." Maybe not in the minors, but in seven innings the Orioles jumped on him for three runs, including Lee May's homer. Jim Palmer won, 4–1. It was the Red Sox' fifth loss in their last six games. After being mired in the mud of fourth place on July 19, fourteen games behind the Red Sox' 62–28 start, the Yankees now were within four games. Roy White had hit a three-run homer off Tiger rookie righthander Kip Young after Mickey Rivers, a skinny centerfielder never known for his arm, had thrown out Rusty Staub at the plate to preserve a 1–0 lead.

"Know what makes you do it?" Rivers told the writers, rubbing his right thumb and index finger together. "Money. It's the only thing that counts now. I got to play good so I can make that money again."

As a member of the Yankees in each of the previous two World Series, Rivers had pocketed a total of $47,693, including $27,758 during the 1977 postseason. Now he and his teammates were hoping to help the Yankees win the American League East after the Red Sox not only had dominated the division for most of the season, but had won six of the eight games between the two teams.

"They got to hear us breathing," Rich (Goose) Gossage, the Yankees' husky relief pitcher, said. "Can you imagine if we pull this off?"

To pull it off, the Yankees knew they couldn't falter in a four-game series in Boston that would begin Thursday night with the Red Sox still holding a four-game lead. Wednesday night the Yankees routed the Tigers, 8–2, without slugger Reggie Jackson, hospitalized with back spasms and a virus. They also won without any public-address progress reports on a 2–0 two-hitter in Baltimore by Luis Tiant, the Cuban righthander with a windup that resembled a spinning top.

"We can see the scoreboard," Bob Lemon snorted. "That's enough."

The scoreboard in Fenway Park would be superfluous. Although the Red Sox had a 52–17 record there this season, their lineup had been riddled with injuries. Designated hitter Carl Yastrzemski had a sprained right wrist and an aching back. Rightfielder Dwight (Dewey) Evans was recovering from a beaning. Third baseman Butch Hobson had a bone chip in his throwing elbow. Second baseman Jerry Remy had a bone chip in his left wrist. Relief pitcher Bill Campbell had an ailing arm. Rick Burleson had returned to shortstop, but during three weeks in July without him the Red Sox were 6–12.

"Nobody ever says a thing," manager Don Zimmer groaned, "about the fact we've had our lineup together for only thirty-five of one hundred and thirty-three games."

Mike Torrez, who would open against the Yankees, had joined the Red Sox as a free agent after winning two games in the 1977 World Series for the Yankees. With a 15–6 record in August, the handsome six-five righthander had been troubled by a swollen middle finger on his pitching hand. He also had been bothered by what he called his teammates' tendency to "swing for the fences rather than doing the little things it takes to win games." That prompted Jim Rice, the Red Sox' leftfielder, to snipe at Torrez.

"We're losing," Rice said, "because he's nibbling and giving up base hits to a bunch of Punch-and-Judy hitters. If he'd get out there and challenge 'em, he'd get them out."

The Yankees, meanwhile, were healthy and happy. Since their fourteen-game deficit on July 19, they had generated a 35–14 streak, a scorching .714 percentage. They also had survived an August 31 scare in Baltimore when X-rays on Ron Guidry's left ankle were negative after he was struck by a batted ball.

"I got ankles like a racehorse," said Guidry, who had broken his ankle three times growing up in Lafayette, Louisiana. "If I break it one more time, they're going to shoot me."

Opposing teams might shoot him, but the Yankees wouldn't. Nicknamed "Louisiana Lightning," the slender twenty-eight-year-old lefthander with the riverboat gambler mustache would carry a team as few pitchers ever have. The year before, principal owner George Steinbrenner had wanted to include Guidry in a trade with the Chicago White Sox for Bucky Dent, but general manager Gabe Paul convinced the principal owner to keep him. Now Guidry was baseball's best pitcher. His 25–3 record would include a 13–0 start. In his 12–3 finish, he would spin seven of his nine shutouts, including three two-hitters in his last five starts. He would strike out 248 batters, including 18 on June 17 against the California Angels, a record for an AL lefthander. With fifteen of his twenty-five victories occurring after a Yankee loss, he defined the word *stopper*. His earned run average would be 1.74.

As dominant as Guidry was, many Yankees credited their comeback to Lemon's arrival on July 25 after Billy Martin was unceremoniously fired.

"It's more relaxed around here," shortstop Bucky Dent said. "We're thinking more about playing the game of baseball. Before, you didn't know what was going to happen. You relax, you can play the game and not worry about other things. You relax and you win. When you win, it's fun."

Before Lemon's arrival, the Yankees had dissolved into a triangle of turmoil involving Billy Martin, Reggie Jackson, and George Steinbrenner.

Although the Yankees had won the 1977 World Series under Martin with Jackson hitting five homers, including three in the sixth-game finale (to equal Babe Ruth's record), the tempestuous manager, the Hall of Fame slugger, and the obstinate owner now were in almost constant conflict. Jackson was depressed because he had been relegated by Martin to being a part-time designated hitter. Martin was fuming at Jackson because the slugger had been in a slump and the Yankees were stumbling in fourth place. Steinbrenner was growling at both Martin and Jackson, and both were growling back. The explosion finally occurred on July 17 with Jackson up, catcher Thurman Munson on first base, and none out in the bottom of the tenth inning against lefthander Al Hrabosky of the Kansas City Royals.

Annoyed that Jackson had been hitless in four previous at-bats,

Martin flashed the bunt sign to third-base coach Dick Howser, who relayed it.

Hrabosky's fastball was too high and too far inside to bunt, but when the Royal infielders noticed that Jackson had squared his stance, they moved in for the next pitch. Seeing that, Martin wigwagged Howser to let Jackson swing away. Howser relayed Martin's order. Not sure that Jackson got the hit sign, Howser hurried to the plate.

"Billy wants you hitting away," Howser said.

"I'm going to bunt," Jackson said sternly.

"He wants you to swing away," Howser said.

On the next pitch, Jackson tried to bunt, but missed. On the third, he bunted foul. On the fourth, he bunted a pop foul to catcher Darrell Porter. On his return to the dugout, Jackson placed his glasses on the ledge behind the bench, perhaps anticipating a confrontation with Martin, but the manager was talking to coach Gene Michael.

"Tell Reggie that Roy White is now the DH," Martin said. "Tell him he can take a shower and go home if he wants."

After the Yankees lost, 9–7, in eleven innings, Jackson calmly told the writers, "I was trying to advance the runner. I thought I'd be helping the ballclub. How can they say I'm a threat to swing the bat? I'm not an everyday player. I'm a part-time player." Minutes later Martin, having thrown a clock into the corridor outside his office and smashed an empty beer bottle against the wall, announced that Jackson had been suspended indefinitely for "deliberately disregarding the manager's instructions." After a conference with Yankee president Al Rosen the next day, the length of the suspension was announced as five days. But when Jackson rejoined the Yankees in Chicago the following Sunday, he talked about how the "magnitude of me, the magnitude of the instance, the magnitude of New York" surrounded him.

"I didn't regard it as an act of defiance," the slugger said. "I didn't know it would get people so upset. If I had known the consequences would have this magnitude, I would rather have swung and struck out and avoided the hassle."

Jackson wasn't in the lineup as the Yankees extended their winning streak to five games, four without him. On his way to the team bus, Martin asked Jack Lang of the New York *Daily News* what Jackson had told the writers. Lang showed the manager his story. Martin fumed. At O'Hare Airport, he flared, telling Murray Chass of *The New York Times* and Henry Hecht of the *New York Post* that, among other things, if Jackson "doesn't shut his mouth, he won't play and I don't care what George says. George can replace me right now if he doesn't like it." Minutes later Martin was calling Jackson a "liar," and then he grouped Jackson with Steinbrenner.

"One's a born liar," the manager said, meaning Jackson, "and the other's convicted."

Martin was alluding to the 1974 guilty plea of Steinbrenner, the chairman of American Ship Building Company, for illegal contributions to President Richard Nixon's 1972 campaign. Fined $15,000, he was suspended from baseball for two years by Commissioner Bowie Kuhn; he was permitted to return on March 1, 1976, nine months early. Now, informed on Sunday night in his Tampa, Florida, home of Martin's remark, Steinbrenner sounded stunned.

"I've got to believe," the principal owner said, "that no boss in his right mind would take that."

Knowing he was about to be fired, Martin resigned the next day in a tearful scene on the balcony above the lobby of the Crown Central Hotel in Kansas City. (Five days later, Steinbrenner would rehire Martin for 1980 as the Yankee manager, with Lemon to become the general manager; by the middle of the 1979 season, Lemon was out and Martin was rehired as manager.) But now, with Martin having re-signed, Yankee president Al Rosen phoned Lemon, his onetime Cleveland Indian teammate and a Hall of Fame righthander who had been a seven-time twenty-game winner. The year before, Lemon had been voted the AL manager of the year with the White Sox, but on June 30 he had been dismissed.

"How soon," Rosen asked him, "can you get to Kansas City?"

Calm and controlled, with a willingness to relax with a drink, Lemon took the tension out of the Yankees clubhouse. "I never took the game home with me," he once said. "I always left it in a bar along the way." He called his players "Meat," as in "Grab a bat, Meat." Which translates to what he told Reggie Jackson shortly after his arrival.

"You're going to hit fourth every day," the new manager said. "Sometimes you'll play rightfield. Sometimes you'll DH. You know what to do. Just hit some over the wall."

That's all Jackson wanted to hear: solid, sensible baseball talk from the manager without any commotion. That's all his Yankee teammates wanted to hear. They were still ten and one-half games behind when Lem arrived. They didn't think they could catch the Red Sox. They didn't imagine they were going to finish the season with a 42–20 surge under their new manager. They just wanted to be allowed to play without the distractions that Martin, Steinbrenner, and Jackson had created. That's exactly what Lem's managerial style allowed them to do.

"You all know how to play; you won the World Series last year," he told them during his first clubhouse meeting. "The season starts now. Just go out and play like you did last year and I'll try to stay out of the way."

They did, and he did. Four days after Lemon's arrival, the Yankees had sliced the Red Sox' lead to eight games. When injuries later helped put the Red Sox in a slump, the Yankees suddenly were in a pennant race. Some of the Yankees credited their rise to the New York newspaper strike that would prevent the *Times*, the *News*, and the *Post* from printing for more than three months. Since the strike began August 10, the Yankees were 22–7.

"The clubhouse," Jackson said, "is more relaxed."

Only four games back, the Yankees opened a four-game series in Fenway Park on September 7, a Thursday night. In conversations among themselves, the older Yankees were boldly confident, especially Lou Piniella and Thurman Munson.

"We're up here to win four," Piniella said.

"We're going to kick their ass," Munson said.

With a cool wind blowing in from beyond the Wall, alias the Green Monster, in leftfield, a pitching duel loomed between Jim (Catfish) Hunter and Mike Torrez.

Instead the Yankees won, 15–3, with twenty-one hits.

Returning to the lineup after two days in Lenox Hill Hospital with his back in traction, Jackson drove in the first run in a two-run first inning. By the second, Torrez had departed. By the third, the Yankees had seven runs when a press box phone rang. "Butch Hobson hasn't even been up yet," a caller said, "and Thurman Munson is already three for three." By the fourth, the Yankees had a 12–0 lead. In the Fenway Park bleachers, fans were chanting, "We want Lee," perhaps hoping to persuade Zimmer from starting rookie lefthander Bob Sprowl in Sunday's game. Then, in the sixth, Munson suddenly sprawled at the plate, clutching his head. He had been beaned by righthander Dick Drago.

"I yelled at him," Drago would say later. "The balls were very slippery all night. A few other pitches got away from me. Maybe it was the cool weather."

Whatever it was, Dwight Evans winced. He still had occasional dizzy spells from his beaning a few weeks earlier. "I can look up," the

Red Sox rightfielder explained, "but if I stay looking up, my head starts spinning." After the game Yankee trainer Gene Monahan minimized the lump on the left side of Munson's head as just a bruise.

"You in there tomorrow?" Lemon asked him.

"Not for more than nine," Munson replied.

Friday night twenty-four-year-old Jim Beattie would be the Yankee starter. When the rookie righthander was shelled for five runs in less than three innings at Fenway Park on June 21, Steinbrenner had snorted, "Beattie spit the bit several times. So did Ken Clay. Who's handling the pitchers? These are supposed to be prize kids. Beattie looked like he was scared stiff." Beattie was demoted to Tacoma of the Pacific Coast League, but now he was back and pitching again in Fenway Park with Steinbrenner perched alongside the Yankee dugout.

"Beattie's not nervous," Yankee outfielder Paul Blair had joked in the clubhouse. "He's just got the wrong uniform on. I wonder why he's wearing *48.*"

Hearing that, Beattie tried to glance over his shoulder at the number on his uniform, then realized that Blair had been teasing. Beattie was wearing number *45* as usual. This time he improved his record to 4–7 as the Yankees knocked out Jim Wright in the second inning of another rout, 13–2, on seventeen hits, including Jackson's three-run homer. When Beattie was removed in the ninth, Steinbrenner stood and clapped.

Beattie couldn't have been happier. Sunday he would marry Martha Johnson in Syracuse, New York, and then rejoin the Yankees on Tuesday in Detroit.

With the Yankees only two games out, the Red Sox were in ruins. They had made seven errors, including Hobson's thirty-eighth. Between innings the Red Sox third baseman had removed the black rubber sleeve on his right elbow and manipulated the bone chips so his arm wouldn't lock. But in the silence of the Red Sox clubhouse, two old pros kept their perspective.

"Nobody died," yelled Luis Tiant, puffing on a cigar. "Play the music."

"I think we've lost sight of something," Yaz said. "We're still in first place."

In a clubhouse meeting before Saturday's game Yaz reminded his teammates of their two-game lead. It didn't help. Guidry spun a two-hit shutout, 7–0, against Dennis Eckersley, who bemoaned Bucky Dent's two-run single in the third that opened a 3–0 lead. Suddenly the Red Sox were only one game up.

"When I was a little kid," Eckersley said, "I wondered how the sixty-four Phillies could blow the pennant. Now I'm in the major leagues. Now I understand."

Sunday a vendor outside Fenway Park was waving "I Hate the Yankees" bumper stickers and barking, "Yaz has one on his car. So does Billy Martin." Inside, in the privacy of the Red Sox manager's office, Yaz suggested that Bill Lee start instead of rookie Bobby Sprowl, but Zimmer opened a desk drawer, held up newspaper clippings of Lee's criticism, sprayed tobacco juice into a cup, and touted Sprowl.

"The kid's got ice water in his veins," Zimmer said.

After only two-thirds of an inning, that ice water had turned to dish water. Sprowl walked Mickey Rivers on four pitches, then he walked Willie Randolph. Thurman Munson bounced into a double play, but Reggie Jackson singled for 1–0. When the rookie lefthander walked Lou Piniella and Chris Chambliss, Zimmer waved for Bob Stanley.

"I know it was quick," Zimmer would say later, "but I didn't want him to get into any more trouble."

Sprowl would only say, "I didn't throw right, that's all." The Yankees won, 7–4, supporting righthander Ed Figueroa with eighteen hits, all singles. With three weeks remaining, the Yankees and Red Sox suddenly shared first place, each with an 86–56 record.

"I'd like to have played every year of my career," Yaz said bravely, "where you've got twenty games to play and you're tied for first place."

But these Yankees had done more than sweep a four-game series at Fenway Park for the first time since the 1943 Yankees had done it. They had outscored the Red Sox, 42–9. They had outhit the Red Sox, 67–30. They had batted .396 as a team, compared to the Red Sox' .171. Of the four Red Sox starters, only Eckersley had lasted beyond the second out in the first inning. The Red Sox had made twelve errors, the Yankees only five. Individually, second baseman Willie Randolph had been on base in sixteen of his twenty-two plate appearances. Bucky Dent drove in seven runs, Reggie Jackson and Randolph each six. Lou Piniella scored eight runs, only one less than the entire Red Sox team. In the Red Sox clubhouse Rick Burleson was seething.

"The Yankees are together," the Red Sox shortstop said. "Nine guys giving their all. Us? We come to the ballpark and one guy's dizzy, another guy's hand hurts. That's bullshit. They've got one guy who comes out of the hospital to play. That's how much this series meant to them."

Looking to a three-game rematch in New York the following weekend, the Yankees now were on a 39–14 surge while the Red Sox were in a 30–32 skid. But with the Yankees off, Monday night the Red Sox regained first place, edging the Orioles, 5–4, as Jim Rice hit two homers. His thirty-ninth homer knocked out Jim Palmer in the sixth. His fortieth, into the centerfield bleachers off Joe Kerrigan in the eighth, broke a 4–4 tie and created a one-half-game lead.

"My job is to drive in runs," Rice said later. "I can't sit around thinking about it. I've got to turn the bat loose."

Tuesday night Torrez lost a five-hitter, 3–2, to Dennis Martinez's three-hitter. With the Red Sox leading, 1–0, in the fifth, first baseman George Scott booted Eddie Murray's grounder. Hobson booted Lee May's grounder. Andres Mora bunted, but Torrez threw it wild past third base.

"I rushed my throw," said the righthander, who hadn't won since August 18. "I knew Murray had gotten a good jump."

That night in Detroit the Yankees lost, 7–4, as righthander Dick Tidrow was rapped for three homers. In the AL office in New York that day, the Yankees also lost the coin toss if a one-game playoff were needed. The playoff would be held at Fenway Park on October 2, the Monday after the season ended. Wednesday night the Yankees finally took over first place when Jim Beattie stopped the Tigers, 7–3, while Dennis Eckersley lost a seven-hitter to lefthander David Clyde in Cleveland, 2–1. By then Thurman Munson was being X-rayed in Henry Ford Hospital. In the first inning he had hunched over after swinging and missing Jack Billingham's fastball. Warming up Beattie before the bottom of the first, the thirty-one-year-old catcher turned and walked to the dugout.

"I can't go," he told Lemon. "My head hurts."

The pain thudded from behind Munson's right eye to the back of his head. Yankee trainer Gene Monahan didn't know if the pain was related to Munson's beaning by Dick Drago in Boston six nights earlier, but the Yankees knew the importance of Munson's presence.

"I hope it's nothing bad," said Jackson, who had feuded openly with Munson the year before. "I don't know if we can win without him."

In 1976 Munson had been voted the American League's most valuable player. He had knocked in more than one hundred runs in each of the three previous seasons. For all of his ornery public personality, his teammates appreciated him as a clutch performer and a clubhouse presence. When X-rays and a brain scan showed no damage, he returned for Thursday night's game. But he didn't play.

"I never experienced anything like that," Munson said of Wednesday night's pain. "My first reaction was that I didn't want to die. I started having headaches two days after Drago hit me, but nothing like this. This wasn't a headache. This was just tremendous pain."

Munson sat in the dugout Thursday night as the Yankees won, 4–2, opening a one-and-one-half-game lead. While the Red Sox were losing in Cleveland, 4–3, Yankee third baseman Graig Nettles smashed two homers and a double as lefthanded relief pitcher Albert (Sparky) Lyle preserved Ed Figueroa's seventeenth victory. Lyle had won the Cy Young Award the year before but this season he had been mostly sidetracked in the bullpen for Goose Gossage's flaming fastball.

"In one year," Nettles had wisecracked to Lyle, "you went from Cy Young to sayonara."

Lyle laughed, but inside he was steaming at the Yankee front office. He would record only nine saves, only two after mid-June. In the off-season, he would be traded to the Texas Rangers in a ten-player deal. But his save in Tiger Stadium had assured the Yankees of some breathing room as they returned to New York for Friday night's opener of a three-game showdown with the Red Sox, who now had lost three straight. When the Red Sox got off their chartered bus outside Yankee Stadium, they saw vendors selling T-shirts blaring "Boston Is Dead" and "Red Socks Choke." Desperate for a hitter who could jump-start the Red Sox' batting order, general manager Haywood Sullivan had been thwarted in his attempts to obtain Rico Carty or Mitchell Page from the Oakland A's or Tony Perez from the Montreal Expos.

"Money has nothing to do with it," Sullivan said. "We just keep getting blocked on the waiver wire."

Zimmer had benched first baseman George Scott, hitless in thirty-four at-bats. "I've gone as far with the man as I can possibly go," the Red Sox manager said. "It isn't just him. It's the only move I can make." Yaz was the new first baseman. Jack Brohamer and Garry Hancock shared the DH role. But with Guidry pitching Friday night, it didn't make any difference. First baseman Chris Chambliss's two-run homer off Tiant in the fourth was enough for the Yankee left-hander's 2–0 two-hitter and a lead of two and one-half games. In the Red Sox clubhouse, one of the Boston writers suggested to Bill Lee, the forgotten lefthander, that the team must be suffering.

"Dead bodies don't suffer," Lee said.

In the Yankee players' lounge, Munson, back in the lineup after Mike Heath had caught Friday night's game, and most of his teammates were watching a closed-circuit telecast of Muhammad Ali regaining the heavyweight title from Leon Spinks in a unanimous fifteen-round decision in New Orleans. But at his locker Guidry discussed his 22–2 record.

"I never dreamed I could pitch this good," he said, his left elbow in a tub of ice. "When this is all over, I'll be able to say, 'Out of all the pitchers in the record book, I had one of the best seasons of any of 'em.' I'm going to dream on that until they lay me in the coffin."

Saturday afternoon 55,091 fans were attracted by another Catfish Hunter–Mike Torrez matchup. Pitching for the first time since suffering his pulled groin muscle in the opener of the Boston series, Hunter was stunned in the first inning by Rice's two-run homer. But the Yankees retaliated with a run on singles by Randolph, Munson, and Jackson. In the fifth, Jackson was in the on-deck circle when Munson tipped a line foul toward him. Trying to stop the ball from sailing into the spectators behind the dugout, Jackson threw up his right hand. The ball smashed into his thumb, tearing the nail loose. Blood stained his batting glove. Gene Monahan quickly taped the nail down.

"Can you hit?" the trainer asked.

"I have no choice," Jackson said.

On a two-two pitch, the slugger known as "Mr. October" lifted a homer barely over the rightfield wall. Returning to the dugout, he accepted congratulations only with his left hand. With the score 2–2, Hunter and Torrez dueled into the ninth. With two out, two on, and Rick Burleson up, Lemon went to the mound.

"How do you feel?" the manager asked.

"Fine," Hunter replied. "Ask Thurman how I'm throwing."

"He's throwing good," Munson said.

Burleson popped up. In the Yankee dugout now, Mickey Rivers, who would lead off, was at the bat rack when coach Yogi Berra walked over. "Last time up," Berra said, nodding toward Carl Yastrzemski in leftfield, "Yaz was playing you in and close to the line. He's giving you the gap." On a no balls–two strikes pitch, Rivers lashed a line drive over Yaz's head into that gap for a leadoff triple. With none out, some managers would have walked both Randolph and Munson to create a force play at the plate, but Zimmer thought differently. Let Torrez pitch to the two righthanded batters, then give him a choice of pitching to whichever lefthanded batter, Jackson or Chambliss, he prefers. Zimmer also had dismissed the idea of going to the bullpen because his best relief pitcher, Bill Campbell, had a bad arm. Now, with the infield in, Randolph bounced to Burleson as Rivers held at third.

With two strikes, Munson poked a low liner to rightfield. Rice made a tumbling catch, but Rivers tagged and scored standing for a 3–2 victory. The Yankees were ahead by three and one-half.

"It's a lot of fun," Bob Lemon was overheard saying now on his office phone to his wife, Jane, who had remained in their Long Beach, California, home. "It's better than sex. As I remember it."

Despite his disappointment, Torrez said, "I'm happy for Cat. When I was with the Yankees last year, as bad as he was hurting, he always wanted the ball." In 1975, after four consecutive seasons as a twenty-game winner for the Oakland A's, Hunter joined the Yankees for a five-year $3.35 million contract when an arbitrator declared him a free agent following a breach of his Oakland contract. While compiling a 17–15 record in 1976, he emerged as only the fourth pitcher to win two hundred games prior to his thirty-first birthday. The others were Cy Young, Christy Mathewson, and Walter Johnson. In 1977 he suffered through a 9–9 record and early this season he was struggling at 2–3 on June 26 when he was anesthetized with sodium pentathol. Dr. Maurice Cowen manipulated Hunter's right shoulder by bending the arm back forty-five degrees.

"Doc told me later," Hunter said, "that the adhesions popped so loud he thought he broke my arm."

Instead, the orthopedist had healed it. By winning his duel with Torrez, the thirty-two-year-old Hunter was on an 8–2 streak. In the Yankee clubhouse, the Hertford, North Carolina, farmer glanced at his onetime Oakland teammate Reggie Jackson, who was leaning against a post, his right hand up, blood oozing down from his battered thumbnail to his wrist.

"That's Reggie," Hunter said, smiling.

"Looks good, doesn't it?" Jackson said.

Sunday afternoon, with 55,088 customers clamoring for a Yankee sweep that would open a lead of four and one-half games, the Red Sox finally rebounded, 7–3. Jim Beattie was battered as Dennis Eckersley, the Red Sox ace, won his seventeenth. After thirty-six hitless at-bats, George Scott got a double. The Yankee lead was trimmed to two and one-half games.

"Saturday was probably the lowest point in my career," Rick Burleson said. "But that's what makes this game different. You play every day. You can bounce back."

Monday night in Detroit the Red Sox kept bouncing, winning,

5–4, on Jerry Remy's eleventh-inning single after Bobby Sprowl, in his third start, had allowed three runs in five innings. But in New York the Yanks beat the Milwaukee Brewers, 4–3, for Ed Figueroa's eighteenth. Since Lemon took over, Figgie was 10–2 and he didn't consider it a coincidence. "Billy Martin always told me he'd pitch me every fourth day, but he never did," the Puerto Rican righthander said. "When Lem goes to the mound, it's to take me out or ask me how I feel. He doesn't tell me to throw a slider or a fastball. Billy did that all the time. Billy told me three or four times in the last inning to throw a fastball, throw a slider, throw this or that. Then he said in the papers I made the wrong pitch. It was his pitch." Now, with Guidry at 22–2, Figueroa had a chance to provide the Yankees with two twenty-game winners for the first time since Whitey Ford and Jim Bouton in 1963.

Tuesday night Yaz was able to take a full swing for the first time in weeks. "Before," he said, alluding to his sore hand, "I had to give the bat a little flip." He clouted a three-run homer off Jim Slaton in the first and a two-run homer off Jack Morris in the fourth. When the Red Sox won, 8–6, and the Yankees were shut out by lefthander Mike Caldwell, 4–0, the difference was down to one and one-half games.

Wednesday night the Red Sox were taking batting practice in Tiger Stadium when somebody said, "The Blue Jays knocked out Guidry in the second." In the opener of a twi-night doubleheader, the Blue Jays, who would lose 102 games in their second season, had stunned baseball's best pitcher. "This thing," Torrez said at the batting cage, "ain't over." By the time the Red Sox stood on the steps of their dugout for the national anthem, the Yankees had lost, 8–1.

"We were all skyed," Torrez said.

But the Red Sox were shelled, 12–2. Torrez failed to win for the seventh straight start. "This is the damndest thing that ever happened to me, especially at this time of year," he said. "I'm throwing well. Maybe I'm just throwing everything up there at the same speed. I know I'm trying. It's a terrible feeling." In Toronto, the Yankees had a similar terrible feeling. Trailing 2–0 in the second game against Tom Underwood, they appeared about to lose a doubleheader to a last-place team. But in the ninth Randolph led off with a single. Munson flied out, but when Jackson walked, Blue Jay manager Roy Hartsfield brought in Victor Cruz, a five-nine righthander from the Dominican Republic with a 7–2 record, nine saves, and a 1.42 earned run average. Cruz had never pitched against the Yankees, and Piniella, Chambliss, and Nettles greeted him with three consecutive singles for three runs.

With the bases loaded in the bottom of the ninth, Gossage fanned pinch hitter Sam Ewing to preserve the 3–2 win and a split. The Yankees were two games ahead with ten games to go.

"The numbers are in your brain, ten games to go, nine to go," Jackson said. "If you're going to be a champion, you've got to win games like this. You can't be losing two to Toronto."

The next night Jackson, after eight strikeouts in thirteen at-bats, supplied a two-run double as the Yankees won, 7–1, behind Hunter and Gossage. But the Red Sox bounced back again, winning, 5–1. Burleson had four singles in Eckersley's eighteenth. The difference was still two games. When the writers entered Zimmer's office, one asked, "How do you feel?"

"I'm all right," the Red Sox manager said, pretending that his Popeye face was twitching. "Why do you ask?"

Friday night the Red Sox' 5–4 loss in Toronto on Rick Bosetti's bases-loaded single in the ninth off Bill Campbell was posted on the Municipal Stadium scoreboard in Cleveland moments before Rick Manning's tenth-inning single off Gossage produced the Yankees' 8–7 loss. In the ninth Munson had struck out, walked calmly to the dugout, then flailed his bat half a dozen times at the two rows of thirteen batting helmets perched on the dugout steps, scattering them all over the dugout. Jay Johnstone, the Yankees' seldom-used outfielder, couldn't resist.

"Pick the row and the helmets Thurman hits," he said in a carnival barker's voice. "Pick the right row and it pays two to one. Pick the first six helmets and it pays four to one. Thirteenth in each row is the house number."

The Yankees could still afford to laugh. They remained two games ahead. But the Red Sox had nothing to joke about. In Zimmer's office in Exhibition Stadium along Lake Ontario, the manager was listening to Butch Hobson.

"Take me out," said the husky third baseman who now had made forty-three errors. "I'm no quitter, but I'm hurting the team, I'm embarrassing the team. I just can't get the ball over to first base. My elbow keeps locking on me."

Saturday, with Jack Brohamer at third base and Hobson as their designated hitter, the Red Sox won, 3–1. Zimmer considered removing Tiant in the ninth with Roy Howell and John Mayberry coming up, but the manager knew that the Cuban righthander hadn't had any luck with relievers trying to save him. Tiant preferred to win by himself or lose by himself. Howell struck out. Mayberry grounded out. Tiant now was 11–8. When Beattie was shelled, 10–1, in Cleveland, the Yankees were only one game ahead. Or the way outfielder Paul Blair looked at it, still one game ahead.

"I remember what Frank Robinson taught us with the Orioles," Blair said. "When you're in first place, you can't afford to panic."

Sunday afternoon Ron Guidry didn't panic. Rebounding from his Toronto nightmare, he spun his third two-hit shutout in four starts, 4–0. His ninth shutout set a Yankee record. Even so, Piniella, angry at his slump, flung his batting helmet, narrowly missing Lemon.

"I don't want anybody throwing helmets like that," the manager told his players later. "Anybody!"

In the ninth Guidry's very presence enabled the Yankee bullpen to listen to a Toronto broadcast of the Red Sox–Blue Jays game.

"We didn't think anybody would need us," Dick Tidrow said later with a laugh. "Not with Guidry pitching."

Torrez needed his bullpen. He couldn't hold a 4–3 lead in the eighth, but the Red Sox tied the score in the ninth without a hit, then won in the fourteenth, 7–6, on Hobson's hot grounder that skipped off the artificial turf into Blue Jay third baseman Roy Howell's throat. With the Yankees still one game ahead, both teams were coming home for six games in the final week: the Yankees against the Blue Jays and the Indians, the Red Sox against the Tigers and the Blue Jays. For the Red Sox, the burden was on Dennis Eckersley, who would acknowledge later that "I was in my own little world, I was going through a divorce" that had been finalized ten days earlier. But now he would be a twenty-game winner if he could stop the Tigers on Tuesday night and the Blue Jays on Saturday afternoon.

"There's no added pressure on me," Eck said Monday, an off day for both teams. "If I'm to win twenty, I have to win both my starts. If we're to win the pennant, we have to win all our games. So there's no added pressure."

Before Tuesday night's game, the Red Sox announced that thirty-nine-year-old Carl Yastrzemski had signed a three-year contract extension through the 1981 season (he would keep playing through the 1983 season). It reflected the front office's faith in the slugger, who never lost faith in his teammates.

"I'm tired of people talking about choking," Yaz said. "Nobody is to blame for what happened to us in the last five weeks. We started the season with twenty-five guys. Twenty-five will stand up if we win. Twenty-five will stand up if we lose."

Tuesday night Eckersley's seven-hitter blanked the Tigers, 6–0, as Rice hit his forty-fourth homer. But the Yankees stayed in step, beating the Blue Jays, 4–1, on Gossage's twenty-fifth save. Wednesday night the Yankees won again, 5–1, on Hunter's six-hitter, while Tiant's twelfth stopped the Tigers, 5–2. George Scott exploded with three hits. Carlton Fisk smashed a two-run triple while catching his 151st game.

"My gloves need stitches. My knees too, my legs are gone," Fisk told the writers. "Monday I went home to New Hampshire for the first time since April and I didn't want to come back. After that fourteen-inning game in Toronto, I felt the season should have been over."

Don Zimmer was not about to rest his thirty-year-old catcher. When one of the writers mentioned Fisk's weariness, the Red Sox manager smiled and said, "He doesn't have to report until five-thirty tomorrow. He can sleep to four. He can sleep all winter." But if the Red Sox were to catch the Yankees, they knew they needed Mike Torrez to win Thursday night. And if there were a one-game playoff with the Yankees on Monday afternoon, Torrez would start.

"I'll be yelling at him," Fisk said. "I've tried just about everything. Going out and telling him to reach down sometimes. Talking to him sometimes. Trying to get him mad at the batter, mad at me, mad at anyone. Hate the catcher. Hate me. Throw the ball and hurt me. That's part of it. I'll be yelling. I can't be nice anymore. I'll be yelling."

Maybe it was Fisk's yelling. Whatever it was, Torrez fired a 1–0 three-hitter Thursday night. Although he walked seven and was bailed out with four double plays, he won on Jim Rice's forty-fifth homer and centerfielder Fred Lynn's throw that nailed Jason Thompson at the plate. Over the four previous seasons Torrez had been at his best in the last three months of the schedule, assembling a 38–11 record. But even with his first victory in nine starts since August 18, the swarthy righthander couldn't escape being the butt of a Boston joke: He had pitched the Yankees to victory in the playoffs and the World Series last year and if he's granted the opportunity, he'll do it again this year. But the only way Torrez would get another start was in a Monday playoff.

"I just hope," Torrez said, "I can get the chance against the Yankees on Monday."

Bob Lemon also was thinking about a playoff. The previous Sunday in Toronto the Yankee manager had used Ron Guidry with only three days' rest, and Thursday night Guidry started again on three days' rest. If there were a Monday playoff, the ace lefthander would have three days' rest. But in walking to the mound for his second straight start on only three days' rest, Guidry was leery, remembering how the last-place Blue Jays had knocked him out in two innings a week earlier. Now he was thinking he didn't want to get five runs down in the first inning after he'd won some big games and his teammates were looking to him. In the fourth he still had a no-hitter, but he knew he didn't have his best slider.

"What do you want me to do about my slider?" he asked Munson.

"Just relax. I'll decide when you throw it. You just throw it."

Guidry threw it for a 3–1 four-hitter that had Reggie Jackson shaking his head in admiration. "I've never seen anybody do what this guy is doing, and I saw Vida Blue in 1971," he said. "But we've got to sweep the Indians this weekend because the Red Sox aren't going to lose another game. Believe me." Friday night the Red Sox crushed the Blue Jays, 11–0, behind Bob Stanley and Dick Drago, as Jim Rice reached four hundred total bases, the first slugger to do that since Joe DiMaggio in 1937. When the Red Sox' victory was posted on the Yankee Stadium scoreboard, the Indians had just broken up a scoreless duel between Jim Beattie and David Clyde on Tom Veryzer's two-out double and Rick Manning's single. In the bottom of the eighth, pinch hitter Cliff Johnson walked. Mickey Rivers bunted pinch runner Fred Stanley to second. With righthanded-swinging Willie Randolph coming up, Indian manager Jeff Torborg brought in righthander Jim Kern.

"Can you imagine," said Mike Torrez, listening to the radio in the Red Sox clubhouse. "Clyde walked one guy and they took him out."

Randolph's grounder took a freak hop to Buddy Bell's left, but running to first the Yankee second baseman pulled up lame, pain searing the back of his left thigh. He thought Bell's throw had hit him in the leg. Then he realized he had pulled his hamstring muscle. Brian Doyle ran for him. When Thurman Munson's single to left drove in Stanley, the word spread in the Red Sox clubhouse.

"It's 1–1 with two on," Zimmer was told.

When Jackson's ground single to right scored Doyle with the go-ahead run, Zimmer heard, "It's two to one, still two on." Moments later Lou Piniella's infield single scored Munson. When Zimmer heard, "It's three to one," the Red Sox manager scowled.

"We're running out of time," he said.

Saturday the Blue Jays' 1–0 lead on Roy Howell's homer off Eckersley in the first inning at Fenway Park was posted on the Yankee Stadium scoreboard just before Rivers led off against Indian righthander Mike Paxton with a line single. Munson singled. Jackson walked. Nettles singled. Chambliss doubled into the leftfield corner. White singled. By then the Red Sox had rallied against righthander Jesse Jefferson to go ahead, 4–1, on Howell's fumble of Burleson's grounder, Remy's double, Rice's walk, Yaz's run-scoring grounder, Fisk's two-run single, Lynn's broken-bat single, and Hobson's sacrifice fly. As the Red Sox trotted out for the second inning, a 5 clanked down next to NY on the Fenway Park scoreboard. In the fifth Jackson homered into the upper deck in rightfield. With a five-hit 7–0 victory, Ed Figueroa was the first Puerto Rican–born twenty-game winner in the big leagues. And with the Red Sox winning, 5–1, for Eckersley's twentieth, the Yankees clinched a tie.

"At least we're going someplace," Lemon said. "Either to Boston for a playoff Monday or to Kansas City for Tuesday's opener of the LCS."

In the White House that Saturday afternoon President Jimmy Carter and Soviet foreign minister Andrei Gromyko discussed a treaty to limit strategic bombers and intercontinental ballistic missiles. On the wall of the Merchants Tire Distributors across from the players' parking lot at Fenway Park, a sign pleaded "God Save the Red Sox." On the clubhouse bulletin board was a prayer to St. Jude, the patron saint of hopeless causes. The Red Sox had won their last seven games, but the Yankees had won their last six.

"Do you believe in fate?" Yaz was asked.

"I believe in Cleveland scoring more runs than the Yankees," he said with a laugh.

"Do you believe in Santa Claus too?"

"There is one, isn't there?" Yaz said.

At his locker, Fisk was saying, "We don't have anything to be frustrated about. Disappointed, yes. We've proved something to the fans and to ourselves. The mark of a good team is to play its best ball in the run. We've done that." Over the last nine games, Fred Lynn certainly had done that, batting .455 with fifteen hits.

"I kept thinking we'd have a playoff," Lynn said, "until the Yankees came back to win last night."

For the Red Sox to create a playoff now, Luis Tiant had to stop the Blue Jays on Sunday while the Yankees lost, but Eckersley was still thinking about a playoff. During the off-season he had come to the Red Sox from the Indians in a six-player deal. Tomorrow one of his ex-teammates, Rick Waits, a twenty-six-year-old lefthander who was the sixth-place Indians' best pitcher, with a 12–15 record, would be going against Catfish Hunter, starting on only three days' rest for the first time in two years.

"Rick Waits can win," Eckersley said. "I know he can win."

Sunday only one out-of-town game was posted on the Fenway Park scoreboard: CLEVE above NY. During the Blue Jays' batting practice, Sam Ewing, an outfielder-DH, was standing near the scoreboard at the bottom of the Wall in leftfield. Quickly and playfully, Ewing pulled down an *8* alongside CLEVE, provoking a roar from the early arriving fans, who assumed the game in New York had really begun. They soon realized it was a prank. But around that time Jeff Torborg assembled the Indians in the visiting team's clubhouse at Yankee Stadium.

"I just want to remind you of the impact of this game on the divisional race," Torborg told them. "You can still salvage some pride."

In the top of the first, Red Sox third baseman Jack Brohamer heard a roar in the Fenway bleachers. He assumed one of the Indians had taken Catfish Hunter deep. He was correct. Indian first baseman Andre Thornton had crashed a two-run homer. The Yankees rebounded with two in their half of the first on Munson's single, Piniella's double, Jackson's sacrifice fly, and Nettles's single. In the Indian second, Gary Alexander led off with a homer and Rick Manning's single delivered another run. With a 4–2 lead, Rick Waits walked to the mound, looked around, and realized he enjoyed being a factor in a pennant race. He would stop the Yankees on five hits, 9–2, while Hunter was shelled.

"My pitches were going where I wanted them to, but there was nothing on them," Hunter would say later. "As soon as I got out there, I knew I had no pop."

Tiant, meanwhile, was blanking the Blue Jays, 5–0, on two hits. Singles by Hobson and Scott, Brohamer's run-scoring grounder, and Remy's double produced two runs in the fifth off Don Kirkwood in the twenty-nine-year-old righthander's last major league appearance. Brohamer's walk and Burleson's homer, his first in three months, added two in the seventh. In the middle of the eighth inning, the Fenway Park message board flashed:

SOX NEXT HOME GAME TOMORROW 2:30.

As if adding an exclamation point, Jim Rice hit his forty-sixth homer. In the Red Sox bullpen, Bob Stanley, listening to a portable radio borrowed from a fan in the stands, heard Yankee broadcaster

Phil Rizzuto say, "I just can't get myself ready for this, going up to Boston" and broadcaster Bill White retort, "I hope the players can." Soon the Fenway Park message board flashed again:

THANK YOU RICK WAITS.

To create the one-game playoff, the Red Sox had finished the season with eight straight victories (four shutouts), including six at Fenway Park, for a 33–3 record there down the stretch. In those eight games, the Red Sox had not made an error until Sunday's finale.

"I've never been prouder of anybody in baseball," Zimmer was saying now. "Don't nobody ever tell me this team choked."

At his locker George Scott said, "There was no question we'd win today. In a big game, Luis Tiant is the greatest pitcher I've ever seen." Across the clubhouse the Cuban righthander was puffing a victory cigar and saying, "It may have been the most important game of my career." At his locker Mike Torrez, tomorrow's starter in the playoff game, was smiling.

"Here I've been given a chance to redeem myself," he said. "If I win this, that's what people will remember. This is a different team than the one the Yankees swept here. I'm a different pitcher than the one that lost six in a row. Thursday's win really helped me. I feel the way I did last October."

Glancing at one of the Boston writers, Torrez winked and said, "Bring your bags to the ballpark tomorrow because we're going to Kansas City." But his record against the Yankees didn't support his confidence. In four previous starts this season, he had beaten them only once, 8–1, in Yankee Stadium on August 3 in a six-inning game shortened by rain. He had been the losing pitcher three times: knocked out in the fourth inning of a 10–4 rout on June 20 in Fenway Park, knocked out in the second inning of a 15–3 rout on September 7 in Fenway Park, edged 3–2 on September 16 in Yankee Stadium. Over his nineteen and one-third innings against the Yankees he had allowed twenty-eight hits with a 7.45 earned run average. And now he would be going against Ron Guidry, baseball's best pitcher.

"Guidry's been as dominant as you can be," Reggie Jackson was saying at his locker. "You couldn't ask to have anybody better going tomorrow. I never saw Sandy Koufax, but we've got the ace of spades going."

In three starts against the Red Sox, the Yankee lefthander was 2–0 with a pair of two-hit shutouts, 7–0 on September 9 in Fenway Park and 4–0 on September 15 in Yankee Stadium. On June 27 in Fenway Park he had pitched six-plus innings in what turned out to be a 6–4 victory in fourteen innings. Over his twenty-four innings, he had allowed only twelve hits and struck out sixteen with a 1.50 earned run average.

As Guidry tossed his glove into his equipment bag for Sunday night's short flight, he spoke easily about the drama of the one-game playoff.

"I thought about it last night, the great season I've had and all," he said. "It would be sort of like topping off the season being sent out to prove who's best. The challenge appeals to me."

"Wouldn't two out of three be a fairer test?" a writer asked.

"One game's enough," he said. "I can only pitch one game."

But that one game was in Fenway Park, not Yankee Stadium. Coming up the tunnel from the Yankee dugout after Sunday's loss, Bucky Dent heard a teammate shout, "George lost the coin toss, now we've got to go to Boston and win." About an hour later, as the Yankees trooped to the buses that would take them to La Guardia Airport, Lou Piniella spotted George Steinbrenner, the Yankees' principal owner. More than any of his teammates, Piniella, who lived near the owner's Tampa home in the off-season and visited him occasionally, was able to tease their bombastic boss.

"You didn't do your job," Piniella said, alluding to the coin toss. "Now we got to do ours."

Steinbrenner smiled. But on the bus Piniella had another wisecrack for the owner. "You're the luckiest guy in the world," he said. "We're not only going to win it for you, but you'll get an extra gate out of it." This time the owner glared.

"Young man," he said sternly, "this is no time for humor."

Rich (Goose) Gossage wasn't laughing. On the bus from Logan Airport to the Sheraton Boston, he pictured himself facing Yaz with two out in the ninth. And after the Yankees were handed envelopes with their room keys, Piniella's sense of humor dissolved into the severity of the situation. Unable to fall asleep, he dressed and walked over to Daisy Buchanan's, a bar and restaurant on nearby Newbury Street.

"Jack Daniel's and water," he told the bartender.

Feeling somewhat guilty that he hadn't stayed in his hotel room the night before what he would later call "the most exciting game of my career," Piniella looked around the bar. Staring back were Thurman Munson, Graig Nettles, and several other teammates.

"We can't sleep either," Nettles said.

The next morning, Monday, October 2, dawned sunny and sparkling. Piniella walked to nearby Fenway Park where police on horseback were already monitoring the beer drinkers. He slipped through the players' entrance, past the empty concession stands, and into the Yankee clubhouse underneath the steel girder stands behind third base. Half the team was already there. While the Yankees sat around waiting for batting practice, Mickey Rivers asked clubhouse man Nick Priori, "The bat me and Bucky are using is chipped. You got any more of that model?" Priori knew what Rivers meant: a Roy White model that the outfielder let Dent and Rivers use. Priori peered into the bat bag and pulled out a Roy White model. Rivers taped the handle the way he and Dent liked it, then told the shortstop, "Don't use that chipped bat anymore. I got a new one that feels good."

"No," Dent said, "I'll stick with the old one."

Dent, as usual, would be batting ninth. By the time he lofted Torrez's inside fastball to Rice in the third inning, the Red Sox had a 1–0 lead on Yaz's homer just inside the rightfield foul pole. In the fifth Dent popped up another inside fastball that Burleson caught. Driving in from his Wellesley Hills home that morning, Torrez had tried to calm the butterflies in his stomach by reflecting on what a difference a year made.

This time a year ago Torrez was about to help the Yankees win the League Championship Series against the Royals, and the World Series against the Dodgers. He was hugging the other Yankees and they were hugging him. George Steinbrenner even embraced him. But the Red Sox offered him a seven-year, $2.7 million contract and now he would be pitching against the Yankees for the divisional pennant.

In the sixth, Burleson doubled into the leftfield corner, moved to third on Remy's bunt, and scored on Rice's single for 2–0. Fisk also singled. Suddenly, with two on and Lynn up, the Red Sox had a chance to knock Guidry out. To break open the game. To win the pennant. On a three-two pitch, Lynn pulled a low inside curveball deep toward the rightfield corner. From the dugout, Zimmer couldn't see the ball but he knew it was near the line. That would mean two runs. Above the Fenway Park roof behind third base, the late afternoon sun slashed into Piniella's eyes. Squinting through the glare, Piniella, who had been playing Lynn closer to the 302-foot foul line than most rightfielders do, hurried over and snared the line drive with a lunging hip-high catch. Grunting in frustration, Lynn wondered why Piniella had been playing him so close to the line. Between innings Piniella had talked to Munson about Guidry's slider.

"It's more the speed of a curveball," Munson told him.

"Yeah, a lefthanded batter can pull it," Piniella said.

In the Yankee dugout now, Piniella told Lemon, "I hope they don't hit another ball to me, I can't see anything out there." But with a 2–0 lead, Torrez, out on the mound for the top of the seventh, appeared in complete command. He had allowed only two hits. He had walked only two and struck out four, including Munson three times. He had pitched outside to the two righthanded sluggers, Munson and Piniella, to keep them from pulling the ball toward the Wall in leftfield where the wind, blowing in, had turned Jackson's high drive in the first inning into a routine fly ball. But now the wind had changed. Now the wind was blowing toward leftfield, toward the Wall, the hard plastic Green Monster, 37 feet high and listed as 315 feet down the line, although in 1975 it had been measured by the *Boston Globe* as not quite 305 feet. With one out, Chambliss singled. White singled. Brian Doyle, the second baseman in Willie Randolph's absence, was the next hitter, but Lemon called him back to the dugout. Jim Spencer, a husky first baseman and DH, would be the pinch hitter. In the on-deck circle, Dent, hitless in his last thirteen at-bats, realized that if Randolph were playing, Lem would have saved Spencer to hit for him, but Lem didn't have another infielder. Spencer lifted a fly ball for the second out.

Walking to the batter's box, Dent was batting .241 with only eleven doubles, one triple, four homers. He had driven in only thirty-seven runs.

Dent took the first pitch, a fastball. Low. Ball one. The second pitch was inside. Dent swung, fouling it straight down, the ball slamming off his left ankle. He hopped in pain. He had needed surgery to remove a blood clot below his left knee during spring training. To protect that leg, which tended to swell quickly if hit, he had worn a shin guard until late in the season, but not today. He kept flexing his left foot, Gene Monahan sprayed a painkiller, ethyl chloride, on the ankle. In the dugout, Lemon wished he had another infielder to pinch-hit for Bucky right now. In the on-deck circle, Rivers turned to the batboy.

"Get that other bat," he said.

When the batboy found the new bat, Rivers pointed to where Dent was about to return to the batter's box. "Hey, homey," Rivers yelled, "you're using the wrong bat. Use this one." Dent turned, handed the bat with the chip in it to the batboy, took the new bat, then settled into his stance. Throughout the delay, Torrez had tossed the ball to shortstop Rick Burleson two or three times but hadn't asked plate umpire Don Denkinger for permission to throw any warmup pitches to keep his arm loose. He had assumed that the delay would be momentary. Instead, it had lasted several minutes. Noticing that Torrez hadn't been throwing, Reggie Jackson remembered how Mike Marshall of the Dodgers hadn't bothered throwing during a six-minute delay in the final game of the 1974 World Series after Oakland fans had thrown trash on the field. Joe Rudi then hit Marshall's first pitch for a home run and a 3–2 lead. Now, with Dent finally in the batter's box, Torrez threw a fastball inside. Not far enough inside. Dent swung. The ball rose toward the Wall, the eyes of 32,925 fans and everybody in a Yankee or Red Sox uniform watching its trajectory.

Half-turning from the mound, Torrez thought Dent hadn't hit the ball that hard. In the dugout, Zimmer thought Yaz would catch it. But at the plate, Carlton Fisk suddenly saw Yaz look up.

Running hard to first base with his head down, Dent was hoping the ball would hit the Wall for a double. As he turned toward second, he saw second-base umpire Al Clark waving his right arm in a circle. The ball had dropped into the net just above the Wall near the foul pole. Home run. As he approached second, Dent slapped his hands together.

Near the first-base line, Torrez stood and stared at the ball in the net. The Yankees led, 3–2, on Bucky Dent's fifth homer.

Except for the noise in the Yankees' dugout and in the nearby box seats where George Steinbrenner, Al Rosen, and other Yankee executives were yelling, Fenway Park was silent. As Piniella waited for Dent to return to the dugout in a swarm of hugs, he noticed that the home run took all the air out of Fenway Park. "You could hear it go poof," he would say later. In the Red Sox clubhouse Dennis Eckersley had been watching workers assemble the television platform for the postgame celebration. Bring on that champagne. But with the Yankees ahead now, the workers hurriedly took the platform apart. Returning to the mound, Torrez walked Rivers on a three-two pitch. Hopping out of the dugout, Zimmer waved to the bullpen for Bob Stanley as Torrez glared. He had struck out Munson, the next hitter, three times but Zimmer hadn't even asked how he felt. Zimmer didn't care. The manager knew that Stanley, a lean six-four righthander, was having a career season: 15–2 with ten saves and a 2.60 earned run average. But

Bucky Dent jumps onto home plate after his three-run homer scored Roy White (6) and Chris Chambliss (10). *UPI Photo*

now Rivers stole second and Munson doubled to left center for a 4–2 lead before Piniella flied to Rice.

In the Red Sox seventh, Hobson struck out, Guidry finishing his follow-through in his hopping motion. But when Scott singled, Zimmer sent up Bob Bailey, a righthanded batter, to hit for Brohamer.

Lemon walked to the mound. He wasn't about to risk the possibility of Guidry letting the pennant get away. Not with Goose Gossage ready. As soon as the Yankees went ahead, Lemon knew he didn't want Guidry to lose. Not after the season he'd had. And with only three days' rest, he might be starting to lose his stuff. But with a two-run lead, Guidry was annoyed that Lemon wanted to take him out just because Scott had singled.

"Damn it," he said. "I can't even give up a hit?"

"I got some fresh meat out there," Lemon told him.

As soon as Gossage had begun throwing in the Yankee bullpen in front of the right-centerfield bleachers, some Red Sox fans cursed him. One even spit on him before Boston policemen dragged that fan away.

Now, as Gossage arrived at the mound, Guidry said, "Good luck," then trotted to the dugout. Winding up and flinging his warmup pitches, Gossage resembled a Brahman bull bursting out of a rodeo gate.

Bailey never had a chance. Strike three, called. Burleson bounced to Dent. The Yankees still had a 4–2 lead.

In the eighth, Jackson, who had been mostly a designated hitter since his right thumbnail had been smashed by the foul ball more than two weeks earlier, wanted to do something. What he did was smash a towering homer off Stanley into the centerfield bleachers for 5–2. After crossing home plate, he stopped at the Yankee box where Steinbrenner and the other Yankee front office people were making the only noise in Fenway Park's graveyard silence. Zimmer waved to the bullpen again, this time for lefthander Andy Hassler. In the bottom of the eighth, the Red Sox pared the score to 5–4 on Remy's double, Yaz's single, Fisk's single, and Lynn's single. Lemon walked to the mound to talk to Gossage.

"You're trying to make me an old man," the manager said, "but I'm already an old man."

Gossage smiled and settled down. Hobson lifted a fly ball. Scott fanned. But with one out in the ninth, Burleson walked. The tying run was at first. Remy drilled a liner to right that Piniella seemed prepared to catch. He was bluffing. He had seen the ball leave the Red Sox second baseman's bat but now the low sun was blinding him. From experience, he drifted to where he thought the ball would land. He didn't want to panic. He didn't want Burleson to think he couldn't catch it. Third-base coach Eddie Yost was waving for Burleson to run, but the Red Sox shortstop hesitated. When he finally noticed the confused expression on Piniella's face, he ran. Too late. As the ball hopped off the grass to his glove side, Piniella saw it, snatched it, and threw hard. Burleson turned back to second.

Even so, the Red Sox had runners on second and first with their two most feared batters coming up, Jim Rice and Carl Yastrzemski.

At third base Graig Nettles, seeing Rice settling into the batter's box with Yaz on deck, remembered how Bobby Thomson hit that pennant-winning homer for the New York Giants in 1951. Gossage flung his fastball. Rice lifted a high fly ball above the sun, but Piniella caught it, deep enough for Burleson to hurry to third after the catch. If not for Piniella's earlier bluff, Burleson would have been on third, and if Rice had produced a similar fly ball, Burleson would have tagged and scored the tying run. But instead of the tying run on the scoreboard, the Red Sox had a runner on third, a haunting reminder of their slump that had created this pennant playoff.

Over the last month, the Red Sox had failed to score a runner from third base with less than two out twenty-four times. They lost five of those games by one run.

Now, as Gossage looked down from the mound, he remembered what he had pictured last night on the bus to the hotel: facing Yaz in the ninth with the pennant on the line. Yaz against the Goose, a premier fastball hitter against a premier fastball pitcher. At third base, Nettles's memory flashed another rerun: as a late-season rookie with the Minnesota Twins in 1967, he was in their dugout during the final game when Yaz's two-run single drove in the tying runs in the Red Sox' eventual victory.

At shortstop, Bucky Dent felt sweat trickling down his back inside his gray uniform. Hit it to me, he mumbled, but no weird hops.

On the mound, Gossage was not about to mess around with breaking pitches. Just wind up and throw the fastball. In the batter's box, Yaz remembered drilling a single off Gossage the previous inning. Yaz hit a high fastball that time, so he assumed Gossage would probably go low this time. He knew that Gossage's explosive fastball would burst through the shadow halfway to the mound. That fastball was so alive, Yaz never knew what it would do. Sometimes it tailed away. Sometimes it took off. Sometimes it jumped in on you. Yaz decided not to try to hit a home run. He checked Chambliss, who was holding Remy near the bag. Just hit the ball through the hole between first and second. Just tie the score.

Uncoiling out of his flailing windup, Gossage fired his best fastball. Yaz took it. Ball one. His legs weak, Gossage stepped off the mound, trying to relax. He decided that even if the Yankees lost, he would be home in the Colorado mountains tomorrow.

The next pitch was just what Yaz wanted and just where he wanted it, a fastball down. But as he swung, the ball exploded toward his hands. His bat lifted a high pop fly behind third base just in foul ground. Staggering slightly, Nettles waved his arms and settled under it. Yaz took a step toward first base, realized it was a foul ball, stopped, looked away momentarily, turned, and watched the ball drop into Nettles's glove.

The Yankees had won, 5–4.

Both arms high, Nettles held the ball aloft in his glove. Gossage jumped straight up. Munson waved his mask. Piniella hurried in from rightfield, both hands raised. Third-base coach Eddie Yost stared at the fans and realized none were moving. They were just standing there, as if in shock. But all the Yankees were running and jumping. All but Bucky Dent, who was staring at the infield dirt. Just as he looked up at Yaz's pop-up, the Yankee shortstop realized that something had slid down his arm. The gold chain that held his gold St. Christopher's medal had broken. Now he was searching the dirt for the medal itself. No luck. Not wanting to wait any longer, he hurried into the clubhouse. But after talking to the writers about his home run, he returned to the empty infield and searched for the medal again. No luck.

Now, as Dent took his uniform off at his locker, he found the medal. It had dropped down inside his pants.

In the Red Sox clubhouse, some of the players were crying as Zimmer addressed them. "Ain't nobody that has to hang their head in this room," the manager said. "What you guys did in winning eight in a row to get to this game was tremendous. What you guys did in going down to the last pitch today was tremendous." He hated the word *choke* and he didn't want to use it, or hear it.

Yaz had listened to Zimmer, but now in the trainer's room, he knew that at least he had swung at his pitch, a fastball down. When he emerged, black glare paint was still under his eyes.

"We came back knowing we couldn't lose even one game, and we didn't," Yaz said, referring to the eight-game winning streak. "We showed our character then. We showed our character today. That's what I'll remember about this year."

Gossage's final pitch?

"Gossage didn't beat us," Yaz said. "Piniella beat us with those two plays. If he doesn't catch Lynn's ball and if Remy's ball gets past him, we win by five or six runs."

At his locker Mike Torrez faced the inquisition about the home run pitch to Bucky Dent.

"I wanted to get the ball more inside," Torrez said. "But still it was really only a fly ball. Only a fly ball. But you guys won't call it that in your stories tomorrow."

Rick Burleson was explaining why he hadn't hurried to third base on Remy's single in the ninth.

"I couldn't go right away," the Red Sox shortstop said. "I didn't know if Piniella was going to catch the ball. Then I saw the expression on his face, saw that he didn't know where the ball was, and I started running. But when I turned and saw he had the ball, it was too late."

Burleson was watching the ball instead of watching third-base coach Eddie Yost.

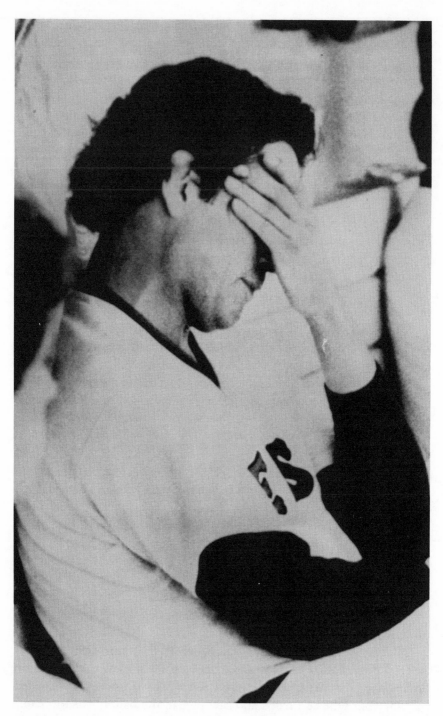

Mike Torrez suffers in the Red Sox dugout. *UPI Photo*

"I was waving for him to keep coming," Yost said. "I saw it was a hit from the beginning. I guess Rick didn't know. He had to hold."

Johnny Pesky, the first-base coach, also knew that Remy's line drive would be a hit.

"Rick was looking at it from another angle," Pesky said. "He just didn't know."

Two months later the forgotten lefthander, Bill Lee, would be traded to the Montreal Expos for Stan Papi, who would never be more than a light-hitting utility infielder for the Red Sox and later the Tigers. Lee would produce a 16–10 record in 1979 for the Expos, his last good year. But now Lee talked about why the Red Sox had lost.

"He lost the pennant," Lee said, nodding toward Zimmer's office. "We should've been home free. A man shouldn't bury veteran ballplayers. He shouldn't have buried me."

Zimmer had ignored Lee, using him only four times in mop-up relief roles in the final weeks, while starting rookie lefthander Bobby Sprowl three times in what turned out to be two losses. Midway through the 1979 season Sprowl would be traded to the Houston Astros, where he would have an 0–1 record over three seasons. He's best remembered in Boston as another long shot that Zimmer, who enjoys the racetrack, had bet on and lost.

"I've gambled all my life and I've been in a lot of photo finishes," the Red Sox manager was saying now. "But this is the toughest one I've ever lost."

Five years later, on joining the Yankees as a third-base coach, Zimmer rented a northern New Jersey home owned by Bucky Dent, whom the Yankees had traded to the Texas Rangers in 1982.

"On every wall there were pictures of that home run swing," Zimmer would say later, with a grin. "I turned all those pictures to the wall."

Surveying the scene in the Red Sox clubhouse now, Dennis Eckersley had absorbed the sadness. "I thought that this was still one of the great years," he would say later. "I thought that we'd get 'em next year." But next year the Red Sox would finish third. By now Reggie Jackson was in the Red Sox clubhouse. He told George Scott, "Both of us should be champions." Not far away George Steinbrenner was surrounded by Boston and New York writers.

"It's a shame," the Yankees' principal owner said, "that this is not the World Series, that our series is not seven games and when we're finished with each other that the season isn't over. We are the two best teams in baseball. We said that on the field today. We won, but you didn't lose."

In the Yankees' clubhouse, Graig Nettles told Bob Lemon, "When Yaz was up, I was saying, 'Pop it up, pop it up . . . Not to me.' " They were on their way to Kansas City for the League Championship Series before defeating the Los Angeles Dodgers in the World Series, four games to two. After they arrived at the Crown Center Hotel in Kansas City, Bucky Dent got a phone call from his friend Joe Illigasch, the CBS director of operations for "60 Minutes."

"Did you get the ball?" Illigasch asked.

"I never thought about it," Dent said.

"I'll get it. I'll call there and get it."

When Illigasch phoned Fenway Park, a member of the grounds crew told him that upon climbing the ladder to empty the net atop the Wall after Monday's game, he found several baseballs in it, as he always did. The others had landed there during batting practice.

"I could give you a ball," the member of the grounds crew said, "but there'd be no way to identify it as the home run ball."

Bucky Dent's home run ball was now just one of many other old baseballs in the darkness of a brown leather ball bag.

1991

Three Time Zones Apart

Atlanta Braves fans do the tomahawk chop. *Atlanta Braves*

BRETT BUTLER HAD never seen or heard anything like it. All around the Los Angeles Dodgers centerfielder, Atlanta Braves fans were waving red-and-blue foam rubber tomahawks while chanting to the beat of tom-tom drums, "Oooooh-ooh, oooh-ooh-ooh-ooh, oooooh-ooh-ooh." Throughout this weekend series, Butler and his teammates had been exposed to the phenomenon of the 1991 National League West pennant race: the tomahawk chop. But instead of being annoyed by the chop, the chant, and the tom-toms in Atlanta–Fulton County Stadium, the Dodgers seemed to be fascinated.

"You felt it in batting practice," Butler would say later. "It was awesome. It was exciting."

It surely was different. In other years, baseball fans occasionally used props to inspire their team. During the 1987 World Series and American League Championship Series, Minnesota Twins rooters waved "homer hankies" supplied by the Minneapolis *Star-Tribune*. In Pittsburgh, announcer Bob Prince popularized the "green weenie" as a hex on Pirate opponents. But now, on Sunday, September 15, the chop, the chant, and the tom-toms were creating a mesmerizing mixture of music and movement as the Braves quickly loaded the bases in the first inning.

More determined than usual, Sid Bream, their lefthanded-hitting first baseman, stepped into the batter's box against Ramon Martinez.

Bream was still seething from what happened in Saturday's game. When the Dodger manager, Tommy Lasorda, brought in lefthander Steve Wilson with the bases loaded in the third, Brave manager Bobby Cox used Brian Hunter as a pinch hitter for Bream, who stalked back to the dugout. Cox had been platooning the two first basemen ever since Bream had returned from midseason surgery on his right knee. The Braves eventually won Saturday's game, 3–2, when Ron Gant's eleventh-inning single scored Keith Mitchell as tomahawks waved and the fans roared.

"At the moment I scored," Mitchell said later, "you couldn't even hear yourself talk."

Despite the victory, Bream, normally mild-mannered and soft-spoken, had burst out of the clubhouse door before it was opened to the members of the news media. Now, in the batter's box on Sunday, he peered out at Martinez, the Dodgers' ace righthander. Only twenty-three years old in only his second full season, Martinez had baffled the Braves in his brief career, winning seven times against only one loss. With a three-one count, Dodger catcher Gary Carter flashed the sign for a changeup, but Martinez misread it. Trying to pitch away from Bream's power, he threw a fastball. Bream pulled it over the right-centerfield fence for a grand slam home run that turned the chop and the chant into cheers demanding a curtain call after he had disappeared into the dugout.

"You've got goose bumps," he said later. "You just hope you don't fall going up the steps."

"But what about Bobby Cox lifting you for a pinch hitter with the bases loaded Saturday?" he was asked. "How did you feel about that?"

"We won't get into that one," he said.

Third baseman Terry Pendleton wasn't reluctant. "Bobby Cox knows this club," he said, "and I know he'd rather have Sid be ticked off about coming out rather than give in to it." Bream's grand slam had ignited a 9–1 victory that prompted lefthander Steve Avery to toss his cap into the crowd and lifted the Braves to a one-and-one-half-game lead over the Dodgers with three weeks remaining. This was quite a turnaround for a franchise that had finished last in the NL West the three previous seasons—before Bream and Terry Pendleton were signed as free agents, before John Schuerholz arrived as the new general manager, before the tomahawk chop had created an instant identity and an instant industry, before the Braves had upstaged the Georgia Tech, University of Georgia, and Atlanta Falcons football teams.

In spring training, not long after the Gulf War ended with Iraq surrendering after a hundred-hour ground battle, a few followers of Deion Sanders, the Braves' outfielder and Falcons' cornerback from Florida State, had swung their arms in a chopping motion and hummed an eerie chant, the way fans of the Florida State Seminoles do. As the season progressed, some Atlanta fans waved toy tomahawks.

When the Braves ascended into the race, Paul Braddy, a foam rubber salesman, visited the Braves' concession manager, John Eifert.

"You should be selling foam rubber tomahawks," Braddy suggested.

"If I can sell 'em for five dollars, I'll take five thousand," Eifert said.

Braddy returned to his suburban Atlanta home, took an electric knife, and cut a chunk of foam rubber into the shape of a small tomahawk. He soon quit his $60,000-a-year job to go into business for himself. He would sell hundreds of thousands of official Braves tomahawks, thereby contributing to a national controversy with Native Americans who were offended by the tomahawks and by the Braves' name. But after the Braves won two of three games from the Dodgers in that weekend series when a club sponsor, Uno-cal, gave away forty thousand tomahawks, their players sensed the value of the chop and the chant.

"They generate a lot of emotion and it carries over," second baseman Mark Lemke said. "The chop and the chant can't hit or pitch or field, but if there's emotion, maybe it helps you to get a hit, make a good pitch or make a play."

Now, with thirteen of their final nineteen games on the road, the Braves had to prove they could win without the chop and the chant, beginning with a seven-game swing through California: two in San Francisco, two in San Diego, and three in Los Angeles in another crucial weekend series. In the NL's geographical denial that East is East, West is West and never the twain shall meet, the Braves would be playing in the same time zone as three of its Western Division rivals for the last time this season.

"West Coast trips can be difficult," Darryl Strawberry was telling writers in the Dodger clubhouse. "It's still a pennant race. Our record at home speaks for itself."

In Dodger Stadium, where they would play thirteen of their last eighteen games, the Dodgers were 44–24 (3–3 against the Braves) but the atmosphere would be calmer.

"I love our fans, they're the best in baseball, but it's just a fact that they're different," Brett Butler said. "They are more spoiled. It's like they've won so much, it's not that big of a deal. They get to the park in the second inning, they leave in the seventh. The fans in Atlanta, because they have never seen anything like this before, are unbelievable. They are awesome. They really charge everything up."

Before the Braves boarded their chartered buses for the ride to the airport Sunday night, catcher Greg Olson bristled when a writer asked if the Braves could rise to the challenge of the California trip.

"All you guys asked us if we could beat the Dodgers when it counted and now it's the West Coast," he said. "Maybe it will be a challenge for us, but we've got the right guys in the right positions."

One of those right guys was thirty-two-year-old Otis Nixon, the leftfielder and leadoff batter, slim and swift. Acquired from the Montreal Expos shortly before the season began, he was leading the NL in stolen bases with seventy-two, including six in one game that tied the major league record established in 1912 by Eddie Collins, the Philadelphia A's second baseman. Nixon had been batting .337 until he slumped in August, but now he was hitting again. He remembered why the Expos had dropped out of the 1989 divisional race that the Chicago Cubs won.

"We didn't know if Mark Langston and Pascual Perez were going to go free agent after that season or not," he said, referring to two Expo pitchers. "There was a lot of talk about that and we let it bother us. We focused on other things instead of focusing on every game and we fell apart. We're going to try not to let that happen here."

Focus on every game. Play 'em one at a time. Don't look ahead. Don't look back. With those or similar words, these have been the clichés of every pennant race since Johnny Evers and Fred Merkle, since Ty Cobb and Ed Walsh. But now, on Monday morning in San Francisco after a long jet flight, Otis Nixon was in his room at the Parc Fifty-Five Hotel when the phone rang.

"Otis, this is John Schuerholz," the Braves general manager said. "Please come to my room. I have something to tell you."

Minutes later, Nixon knocked on the general manager's door. Schuerholz opened it, then motioned for Nixon to sit down.

"Otis, I've got bad news," the general manager said. "I've just been informed by the commissioner's office that you failed a drug test on September 7 when we were in New York. You've been suspended for sixty days. Suspended immediately."

Schuerholz explained that the club had arranged for Nixon to move to another hotel to avoid the news media.

"Otis was very quiet, very timid," Schuerholz would say later. "He didn't deny it. He didn't say a word."

As a minor leaguer with the Buffalo Bisons in the Cleveland Indians' farm system, Nixon had been arrested in 1987 for cocaine possession. He pleaded guilty to a reduced charge of obstructing justice, was fined $500, and underwent a thirty-day rehabilitation program. While with the Expos and the Braves, he had been tested frequently, as often as two or three times a week. But in July, after have passed more than 250 drug tests over four years, one of his tests turned up positive. In an August 1 hearing in Commissioner Fay Vincent's office, he insisted that he had not used cocaine.

"He looked at me across the table," Deputy Commissioner Steve Greenberg said later of that meeting. "He looked me in the eye and said, 'I did not use [cocaine]. I cannot explain what happened on that test. I'm not disputing the test, but I can't understand it. I haven't used since 1987.' Two days later, he tested normal. It was like a blip on the screen."

But in San Francisco now, Nixon did not dispute the commissioner's ruling. Aware that he had been suspended and would lose $67,500 of his $585,000 salary, he packed his bags, checked out of the Parc Fifty-Five, checked into a nearby hotel for a few hours, then took a taxi to San Francisco International Airport where the Braves had made a reservation for him on a flight to Atlanta. He arrived at the gate just as the jetway door was about to be closed.

"No first-class seats left?" he asked.

"First class is full," he was told.

"I'll take a tourist seat," he said.

When the jetliner rolled to the gate at Hartsfield International Airport that night, Nixon didn't get off with the rest of the passengers. Wearing black sunglasses, a black shirt, black slacks, and black shoes, he descended a jet stairway and entered an automobile waiting on the tarmac. Against the Giants, his teammates were blowing a three-run lead in an 8–5 loss. When the Dodgers used nine pitchers, including five in the ninth inning, to defeat the Cincinnati Reds in twelve innings, 6–5, on Jeff Hamilton's bases-loaded single, the Braves' lead had shrunk to one-half game. And without Otis Nixon, their chances in the pennant race had shrunk despite Bobby Cox's stiff upper lip.

"We're fine," the Braves manager insisted. "I feel very confident with Lonnie Smith as our leftfielder."

At thirty-five, Smith was not a base stealer but he could hit. He had batted over .300 six times with the Braves, Kansas City Royals, St. Louis Cardinals, and Philadelphia Phillies despite drug problems that required a 1984 stay in rehab. Never a good outfielder, his nickname was "Skates" because he occasionally would slip and fall when approaching a fly ball. In Monday night's loss, one of those falls had led to two runs. But he suddenly had been thrust into the lineup as the new leadoff batter. More than any of his teammates, he understood Nixon's situation.

"I know what it feels like," Smith said. "I've been there. I've been through more torment than anyone could imagine unless they've been in a war."

Tuesday night Nixon appeared at the downtown Champions sports bar where his friend Deion Sanders, now a Falcons cornerback after having been a part-time Braves outfielder, taped his weekly television show. While Nixon played pool, other TV sets showed the Braves losing to the Giants again, 3–2. When Bobby Ojeda of the Dodgers stopped the Reds, 5–3, on homers by Eddie Murray and Kal Daniels, the Braves had dropped into second place by one-half game. Two games without Nixon, two losses.

Dodger manager Tommy Lasorda had his own problems. His bullpen closer, Jay Howell, would not be able to return for the stretch drive because of a sore elbow. His ace, Ramon Martinez, needed a cortisone injection to relieve the soreness in the bicep of his pitching arm, struck on August 20 by Padre third baseman Jack Howell's liner. But first baseman Eddie Murray was thriving in the crucible of the pennant race. He was batting .382 in September with five homers and eighteen runs batted in.

"September is the toughest month to play in," Murray said. "With all the new pitchers, you face guys trying to make the team for next year, guys you don't know. It's hard. I don't know when I'll get another chance to be this close."

Lonnie Smith also understood what it meant to be close to a pennant, close to a League Championship Series, close to the World Series. When the Royals lost Willie Wilson during the final weeks of the 1985 season with a reaction to a penicillin shot, Smith batted .318 in September while stealing six bases, scoring fourteen runs, and driving in twelve.

"We would not have won that pennant," recalled John Schuerholz, then the Royals' general manager, "without Lonnie Smith."

Wednesday night in San Diego the Braves opened with five runs in the first as their ace, Tommy Glavine, recorded his nineteenth victory, 6–4. In three games since Nixon's departure, Smith now had a total of three hits in nine at-bats, but he knew what some people were whispering.

"I'm the bad boy, remember?" he said before Thursday's game. "I can't catch. I can't run. I'm not an offensive threat. I'm not perfect. But I can still play this damn game."

Against the Padres that night Smith had a homer, two singles and scored the winning run in the tenth inning on David Justice's single in a 4–2 victory. But the Dodgers swept their two-game series with the Houston Astros, maintaining their lead of one-half game. Since returning from Atlanta, the Dodgers had won four straight for a 48–24 record at Dodger Stadium, where Tim Belcher would open Friday against Steve Avery, who in his brief career had a 3–0 record against the Dodgers. But before Friday night's game Tommy Lasorda tried to minimize Avery's success.

"Has he lost a game this season?"

"Yes," he was told.

"Has he beaten everybody?"

"No," he was told.

"OK, then," Lasorda said.

But the Dodgers didn't beat him. Then only twenty-one years old, the six-four lefthander fired a 3–0 six-hitter for his seventeenth win. While trotting between first and second on his thirtieth homer, Ron Gant pumped his fist and literally leaped into history: he had joined Willie Mays (1956–1957) and Bobby Bonds (1977–1978) as the only major leaguers to hit thirty homers and steal thirty bases in successive seasons.

"The thirty-thirty record was one reason I leaped," Gant would say later. "But the big reason was, we needed a big blow."

Gant's homer preceded Avery's moment of truth: sixth inning, bases loaded, two out, Juan Samuel up. He flied out.

"That seemed to take a lot out of the Dodgers," Avery said. "They weren't quite as aggressive the rest of the game."

They weren't in first place anymore either. The Braves were up there now, by one-half game. The next night lefthander Charlie Leibrandt had a 1–0 lead in the eighth when Pendleton fumbled a grounder and shortstop Rafael Belliard threw wild, leading to the tying run. With the bases loaded and Strawberry up, Bobby Cox hurried out to remove Leibrandt as Pendleton turned to the lanky lefthander and mouthed his apology.

"That's mine," the third baseman said, meaning that his error had created the tying run. "That's mine."

The threat ended when Strawberry struck out. But in the ninth, Kal Daniels's single and Samuel's triple off lefthander Mike Stanton produced a 2–1 victory, a one-half-game lead, and a sudden superstition. When the Dodgers arrived for Sunday's game, they realized that Saturday's celebrity batboy, actor Tony Danza, had not returned. Danza was hosting a party at his home when the phone rang.

"After eight years, I finally threw a party," the star of the television show "Who's the Boss?" would say. "All these producers were there. I'm thinking, 'There's no way I can make the game today.'"

Danza arrived and the Dodgers won, 3–0. Ramon Martinez, with six days' rest strengthening his sore bicep, allowed only two hits in seven innings and crashed a home run off Glavine, his first in the majors. During the 1990 season he had bet Eddie Murray a dinner that he would hit a home run, and now he put a note in the first baseman's locker.

"Eddie," it read. "When is dinner? Ramon."

The Dodgers had jumped one and one-half games ahead with only two weeks remaining: eleven games for them, twelve for the Braves. In the Dodgers' glow, righthander Kevin Gross talked about how to use the Los Angeles block for the tomahawk chop.

"First, you raise your left forearm up just across eye level; that blocks the tomahawk," he said. "Then you bring your right fist up into the solar plexus. That knocks the wind out of them. Then you can either leave or bury the Braves."

The Braves weren't about to be buried. Knowing that Nixon's suspension had deprived Cox of a swift base runner, John Schuerholz had an idea: borrow Deion Sanders from the football Falcons to be a pinch runner.

In his fifty-one games Sanders had batted only .193 but had nine stolen bases. With the Braves returning to Atlanta, Sanders would be available for three night games with the Reds after the Falcons' afternoon practices. When the Braves visited Cincinnati the following week and finished the season in Atlanta against the Astros, he would be available because the Falcons had a bye that week in the National Football League schedule.

"It's my decision," Sanders said. "All the Falcons can do is lay a fine on me, which I'm used to. I'll do anything I can to help the Braves win it. I'm ready to walk the last mile with them."

On a battered wooden table in the dark runway to the Braves' dugout, Sanders signed a short-term contract late Tuesday afternoon before rain created a Wednesday doubleheader. In San Diego, after learning that shortstop Alfredo Griffin would be lost for the season with a sprained knee, the Dodgers won, 5–2, for Mike Morgan's fourteenth win. Hit-and-run plays ordered by Lasorda produced three runs as third-base coach Joey Amalfitano told the manager, "Tommy, you're hot tonight." Lasorda shrugged it off.

"In a pennant race, you can't be conservative," he said. "Some people become conservative because they're afraid of doing something wrong. That's the wrong attitude to take."

Hours after the Braves had dropped two games behind, rookie outfielder Keith Mitchell bounced his car off an interstate highway divider. He was arrested for driving under the influence and driving with a revoked license. In a separate accident, rookie first baseman–outfielder Brian Hunter also was arrested for driving under the influence. When the Braves gathered Wednesday for their twi-night doubleheader, Terry Pendleton took aside the two rookies, each free on bond.

"It's pennant time and we don't need distractions like this," the veteran third baseman told them in a firm voice. "If something like this happens again or if you have a problem, call me."

Mitchell appreciated Pendleton's concern. "He was cool about it," the rookie said. "He made us realize some things." Around that time Deion Sanders was jogging off the practice field at the Falcons' complex in nearby Suwanee. To prepare for Sunday's game against the New Orleans Saints, he had been at the complex since nine o'clock that morning, starting with a special-teams meeting and a defensive unit meeting. Now, after a shower, he climbed into the WXIA Channel 11 helicopter.

"I've never been on one of those things before," he said later. "I was scared as hell."

After the helicopter landed in a steady drizzle at the state capitol building near the stadium, the first athlete ever to be playing major league baseball and pro football *simultaneously* hopped into a Channel 11 staff car. As the car approached the stadium tunnel to the Braves' clubhouse, a security guard waved it away.

"Hey," a voice in the car yelled, "we've got Deion."

With a flourish, the guard waved the car through. Sanders, carrying a football, hurried into the clubhouse to put on his uniform. Out on the field, the opener of the twi-night doubleheader with the Reds had already begun. Inserted as a pinch runner in a late inning, Sanders stole second base. The Braves won, 2–1, in the tenth on Ron Gant's run-scoring single but lost the second game, 10–9, in ten innings. When the Dodgers lost in San Diego, 8–2, their lead had been sliced to one and one-half games. But on Thursday, with the Dodgers not scheduled, the Braves lost again, 8–0, to Jose Rijo's eight-hitter. Now they were two games behind, but Rijo sympathized with them.

"I know how much the game meant to the Braves and I feel sorry for what I did," the Reds' righthander said. "I'd love to see the Braves in the playoffs. I think they deserve it. The Dodgers have been there so many times."

With a two-game lead and only nine games remaining, the Dodgers were counting on being there one more time. But as they awaited Friday night's start of a weekend series with the Giants, they were wary of the longtime rivalry that blazed in Ebbets Field and the Polo Grounds before the franchises moved to California after the 1957 season. In 1962 the Dodgers held a four-game lead over the Giants before a 3–10 finish created a pennant playoff. In the third game of that playoff series, the Dodgers had a 4–2 lead going into the ninth inning but the Giants rallied for four runs and the pennant. In 1971 Juan Marichal of the Giants preserved a one-game lead over the Dodgers by stopping the Padres in the season finale. In the 1982 season finale Giant second baseman Joe Morgan's home run off Terry Forster spoiled the Dodgers' bid to force a one-game divisional playoff with the Braves and created a Candlestick Park celebration.

"You would've thought the Giants had won the division," recalled Jerry Reuss, then a Dodger lefthander. "But it wasn't that the Giants had won. It was that the Dodgers had lost."

As this pennant race sizzled, several Giants had warned the Dodgers to eliminate the Braves before the final weekend series at Candlestick Park or "We'll knock you out of the race again." But with only nine games remaining, the Braves knew they were in jeopardy, particularly those three who had been through pennant races before: Terry Pendleton, Sid Bream, and thirty-four-year-old lefthander Charlie Leibrandt. Not long after the Braves walked into the Houston Astrodome for Friday night's opener, Pendleton and Bream approached Bobby Cox.

"We'd like to have a meeting," Pendleton said.

"Just the players," Bream said. "Nobody else."

"It's all yours," Cox said. "Have a good one."

With his teammates sitting at their lockers after batting practice, Pendleton stood and looked around. "We're two back with only nine to play," he said. "We can't afford to lose another game. We've got to get rolling now. These chances don't come along every year. You never know when you're going to get another chance to win a division. You've got to take full advantage of it. You don't want to look back and know you wasted a chance to win."

Now Bream stood up. "We have nine games to go," he said, "and we have to believe in our hearts that if it takes winning all nine games, we'll win all nine."

Across the clubhouse, Leibrandt said, "With the Dodgers on the coast for the rest of the season, we get to post our score first. If we can win our game, that adds to the pressure on the Dodgers to match it. When I was with the Royals, I remember being in California and seeing those eastern scores go up. Every game we win will make it tougher for the Dodgers to win."

The Braves had their orders. Don't waste their opportunity. Win their remaining nine games. Use the time zone difference to put pressure on the Dodgers.

Instead, the Braves immediately put pressure on themselves. Through seven innings, the Braves had been shut out by Ryan Bowen, a rookie righthander with a 5–4 record. But when Lonnie Smith led off the eighth with a double off the leftfield wall, righthander Xavier Hernandez relieved. Mark Lemke singled, scoring Smith. Pendleton singled, prompting Astro manager Art Howe to bring in lefthander Rob Mallicoat. David Justice's line single loaded the bases. The fourth Astro pitcher of the inning, righthander Mark Portugal, got Ron Gant on a pop foul before consecutive singles by Bream, Greg Olson, and pinch hitter Jeff Blauser completed a four-run rally that stood up for a 4–2 win. But the Dodgers beat the Giants, 6–2, surviving two errors by Jose Offerman, the rookie shortstop from the Dominican Republic who hid in the clubhouse runway before three teammates consoled him.

"I just wanted to be alone," Offerman said. "But they told me not to think about it too much. They let me know we still had a game to play."

Saturday afternoon in Los Angeles the Dodgers lost to the Giants, 4–1, on Will Clark's two-run homer and lefthander Trevor Wilson's three-hitter after Kal Daniels succumbed to the pressure of the pennant race. With two on and two out in the first inning, the Dodger leftfielder was called out on strikes by umpire Joe West.

"You know how it is during a pennant race," Daniels said later. "I wanted to come through in the clutch so bad. I wanted to get that run home so bad."

Daniels argued, loudly and obscenely. With an appreciation of the pennant race, West walked away, but Daniels, as he acknowledged later, "said something I shouldn't have said," something that umpires deem grounds for an automatic ejection.

"I would not say something like that again," Daniels said. "I should not have said it. I know that. But at the time I just couldn't help myself."

Some of Daniels's teammates quietly complained about his loss of self-control that deprived them of one of their best hitters. If he had not been ejected, maybe the Dodgers would have won that game. If he had not been ejected, his replacement, Mitch Webster, would not have been called out on strikes three times, another victim of pennant race pressure.

"It was like I didn't have an idea up there," Webster said. "It was like my hands were stuck."

With an opportunity now to cut the Dodgers' lead to one game that night, the Braves again rallied to win, 5–4. Alejandro Peña, who had replaced the ailing Juan Berenguer in the bullpen, fanned Jeff Bagwell with the tying run on third in the ninth. Sunday afternoon in the Astrodome the Braves needed thirteen innings for a 6–5 victory. With the tying run on third and the winning run on second, Jim Clancy, a thirty-five-year-old righthander who had pitched for the Toronto Blue Jays when Cox was their manager, got rookie shortstop Andujar Cedeño on a soft liner to Blauser for the final out. In the clubhouse, Blauser noticed many of his teammates drinking milk.

"They must be trying," he said, laughing, "to calm their ulcers."

Soon the Braves were on a jet to Cincinnati for Monday's opener of a three-game series. By the time the jet landed they might be tied for first place. Going into the bottom of the ninth inning, losing 2–1 to Dave Righetti, some of the Dodgers thought so too. Several were in the shower. Eddie Murray was at his locker, taking off his uniform. Tommy Lasorda, having been ejected, was in his office with a plate of enchiladas, watching Mike Scioscia lead off the ninth with a single. Jose Offerman ran for him. Stan Javier singled. In the clubhouse now, Murray yelled, "If we're going to win this thing, we're going to win it all together."

With a Dodger jacket over his T-shirt, Murray hurried to the dugout along with Mike Morgan, wearing cowboy boots, and Jim Gott, an icebag strapped to his right shoulder.

On Brett Butler's grounder, Offerman stayed alive in a rundown between home and third long enough for Javier to move to third and Butler to second as the potential winning run. Then occurred one of baseball's most unusual singles.

As Mike Sharperson slapped a quick two-hop grounder toward third baseman Matt Williams, his bat broke.

Above the infield grass, the barrel of the Louisville Slugger C-243 model whirled like a helicopter's propeller as Williams moved to field the ball. But with the bat barrel spinning toward his face, Williams ducked. Incredibly, the broken bat barrel struck the ball.

"I had a chance to grab the ball," Williams said later, "just before the bat got there."

The ball hopped past him. Sharperson hurried across first base for a single as Javier scored the tying run. Moments later Darryl Strawberry, hitless in ten previous at-bats in the series, singled to right center. With a 3–2 victory, the Dodgers had retained their one-game lead and Lasorda's enchiladas suddenly tasted much better. Quietly, the Braves checked into the Terrace Hilton Hotel in Cincinnati, still one game behind.

"Freaky things have happened to us all season," Dodger center-fielder Brett Butler said. "This one was, I don't know, superfreaky."

But the Dodgers had a gripe. One of the Reds' best relief pitchers, lefthander Norm Charlton, had been suspended for seven games and fined $1,000 for admitting he had thrown at Dodger catcher Mike Scioscia, whom he accused of stealing signs. Pending a hearing, Charlton had not served the suspension. Now that the Braves were coming to Cincinnati, he suddenly decided to start serving it.

"The thing I don't like," Dodger executive vice president Fred Claire said, "is when a player can dictate the process."

National League president Bill White did the dictating. He ordered Charlton to remain in his Reds uniform for the three-game series that conceivably could decide the division title. If the Braves lost three in Cincinnati while the Dodgers were sweeping three from the Padres, the Dodgers would clinch. For the Braves, the Monday night opener began ominously when John Smoltz's first eight pitches were balls. Two on, nobody out.

"Right there," the lanky righthander said later, "I made a mechanical adjustment with my curveball."

Midway through the season Smoltz had made a mental adjustment. Schuerholz suggested that he consult Dr. Jack Llewellyn, a Marietta, Georgia, sports psychologist. Once 2–11, Smoltz now had put together a 10–2 streak. And with the mechanical adjustment on his curveball, he stopped the Reds on two hits and struck out ten before Mike Bielecki, obtained the day before from the Chicago Cubs along with catcher Damon Berryhill, pitched the ninth inning of the 4–0 victory.

"Smoltz's curveball," catcher Greg Olson said, "was the nastiest I've seen all season."

Watching the Braves on television in the Dodger Stadium club-house, Darryl Strawberry said, "Me, Eddie Murray, and Kal Daniels, this race is now dependent on us. If this team is going to get the job done, we've got to get it done. Every night." In a 7–2 rout of the Padres that night, Strawberry crashed his twenty-sixth homer and Murray collected his 2,500th hit as Orel Hershiser pitched a two-hit shutout for seven innings.

"If we need to win Sunday's finale," Lasorda said, "Hershiser is my pitcher."

With five games remaining, the Dodgers still held a one-game lead. As they gathered for Tuesday night's game, they were dreaming of a two-game lead. Joe Oliver's grand slam off Charlie Leibrandt in the first inning in Cincinnati had provided Jose Rijo with a 6–0 lead. But run by run, the Braves crawled back, closing to within 6–5 in the seventh. Charlton, in relief, let two inherited runners score, one on a fly ball that centerfielder Mariano Duncan, usually a shortstop, failed to catch. With none out in the ninth and Rob Dibble pitching, pinch runner Deion Sanders, shuttling between Falcons meetings and practices in Atlanta and the Braves games in Cincinnati, stole second base. Terry Pendleton lifted a short fly to center. On his way back to the dugout, Pendleton trotted by David Justice.

"Pick me up," Pendleton said.

Justice knew what Pendleton meant: drive in that tying run. His previous time up, Justice had popped up. But now he reminded himself to swing smoothly. On Dibble's first pitch, a fastball down the middle, the Braves rightfielder crushed a homer into the rightfield stands that put the Braves ahead, 7–6. Moments later, in the first inning of their game with the Padres, the Dodgers knew about Justice's twenty-first homer. And when Alejandro Peña, once a Dodger, nailed down his ninth save since joining the Braves, the Dodgers knew they had to win to preserve their one-game lead. They did, 3–1, their eleventh victory in fourteen games, but some were openly wondering about the Reds' will to win. "I think the Reds just kind of laid down for the Braves," infielder Lenny Harris said. "We all know the only people who want to see us win is us." Lou Piniella, the Reds' manager, defended his team, citing the loss of several injured players. But of twenty-five Reds players polled, twenty acknowledged rooting for the Braves; the other five had "no comment." Even the Braves had not expected to win after trailing 6–0 in the first.

"Winning a game when you're six runs down against Rijo, Charlton, and Dibble," said Bobby Cox, "is just about impossible."

David Justice is greeted in the Braves' dugout after his game-winning homer in Cincinnati.
AP/Wide World Photo

The next night, the Braves jumped on Scott Scudder, a twenty-three-year-old righthander with a shaky 6–8 record. As several Dodgers watched on television in their clubhouse three time zones away, Scudder began by hitting Lonnie Smith with a pitch. Lemke popped out, but Pendleton tripled and Justice doubled for a 2–0 lead. Gant struck out, but Bream walked. Olson singled for 3–0, and when Scudder walked Belliard, the Dodgers were fuming.

"He's afraid; he's afraid to pitch to 'em," Lasorda yelled at the television screen in his office. "Get him out of there. Look at his eyes. He's afraid. Get him out of there."

When Scudder also walked the Braves starter, Tommy Glavine, forcing in the fourth run, manager Lou Piniella got him out of there. Smith clipped righthander Kip Gross for a two-run single to complete the 6–0 burst that should have eased Glavine's burden. But as the slim

Tom Lasorda watches the Braves on television in his movie star–studded office.
Tom Zimmerman

lefthander walked to the mound, he remembered how Jose Rijo had blown a 6–0 lead the night before.

"I told myself, 'Don't you let that happen,' " Glavine recalled. "I told myself, 'Don't ease up. Don't let this game get away.' "

Glavine prevailed, 6–3, the first Braves pitcher to win twenty games in a season since knuckleball righthander Phil Niekro in 1979. Now the Dodgers had to win again to stay in first place. Strawberry's single provided Tim Belcher with a 1–0 lead in the first, then he hit a two-run homer in the fifth, his fifth homer in the September stretch. But hoping to break a 3–3 tie in the seventh, Lasorda removed Belcher for a pinch hitter.

"I was going for the runs," Lasorda explained later. "That's the difference between the National League and the American League, where you have the designated hitter. In the National League, you've got to make that decision."

That decision would haunt the Dodger manager. In the eighth, with Kevin Gross and then Roger McDowell pitching, the Padres scratched together six runs on seven singles, including two bunts and three hits that never reached the outfield grass. On the chartered jetliner returning the Braves to Atlanta that night, Ron Gant had his cellular phone to his ear. Like the players on most baseball teams, the Braves usually play cards on their flights. But not tonight. Gant had dialed the Dodger game on radio and now he was delivering a play-by-play of the Padres' six-run inning that produced a 9–4 victory.

"We're tied," Terry Pendleton kept saying. "We're tied."

Walking off the field in Dodger Stadium, Padres reliever Larry Andersen was so happy, he thought about doing the tomahawk chop. "But then," he would say later, "I told myself, 'That would be bush.' " With each team's record at 92–67, the pennant race was boiling down to the final weekend of the schedule: the Braves were home for three games against the Astros while the Dodgers were in San Francisco for three games with the Giants, their bitter rivals for more than a century. More than any of his Dodger teammates, Brett Butler, once a Giant, understood what it would be like in Candlestick Park.

"The fans' involvement will be tenfold whatever it is in Atlanta," the Dodger centerfielder said. "The Braves want to win. The Giants want to spoil. They're motivated by hatred and by spoiling."

If a playoff were necessary, it would be Monday at Dodger Stadium. But on Friday night, the Braves dominated the Astros, 5–2. Steve Avery had a no-hitter until outfielder Luis Gonzalez doubled down the leftfield line with two out in the seventh.

"I like to be out there in big games like this," Avery was saying now in the Braves' clubhouse. "I get pumped. All those people won't let you relax. That feeling can add a few miles an hour to your fastball."

Just then the Braves, watching ESPN on their clubhouse television set three time zones away, roared when Will Clark hit a two-run homer off Ramon Martinez in the first inning. Greg Olson hurried into Bobby Cox's office. "When I got on first in San Francisco two weeks ago," the catcher told the manager, "Will told me, 'Don't worry, I love hitting against the Dodgers. I hate 'em." Matt Williams and Kevin Bass also would homer in a 4–1 victory. In their previous twenty-seven innings against Bud Black, the Dodgers had pounded him for fourteen runs. But in six innings this time Black held them to one run. Suddenly the Dodgers were a game behind. Suddenly the Braves could clinch the division with two victories or with one victory coupled with a Dodger defeat. Suddenly the Braves could clinch a tie with a victory Saturday afternoon.

"No doubt the pressure's on the Dodgers now," Avery said. "We have the advantage of playing earlier, and every time we win it puts a little more heat on them."

Because of television commitments on Saturday, the Braves would be playing about an hour earlier. Their starter, John Smoltz, had fallen asleep Friday night with the Giants ahead, then had dreamed that the Dodgers had rallied to win. In his mind, the race was still tied when he sat down to breakfast. His visiting father-in-law, Bob Struble, knew differently.

"It's nice to be a game up," he said.

"No," Smoltz said, "we're still tied."

"The Dodgers lost last night. You're a game ahead."

"We are?" Smoltz said.

That afternoon Smoltz fired an eight-hitter, winning 5–2, for a 14–13 record. Ron Gant hit his thirty-second homer, drove in another run, and scored another. The scoreboard showed the Dodgers losing again, 4–0. As soon as David Justice caught the final out, the Braves

The Braves celebrate the National League West title. *Atlanta Braves*

smothered Smoltz, then stood together for nearly four minutes on the grass to the first-base side of the mound, staring at the Dodger game on the Diamond Vision screen above centerfield. Moments later Eddie Murray grounded to second baseman Robby Thompson to complete Trevor Wilson's two-hitter. As the Braves celebrated their division pennant, Otis Nixon was watching them on television at the Anchor Hospital rehab center in a room he shared with three others.

"I was just happy that my teammates had won the pennant," Nixon would say later. "I was very happy for them."

By winning the National League West, the Braves had gone from last place to first place. Worst to first, so to speak.

"That worst to first has nothing to do with us," David Justice was saying now as the Braves celebrated in their clubhouse. "I mean, we had our season, most of us, and we were just happy to be here. That worst to first, that's somebody else."

Worst to first also described the 1991 Minnesota Twins, the American League champions. In a World Series that many historians considered baseball's best, the Twins finally defeated the Braves in the tenth inning of a 1–0 seventh game.

But with three straight losses, the Dodgers had gone from first to elimination. Tommy Lasorda was trying to deflate the Giants' joy.

"If I was San Francisco," the Dodger manager said, "and I finished twenty games behind, I don't know why I'd be happy about anything."

In the Giants' clubhouse, Will Clark was alone at his locker, enjoying the moment, when Bill Plaschke of the *Los Angeles Times* approached and asked if he felt sorry for the Dodgers.

"Do I feel sorry for the Dodgers?" he repeated, then he cackled, "Ha, ha, ha, ha, ha, ha, ha."

1993

The Last Pure Pennant Race

In baseball's burning of Atlanta, the flames that destroyed eight luxury suites and part of the press box were "an omen" to the Braves' owner, Ted Turner. *Atlanta Braves / J. Sebo*

OHN SMOLTZ COULDN'T sleep. Not now. Not after he had jeopardized the Atlanta Braves' grip on first place. In a night game against the Houston Astros on Thursday, September 30, 1993, he had been removed by manager Bobby Cox in the fifth inning, the fifth consecutive start in which he had permitted five earned runs. His teammates' three-run rally in the ninth could not prevent a 10–8 loss.

"It's the most disappointed I've ever been in my life," the twenty-six-year-old righthander was telling his wife Diane in their Alpharetta, Georgia, home. "I'm not afraid to fail, but I didn't give myself a chance to succeed."

Every so often Smoltz would phone a sports-score service to learn the progress of the San Francisco Giants' game in Los Angeles, which was not being televised in the Atlanta area. If the Giants won, they would share first place in the National League West with the Braves, each with three games remaining on the final weekend of the season: the Braves against the Colorado Rockies in Atlanta, the Giants against the Dodgers in Los Angeles. If the two teams finished in a tie, the Braves would go to San Francisco for a one-game playoff Monday night at Candlestick Park, a playoff that Smoltz would start, a playoff that Smoltz had been thinking about when he went to the mound that Thursday night.

"I let public opinion and outside influences affect my pitching," he told his wife. "I became more location-conscious."

The more Smoltz tried to cut the corners of the plate, the harder he threw, the wilder he was. Now, like most of his teammates, he was anxious to learn the Giants' score. Some were watching CNN, where gunfire between American soldiers and Somali snipers was the lead story; some were waiting for ESPN's late SportsCenter news show. But in his Duluth, Georgia, home, Terry Pendleton was sleeping. He seldom watched baseball on television. He had not waited up for the score after driving alone up Interstate 85 from Atlanta–Fulton County Stadium in his silver Mercedes-Benz.

"Driving along," the thirty-three-year-old third baseman would say later, "I told myself, 'Listen, you haven't had a good year. If you had, we'd be six or seven games up. The least you can do is come out there tomorrow night and do everything you possibly can to help this club.'"

Two years earlier Pendleton had earned the Most Valuable Player award. This season his batting average had skidded to .148 during the first few weeks. On May 26 in Cincinnati he had walked off the field in the middle of an inning, annoyed that righthander Marvin Freeman had not retaliated after centerfielder Deion Sanders, whom Otis Nixon would replace in early July, had been hit by a pitch. Pendleton was fined. But now the chunky third baseman was up to .267 with 16 homers and 75 runs batted in. As he slept, the Giants won, 3–1, for righthander Bill Swift's twenty-first victory. With both teams tied, Monday night's playoff loomed larger than ever.

"If we win, we continue to play," Giants third baseman Matt Williams said of the three remaining games with the Dodgers and Monday's playoff. "We control it."

The Giants understood control. Also the loss of control. With a ten-game lead on the morning of July 23, the Giants were in complete control of the last pure pennant race.

Baseball's club owners had voted to realign the National League and the American League into three divisions each, with the Braves transferring to the NL East. The three divisional winners would qualify for the playoffs along with the second-place team with the best record.

For the first time, beginning in 1994, a second-place team could win the World Series. For the first time, first place would no longer mean everything.

When the Braves lost to the Pirates, 8–7, on July 22 after lefthander Mike Stanton blew a three-run lead in the ninth, their third consecutive NL West title seemed out of reach. But on July 18, in the trade that would turn the Braves upward and onward, general manager John Schuerholz obtained first baseman Fred McGriff from the San Diego Padres for three minor league prospects: outfielder Melvin Nieves, outfielder Vincent Moore, and righthander Donnie Elliott.

"What bothers me," Giants general manager Bob Quinn told his manager, Dusty Baker, "is that San Diego didn't get more for him."

At a lean six-three and 215 pounds, the twenty-nine-year-old

McGriff was the only slugger since the dead-ball era to lead both leagues in homers. He hit 35 for the Padres in 1992 after having hit 36 for the Toronto Blue Jays in 1989. But the Padres, desperate to trim their payroll, wanted to unload McGriff's $4.25 million salary.

"I'm dangling out there, I know I'm going somewhere," McGriff had said. "I just hope it's to a team in a pennant race."

When the Braves got McGriff, they weren't really in the race. But the Giants, like every other team in baseball, feared the slugger who had 191 homers in the previous six seasons, more than any other major leaguer. More than Mark McGwire, more than Jose Canseco, more than Joe Carter. At the time of the trade he had a career total of 209 homers, on pace for at least 400 in his career.

"I just hope," Dusty Baker said, "the Braves got McGriff a month too late."

In the hours before a July 20 night game, McGriff strolled into the Braves clubhouse in Atlanta to find his name in the cleanup slot in the batting order. "It just seems," Bobby Cox explained, "like the right place for him." Now in the batting cage underneath the stands, McGriff heard a security guard yelling, "Fire, fire. There's fire upstairs. Get out on the field." McGriff hurried through the tunnel to the dugout and looked up. Flames were destroying eight luxury suites and part of the press box. Staring at the blaze, Ted Turner spoke to Terry Pendleton.

"There's our omen," the Braves owner said. "We're going to win this thing."

That night the game was delayed for two hours, but the flames symbolized the arrival of the slugger who lighted a fire under the Braves and put the torch to the Giants' season. Although the Braves soon fell ten games behind, they won twelve of their first fifteen games with McGriff in the lineup. But as late as August 11, the Braves were nine games out. When they arrived in San Francisco for a three-game series on August 23, they were seven and one-half games out.

"We know what we have to do," Pendleton said. "We have to sweep."

In the Monday night opener Steve Avery stopped the Giants, 7–4, on an eight-hitter. Tuesday afternoon the Braves won, 6–4, behind Tommy Glavine as Pendleton homered and drove in three runs. Wednesday afternoon McGriff and David Justice each swatted two homers in a sixteen-hit barrage that routed Bill Swift as Greg Maddux coasted, 9–1.

"That's where it all started," Maddux would recall. "We knew we needed a sweep."

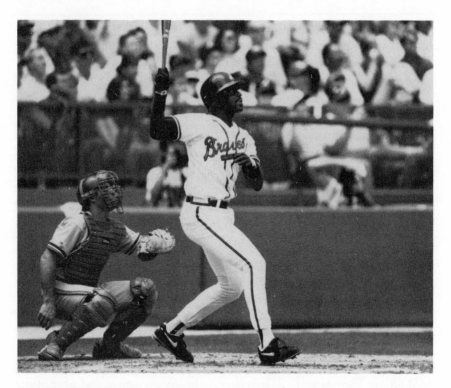

Fred McGriff. *Atlanta Braves/J. Sebo*

Maddux had joined the Braves as a free agent for a five-year, $28 million contract, some $6 million *less* than the Yankees' offer. "Atlanta," he explained, "was where I wanted to be." He would be voted the Cy Young award for the second consecutive season, having earned it with a 20–11 record for the Chicago Cubs in 1992. And now, after their sweep in San Francisco, the Braves were only four and one-half games out with thirty-four to play. Plenty of time for the Braves to keep climbing. Plenty of time for the Giants to keep falling, especially since they had been prevented by the Braves from pursuing Dennis Martinez, the Montreal Expos' ace righthander. The day before the July 31 trade deadline, John Schuerholz decided to claim Martinez on waivers.

"Two things can happen, both of them good," he told Dean Taylor, his assistant. "We'll get him or the Giants won't."

Because the Braves were in second place, their claim took precedence. Schuerholz offered first baseman Brian Hunter to the Expos, but when Martinez learned that he would be only an occasional fifth starter and that the Braves weren't offering him any extra money, he used his rights as a ten-year player in his fifth year with the Expos to reject the trade.

Three weeks later the Giants, desperate for pitching with left-hander Bud Black out with a damaged elbow after an 8–2 start, made a move that was listed in "transactions" but eventually would be in headlines. They brought up twenty-one-year-old righthander Salomon Torres from their Phoenix farm team.

When the Braves routed the Giants' ace, righthander Bill Swift, in the opener of a three-game rematch in Atlanta on August 31, they were only three and one-half games out. The next night a Giant rookie infielder, John Patterson, hit his first major league homer in the ninth inning off righthander Mark Wohlers for a stunning 3–2 victory. But the Braves took the third game, 5–3, when rookie Tony Tarasco doubled and scored the winning run on lefthander Ron Gant's liner off righthander Dave Burba's derriere.

On Friday night, September 10, the Braves finally ascended into a first-place tie with a 3–2 victory in San Diego as McGriff hit his thirty-second homer. The next day the Braves moved one game up, winning, 13–1, behind John Smoltz's eight-hitter. When the Braves jumped four games ahead with a 2–1 victory over the New York Mets on Gant's double in the eleventh inning, it appeared they would run away with the pennant.

But the Giants, tortured by an eight-game losing streak at Candlestick Park, responded by winning eleven of twelve games. Just as the Giants' new owners had responded in 1992 when the franchise appeared headed for the Tampa–St. Petersburg area in Florida. Twenty investors from the Bay Area had put up $100 million to purchase the club from Bob Lurie, thereby keeping the team in San Francisco and maintaining the intra-California rivalry with the Dodgers, a holdover from their New York–Brooklyn roots. Peter Magowan, the forty-one-year-old chief executive officer of the Safeway supermarket chain, emerged as the new president and managing general partner.

"We did this more as a civic gesture," Magowan said. "I don't think any of us made the miscalculation that we would get a good return on this investment."

Magowan and his executive vice president, Larry Baer, quickly decided that the Giants should invest another $43.75 million. Outbidding the Braves and the Yankees, they signed free agent Barry Bonds to a six-year contract. As the Giants stormed to their ten-game lead, Bonds turned out to be a bargain despite his thorny personality.

"I'm not afraid to be lonely at the top," the twenty-nine-year-old leftfielder growled. "Just the game. Just performance. That's all I'm interested in."

The season before, the Giants had a 72–90 record, a fifth-place flop. Even with a new owner in Magowan, a new general manager in Bob Quinn, a new manager in Dusty Baker, and several other new players, the Giants were giants again primarily because of Bonds, generally considered to be the best player in baseball. His only flaw had been his failure to produce for the Pittsburgh Pirates in the three previous NL Championship Series, two against the Braves: an overall .191 average with only one homer, only three runs batted in.

"In the playoffs, I sucked," he said.

Now, on the season's next to last weekend, Bonds hit four homers as the Giants streaked to within one and one-half games. In their 5–2 victory over the Padres on Sunday afternoon, Swift joined John Burkett as a twenty-game winner. But when Padres manager Jim Riggleman announced that his ace righthander, Andy Benes, who was 15–14, would start Monday night's game instead of rookie Tim Worrell, who was 1–7, whispers circulated that Bobby Cox had suggested the switch. Riggleman denied it, loudly.

"No manager would call another manager and tell him who to play," Riggleman said. "It's an insult to Bobby Cox to say something like that. If I had a conversation like that with another manager, I would do just the opposite for the nerve of somebody calling."

But when Matt Williams socked a two-run homer in the first, the Padres were on their way to an 8–4 loss and the Giants suddenly were one game out. Tuesday night the Braves lost to the Astros, 5–2, as Doug Jones struck out shortstop Jeff Blauser with the bases loaded to preserve Pete Harnisch's sixteenth victory. When the Giants stopped the Colorado Rockies, 6–4, on second baseman Steve Scarsone's three-run homer for Burkett's twenty-first victory, they had pulled into a first-place tie with the Braves, each with a 100–57 record, each with five games remaining.

"I think I know," Dusty Baker said, "how Lazarus felt."

If the Giants were to win Wednesday afternoon, they would hop into first place by one-half game before the Braves played the Astros that night. Salomon Torres, the touted rookie righthander with a 3–3 record after having been brought up from Phoenix, would be Baker's starter. The previous Saturday he had blanked the Padres on three hits for eight innings in a 3–1 victory. Weeks earlier, when Bob Quinn was talking to the Seattle Mariners about lefthander Randy Johnson, the Giants general manager had been willing to include Torres in the package. But when the Expos had asked for Torres in talks about Dennis Martinez, he refused.

"No way," Quinn told Expos general manager Don Duquette. "Not for Martinez."

In his previous starts, Torres had been vulnerable in the early innings. Hoping to solve that problem for Wednesday's game, pitching coach Dick Pole had him throw about 15 more warmup pitches than usual. But on the rookie's fifth pitch in the first inning, Nelson Liriano, the Rockies' shortstop, sliced a home run inside the rightfield foul pole. Only his second homer all season. In the second inning, centerfielder Daryl Boston hit his first of two homers. In the third Torres walked three as the Rockies took a 4–1 lead. But with one out in the Giants' fifth, the bases were loaded when Matt Williams dug in against Steve Reed, a twenty-seven-year-old righthander selected by the Rockies from the Giants in the expansion draft.

Ball one. Ball two. Ball three. To many others, the fourth pitch appeared high and outside. Plate umpire Bruce Froemming yelled, "Strike."

Had it been ball four, the walk would have forced in a run for 4–2 and kept the bases loaded with Bonds up. Instead, on a 3–1 count, Williams bounced to third baseman Charlie Hayes, who stepped on the bag and fired to first for a double play. Emerging from the dugout, Baker talked to Froemming about that fourth pitch to Williams.

"The catcher," Baker said, "had to lunge."

"It was a strike," Froemming said, firmly.

Baker returned to the dugout. "What are you going to say to that?" he shrugged after the 5–3 loss. "I couldn't afford to get thrown out. If I'd been belligerent, he would've been belligerent back. But that call changed everything." During this last home game, which raised the Candlestick Park attendance to a record 2,606,354, signs demanding "Keep Will" were waved at the first baseman who would become a free agent after an off year: .283, 14 homers, 73 runs batted in.

"Did you see the signs?" Clark was asked.

"What do you think, I'm blind?" he said. "The fans and I had a good little understanding. I've appreciated their support, especially this year because it's been a trying year. It's pretty touching, you might say. I take it to heart."

But in wasting the opportunity to take a temporary one-half-game lead, the Giants had dropped one-half game behind.

Three time zones away in Atlanta, thousands had watched the final innings of the Giants' loss on the DiamondVision screen high in centerfield before the Braves stopped the Astros, 6–3, for Tom Glavine's twenty-first victory. As their fans did the tomahawk chop, some with new battery-powered neon tomahawks that cost $180, the Braves again were one game ahead with four to play.

Thursday night John Smoltz's wildness would sabotage the Braves, 10–8, while the Giants won the opener of their four-game series at Dodger Stadium, 3–1, for Swift's twenty-first victory. Again they were tied.

Friday morning Smoltz would drive to the Golf Club of Georgia, hop into a cart, and play the new Creekside course there. By himself. "I wanted to focus," he would say later, "on what I had to do Monday night" in the playoff that seemed inevitable now, the playoff that he would start against Swift, the playoff that would be in San Francisco because in the conference-call coin toss to determine the site, John Schuerholz had called "heads" and it had come up tails.

"That morning," the Braves general manager explained, "my thirteen-year-old son Jonathan told me to call heads."

Now, as the Braves gathered for Friday night's game, Terry Pendleton was putting on his uniform when Fred McGriff strolled by. "My back's sore from carrying you," the first baseman said with a straight face. "It's time you did something."

Pendleton laughed and said, "I'll help you out."

In the first inning Pendleton's single drove in a run for a 2–0 lead. In the third he whacked Greg Harris's first pitch for a three-run homer that increased the lead to 6–2. In the eighth he produced another run with a ground out in the 7–4 victory that Greg McMichael closed for Steve Avery, now 18–6. On his way to the shower, McGriff strolled by Pendleton.

"It's about time," McGriff said.

By now many of their teammates were watching the early innings of the Giants' game on ESPN in the players' lounge. With Monday night's playoff appearing even more inevitable, Smoltz was reminded of the banner that hung from the upper deck.

"Pitch Mercker Now or Monday," it demanded.

Kent Mercker, the fifth starter most of the season but now in the bullpen, joked, "It cost me $80 in supplies just to make it."

"You'd have thought," Smoltz said, "that Kent would get his family better seats."

In Dodger Stadium, meanwhile, Bobby Thomson and Willie Mays were sitting alongside Giants president Peter Magowan behind the Giants' dugout. On October 3, 1951, Magowan was a nine-year-old student at St. Bernard's on East 98th Street in New York City, only fifty-seven blocks from the Polo Grounds. That afternoon Thomson's home run off Dodger righthander Ralph Branca won the pennant for the franchise Magowan would save from moving to Florida four decades later. Magowan had arranged for Thomson and Mays, who was on deck that day in 1951 and now had a lifetime contract as a Giants icon, to attend the Dodger series as good luck charms.

"Sunday is October 3, so Peter thought maybe a former October 3 guy might help," Thomson told the writers. "I don't know what I can do, but I'll sit here and keep my fingers crossed."

Magowan remembered staying in school to listen to that 1951 game on the radio, especially with most of his classmates' loyalty split between the Giants and the Dodgers.

"When the Giants won, I went home elated," Magowan recalled. "But my dad had been at the game and he told me that three of his friends had left in the top of the ninth. He said, 'Let that be a lesson to you in life. Never give up.' Believe me, I've remembered that. When we were about to lose the Giants to St. Petersburg, I thought about that. When I thought we had Barry Bonds signed and the whole deal almost came unstuck, I thought about that again. And when we were four games behind the Braves, we didn't give up again."

When the Dodgers jumped to a 4–0 lead Friday night, Bonds wouldn't let the Giants give up. In the third inning his three-run homer off Ramon Martinez created a 4–4 tie. In the fifth, with first base open, Dodger manager Tommy Lasorda brought in rookie left-hander Omar Daal but decided not to walk Bonds because "the bases loaded is too tough a situation to put a pitcher in." Bonds hit another three-run homer for a 7–4 lead. In the seventh his double off Steve Wilson knocked in the decisive run in an 8–7 victory that preserved the first-place tie.

"To have a game of this magnitude at this time of the year," Dusty Baker said, "that right there is what MVP's are. This erases all doubt."

Baker's doubts about his starting pitcher in Sunday's finale also had been erased. It would be Salomon Torres's turn, but the Giants manager had considered using Jim Deshaies or Scott Sanderson. "I'm praying on it," Baker had been saying, "and asking the good Lord to help me make a good decision. I wouldn't mind Him hurrying up." But after Friday night's victory the manager announced, "Salomon's preparing for it and that's what we're going to do." He also reminded his players that Saturday's game would start at noon for CBS television.

"Make sure you get to bed early," Baker said. "If you usually drink three beers, drink two. Get your rest."

More than any of his teammates, Rod Beck needed rest. Working for the seventh time in the last eight games, the husky righthander with the drooping mustache had surrendered a two-run homer to Eric Karros in the ninth, the fourth homer off him in the last five games. But with forty-seven saves, the Giant known as Shooter was Baker's bullpen closer.

"Sleep in tomorrow morning," Baker told him. "You don't have to be here with everybody else. Just be ready to pitch."

With the Braves starting at three o'clock in Atlanta on Saturday for television, the co-leaders had rare simultaneous games. The Braves took the suspense out of theirs with a 10–1 rout. Terry Pendleton drove in three more runs with a triple and a single for Greg Maddux's twentieth victory.

"I remember looking at the scoreboard when it was 2–0 Giants and when they went up 3–2," Maddux said. "Then I got a little upset at myself for looking up."

By the eighth the Giants were leading, 5–3, when the Dodgers loaded the bases with two out. Baker waved to the bullpen for Rod Beck, and Lasorda sent up lefthanded-swinging Dave Hansen as a pinch hitter for outfielder Raul Mondesi. On the second pitch, Hansen drove the ball high toward the rightfield stands. Baker hopped to the top step of the Giants' dugout.

"Lord, please, no, no," the Giants manager muttered.

Rightfielder Dave Martinez had driven in three runs with a double and a force-out as the replacement for Willie McGee, who had pulled a rib cage muscle during Friday night's game. But now Martinez, his glove high, was hurrying toward the low wall behind him. As he looked up, he could feel fans' hands on the back of his gray uniform shirt.

"They must've been Giant fans," he said later. "Dodger fans might have tried to pull my hat down."

Hansen's long fly ball settled into Martinez's glove for the third out. In the Dodgers' dugout Lasorda flung his blue cap at the bench. But when the ball was still in the air, Beck had walked calmly off the mound toward the dugout.

"Like it was no big thing," Baker said after Beck's two strikeouts and a ground out in the ninth preserved the 5–3 victory that evened the season series at 6–6. "But that's Shooter."

Sitting wearily at his locker, his arm tired, his hip sore, his legs rubbery, Beck said, "I had no idea where the ball would land. He missed it by one grain of the bat. But this is what dreams are made of. This is pennant race time. We've won a hundred and three games and we're still tied. That's ridiculous, but it's great. I've been in the ice tub and the beer tub regathering it for tomorrow." Almost as much as Barry Bonds, the twenty-five-year-old closer had kept the Giants alive by coming out of the bullpen in eight of the last nine games. In addition to his 48 saves, he had a 3–1 record and a 2.16 earned run average. In his 79⅓ innings, he had allowed only 57 hits, struck out 86, and walked only 13.

"If I don't use Beck and lose the game, I'm going to be criticized," Baker told the writers. "If I do use Beck and lose the game, I'm going to be criticized. I'd rather be criticized going with my best."

With his bullpen worn and weary, Baker was hoping that Salomon Torres would supply at least six or seven strong innings Sunday, maybe nine. The rookie from the Dominican Republic had begun the season with a 7–4 record and a 2.70 earned run average for the Shreveport Captains of the Texas League. Promoted to the Phoenix Firebirds of the Pacific Coast League, he was 7–4 with a 3.50 earned run average. In seven Giants starts, he had a 3–4 record with a 3.70 earned run average. Torres had never pitched against the Dodgers, but Baker considered Deshaies and Sanderson more of a risk. Deshaies, a thirty-three-year-old lefthander who was 2–2 after coming over from the Minnesota Twins on August 28, had a high fastball susceptible to righthanded sluggers such as Mike Piazza, Eric Karros, and Cory Snyder, especially in Dodger Stadium where the ball usually carries in the afternoon. Sanderson, a thirty-seven-year-old righthander obtained from the California Angels on August 3, had been 4–2 with the Giants, but he needed precise control to be effective. Baker also believed that his hitters would score against Kevin Gross, a thirty-two-year-old right-hander with a shaky 12–13 record, only two complete games, and a 4.28 earned run average, the highest of any Dodger starter. Will Clark, in particular, had been on a tear, with eight hits in his last ten at-bats. Over the last nine games, he was batting .500 with eighteen hits in thirty-six at-bats. Baker wasn't worried about getting runs, only about preventing runs.

"You can go with experience or you can go with talent and I'm taking a page from Jim Leyland's book," Baker told the writers, referring to the Pirate manager. "Jim says when you're in doubt, go with talent."

That evening Baker took talent out to dinner. Torres and his Dutch roommate, outfielder Rikkert Faneyte, also up from Phoenix, joined the manager and Angel Prada, the sports editor of *La Voz Libre*, and ten others at a long table at El Colmao, a storefront Cuban restaurant on West Pico Boulevard, a Hispanic neighborhood that had the boyish-faced righthander smiling.

"This," he said, "looks like the Dominican."

Baker was hoping to relax Torres with the type of food he grew up eating in San Pedro de Macoris, the sprawling Dominican city that has produced so many major league players. Torres ordered a shrimp entree but when it arrived, he shook his head. Too soupy. He pointed to Baker's plate, which featured a beef entree.

"I'd rather have that," he said.

Torres soon was dining heartily on *picadillo a la criolli*, black beans and rice, avocado salad, fried bananas, and green bananas with a big glass of orange juice. As the group left the restaurant, Nancy Donati of the Giants front office told the rookie, "Good luck tomorrow."

"Thank you," Torres said. "I have a very good feeling about the game."

Three time zones away in their suburban Alpharetta home, Carri Glavine, whose husband would pitch tomorrow, noticed that he had never seemed so restless.

"What's wrong?" she finally asked. "Are you mad at me?"

"No. I just feel like the whole world is on my shoulders."

His world and the Braves' world. Tommy Glavine was now a three-time twenty-game winner and a Cy Young Award winner in 1991, but he had been unable to silence the whispers that he was not a big-game pitcher. He had a 2–2 record in four World Series starts, but he had been 0–4 in four NLCS starts against the Pirates. His record down the stretch in past pennant races was also suspect: 1–3 a year ago, 3–3 two years ago. Now the slender southpaw would be starting this season's biggest game.

"Don't count your money yet," Rockies centerfielder Daryl Boston had been shouting at the Braves. "Don't count your money yet."

The odds had shortened on a Braves' sweep. Although the Rockies had lost all twelve of their games with the Braves, before their arrival in Atlanta they had won thirty-one of forty-nine. Only the Expos and the Braves were finishing the season stronger. The Rockies' starter would be a former Brave with a 5–8 record, righthander David Nied, the first player taken in the expansion draft. In his only previous start against the Braves, on May 6 in Denver, the twenty-four-year-old righthander had been strafed for five runs in five innings in a 13–3 loss.

"I know some guys have hard feelings toward their old organization, but I don't," Nied said. "I've got a lot of friends over there. I've been pulling for those guys the whole time. Until now."

When the Braves arrived for Sunday's game, they were carrying suitcases and travel bags. If the season ended in a tie, they would board a Delta charter for the flight to San Francisco and Monday night's playoff.

"I don't want to go," Pendleton said, "but if we have to go, I'll be the first one on the plane."

With their game starting three hours before the Giants' game, Fred McGriff said, "We've got to throw the win up there early so they see it." In the third, singles by McGriff and Pendleton drove in two runs. Nied departed in the fourth after Gant's two-run double, giving the leftfielder 117 runs batted in along with 36 homers. The Rockies rallied, scoring a run in the fifth, another in the sixth. When their little second baseman, Roberto Mejia, homered off Glavine with two out in the seventh, Bobby Cox brought in Steve Bedrosian, who struck out pinch hitter Alex Cole.

In the bottom of the seventh, David Justice slugged his 40th homer for his 120th run batted in, joining Henry Aaron, Jeff Burroughs, and Dale Murphy as the only Atlanta players to hit 40 homers and drive in 100 or more runs in the same season. Greg McMichael preserved the 5–3 score for Glavine's 22nd victory and the Braves' 104th, but no celebration erupted.

Instead, the Braves hurried up the tunnel to their clubhouse where they would monitor the Giants' game, which ESPN was televising. Outside, the 48,904 fans had been invited to watch the Giants' game on the centerfield screen. At least five thousand would stay. By then Tommy Lasorda had exhorted his Dodgers to do unto the Giants as the Giants had done unto them in 1991 when Will Clark cackled, "Ha, ha, ha, ha, ha, ha, ha"; in 1982 when Joe Morgan's three-run homer off Terry Forster enabled the Braves to win the division; in 1962 when righthander Stan Williams walked Jim Davenport to force in the Giants' winning run at Dodger Stadium in the decisive third game of a pennant playoff; and in 1951 when Bobby Thomson's three-run homer off Ralph Branca in the ninth inning won the decisive third game of that pennant playoff.

"They broke our hearts each time," Lasorda told his players. "Now we're going to break their hearts. Winning this game will make my year."

Dusty Baker didn't address his players before Sunday's game. In the clubhouse before Thursday's game the former outfielder, who played eight seasons for the Dodgers after four seasons with the Braves, had told them, "I'd rather win it here in Dodger Stadium." With the Braves having finished with 104 victories, that was no longer possible. But most of what the Giants manager told his players Thursday still stood.

"We're in a position to make our own destiny," he had said. "We want to win a hundred and four games to break the franchise record. If we have to, we want to go home and win Monday's playoff."

During batting practice hundreds of Giants fans, down from San Francisco, chanted "Beat L.A., beat L.A." in Dodger Stadium's steamy, smoggy heat. But the Dodger fans had history on their side. Not since 1923 had the Giants swept a four-game series in the Dodgers' ballpark. Hoping to avert his early-inning problems, Torres again threw about fifteen more warmup pitches than usual. In the dugout he went over the pitchout and pickoff signs with Baker and catcher Kirt Manwaring, and then the manager spoke quietly to the rookie, whom he knew to be a Seventh Day Adventist.

"Don't try to control everything," Baker told him. "Just let Him control it."

But the Giants manager did not tell any of his players about his fantasy that now was no longer possible on Sunday but might still occur in Monday night's playoff: Robby Thompson hitting a pennant-winning homer just as Bobby Thomson had in 1951. "How dramatic," he acknowledged later, "would that be?" Smashed in the face by Padre righthander Trevor Hoffman's fastball on September 24 at Candlestick Park, the scrappy second baseman had missed eight games with a broken left cheekbone and a bloodshot, blackened left eye when the Giants needed his .314 average, 19 homers, and 65 runs batted in. Fitted with a clear plastic mask, he had taken batting practice and grounders before Thursday's game.

"It's more than the fear of getting hit by a pitch or having a ground ball hit you in the face," Baker told the writers. "It affects him when he swings, when he runs. It hurts when he tightens his jaw when he's hitting."

Before the Friday night game, Thompson had begged Baker to allow him to play. "No," the manager said. Before the Saturday afternoon game, Thompson tried again. "No," the manager said. But after that game Baker, who considered Thompson "the spiritual leader" of the infield, left a voice-mail message for his second baseman at their Hyatt Regency hotel.

"We need you Sunday," Thompson heard the manager say. "You're playing. Be careful."

Being careful has never been Thompson's style. When he lifted a foul pop to Piazza in the first inning, he wore a helmet with a larger than usual ear flap to protect his cheekbone, but he didn't wear his clear plastic mask. When he trotted to second base, the mask shielded his discolored left eye and cheekbone, but in third he dove into the dirt for Dave Hansen's sharp grounder up the middle.

"I thought I had it," Thompson would say later.

He didn't. Kevin Gross, who had led off the third against Torres with a single, scored from third and the Dodgers had a 1–0 lead. Karros's double soon made it 2–0. When the Dodgers added a third run in the fourth on Jose Offerman's single, Baker waved to the bullpen for Trevor Wilson.

"I've got to come get you, man," the manager said softly to Torres at the mound. "I don't want to, but I've got to."

Baker patted Torres on the butt, and the rookie jogged to the dugout. The manager had gambled on talent and lost. All those black beans and fried bananas had not helped Torres from walking five and being riddled for five hits. Even so, a 3–0 deficit wasn't overwhelming. In the fifth, shortstop Royce Clayton and catcher Kirt Manwaring opened with singles. Second and first, nobody out, a chance for a big inning. But with Wilson coming up, Baker didn't use a pinch hitter.

"Trevor is a good bunter," the manager would explain. "I didn't want to waste another player to bunt. We got two runners in scoring position. We get a hit there and it's a 3–2 game. As it was, we got one run."

With two out and Manwaring on third, Thompson was up. Baker would have taken that fantasy homer then, but Thompson lifted a fly ball to center. Trailing, 3–1, Baker didn't want the lefthanded Wilson pitching to the Dodgers' righthanded sluggers, so he brought in Dave Burba to work the fifth. The husky righthander had a 10–3 record, but in only ninety-four innings he had been rapped for twelve homers. Moments later, the first pitch of his ninety-fifth inning disappeared over the right-centerfield fence—Mike Piazza's thirty-fourth homer, a record for a Dodger rookie. Karros walked. Leftfielder Henry Rodriguez popped out, but Cory Snyder homered, the ball bouncing near where Piazza's had landed. Suddenly the Dodgers had a 6–1 lead. In the bullpen Rod Beck took a deep breath.

"We could've dealt with a three-run deficit," he would say later. "But all of a sudden it was five."

Salomon Torres. *San Francisco Giants/Martha Jane Stanton*

Lasorda wasn't celebrating yet. "We've still got a game to play," he barked at his players. "Bear down." With one out in the sixth, Burba walked both Jose Offerman and Tim Wallach. Baker waved to the bullpen for righthander Mike Jackson. Piazza lined to Bonds, but Karros singled to left, scoring Offerman for a 7–1 lead. Scott Sanderson pitched a scoreless seventh but in the eighth, with lefthander Dave

Righetti pitching, Offerman walked, Wallach singled, and Piazza hit a three-run homer. Watching television in the Braves' clubhouse, David Justice whooped.

"It's over," he said. "Bonds can't hit an eight-run homer."

Moments later Eric Karros tripled. As the Giants' seventh pitcher, Jim Deshaies, arrived at the mound, Will Clark and Robby Thompson, each about to become a free agent, squatted together on the infield dirt.

"We were just talking," Thompson would say later. "About the game . . . and the game . . . and the game."

Near third base, Matt Williams also was squatting, a study in solitude and sorrow, his 38 homers and 110 runs batted in all for naught, the 10–1 inning-by-inning numbers on the small scoreboard behind him. Soon it was 12–1 on Raul Mondesi's two-run homer. But when Snyder pulled back from a high inside pitch, Williams heard angry shouts from the nearby Dodger dugout.

"You're next," he heard. "You're the first one up. You're next. Stay loose."

Williams thought he recognized one of the voices as that of Orel Hershiser, but several Dodgers were yelling at Williams, threatening to retaliate for Deshaies's inside pitch. Lasorda reacted.

"Don't start a riot," the manager ordered. "Just finish the game."

In Atlanta, the Braves weren't celebrating yet, but the thousands who had remained in the stadium were. On the stadium screen a shot of Lasorda had been captioned, "Our Pal."

And when Kevin Gross got the final out in the ninth, Lasorda acted as if the Dodgers had just won the pennant instead of the Braves.

"I love Dusty Baker, I love Peter Magowan," Lasorda said. "I know they feel bad, but this is something we wanted very much to do. I know the people of Atlanta were depending on us. We did our job. And I want all the fans in San Francisco to feel today like we felt in 1991 and 1982 and 1951 and 1962. Now they will remember this day a lot more than we will."

In the Giants' clubhouse, their 103 victories not enough, the players didn't want to remember.

Will Clark grumbled, "We got our ass kicked." Dave Burba, his voice breaking, mumbled, "I know I didn't lose the game by myself, but I didn't help it. I felt weak. The walks, the two homers. That's never happened to me before. That's what hurts." But losing to the Braves had happened before to Barry Bonds, as a Pirates outfielder in two National League Championship Series. Now, despite his league-leading 46 homers, his league-leading 123 runs batted in, his fourth best .336 average, and what would be his third Most Valuable Player award, his team had lost to the Braves again.

"One of us had to lose; unfortunately, it's always us, or me," Bonds said. "Only good thing about it is, I didn't have to see Atlanta on the same field, didn't have to see them parade around like the last two years. But they know I'm coming after 'em."

In the manager's office, Dusty Baker shrugged. "When it hurts that bad, you don't want to talk about it," he said. "We won fourteen of our last seventeen and it wasn't enough. You ever lose a girlfriend? Every song reminds you of her." The next day, coincidentally, when a phone call to the Giants office in San Francisco was put on hold, Whitney Houston was heard singing, "Didn't we almost have it all?" Now, on Baker's desk, the phone rang.

"Dusty," the voice said. "Tommy."

"Hi, Tommy," the Giants manager said.

"Dusty, I want you to hold your head high. You did a good job."

"I hear you," Baker said.

"I feel bad it had to end this way for you when you won a hundred and three games, but we had to play hard."

"I wouldn't have expected anything different."

"Now you know," Lasorda said, "how we felt in '91."

"I sure do," Baker said. "Thanks for calling."

Soon all the Giants were on their chartered buses for the ride to Los Angeles International Airport. All but one. Salomon Torres, charged with each of the Giants' three losses in their final seventeen games, had dressed quickly and left the clubhouse before it was opened to the writers and broadcasters. Monday he would tell Bob Quinn, "I don't feel I want to play baseball anymore," but the general manager comforted him. Later that week he told Quinn, "I will be the Rookie of the Year in 1994." But after Sunday's loss, he boarded a commercial flight, arriving at San Francisco International Airport long after his teammates had been greeted by hundreds of fans. On a hastily erected platform, Matt Williams addressed them.

"If you ask any man on this stage what it felt like to listen to that," he fumed, alluding to Dodger voices, "well, I'd be surprised if the Dodgers win one game next year. Just one. Orel Hershiser sat over there in the opposing dugout and ragged on me all day. But if he ever pitches again, there's line drives right back up the middle."

Later that week Hershiser phoned the Giants third baseman. "Orel assured me," Williams told Ross Newhan of the *Los Angeles Times*, "that he wasn't the person making the comments. We aired it out, and I took him at his word. I mistook him for someone else. I went about expressing my frustration in the wrong way. I chose the wrong words. I was upset that we lost and upset with what transpired. If I downgraded the Dodger organization, coaches, and players in any way, which I think I did, I apologize."

By then the Braves had begun the NL Championship Series, which they would lose to the Philadelphia Phillies in six games, but they still glowed with the satisfaction of having won the last pure pennant race.

"It's the most rewarding of our three consecutive divisional titles," Bobby Cox had said during the Braves' clubhouse celebration Sunday night, "because of the number of games we had to win."

That winning number, 104, never would have been attained without Fred McGriff batting cleanup. Over the season he hit .291 with 37 homers and 101 runs batted in. But after his arrival coincided with the flames in the luxury suites, the Braves stormed to a 51–17 finish as he batted .310 with 19 homers and 55 runs batted in. With champagne splashing around him that Sunday night, he smiled and said, "I guess I helped a little bit." At his locker, Terry Pendleton put the last pure pennant race in perspective.

"It'll never be the same as this," he said. "It'll never be as good as this again."

Bibliography

BOOKS

Asinof, Eliot. *Eight Men Out*. New York: Holt, Rinehart and Winston, 1963.

The Ballplayers, New York: William Morrow, 1990.

The Baseball Encyclopedia, New York: Macmillan, 1990.

Caray, Harry, and Bob Verdi. *Holy Cow!* New York: Villard Books, 1989.

Carew, Rod, with Ira Berkow. *Carew*. New York: Simon & Schuster, 1979.

Cobb, Ty, with Al Stump. *My Life in Baseball*. New York: Doubleday, 1961.

Coleman, Ken, and Dan Valenti. *The Impossible Dream*. Lexington, Mass.: Stephen Greene Press, 1987.

Cohen, Richard M., and David S. Neft. *The World Series*. New York: Macmillan, 1986.

Creamer, Robert W. *Babe*. New York: Simon & Schuster, 1974.

———. *Baseball in '41*. New York: Viking, 1991.

DiMaggio, Dom, with Bill Gilbert. *Real Grass, Real Heroes*. New York: Zebra Books, 1990.

Dolson, Frank. *The Philadelphia Story*. South Bend, Ind.: Icarus Press, 1981.

Durocher, Leo, with Ed Linn. *Nice Guys Finish Last*. New York: Simon & Schuster, 1975.

Eskenazi, Gerald. *The Lip*. New York: William Morrow, 1993.

Feller, Bob, with Bill Gilbert. *Now Pitching*. New York: Birch Lane Press, 1990.

Fleming, G. H. *The Dizziest Season*. New York: William Morrow, 1984.

Gilbert, Bill. *They Also Served*. New York: Crown, 1992.

Graham, Frank. *The Brooklyn Dodgers*. New York: G. P. Putnam's Sons, 1945.

———. *Connie Mack*. New York: G. P. Putnam's Sons, 1945.

———. *McGraw of the Giants*. New York: G. P. Putnam's Sons, 1944.

———. *The New York Giants*. New York: G. P. Putnam's Sons, 1952.

———. *The New York Yankees*. New York: G. P. Putnam's Sons, 1943.

Gregory, Robert. *Diz*. New York: Viking, 1992.

Greenberg, Hank. *The Story of My Life*. New York: Times Books, 1989.

Gropman, Donald. *Say It Ain't So, Joe*. Boston: Little, Brown, 1979.

Halberstam, David. *Summer of '49*. New York: William Morrow, 1989.

Holmes, Tommy. *Dodger Daze and Knights*. New York: David McKay, 1953.

Honig, Donald. *Baseball When the Grass Was Real*. New York: Coward, McCann, and Geoghegan, 1975.

Jackson, Reggie, with Mike Lupica. *Reggie*. New York: Villard Books, 1984.

Johnson, Dick, and Glenn Stout. *Ted Williams*. New York: Walker, 1991.

Kahn, Roger. *The Boys of Summer*. New York: Harper & Row, 1971.

Lee, Bill, with Dick Lally. *The Wrong Stuff*. New York: Viking, 1984.

Lieb, Frederick G. *The St. Louis Cardinals*. New York: G. P. Putnam's Sons, 1944.

Linn, Ed. *The Great Rivalry*. New York: Ticknor & Fields, 1991.

Lowrey, Philip J. *Green Cathedrals*. New York: Addison-Wesley, 1992.

Mays, Willie, and Lou Sahadi. *Say Hey*. New York: Simon & Schuster, 1988.

Mead, William B. *Even the Browns*. Chicago: Contemporary Books, 1978.

McCallum, John D. *Ty Cobb*. New York: Praeger, 1975.

The National Pastime. Cooperstown, N.Y.: Society for American Baseball Research, 1988.

Paige, LeRoy (Satchel), as told to David Lipman. *Maybe I'll Pitch Forever*. Lincoln, Neb.: Bison Press, 1993.

Parrott, Harold. *The Lords of Baseball*. New York: Praeger, 1976.

Ritter, Lawrence. *The Glory of Their Times*. New York: William Morrow, 1966.

Rose, Pete, and Roger Kahn. *Pete Rose: My Story*. New York: Macmillan, 1989.

Shannon, Bill, and George Kalinsky. *The Ballparks*. New York: Hawthorn, 1975.

Shaughnessy, Dan. *The Curse of the Bambino*. New York: Dutton, 1990.

Snider, Duke, with Bill Gilbert. *The Duke of Flatbush*. New York: Zebra Books, 1988.

Sowell, Mike. *The Pitch That Killed*. New York: Macmillan, 1989.

Stockton, J. Roy. *The Gashouse Gang.* New York: A. S. Barnes, 1945.

Thomson, Bobby, with Lee Neiman and Bill Gutman. *The Giants Win the Pennant!* New York: Kensington, 1991.

Total Baseball. New York: Warner, 1989.

Veeck, Bill, with Ed Linn. *Veeck, as in Wreck.* New York: G. P. Putnam's Sons, 1962.

Williams, Dick, and Bill Plaschke. *No More Mr. Nice Guy.* New York: Harcourt Brace Jovanovich, 1990.

Yastrzemski, Carl, and Gerald Eskenazi. *Yaz.* New York: Doubleday, 1990.

NEWSPAPERS

The New York Times, 1908, 1920, 1934, 1938, 1940, 1941, 1944, 1948, 1949, 1951, 1964, 1967, 1991, 1993.

The New York *Daily News,* 1941, 1944, 1949, 1951, 1964, 1967.

Newsday, 1978.

Atlanta *Journal-Constitution,* 1991, 1993.

Boston Globe, 1978.

Boston Herald, 1948, 1949, 1967.

Brooklyn Eagle, 1934, 1941, 1951.

Chicago Tribune, 1908, 1920, 1938, 1967.

Cincinnati *Enquirer,* 1964.

Cleveland *Plain-Dealer,* 1908, 1920, 1940, 1948.

Detroit News, 1908, 1940, 1944, 1967.

Los Angeles Times, 1991, 1993.

Minneapolis *Tribune,* 1967.

Philadelphia Inquirer, 1964.

Pittsburgh *Post-Gazette,* 1938.

St. Louis Post-Dispatch, 1934, 1941, 1944, 1964.

San Francisco *Chronicle,* 1991, 1993.

San Francisco *Examiner,* 1991, 1993.

San Jose *Mercury-News,* 1993.

Index

Doerr, Bobby, 169, 176, 177, 191, 197, 200, 204, 206, 207, 318
Donahue, Jiggs, 20, 21
Donlin, Mike, 25, 39
Donovan, Wild Bill, 16, 19, 31, 36, 37, 38
Dougherty, Patsy, 20, 21, 28, 34
Downs, Jerry (Red), 34
Dressen, Charlie, 137, 214, 216, 217, 218il, 221, 222, 223, 224, 225, 226, 228, 229, 230, 231, 232, 233, 234, 235, 236, 237, 238, 240, 241, 242, 243, 245, 246, 247, 248, 251, 252, 253, 254
Drysdale, Don, 258, 262
Durocher, Leo, 80, 81, 85, 90, 130–31, 133, 134, 135, 136, 137, 138, 141, 142il, 143, 144, 146, 147, 148, 211, 212, 214, 215, 216, 217, 219, 220, 222, 223, 227, 228, 231, 232, 233, 234, 235, 236, 239, 241, 242, 244, 245, 247, 250, 251, 254, 261, 263, 264, 280, 283
Dusak, Erv, 144

E

Earley, Tom, 134
Eckersley, Dennis, 334, 335, 336, 339, 341, 342, 343, 344, 345, 346, 351
Edwards, Bruce, 218
Edwards, Hank, 168
Edwards, Johnny, 273
Ehmke, Howard, 52, 181
Eisenstat, Harry, 121
Elliott, Bob, 172
Ellis, Sammy, 266, 281, 282
Engle, Clyde, 40
Ennis, Del, 231, 237, 238
Erickson, Paul, 132, 133
Ermer, Cal, 293, 300, 304, 305, 306, 309, 312, 314, 318, 319, 321
Erskine, Carl, 217, 223, 226, 229, 232, 235, 237, 241, 245, 246, 249, 251
Evans, Dwight, 329, 333

Evers, Johnny, 7, 8, 9il, 11, 12, 13–14, 26, 39, 41, 364

F

Faber, Red, 51, 52, 56, 60, 70, 71il, 73, 76
Fain, Ferris, 199
Fairly, Ron, 261
Feller, Bob, 111, 112, 113, 114, 115, 118, 119, 121, 123, 124, 125, 126, 155, 166, 169, 170, 172, 173, 174, 175, 176, 181
Felsch, Happy, 51, 56, 59, 61, 62, 70, 71il, 72, 73, 75
Ferriss, Dave (Boo), 179
Fette, Lou, 100
Fisher, Jack, 167
Fisk, Carlton, 98, 343, 345, 349, 351, 353
Fitzsimmons, Freddie (Fat Freddie), 84, 88, 92, 135, 247
Fletcher, Elbie, 108, 147
Flick, Elmer, 16, 31
Flood, Curt, 267, 268, 275, 286
Ford, Whitey, 340
Fowler, Dick, 198
Foxx, Jimmie, 84, 98, 296
Foy, Joe, 294, 301, 302, 322
Franks, Herman, 143
Freehan, Bill, 293, 296, 297
Fregosi, Jim, 305, 316, 322
French, Larry, 103
Frick, Ford, 135, 139, 225, 235, 287
Frisch, Frank, 80, 81, 82, 83, 85, 87, 88, 90, 219
Furillo, Carl, 217, 221, 222, 223, 226, 232, 236, 237, 239, 244

G

Gaedel, Eddie, 162
Galan, Augie, 100
Galehouse, Denny, 149il, 154, 159, 161, 179, 180, 180il, 181, 182, 183
Gandil, Chick, 52, 59, 63, 64, 66, 67, 68, 70, 71il, 72, 74

Hodges, Clarence (Shovel), 73
Hodges, Gil, 212, 217, 223, 225, 236, 237, 238, 239, 242, 244, 245, 246, 247, 251, 303
Hofman, Solly, 11
Hogg, Billy, 16
Hollingsworth, Al, 149*il*, 162*il*
Hopp, Johnny, 144
Hopper, Clay, 145
Hornsby, Rogers, 51, 83, 152
Horton, Willie, 292, 320
Houk, Ralph, 197, 286, 287, 301
Houston Astros, 357, 367, 368, 371, 377, 383, 388, 390
Howard, Del, 14
Howard, Elston, 317, 318
Howell, Harry, 31
Hoyt, Waite, 91
Hrabosky, Al, 330, 331
Hubbell, Carl, 83, 84, 85, 88, 91, 98, 133, 137, 233
Hudson, Johnny, 130, 131
Hudson, Sid, 119, 195
Hughson, Cecil (Tex), 179, 205
Hunter, Brian, 361, 369, 386
Hunter, Jim (Catfish), 309, 333, 338, 339, 341, 343, 346
Hutchinson, Fred, 117, 123, 171, 263, 266, 285, 287

I

Irvin, Monte, 211, 214, 216, 219, 220, 224, 225, 232, 236, 240, 244, 245, 246, 252, 253
Isbell, Frank, 21, 28, 34, 36, 37

J

Jackson, Joe (Shoeless Joe), 51, 56, 59, 61, 62, 64, 65, 66, 67, 68, 69, 70, 71*il*, 73, 75
Jackson, Reggie, 329, 330, 331, 332, 333, 334, 335, 336, 338, 339, 340, 341, 344, 345, 346, 347, 350, 351, 353, 357

Jackson, Travis, 87
Jakucki, Sig, 149*il*, 151, 152, 153, 156, 159, 161, 162*il*
Jamieson, Charlie, 50, 62
Jansen, Larry, 216, 225, 230, 231, 232, 242, 244, 253
Javier, Julian, 268, 275, 285
Jennings, Hughie, 15, 16, 35, 36, 37, 38
Jensen, Woody, 102, 103, 104
Johnson, Alex, 267, 282
Johnson, Art, 144
Johnson, Ban, 46, 47, 50, 52, 59, 62
Johnson, Billy, 193, 205
Johnson, Deron, 279, 281, 282
Johnson, Earl, 117, 176, 177, 179, 189
Johnson, Walter, 15, 21, 24, 339
Johnston, Doc, 45, 50
Jones, Dalton, 291, 296, 314, 318
Jones, Fielder, 28, 32, 34
Jones, Sheldon, 216
Joost, Eddie, 138, 139
Joss, Addie, 15, 22, 28, 29, 30, 30*il*, 31, 34, 36, 37
Judnich, Walter (Wally), 171, 175
Jurges, Billy, 99, 102, 104
Justice, David, 367, 371, 374, 375, 375*il*, 378, 379, 385, 395, 399

K

Kaline, Al, 292, 297, 299
Kansas City Athletics, 299, 300
Kell, George, 207
Keller, Charlie, 111, 201
Kellner, Alex, 197
Keltner, Ken, 113, 166, 168, 174, 175, 182, 182*il*
Kennedy, Bob, 182
Kennedy, Vern, 122
Kerr, Dickie, 51, 52, 55, 56, 58, 60, 62, 68, 70, 71*il*, 73
Kerr, John (Buddy), 216
Killebrew, Harmon, 299, 299*il*, 300, 306, 307, 309, 312, 313, 314, 317, 319, 320
Killian, Ed, 16, 20, 34

415